ARS HABSBURGICA

HABSBURG WORLDS

VOLUME 6

General Editor
Violet Soen, *KU Leuven*

Editorial Board
Tamar Herzog, *Harvard University*
Yves Junot, *Université Polytechnique Hauts-de-France*
Géza Pálffy, *Hungarian Academy of Sciences, Institute of History*
José Javier Ruiz Ibánez, *Universidad de Murcia, Red Columnaria*
Barbara Stollberg-Rilinger, *Westfälische Wilhelms-Universität*
Joachim Whaley, *University of Cambridge*

Ars Habsburgica

New Perspectives on Sixteenth-Century Art

edited by
FERNANDO CHECA &
MIGUEL ÁNGEL ZALAMA

BREPOLS

Cover illustration: *Honor* from the series *The Honors*, tapestry designed before 1520, woven between 1525 and 1532. Design attributed to Bernard van Orley. Metropolitan Museum of Art, New York. Purchase, 2014 Benefit and Director's Funds, several members of The Chairman's Council Gifts, Brooke Russell Astor Bequest, Ambassador and Mrs. W. L. Lyons Brown, Mr. and Mrs. Richard L. Chilton Jr., and Josephine Jackson Foundation Gifts, 2015. The work is under Public Domain.

© 2023, Brepols Publishers n.v., Turnhout, Belgium.

All rights reserved. No part of this publication may be reproduced, stored in a retrieval system, or transmitted, in any form or by any means, electronic, mechanical, photocopying, recording, or otherwise without the prior permission of the publisher.

D/2023/0095/172
ISBN 978-2-503-59594-8
eISBN 978-2-503-59595-5
DOI 10.1484/M.HW-EB.5.124875
ISSN 2565-8476
eISSN 2565-9545

Printed in the EU on acid-free paper.

Contents

List of Illustrations	7
Introduction: *Ars Habsburgica*, or New Perspectives on Sixteenth-Century European Art Fernando CHECA & Miguel Ángel ZALAMA	11
Habsburg Politics and Cultures in the Sixteenth Century. The Cosmopolitan Iberian Experience of Empires and Kingdoms Fernando BOUZA	15
A Theory of Art for the 'Habsburg Renaissance' Fernando CHECA	27
Rethinking Vasari. Art and Arts in the Sixteenth Century Miguel Ángel ZALAMA	41
The Antithesis between the Vasarian Canon and the Habsburg Model of the Arts. Defining National Identity in the Italian *Risorgimento* Matteo MANCINI	57
Luxury and Identity in the Sixteenth-Century Habsburg Courts Jesús F. PASCUAL MOLINA	73
Food as a Strategy of Power. The Political Role of Banquets in Prince Philip's *Felicissimo Viaje* (1548–1551) Vanessa QUINTANAR CABELLO	91
His Polis. The Habsburg Naval Epic in the Mediterranean Víctor MÍNGUEZ	109
Habsburg Mars. The House of Austria and the Artistic Representation of Land Warfare Antonio GOZALBO NADAL	127

Sixteenth-Century Notions of *Spolia* and Triumph Representation
Antonio URQUÍZAR-HERRERA   143

The *Armamentarium Heroicum* of Archduke Ferdinand of Tyrol
Christian BEAUFORT-SPONTIN   165

The Habsburg Dynasty and Emblematic Literature. A Historiographical Assessment
Patricia ANDRÉS GONZÁLEZ   177

Books and Libraries in the Construction of the Habsburg Dynasty's Image During the Sixteenth Century
José Luis GONZALO SÁNCHEZ-MOLERO   199

Epic and Truth. Writing for the Habsburgs in Sixteenth-Century Spain
María José VEGA   221

Philip II as *Rex Pacificus*. Belligerence and Pacifism in Epic Versions of the Battle of Saint-Quentin (1557)
Lara VILÀ   237

Notes on the Contributors   253

Index of names   257

List of Illustrations

Fernando Bouza

Fig. 1.1.	*Religion assisted by Spain* by Titian, 1572–1575. © Museo Nacional del Prado.	20

Miguel Ángel Zalama

Fig. 3.1.	Front page of *Le vite* by Giorgio Vasari, Florence, Giunti, 1568.	43
Fig. 3.2.	*The Capture of Tunis* tapestry from *The conquest of Tunis* series, Jan Vermeyen and Pieter Coecke van Aelst, 1543-1548. Madrid, Patrimonio Nacional © Digital image courtesy of the Getty's Open Content Program.	52
Fig. 3.3.	*The revelation of St. John* tapestry from the *Apocalypse* series. Willem de Pannemaker, c. 1550. Madrid, Patrimonio Nacional © Digital image courtesy of the Getty's Open Content Program.	53

Matteo Mancini

Fig. 4.1.	Alessandro Manzoni, *I Promessi sposi*, 1840, prints by Francesco Gonin.	62
Fig. 4.2.	Face of Lucia Mondella, print by Francesco Gonin, in Alessandro Manzoni, *I Promessi sposi*, 1840.	62
Fig. 4.3.	*Immaculate Conception* by Diego Velázquez, 1618. © National Gallery of Art, London.	63
Fig. 4.4.	Face of *L'innominato*, print by Francesco Gonin, in Alessandro Manzoni, *I Promessi sposi*, 1840.	63
Fig. 4.5.	*Portrait of Juan de Pareja* by Diego Velázquez, 1650. ©Metropolitan Museum of Art, New York.	65

Jesús F. Pascual Molina

Fig. 5.1.	*A goldsmith in his shop*, by Petrus Christus, 1449. © Metropolitan Museum of Art, New York.	75

Fig. 5.2. *Jean Wauquelin presenting his Chroniques de Hainaut to Philip the Good*, frontispiece in miniature from the *Chroniques de Hainaut*, atrib. to Rogier van der Weyden 1448. © Royal Library of Belgium. 77

Fig. 5.3. *The Virgin of the Catholic Monarchs*, Master of the Virgin of the Catholic Monarchs, 1491-1493. © Museo Nacional del Prado. 79

Fig. 5.4. *Bust of young Charles V*, anonymous, c. 1520. Valladolid, Museo Nacional de Escultura. © Photo by the author. 83

Vanessa Quintanar Cabello

Fig. 6.1. *Still life of fish and oysters with a cat*, Alexander van Adrianssen, first half of the XVII century. © Museo Nacional del Prado. 92

Fig. 6.2. *Ceres and two nymphs*, Peter Paul Rubens and Frans Snyders, 1615-1617. © Museo Nacional del Prado. 102

Fig. 6.3. *The sense of taste*, Peter Paul Rubens and Jan Brueghel the Elder, 1618. © Museo Nacional del Prado. 105

Víctor Mínguez

Fig. 7.1. *Rodela (shield) of the Apotheosis of Charles V*, anonymous, c. 1535-1540. © Real Armería, Madrid. 110

Fig. 7.2. *Imprese 68 His Polis*, from *Idea de vn Principe político christiano representada en Cien empresas* by Diego Saavedra Fajardo, Munich, 1640. 113

Fig. 7.3. *Capture of La Goleta*, Frans Hogenberg, drawings by Vermeyen, 1540-1590. 117

Fig. 7.4. *Departure of the fleet of the Holy League from the port of Messina*, Luca Cambiaso, 1581-1582, Real Monasterio del Escorial. © Patrimonio Nacional. 122

Fig. 7.5. *Philip II offering the infante Fernando to Victory* by Titian, 1573-1575. © Museo Nacional del Prado. 124

Antonio Gozalbo Nadal

Fig. 8.1. *Capture of Francis I*, tapestry from the series *Tha Battle of Pavia*, design by Bernard van Orley, manufactured in Bruxelles by William Dermoyen, between 1528-1531. © National Museum of Capodimonte, Naples. 129

Fig. 8.2. *Panoramic view of Vienna during the first Turkish siege*, by Nikolaus Meldemann, 1530. © Wien Museum. 131

Fig. 8.3. *Emperor Charles V at Mühlberg*, Titian, 1548. © Museo Nacional del Prado. 135
Fig. 8.4. General view of the Hall of Battles at El Escorial. 138
Fig. 8.5. *Jemmingen Battle*, by Franz Hogenberg, 1568. © Biblioteca Nacional de España, Madrid. 140

Antonio Urquízar-Herrera

Fig. 9.1. *Dulle Griet*, Pieter Bruegel, 1563. © Museum Mayer Van der Bergh (Antwerp). 144
Fig. 9.2. Details of *spolia*, from *Arch of Honor. Triumphal arch* of Maximilian I, various artists, 1515-1518. © Metropolitan Museum of Art, New York. 146
Fig. 9.3. Detail of *spolia* (1). Onofrio Panvinio, *Comentario dell'vso, et ordine de' trionfi antichi*, Venice: Michele Tramezzino, 1571. 153
Fig. 9.4. Detail of *spolia* (2). Onofrio Panvinio, *Comentario dell'vso, et ordine de' trionfi antichi*, Venice: Michele Tramezzino, 1571. 154
Fig. 9.5. Portrait of *Johann Baptista de Tassis* from Jakob Schrenck von Notzing, *Augustissimorum Imperatorum ... verissimae imagines ... quorum arma, aut integra, aut horum partes ... heroica facinora patrarunt ...*, Innsbruck: Johannes Agricola, 1601. 160

Christian Beaufort-Spontin

Fig. 10.1. Frontpage of the *Armamentarium Heroicum*, Dominicus Custos after Giovanni Battista Fontana, 1601. 173

Patricia Andrés González

Fig. 11.1. Recto of a Sheet with Maximilian, from *The Genealogy of Emperor Maximilian* I, Hans Burgkmair, 1509-1512. © Metropolitan Museum of New York. 182
Fig. 11.2. Medals of *Philip II and Mary I of England*, Jacopo da Trezzo, 1555. © National Archaeological Museum, Madrid. 185
Fig. 11.3. Left: *Freydal, The Book of Jousts and Tournament of Emperor Maximilian I: Combats on Horseback*, Plate 79, c. 1515. © National Gallery of Art, Washington; Right: 'Theuerdank Nearly Shoots Himself with a Crossbow', from *Theuerdank*, Hans Burgkmair, 1517. © Metropolitan Museum of Art, New York. 190

Fig. 11.4. *Turnierbuch. Ritterspiele gehalten von Kaiser Friedrich III und Kaiser Maximilian I in den Jahren 1489–1511*. Hans Burgkmair, the younger. © Bayerische Staatsbibliothek. 191

Fig. 11.5. Frontpage of *Idea de vn principe politico christiano*, by Diego de Saavedra Fajardo. © Biblioteca Nacional de España, Madrid. 196

José Luis Gonzalo Sánchez-Molero

Fig. 12.1. *Portrait of Charles V* by Cristoph Amberger, *c.* 1532. © Staatliche Museen zu Berlin, Gemaldegalerie. 201

Fig. 12.2. *The librarian*, painting by Arcimboldo, *c.* 1566. © Skokloster Castle, Sweden. 202

Fig. 12.3. *The young White King learns black magic*, from the *Weisskunig*, woodcut by Hans Burgkmair, 1516. 205

Fig. 12.4. Façade of El Escorial, detail of the situation of the Royal Library. © Photo by the author. 216

Fig. 12.5. Portrait of *Philip II*, Juan Pantoja de la Cruz, *c.* 1590, Library of El Escorial. © Patrimonio Nacional. 218

Lara Vilà

Fig. 14.1. Woodcut from *Le triomphe d'Anvers faict en la susception du Prince Philips, Prince d'Espaign[e]* written by Cornelius Grapheus, Page Liiii recto, by Pieter Coecke van Aelst, 1550. © Metropolitan Museum, New York. 241

Fig. 14.2. *The Queen of Sheba visits King Solomon*, painting by Lucas de Heere, Ghent Saint Bavo Cathedral. © Photo by Pol Mayer. 244

Fig. 14.3. *The Last Supper*. Detail from the stained-glass window number 7 in the Sint Janskerk at Gouda, Netherlands, by Dirk Crabeth, 1557. © Photo by Rolf Kranz. 245

FERNANDO CHECA & MIGUEL ÁNGEL ZALAMA

Introduction: *Ars Habsburgica*, or New Perspectives on Sixteenth-Century European Art

Over the last several decades, art historians have been revising many accepted ideas about the general interpretation of Renaissance art. Many of these scholars agree that it is necessary to rethink the predominantly Italocentric model of the art of that period, and with it the idea that its aesthetics were heavily steeped in classicism They criticise the tradition of scholarship that focuses on 'national' schools and arts, usually defined according to their greater or lesser degree of 'Italianism'.[1] These approaches began in the 1980s, have become increasingly common in recent years, and have provided a comprehensive vision of the period as far richer and more complex than was conventionally believed.

The main lines of recent research coincide, above all, in their insistence on extending scholarship to 'other' renaissances, in addition to the customary categories of Italian art, Flemish art and Renaissance in northern Europe. They take into account the new discourses that emerged in eastern Europe—Jan Białostocki's studies were pioneering in this respect[2]—and the Iberian kingdoms, as well as developments in the Americas, Africa and the Far East.[3] But it is not merely a question of broadening the geographical scope of scholarship; first and foremost, it is about acknowledging the interconnections, interactions and movements between these contexts in order to gain a fuller understanding of the art of the period: the new trade routes, the travels of artists and artworks, and the movements of the patrons themselves.[4] The sixteenth century was a dynamic age which, for

---

1 Claire J. Farago, *Reframing the Renaissance: Visual Culture in Europe and Latin America 1450–1650* (New Haven/London: Yale University Press, 1995).
2 Jan Białostocki, *The Art of the Renaissance in Eastern Europe: Hungary, Bohemia, Poland* (Oxford: Phaidon, 1976).
3 Thomas DaCosta Kaufmann, 'From Treasury to Museum: The Collection of the Austrian Habsburgs', in *The Culture of Collecting*, eds. John Elsner and Roger Cardinal (London: Reaktion Books, 1994), 137–154; Thomas DaCosta Kaufmann, 'The Kunstkammer: Historiography, Acquisition, Display', in *A Arte de Coleccionar. The Art of Collecting*, ed. Hugo Miguel Crespo (Lisbon: Ar/Pab, 2019), 17–33.
4 Peter Burke, *Hybrid Renaissance: Culture, Language, Architecture* (Budapest/New York: Central European University Press, 2016).

the first time, encompassed the world.⁵ These historical realities gave rise to new political, cultural and artistic identities which, from an art history perspective, can no longer be explained by abstractions and conceptualisations such as the 'national school', 'centre vs. periphery' or 'classicism vs. anti-classicism'—the themes that dominated historiographical debate from the nineteenth century to the 1980s.

Ars Habsburgica aims to expand on these ideas by proposing a perspective which we believe is of crucial importance for understanding the phenomenon of artistic activity in the Renaissance. Specifically, it aims to consider the role that the Habsburg dynasty and its diverse courts played during this period, including not only its Iberian realms, but also its Italian, Flemish, central European and imperial territories. To narrow the focus of this vast theme, we have deliberately excluded the dynasty's transatlantic territories, but the book does discuss artistic events in places not normally considered in relation to the Habsburgs, such as England.

As is well known, the seminal nineteenth-century contributions of Jacob Burckhardt (1860) and Jules Michelet (1879) had, and continue to have, a major impact on Renaissance historiography.⁶ Julius von Schlosser's works on the history of collecting and art literature, published in 1908 (*Die Kunst und Wunderkammern der Spätrenaissance*) and 1924 (*Die Kunstliteratur*), have also been tremendously influential.⁷ Our volume offers new points of view that will contextualise, in a fresh way, certain framework notions of the Renaissance in general and the specific cultural world of the Habsburgs.

The essay by Fernando Bouza offers an historical analysis of the sixteenth-century Habsburg universe as a complex cultural setting, while eminently historiographical essays by Fernando Checa, Miguel Ángel Zalama and Matteo Mancini interrogate the historiographical tradition. Checa proposes a model of source studies that points to a Habsburg 'art theory'; Zalama moves beyond the idea of Giorgio Vasari's system of the arts and posits a 'Habsburg idea' of artistic activity; and Mancini presents a new approach to Italian sources on the Renaissance which overcomes nineteenth-century historiographical perspectives on the artistic production of Renaissance Italy and its relationship with Spain.

This book articulates sixteenth-century concepts of art, not so much in terms of national identities, but rather considering the world of the court

---

5 Serge Gruzinsky, *Les quatre parties du monde. Historie d'une mondialisation* (Paris: Éditions de la Martinière, 2004).
6 Jacob Burckhardt, *The Civilization of the Renaissance in Italy* (London: Albert & Charles Boni, 1878). Jules Michelet, *Histoire de France*, vol. IX (Paris: La Renaissance, 1879).
7 Julius Ritter von Schlosser, *Die Kunst-und Wunderkammern der Spätrenaissance* (Leipzig: Klinkhardt & Biermann, 1908); Julius Ritter von Schlosser, *Die Kunstliteratur: ein Handbuch zur Quellenkunde der neueren Kunstgeschichte* (Vienna: A. Schroll, 1924).

as an artistic and cultural production space as well as a political sphere. This interpretation is in line with the classic studies of Norbert Elias and Frances Yates, as well as the more recent contributions of Amedeo Quondam, Carlo Ossola and Thomas DaCosta Kaufmann.[8] The methodological starting point is to determine how acceptable these traditional ideas are at this point in the twenty-first century, as we apply historiographical models different from those of the past and focus our attention on the artistic and cultural activity of the Habsburg dynasty.

The goal is to question the so-called Vasarian paradigm, the greatest and most-polished example of art-historical Italocentrism, on which much of the art history of the sixteenth century has been based. These aspects are addressed by Jesús F. Pascual and Fernando Bouza, whose essays explain how places like Spain, Portugal or England were linked by Habsburg cultural policy at certain junctures. Highly evocative image policies were developed in these places, in which artistic genres such as arms, armour and tapestries played a decisive role. The same can be said of Vanessa Quintanar's work, which approaches the subject by examining the familiar world of court festivities, especially the banquet and food, as a 'strategy of power'.

The Habsburg court and political system produced many works united by the theme of power, represented via a new iconography and images of war. Warfare and belligerence are the topic of essays by Víctor Mínguez, Antonio Gozalbo, Antonio Urquízar and Christian Beaufort-Spontin, who also analyses certain aspects of the practice of collecting arms and armour. The image of naval and land warfare, trophies and armour are specifically addressed in these contributions. They explore war as a fundamental element of Habsburg culture at a time when the very concept underwent a decisive change: the new idea of war not only influenced the military 'art' and the construction of fortifications, ships and firearms, but also affected literature, armour, flags, etc., and is amply reflected in epic poetry, painting and tapestries as an inherent Habsburg quality. In short, it would not be inaccurate to speak of an *Ars Bellica Habsburgica* in the sixteenth century.

Literature, books and the cultural sphere in general were also of central significance for the development of an art theory linked to the image of Habsburg power. María José Vega's essay examines themes related to 'textual cartography', the circulation of written ideas and books in the Habsburg world, looking beyond international relations to focus on the

---

8 Norbert Elias, *The Court Society* (New York: Pantheon Books, 1983 [1969]); Frances Yates, *Astraea: The Imperial Theme in the Sixteenth Century* (London: Routledge & K. Paul, 1975); Amedeo Quondam, *'Questo povero cortegiano'. Castiglione, il libro, la storia* (Rome: Bulzoni, 2006); Carlo Ossola, *L'Automne de la Renaissance: Idée du Temple de l'art à la fin du Cinquecento* (Paris: Les Belles Lettres, 2018); Thomas DaCosta Kaufmann, *Toward a Geography of Art* (Chicago: University of Chicago Press, 2004).

idea of the circulation and exchange of books and the textual form itself. Lara Vilà's chapter explores the connections between text and image, studying the image of Philip II as 'Rex Pacificus' and how it was shaped through references to Solomon and royal virtues. In his essay, José Luis Gonzalo investigates the fundamental role of books and libraries, particularly that of El Escorial, in shaping an image of Habsburg power and as a cultural medium for enacting certain court policies, while Patricia Andrés focuses on the creation of a 'hieroglyphic image' of the court through emblem books.

The ideas that the essays in this book present are derived from projects, meetings and seminars conducted in recent years by a substantial group of Spanish art history researchers who share an interest in these topics. Colleagues from universities and museum curators, Spanish and foreign, were also invited other to broaden and enrich these new perspectives on the *Habsburg Renaissance*. We thank the editors at Brepols Publishers, as well as the editorial board for their continuing support. The much appreciated assistance of Joachim Whaley and William O'Reilly made this book ready for a worldwide readership. This volume has been coordinated by Jesús F. Pascual Molina.

FERNANDO BOUZA

Habsburg Politics and Cultures in the Sixteenth Century

The Cosmopolitan Iberian Experience of Empires and Kingdoms[*]

According to Donald R. Kelley, the Swiss scholar Christophe Milieu (†1570) made what is 'perhaps the most striking contribution to cultural and literary historiography in the Renaissance'.[1] In addition to being the first to use the term *historia literaturae*,[2] Milieu (also known as Christophorus Mylaeus) is remarkable because he argued that historical reason (*historica ratio*) was 'the best way to organize the "universe of things"'.[3]

To prove his point, after sketching out his ideas in 1548, Milieu expanded on them in *De scribenda universitatis rerum historia libri quinque*, five books on how to write the history of the universe of things, published in Basel in 1551. If his goal was to create a universal history,[4] it seems only fitting that the Swiss scholar dedicated his work to the Most Serene Princes Maximilian and Philip of Habsburg. The latter took the throne as Philip II (1527–1598), and the former became Holy Roman Emperor Maximilian II (1527–1576); both were called to wield, or reclaim, universal power.[5]

---

[*] This work is part of the research conducted for the project PID2020-113906GB-I00 [*Las prácticas culturales de las aristocracias ibéricas del siglo de oro: en los orígenes del cosmopolitismo altomoderno (siglos XVI-XVII)*], supported and funded by the Spanish government.
[1] Donald R. Kelley, *Faces of History: Historical Inquiry from Herodotus to Herder* (New Haven: Yale University Press, 1998), 154.
[2] Donald R. Kelley, 'Writing Cultural History in Early Modern Europe: Christophe Milieu and his Project', *Renaissance Quarterly*, 52:2 (1999), 342–365 (esp. 342).
[3] Kelley, Faces, 154.
[4] Wilhelm Schmidt-Biggemann, *Topica universalis. Eine Modellgeschichte humanistischer und barocker Wissenschaft* (Hamburg: Felix Meiner Verlag, 1983), 21–30.
[5] Cristophe Milieu, *De scribenda universitatis rerum historia libri quinque* (Basil: Oporinus, 1551), '[Epistola] Serenissimis Principibus Philippo Hispaniarum atque Maximiliano Bohemiae Regi'.

Fernando Bouza • Complutense University of Madrid

In 1564, Maximilian was elected emperor of the Holy Roman Empire and, as *Kaiser*, became the highest-ranking civil authority in all of Christian Europe.[6] According to the political categories that applied, his universal superiority was derived from his status as the last surviving descendant of the Roman emperors by virtue of *translatio imperii*, the idea that 'the empire had been transferred from hand to hand and place to place', from the Roman Caesars of old to the Germanic Kaisers, 'and had therefore survived'.[7]

The 'Holy' aspect of his status reflected the fact that he claimed supreme power by virtue of being the active defender of Christendom from its enemies. The ever-suffering and stricken *Christianitas afflicta* was, in the confessional sixteenth century, facing the double threat of heretical schism and attack by forces of the Ottoman empire.[8]

For his part, from 1554–1555 Philip II gradually brought under his dominion different territories in Italy, Flanders, Burgundy, Spain and the Americas which were inherited from his father, Charles V (1500–1558). In 1531, Charles decided to reserve the imperial title for his brother Ferdinand I (1503–1564), thus dividing the extraordinary, accumulated possessions that the union between the Habsburgs and the Trastámaras of Castile and Aragon had placed in his hands as German emperor and Spanish king.

Maximilian and Philip were closely related on several counts. In addition to being cousins, they were brothers-in-law and in 1570 their dynastic ties were further reinforced by Philip's marriage to his niece, Archduchess Anna of Habsburg, the eldest daughter of Maximilian and Empress Maria Anna, Philip II's sister.

The famous saying 'Let others wage war, you, happy Austria, marry, | for Realms, which Mars gives to others, Venus bestows on you' recalls the great advantages that the House of Habsburg, or House of Austria as it was also known, obtained from several strategic marriages, including that of Maximilian I and Mary of Burgundy in 1477[9] and of the Archduke Philip the Fair and Joanna of Castile in 1496.[10] However, as the case

---

6 Barbara Stollberg-Rilinger, *The Holy Roman Empire: A Short History* (Princeton: Princeton University Press, 2018); James Muldoon, *Empire and Order: The Concept of Empire, 800–1800* (Basingstoke: Macmillan Press, 1999).
7 John G. A. Pocock, *Barbarism and Religion, Volume Three: The First Decline and Fall* (Cambridge: Cambridge University Press, 2003), 127.
8 Heinrich Lutz, *Christianitas afflicta. Europa, das Reich und die päpstliche Politik im Niedergang der Hegemonie Kaiser Karls V (1552-1556)* (Göttingen: Vandenhoeck & Ruprecht, 1964).
9 H. G. Koenigsberger, *Mars and Venus: Warfare and International Relations of the Casa de Austria* (London: Spanish Embassy, 1995).
10 Xavier Gil, 'The shaping of the Iberian polities in the late fifteenth and early sixteenth centuries', in *The Iberian World 1450–1820*, eds. Fernando Bouza, Pedro Cardim and Antonio Feros (London/New York: Routledge, 2020), 7–33.

of Philip II's childless union with his father's cousin Mary Tudor (1516–1558) proved, 'the magic formula' of Habsburg marital policy was not always successful;[11] and for all their strategic matchmaking, as Helmut G. Koenigsberger noted, the Habsburgs never forgot about war, conquest or domination.[12]

Marriage alliances were simply another tool in the hegemonic politics of every European dynasty. Consequently, inheritance was at the root of several dynastic successions that rocked the international stage, such as Henry of Bourbon's ascent to the French throne in 1589, or when a Stuart, James VI of Scotland, succeeded a Tudor, Elizabeth I, on the English throne. Another inheritance made Portugal part of Philip II's domains when Sebastian I of the House of Aviz died in 1578 at the Battle of Alcácer Quibir (Ksar-el-Kebir) in North Africa.

Philip II also thereby added Portugal's empire on the African coast, the routes and some coastal regions and islands of the Indian Ocean, and Brazil to the possessions he had inherited from his father Charles I as king of Spain, which had already been enlarged in different parts of the Americas and in the Philippines prior to 1580. Philip II was now ruler of a monarchy of unequivocally universal dimensions. Shortly after his proclamation by the *Estado da Índia* at Goa on 3 September 1581, the new king received a letter from a local prince who told him 'o seu nome se soa desde nasente do sol athe omde se poem' [your name resounds from where the sun rises to where it sets].[13]

The decorative programme designed for the royal hall in Lisbon's Torreão do Paço visually evoked the universal dimensions of the global power that was placed in Philip II's hands in 1580. The new tower which the monarch added to the existing Portuguese royal palace was to be painted with frescoes showing 'un Hércules con su piel de león' and 'por el suello el mundo en pedaços […] y en todas las superficies de los pedaços se pintarán mares y tierras y hércules encurvado juntando todos estos pedaços con galhardia' [a Hercules with his lion's skin (and) on the floor the world in pieces … and on the surfaces of every piece painted seas and lands and Hercules bending down to gather all those pieces with gallant grace]. The meaning of this decoration was unmistakeable, for Hercules 'a de ser moço con poca barva y ruvia remendando la filosofomía [fisognomía] de su magestad' [must be a youth with a sparse blonde beard recalling the physiognomy of His Majesty].[14]

---

11 Garrett Mattingly, *Renaissance Diplomacy* (Boston: Houghton Mifflin, 1955), 188, quoted in Muldoon, Empire and Order, 180.
12 Koenigsberger, *Mars and Venus*.
13 Fernando Bouza, *Felipe II y el Portugal dos povos. Imágenes de esperanza y revuelta* (Valladolid: Universidad de Valladolid, 2010), 46.
14 Bouza, *Felipe II*, 45.

Although he could not claim the supreme distinction of emperor, then held by his nephew Rudolf II (1552–1612), the Spanish and Portuguese Hercules could present himself as the true defender of a Christendom plagued by heretics and infidels from every part of the globe. He felt especially entitled to this role since, in his eyes, all emperors from Maximilian II onwards[15] had ceased to fulfil their preeminent duty of leading the church in its fight against Protestantism.

The aforementioned *translatio imperii* undoubtedly benefited the imperial branch of the House of Habsburg. There was also a *translatio fidei* and a *translatio scientiae*, the transfer of faith and knowledge across time and space, forever moving from east to west like the sun.[16] The global extension of his domains made Philip's monarchy a genuine empire.[17] Furthermore, according to the categories of the age, the dual condition of *translatio fidei* and *translatio scientiae* permitted Philip II to claim sovereignty over what Pablo Fernández Albaladejo called an 'empire *per se*', a reformulation of modern universal power.[18]

Philip II could boast of being not only a defender of the faith, like so many other European princes, but also the genuine executor of *translatio fidei* because he was exporting the true faith from Europe to the Indies.[19] He could also present himself as a protector of learning, a second Solomon who would build the library of El Escorial as a haven for errant books and codices from around the world.

The monastery of El Escorial near Madrid is the best evidence of the close connection between *translatio fidei* and *translatio scientiae*. Around 1590, the historian Luis Cabrera de Córdoba wrote in his poem *Laurentina* about the abundance of excellent books 'en todos los idiomas diferentes | así con arte como de vulgares' [in every different language | erudite and common alike] that had come to El Escorial 'de [*i.e.* desde] naciones diversas y de gentes' [from diverse nations and peoples] seeking the refuge that Philip II afforded, for 'que de ellas [naciones] se han venido aquí

---

15 Paula S. Fichtner, *Emperor Maximilian II* (New Haven: Yale University Press, 2001).
16 Peter Burke, 'The Myth of 1453: Notes and Reflections', in *Querdenken: Dissens und Toleranz im Wandel der Geschichte: Festschrift Hans Guggisberg*, ed. Michael Erbe (Mannheim: Palatium, 1996), 23–30.
17 Anthony Pagden, *Lords of All the World: Ideologies of Empire in Spain, Britain and France, c. 1500–c. 1800* (New Haven: Yale University Press, 1995); Muldoon, *Empire and Order*; John H. Elliott, *Empires of the Atlantic World: Britain and Spain in America, 1492–1830* (New Haven: Yale University Press, 2006).
18 Pablo Fernández Albaladejo, 'Imperio de por sí: la reformulación del poder universal en la temprana Edad Moderna', in *Fragmentos de Monarquía. Trabajos de historia política* (Madrid: Alianza, 1982), 168–183; Eva Botella-Ordinas, '"Exempt from time and from its fatal change": Spanish imperial ideology, 1450–1700', *Renaissance Studies*, 26-4 (2012), 580–604.
19 David A. Boruchof, 'New Spain, New England, and the New Jerusalem: The "Translation" of Empire, Faith, and Learning (*translatio imperii, fidei ac scientiae*) in the Colonial Mission Project', *Early American Literature*, 43-1 (2008), 5–34.

huyendo | porque, como la fe, se iban perdiendo' [they have fled here from those nations | because, like faith, they were gradually being lost].[20]

In sixteenth-century Europe, all political power was closely bound up with religion. Ultimately, the strength of rulers and authorities was only legitimate if used to promote the salvation of their subjects' immortal souls. The confessional schism resulting from the Protestant and Catholic reformations only strengthened the bond between altars and thrones, between the sword and the Word.[21]

Spain succouring Religion, also known as 'Religion saved by Spain', the picture that Titian painted between 1572 and 1575 and now in the Museo del Prado, is a good example of the visual allegorical representation of Philip II as a militant defender of the faith. The painting's history is quite complex, but we know that Titian sent Maximilian II a painting with a similar composition which, though now lost, was recorded in a print made by Giulio Fontana in 1568. In that work, Religion was succoured not by the Spain of Philip II, but by the empire of Maximilian II.[22]

The image of a prince using his power to defend the faith was also popular in Protestant Europe. A good example is the print attributed to Marcus Gheeraerts the Elder (*c.* 1520–*c.* 1587) that depicts Willem van Oranje (William of Orange) as Saint George, armed and on horseback over the United Provinces, defending a tormented woman from the dragon of Spanish tyranny. The woman is the personification of the Netherlands, and by her side we see the lamb of the Church of Christ ('De Kerke Christi').[23]

Philip II's Counter-Reformation confessionalisation did not mean that his relations with papal Rome were always excellent. In fact, both he and his father, Charles V, had complicated relationships with the supreme pontiffs. Occasionally their interests clashed with the pope's in power struggles on the Italian political stage, and they tried to divert a part of the lucrative income that clergymen received in Spanish territories to fill the royal coffers.

The curious rumour that neither the emperor nor his son was admitted to heaven when he died, in 1558 and 1598 respectively, is a telling reminder that their dealings with the Catholic Church were perplexing. According to the rumour, Charles was doomed to remain in purgatory for several years because he had been responsible for the Sack of Rome (1527)

---

20 Luis Cabrera de Córdoba, *Laurentina*, ed. Lucrecio Pérez Blanco (San Lorenzo del Escorial: Ciudad de Dios, 1975).
21 Richard Mackenney, *Sixteenth Century Europe: Expansion and Conflict* (New York: Saint Martin's Press, 1993).
22 Erwin Panofsky, *Problems in Titian: Mostly Iconographic* (New York: New York University Press, 1969), 186–190.
23 Daniel R. Horst, *De Opstand in zwart-wit: propagandaprenten uit de Nederlandse Opstand [1566–1584]* (Zutphen: Walburg Press, 2003), 239 and 350.

Fig. 1.1. *Religion assisted by Spain* by Titian, 1572–1575. © Museo Nacional del Prado.

and because of his policy of selling lands that had been granted to religious military orders. Philip II was also apparently turned away from heaven's gates for a time because he had sold church assets in an attempt to bolster his floundering treasury in the 1570s, not to mention the fact that he had laid siege to Rome in the time of Paul IV.[24]

Despite these disputes, Spanish kings and queens had been known as Catholic monarchs since the days of Isabella and Ferdinand. The Holy Roman Empire had an evident confessional diversity after the Peace of Augsburg of 1555, which sanctioned Lutheranism in those territories where the rulers chose to make it their official religion, and tolerated

---

24 Fernando Bouza, 'Felipe II sube a los cielos. Cartapacios, pliegos, papeles y visiones', in *Historia y perspectivas de investigación. Estudios en memoria del profesor Ángel Rodríguez Sánchez*, ed. Miguel Rodríguez Cancho (Mérida: ERE, 2002), 301–306.

numerous Jewish communities.[25] By contrast, sixteenth-century Spain witnessed a progressive and painful process of religious homogenisation.

The country's Muslim population was forced to renounce its Islamic faith between 1502 (in Castile) and 1526 (in Aragon), although the forced conversion of the Moriscos did not prevent them from continuing to observe the tenets of Islam in secrecy or from maintaining their cultural customs. Spain only tolerated the presence of so-called *moros de paz* or 'Moors of peace', generally ambassadors or traders from the Barbary coast.[26] The Jews had already been expelled in 1492, but a small Jewish quarter survived in the North African city of Oran, where the so-called 'Jews of the king of Spain' lived.[27] The confessional closing of ranks around Roman Catholicism and obedience to one sovereign ruler were the two things that Philip II's subjects had in common. The many and varied territories under his power constituted a composite monarchy,[28] referred to as the Spanish monarchy or, after 1580, the Spanish-Portuguese monarchy. A product of inheritance, conquest and negotiation, this monarchy was an aggregate of territories that maintained their own prerogatives and freedoms in terms of jurisdiction, privileges, representative and ceremonial institutions, majestic regalia, currency, language, taxation and even defence. This is illustrated by the fact that Philip II became Philip I in Portugal and there set aside his habitual black garments, at least for major ceremonies, and took up the prescribed regalia of majesty of his new kingdom, such as the royal sceptre, which did not exist in Castile. In the same way, the royal coat of arms was modified to incorporate the symbols of the new dominion, making sure to bestow on it a privileged position that would clearly identify it as a territory which retained its status as a separate kingdom. A splendid example of the new composition is found on the Tomar Cross, which Philip II of Spain (I of Portugal) gave to the Convent of the Order of Christ at Tomar, commemorating the solemn ceremony that acknowledged his accession to the Portuguese throne.

The Holy Roman Empire, too, was extraordinarily diverse, a mosaic of hundreds of jurisdictional realms which actually numbered more than 1,500 if we include the smaller feudal domains that acknowledged their dependence on the emperor. Compared with the 'classic' national states such as France or England, this empire or monarchy has long been regarded as an inexplicable anomaly in political science.

---

25 *In and Out of the Ghetto: Jewish-Gentile Relations in Late Medieval and Early Modern Germany*, eds. Ronnie Po-chia Hsia and Harmut Lehmann (Cambridge: Cambridge University Press, 1995).
26 Bernard Vincent, 'Les musulmans dans l'Espagne moderne', in *Les musulmans dans l'histoire de l'Europe. I. Une intégration invisible*, eds. Jocelyne Dakhlia and Bernard Vincent (Paris: Albin Michel, 2011), 611–634.
27 Jean-Frédéric Schaub, *Les juifs du roi d'Espagne. Oran, 1509–1669* (Paris: Hachette, 1999).
28 John H. Elliott, 'A Europe of Composite Monarchies', *Past & Present*, 137 (1992), 48–71.

As early as 1667, its oddity led the German jurist Samuel Pufendorf (1632–1694) to describe the Spanish empire as *monstro simile*— a monstrosity.[29] However, in recent years, historiography has debunked the perception of these supposedly irregular political formations—the Holy Roman Empire[30] and the Spanish monarchy[31]—as aberrant monstrosities.

The first indication that the empire and the monarchy were not monstrous political entities may be their longevity. The Holy Roman Empire survived until 1806, and the composite monarchy endured at least until the early-eighteenth century when the House of Bourbon came to the throne.

The sixteenth century was still a period of hegemony for the Spanish monarchy; despite facing serious conflicts in Flanders and elsewhere, its structure was not under the enormous pressure of the great crises that arose in the following century, when it would be forced to prove its undeniable resilience.[32] However, this period raises questions about how that composite monarchy actually managed to govern jurisdictionally diverse territories and even make the qualitative leap of adding Portugal to its possessions.

First, the monarchy developed a system of deputies who, as direct agents of the king, represented the monarch in territories including Portugal, Aragon and Naples, where they were required because of the nature of their realms as kingdoms and not mere provinces. Appointing viceroys and governors, the monarchy became a series of domains ruled by an absent king where the domains retained their own privileges, local bureaucracy and even their own courts, maintaining the rituals of their distinctive ceremonial traditions. A case in point is the Lisbon court of Archduke Albert of Austria (1559–1621), Viceroy of Portugal from 1583 to 1594.

Second, the monarchy remained firmly rooted in Castile, the mainstay of the royal treasury by virtue of its tax-collecting capacity and, most importantly, the realm to which the silver-rich Viceroyalties of New Spain and Peru were attached. Moreover, Castile was the seat of the royal court, installed in Madrid in 1561. The acquisition of Portugal opened the possibility of making Lisbon the court of the new dual monarchy, as its location on the Atlantic coast was considered more advantageous than inland Madrid. This never happened, less because of the inconvenience of

---

29 Alfred Dufour, 'Pufendorf', in *The Cambridge History of Political Thought (1450–1700)*, ed. James H. Burns (Cambridge: Cambridge University Press, 1991), 561–588 (esp. 583).
30 Peter H. Wilson, 'Still a Monstrosity? Some Reflections on Early Modern German Statehood', *The Historical Journal*, 49:2 (2006), 565–576.
31 *Polycentric Monarchies: How Did Early Modern Spain and Portugal Achieve and Maintain a Global Hegemony?*, eds. Pedro Cardim, Tamar Herzog, José Javier Ruiz Ibáñez, and Gaetano Sabatini (Brighton: Sussex Academic Press, 2012).
32 Christopher Storrs, *The Resilience of the Spanish Monarchy 1665–1700*, (Oxford: Oxford University Press, 2006).

moving to a new city than because it meant abandoning the Castilian heart of the monarchy.

The Castilian court was home to several tribunals or councils that advised the monarch on the varied affairs of state and governance, although the domains of the composite monarchy maintained their own systems of justice and government, as was the case in Portugal, the Netherlands, Franche-Comté, Milan, Naples and Sicily.

Some of the councils residing alongside the absent king can be likened to our modern-day bureaucracy, although the legal officials of that era were far from loyal public servants. Others, however, handled matters related to the government of specific territories, such as the councils of Castile, the Indies, Flanders, Italy, Aragon and, after the dual union of 1580, Portugal. Some of them, like Aragon and Portugal, existed as privileges of their respective kingdoms, serving as reminders of these territories at the royal court and not merely as administrative tribunals.

In addition, the Castilian court included those who served the different royal households, starting with the king and queen. They employed people from many different realms and territories, creating a cosmopolitan court environment which ladies and gentlemen from across the monarchy's domains and beyond aspired to join. In this respect, it is interesting to recall that one of the privileges Philip II granted to Portugal was allowing certain young women of the Portuguese nobility to serve the Infantas at court, giving rise to the famous *meninas*.

Spain made its presence felt in different territories by the constant threat of violence, often perpetrated by troops stationed at strategically-located garrisons or castles to control the population. It also sent legal officials to mete out justice or collect taxes in the Crown's name, thereby keeping a tight rein on even the most far-flung domains.

An impressive system of written communications and dispatches was created to overcome the inconveniences posed by the enormous distances covered; it could even be said that the Spanish-Portuguese monarchy, attempting to bind its many parts together, created an empire of ink—a written empire.

A steady stream of reports was sent from the territories to decision-making centres such as Madrid, Seville and Lisbon, while royal orders and petitions flowed outwards in the opposite direction. The printing press also helped to distribute royal orders, particularly in Spanish America, first to Mexico (1539) and later to Peru (1584), where the first text ever printed was a royal proclamation of Philip II. Finally, this empire of ink also established channels by which subjects of any status could write to the monarch or his tribunals.[33]

---

33 Fernando Bouza, 'Cultures and communication across the Iberian world (fifteenth–seventeenth centuries)', in *The Iberian World 1450–1820*, 211–244 (esp. 228–239).

Yet however overbearing and coercive they may have been, the military and official legal forces were not the most important means of maintaining control in a large part of the monarchy's domains (after periods of conquest or rebellion). One of the main reasons why the monarchy was able to endure in such different and distant places, from Franche-Comté to Portugal, was its extraordinary talent for reaching agreements with the local ruling class.

By conducting negotiations that culminated in formalised pacts and charters, the Spanish Habsburg monarchy worked because it had the support of local nobles and leaders who facilitated the governance of its constituent parts. In exchange for their support, these ruling classes expected to maintain their privileged status in each domain and cultivate opportunity to prosper at court or in the service of a universal monarch.

Although this monarchy/empire was characterised by the existence of internal borders, clearly established in the jurisdictional charters of each constituent realm, it was also a unified reality for certain groups whose members could move unimpeded throughout its domains. These clearly identifiable groups included courtiers, urban patricians, merchants, traders and businessmen, lawyers and officers of justice, diplomats, soldiers and sailors, missionaries and clergymen, collectors, inventors and artists. It can therefore be said that numerous *res publicae* rested on that composite monarchy and gave to it the spatial continuity not provided by legal charters.

The monarchy's operating mechanism benefited enormously from the dense web of interpersonal networks woven around merchants in such vital matters as the circulation of news and financial revenue. A small cluster of individual biographies, however, reveal that it was possible to live by hopping from one European court or realm to the next, in the service of the monarch, the royal family, the provincial aristocratic courts, or even the market. By way of example, we might recall the cases of Cardinal Antoine Perrenot de Granvelle, Ruy Gómez de Silva, Sofonisba Anguissola, Cristóvão de Moura, Antonis Mor, Jacopo da Trezzo, Joris Hoefnagel, Pompeo Leoni and, above all, Doménikos Theotokópoulos, El Greco.

However, in addition to these celebrated individuals—whose experiences ran parallel to those of Arcimboldo of Milan and the Flemish artist Bartholomeus Spranger, who travelled to Vienna and Prague for work—many other lives attest to the appeal of residing, or seeking employment, in the monarchy of Philip II. The list is extensive, ranging from ladies-in-waiting like Jeanne de Chassincourt (Jacincourt); Juliana de Alencastre and the sisters Anna, Barbara and Hippolyta Dietrichstein; to printers and engravers (the Craesbeecks and Pieter Perret); natural philosophers (Leonardo Fioravanti and Giovanni Battista Gesio); scholars (Pierre Pantin and Andreas Schottus); musicians (Philippe Rogier and

Géry de Ghersem); and individuals such as Elisabetta Bonacina, Jacopo da Trezzo's servant, the court fool Agostino Profiti, and the highly esteemed tailor René Geneli. Eugenio Salazar was probably quite right in saying that the royal court had become a magnet for myriad people who dressed and wore their hair and moustaches in the style of their respective native lands, moreover exhibiting 'tanta diversidad de lenguas entre ellos, como entre los que edificaban la torre de Babel' [among them a diversity of tongues to rival that of the builders of the Tower of Babel].[34]

In this monarchy of *res publicae*, there were excellent connections between major cities like Seville, Antwerp, Burgos, Madrid, Brussels, Naples, Milan and Lisbon, which in turn had links to important urban centres in Asia, such as Goa; or the Americas, such as Mexico City and Lima. For reasons already indicated above, the venerable, lavish court of Lisbon, a Babelian city with a cosmopolitan atmosphere[35] which Francisco Porras de la Cámara visited in 1591, played a very prominent role in this monarchy/empire after 1580.[36]

Porras arrived as part of the delegation sent to Lisbon by the city council of Seville to ensure a steady supply of grain for making bread to feed the Andalusian metropolis. His case illustrates the fact that interurban relations were not hampered by jurisdictional borders; indeed, the traffic of goods and metals that had linked Seville and Lisbon throughout the sixteenth century, long before the kingdoms were united in 1580, continued seamlessly after that date. On the banks of the Tagus, Porras's delegation was received by a group of Christian businessmen newly arrived from Antwerp who were doing business in both Portugal and Castile, competing with Genoese and German merchants to profit from the lucrative Atlantic and Indian trade.

During his time in Lisbon, the Sevillian was struck by the astonishing diversity of the Portuguese court, taking note of life in the palace, its bustling commercial streets, and the land and sea exercises conducted by troops from the Castilian garrison. He also noticed the music and songs of the African slaves, the comedies and the squares 'que se poblaban de gentes de todas naciones y reinos e lenguas e profesiones del mundo'

---

34 *Epistolario español. II*, ed. Eugenio de Ochoa (Madrid: Rivadeneyra, 1870), 283–284.
35 Sheldon Pollock, 'Cosmopolitanism and Vernacular in History', in *Cosmopolitanism*, eds. Carol A. Breckenridge, Dipesh Chakrabarty, Homi K. Bhaba and Sheldon Pollock (Durham, NC: Duke University Press, 2002), 15–53.
36 *The Global City: On the Streets of Renaissance Lisbon*, eds. Annemarie Jordan-Gschwend and K. J. P. Lowe (London: Paul Holberton Publishing, 2015); Saúl Martínez Bermejo, 'Lisbon, new Rome and emporium: Comparing an early modern imperial capital, 1550–1750', *Urban History* 44(4) (2017), 604–621. An edition of the *Jornada de Lisboa de 1591*, the original manuscript of which is held at the Real Biblioteca in Madrid, MSS II/2243, is currently in preparation.

[filled with people of every nation and kingdom and language and profession in the world].[37]

He seemed to be particularly impressed by the influence of the *Estado da Índia*, which was everywhere in Lisbon, and took pains to describe it. For instance, he recounted the ceremonies of the solemn celebration of the feast of Santo Tomé (the Apostle Thomas) in the royal chapel, organised by the company in charge of Asian trade, the *Casa da Índia*. The chapel floor was covered with silk carpets from India and Anatolia, on which large zoomorphic censers representing lions, dragons and eagles had been placed. Porras was particularly surprised by the nine large basins of spices —pepper, ginger, cinnamon, nutmeg and other 'escogidísimas drogas al fin como para ofrecer a Dios' [fine drugs carefully selected as if for offering to God]—placed before the main altar, where there were also two tigers and two tortoises with perfume emanating from their stripes and openings in their shells. Finally, the voices of twenty singers and the strains of two organs completed a truly stunning spectacle.

The Iberian and cosmopolitan experience of the Spanish-Portuguese monarchy reached its apogee in Lisbon as a showcase of imperial power. Its renovated royal palace was certainly not a bad choice of location to paint Philip II as the new Habsburg Hercules, gathering up with 'gallant grace' all parts of a world where were divided and shattered in pieces on the palace floor.

---

37 Isabel de Castro Henriques, *Historical Guide to an African Lisbon: 15th to 21st Century* (Lisbon: Colibri, 2021).

FERNANDO CHECA

A Theory of Art for the 'Habsburg Renaissance'

The idea of a literary source for art in the early modern era gained acceptance in 1924, when the Austrian historian Julius von Schlosser published his famous book *Die Kunstliteratur* [Art Literature], to which he added the subtitle *Ein Handbuch zur Quellenkunde der Neueren Kunstgeschichte* [A Handbook for Studying the Sources of Modern Art History].[1]

In his book, Schlosser placed Giorgio Vasari and his *Lives of the Most Excellent Painters, Sculptors and Architects* at the heart of an entire theoretical system that was practically canonical for much of the twentieth century. We find a precedent for this idea in the *Vasaristudien* of Wolfgang Kallab, a book left unfinished by the author and completed by Schlosser himself in 1908.[2]

In Schlosser's opinion, 'the forefather of art literature in the true sense of the word' had been the Florentine sculptor Lorenzo Ghiberti and his *I comentarii*, on which Schlosser wrote his doctoral thesis. Ghiberti was the first to sketch the outlines of a genuine history of art, later retraced and completed by Vasari and his followers. Ghiberti also pioneered a very specific Italian style of art prose and created a vocabulary for the new art. Schlosser thought that Leon Battista Alberti, whom he regarded as the greatest treatise writer of the fifteenth century, continued the methodology introduced by Ghiberti, expanded on his ideas, and ushered in a new way

---

1 Julius von Schlosser, *Die Kunstliteratur: Ein Handbuch zur Quellenkunde der neuen Kunstgeschichte. Vol. 1* (Vienna: Kunstverlag Anton Schroll & Co., 1924). Recent studies about J. von Schlosser: Raphael Rosenberg, 'Delineating the history of art literature by genre: Julius von Schlosser revisited', in *Journal of Art Historiography*, 24 (2021), 1–20, and Christopher Wood, *A History of Art History* (Princeton: Princeton University Press, 2019), 318–328.
2 Wolfgang Kallab, *Vasaristudien, mit einem Lebensbilde des Verfassers aus dessen Nachlasse herausgegeben von Julius v. Schlosser* (Vienna: Karl Graeser & Leipzig: B. G. Teubner, 1908).

Fernando Checa • Complutense University of Madrid

Ars Habsburgica, ed. by Fernando Checa & Miguel Ángel Zalama, Habsburg Worlds, 6 (Turnhout: Brepols, 2023), pp. 27–40
BREPOLS ✥ PUBLISHERS   10.1484/M.HW-EB.5.135331

of thinking about and expressing artistic reality that applied to both visual arts and architecture. Schlosser likewise underscored the normative quality that these writers ascribed to artistic activity, and how this activity should be related to antiquity, and noted the importance of the artist's biography in this process as a means of explaining art history, as well as the history of Italy and its cities.

Years later, other studies called attention to the formal structure of the theories expressed in these writings, which they traced back to the classical divisions of the art of rhetoric. This perspective was pioneered in an article by Creighton Gilbert, published in the journal *Marsyas* in 1943.[3] Gilbert established the first genealogy of the tripartite division of painting proposed by authors like Leon Battista Alberti and Paolo Pino—in other words, the idea that painting was divided into 'invention', 'design' or 'drawing', and 'colouring'—by linking these categories to the three parts into which the ancients had divided the art of rhetoric: *inventio, dispositio* and *elocutio*. This is not the place for even a brief historiographical review of the subject, although we should recall that twenty years later, in 1963, Richard Krautheimer published his 'Alberti and Vitruvius', which drew a connection between Alberti and Vitruvius and the methodological classifications of artistic reality according to the aforementioned tripartite rhetorical scheme. Essentially, he associated the Vitruvian triad of *firmitas, utilitas,* and *venustas* [strength, utility, and beauty] for architecture with the *inventio, dispositio,* and *elocutio* [invention, arrangement and style] of rhetoric.[4]

This system of thought is a historiographical construct that was quite successful throughout the twentieth century, but it excludes other types of literary sources which, because their contents are not structured in a similar way, were not useful for establishing a theoretical basis of the subject that concerns us here—namely, the 'Habsburg Renaissance'. This particular Renaissance, therefore, lacked a written theoretical foundation, a unique 'art literature' of the type so richly and abundantly described in Schlosser's book. Rather, as this chapter will attempt to prove, the great works of art produced in the service of the Habsburgs over the course of the sixteenth century found their 'theoretical' commentary in general discourses that were ignored in the twentieth-century historiographic system. Consequently, a different classification and canon of sources must be devised to provide a theoretical basis for a proposed 'Habsburg Renaissance'.

---

3 Creighton Gilbert, 'Antique Frameworks for Renaissance Art Theory: Alberti and Pino', *Marsyas*, 3 (1946), 87–106.

4 Richard Krautheimer, 'Alberti and Vitruvius', in *Studies in Western Art*, II (Princeton, NJ: Princeton University Press, 1963), 42–52; reprinted in *Studies in Early Christian, Medieval and Renaissance Art* (New York: New York University Press / London: University of London Press, 1969), 323–332.

With this in mind, we would like to highlight four sources of primary importance for crafting a Renaissance image of power around the Habsburg dynasty.

Languages of triumph: Juan Cristóbal Calvete de Estrella and his *Felicissimo viaje*... (1552)

In addition to being an inexhaustible resource for iconographic studies, accounts of court festivities and triumphal entries can provide vital insight into the functions and meaning of artistic images in the sphere of the House of Habsburg and what Larry Silver, speaking of the art created around Emperor Maximilian I, called 'visual ideology'.[5]

Consequently, the humanist Juan Cristóbal Calvete de Estrella –member of the house of emperor Charles V and prince Philip II– should be regarded as one of the fundamental theoreticians in the visual construction of the 'Habsburg Renaissance', primarily thanks to two seminal works: his description of Prince Philip's progress through Italy and the Netherlands between 1548 and 1551, published in 1552, and his account of the imperial catafalque for the obsequies of Charles V in Valladolid in 1559.[6]

In the first of these books we find several pertinent aspects:

a   A *theory of triumph*, in the explicit sense of a revival of classical antiquity, and in light of the civic importance of places where triumphal entries were made and their association with imperial power. The value of festivities and the ephemeral helps us to understand the idea of a fundamentally magnificent and highly political world in constant motion around the House of Austria, where the aesthetics of celebration and triumph exceeded the traditional Flemish *joyeux entrées* and overcame everything. To give just one example, Calvete, when speaking of the prince's sea voyage from Catalonia to Genoa, commented on the ornamentation of the vessels and said that the ships resembled 'triumphal arches with the rich standards and flags visible on them'.[7]

---

5   Larry Silver, *Marketing Maximilian: The Visual Ideology of a Holy Roman Emperor* (Princeton, NJ: Princeton University Press, 2008). In addition to Silver, there have been other studies about the construction of a Maximilian's 'visual culture', such us Heinz Noflatscher, Michael A. Chisholm, and Bertrand Schnerb (eds.), *Maximilian I. (1459–1519): Wahrnehmung - Ubersetzungen – Gender* (Innsbruck: Studien Verlag, 2011).
6   Juan Cristóbal Calvete de Estrella, *El felicissimo viaje del muy alto y muy poderoso principe don Phelippe*, ed. Paloma Cuenca (1552; Madrid: Sociedad Estatal para la Conmemoración de los Centenarios de Felipe II y Carlos V, 2001); and Juan Cristóbal Calvete de Estrella, *El túmulo Imperial, adornado de historias y letreros y epitaphios en prosa y verso latino* (Valladolid: Diego Fernández de Córdoba, 1559).
7   Calvete de Estrella (2001), 31, note 6.

b   The work helps us to understand the importance and distinctive features of a specific *type of court artist*, also easily identifiable in the Habsburg world, by listing among the prince's companions the musician Antonio Cabezón, 'singular organist', the painter and miniaturist Diego de Arroyo, renowned, he says, in the manual arts, 'whom no man of our age surpasses in illumination and painting', and Juan de Serojas, 'unique in handicrafts that can be wrought'.[8]

Artists of this type were also plentiful at the court of Emperor Maximilian I, where we find the miniaturist and painter Jörg Kölderer,[9] whose presence at the Habsburg court in Valladolid was noted by Jesús Pascual Molina.[10] The appearance of such artists, specialised in the pageantry and decoration of court festivities, and their mention in these sources can also be linked to the arts system that developed in the Habsburg world.

c   Calvete's book is one of the most important sources for studying the artistic representation of kings and princes in the Renaissance, for it develops a *theory and practice of Habsburg magnificence* at a decisive moment in the evolution of a certain kind of Renaissance art in connection with the House of Austria of the late 1540s.

The classical element in this type of imagery is highly significant, as illustrated by the continual importance attached to the mythological character of Hercules, succession myths in biblical and classical literature, the reiterated appearance of allusions to and images from the *Aeneid* (essential to the visual construction of the 'Habsburg Renaissance' in the late 1540s and early 1550s), and the figurative relevance of dynastic, imperial and royal genealogies. These elements were decisive in the visual configuration of artistic programmes from the time of Maximilian I and would remain so for many years. The book also contains a number of fascinating references to different visual representations of the prince: seated, on horseback, standing, in armour, imitating bronze, imitating marble, etc.

d   Calvete also offers a very interesting assessment of the *artistic languages of magnificence of the Italian Renaissance* from the perspective of a

---

8   Calvete de Estrella (2001), 33.
9   Silver (2008), 14–17, note 5. More recently, Silver has analyzed in more detail those topics in Larry Silver, 'Did Germany Have a Medieval Herbstzeit?', in Peter Arnade, Martha Howell and Anton van der Lem (eds.), *Rereading Huizinga: Autumn of the Middle Ages, a Century Later* (Amsterdam: Amsterdam University Press, 2019), 143–168.
10 Jesús Félix Pascual Molina, *Fiesta y poder. La corte en Valladolid (1502–1559)* (Valladolid: Universidad de Valladolid, 2013); Jesús Félix Pascual Molina, 'Los oficios artísticos en la casa real en España durante el siglo XVI, y su relación con la fiesta cortesana', in Begoña Alonso Ruiz, Javier Gómez Martínez, Julio J. Polo Sánchez, Luis Sazatornil Ruiz and Fernando Villaseñor Sebastián, eds., *La formación artística: creadores-historiadores-espectadores*, vol. I (Santander: Editorial Universidad de Cantabria, 2018), 107–119.

Spanish Habsburg courtier in the mid-sixteenth century, a man of Erasmian education and ideas, in his description of the triumphs at Genoa, Milan, Mantua and Trento. This language differs noticeably from his account of triumphal entries into Flemish cities, for example Brussels and Antwerp, and his detailed description of Binche Palace and the festivities that Mary of Hungary organised there. Nor does he overlook the importance of the Flemish 'chambers of rhetoric' which, prior to their prohibition in 1567, often inspired the iconographic and historical themes chosen for triumphal arches and for the ephemeral 'theatres' that figured so prominently in Prince Philip's 1549 arrival in Antwerp.[11]

This book is therefore one of the best keys to understanding the significance and the perception that both realms, Italy and Flanders, acquired in the artistic imagination of Habsburg power, which would have far-reaching consequences for future art. The chronicler gives a particularly eloquent description of the *Palazzo Te* in Mantua, designed like a labyrinth, which can be compared with his account of the palace and city hall of Brussels and their paintings—painstakingly described by Calvete and now lost—in which Rogier van der Weyden elaborated on the idea of the administration of justice in the classical world. His incredibly lengthy report of the culmination of the prince's journey at Binche Palace is also one of the defining, if not the most important, moments of the 'Habsburg Renaissance'.

Languages of history: military chronicles and poetic language. The *Conquest of Tunis* tapestry series by Jan Cornelisz Vermeyen

In the Habsburg cultural and visual world, it was fairly common for the chronicle of a historical event, usually war-related, also to provide inspiration and interpretation for the artistic image.

While the military chronicle could often be a source of iconography and accurate information on specific events, here we shall highlight the Habsburg Renaissance's preference for narrative as an artistic language, rather than symbolism or allegory. However—and this is a key point—the choice should not be construed to imply lack of interest in interpretation as opposed to supposed 'realism', but rather a conscious *parti pris* in the artistic image's construction.

The written account of the German war in which the troops of Charles V defeated the Schmalkaldic League in 1547, commissioned by

---

11 Stijn Bussels, *Spectacle, Rhetoric and Power: The Triumphal Entry of Prince Philip of Spain into Antwerp* (Amsterdam/New York: Rodopi, 2012).

the emperor from Luis de Ávila y Zúñiga, was undoubtedly the primary source of Titian's *Equestrian Portrait of Charles V at Mühlberg*, in terms of both iconography and the use of artistic language.[12] However, here we will focus on one of the most important examples of Habsburg art from the late 1540s: the series of twelve tapestries known as *The Conquest of Tunis*, the cartoons for which were designed by Jan Cornelisz Vermeyen and which Mary of Hungary commissioned in early 1545 from the tapestry weaver Willem de Pannemaker.[13]

Particularly significant is the inscription that appears on the first tapestry in the series, called *The Map*, held by a likeness of the series' own artist, Jan Cornelisz Vermeyen. It reads as follows:

> The conquest in Africa in 1535 of Charles, the fifth Holy Roman Emperor [...] had serious causes that the chroniclers of the time recount more fully in their histories. These causes left aside, the course of events is represented in this work as exactly as possible. As it is necessary for a clear understanding to know the country in which the events took place and what preparations had been made, the action is treated in this tapestry according to nature, all that concerns cartography/cosmography, leaving nothing to be desired. In the distance the coasts of Africa, like those of Europe and its boundaries, are seen with their chief ports, their broad gulfs, their islands, their winds, at exactly the same distances at which they really lie, the author having taken more care over their precise situation than over the requirements of painting. All has been done, for the countries as well, in strict accordance with cartography/cosmography, and the painter has observed the canons of his art, considering that the spectator's viewpoint is from Barcelona, where the embarkation for Tunis took place. This town lies between the spectator and the south, with the north behind, over the left shoulder. With accuracy thus established, the peculiarities of the other tapestries can be better understood.[14]

---

12 Luis de Ávila y Zúñiga, 'Comentario de la guerra de Alemania', in *Historiadores de sucesos particulares*, Biblioteca de Autores españoles, XI (1549; Madrid, 1852); Fernando Checa Cremades, *Tiziano y las cortes del Renacimiento* (Madrid: Marcial Pons Historia, 2013), 259–260.

13 Hendrik J. Horn, *Jan Cornelisz Vermeyen, Painter of Charles V and His Conquest of Tunis: Paintings, Etchings, Drawings, Cartoons & Tapestries* (Doornspijk: Davaco, 1989), 118. For the cartoons, see the study by Katia Schmitz-von Ledebur, 'Emperor Charles V Captures Tunis: a Unique Set of Tapestry Cartoons', in *Studia Bruxellae*, vol. 11, no. 1 (2019), 387–404. About the context of the imperial campaign, and its impact, see some of the studies in Ingrid Ciulisova, Herbert Karner and Bernardo J. García García (eds.), *The Habsburgs and their Courts in Europe, 1400–1700: Between Cosmopolitanism and Regionalism* (Vienna: Österreichische Akademie der Wissenschaften, KU Leuven, 2014).

14 Horn, 230.

The intention of the series' visual language is to achieve a high degree of historical accuracy, not only with regard to events—for which, as we shall see, the artist resorts to the language of historical chronicles—but also with regard to places and topography, deeming it necessary that the tapestries should enable viewers to 'know the country in which the events took place'. The artist wanted the subject of this hanging depicted in a manner so true to nature that in 'all that concerns cartography/cosmography' it leaves 'nothing to be desired'. This desire for accuracy even trumped the author's aesthetic and artistic interests, 'having taken more care over their precise situation than over the requirements of painting'.

The inscription clearly denotes the use of a representative double language, which varied depending on the types of events narrated. While everything related to the sea voyage follows a chorographic and topographical narrative system, the description of the campaign uses 'the languages of art', which naturally afford greater freedom.

The idea of a double language—topographical and precise with regard to the geographical aspects of the series, and poetic and 'creative' when using the 'languages of art' to chronicle military events—recalls Aristotle's famous passages in *Poetics*, where he distinguished between the languages of poetry and history. The Stagirite noted:

> It is, moreover, evident from what has been said that it is not the function of the poet to relate what has happened, but what may happen —what is possible according to the law of probability or necessity. The poet and the historian differ not by writing in verse or in prose. [...] The true difference is that one relates what has happened, the other what may happen. Poetry, therefore, is a more philosophical and a higher thing than history: for poetry tends to express the universal, history the particular.

He later remarked:

> The poet being an imitator, like a painter or any other artist, must of necessity imitate one of three objects—things as they were or are, things as they are said or thought to be, or things as they ought to be. The vehicle of expression is language—either current terms or, it may be, rare words or metaphors. There are also many modifications of language, which we concede to the poets. (Aristotle, *Poetics*, 9 and 25).

In the second century AD, Lucian of Samosata understood that history should be explained clearly and that facts should be presented as lucidly as possible:

> Using neither unknown nor out-of-the-way words [...] but such as ordinary folk may understand and the educated commend'. However, in his treatise on *How To Write History*, he proposed a balance between factual accuracy and narrative which we might call a 'poetic' system,

where the historian's mind acquires a touch of poetry when his subject is lofty and sublime, especially, Lucian says, 'when he has to do with battle arrays, with land and sea fights; for then he will have need of a wind of poetry to fill his sails and help carry his ship along, high on the crest of the waves. Let his diction nevertheless keep its feet on the ground, rising with the beauty and greatness of his subjects and as far as possible resembling them, but without becoming more unfamiliar or carried away than the occasion warrants.

The different ways in which Vermeyen portrayed himself in the cartoons for the series also articulate these language variations and the relationships between images and words, one of the central pillars of the entire tapestries narrative system.

In the first tapestry of the series, we see a full-length, life-sized portrait of the artist gazing out at the viewer and wielding not a brush but a compass, thereby underscoring the importance of geography and topography in the series, as well as the intellectual and scientific nature of his creation.

The cartoonist emphasises the descriptive language which chronicles the story of his tapestries by inserting his own likeness, frequently though not overly conspicuously, in the midst of the field of battle, sketching events as they occur: a Vermeyen determined to give a true and faithful account of what happened.

Finally, in the ninth tapestry Jan Cornelisz again casts himself in a leading role, placing his enlarged figure beside that of an even more prominent personage, probably the cosmographer and chronicler Alonso de Santa Cruz, in the midst of writing his text. This is undoubtedly a reference to the written account, now visually presented in perfect balance with the image.

A comprehensive theory of the Habsburg Renaissance: Fray José de Sigüenza's *Historia de la orden Jerónima* (1605)

Fray José de Sigüenza's history of the Order of Saint Jerome, published in 1605, is undoubtedly the most important source for a full understanding of the idea of the 'Habsburg Renaissance'.

In keeping with the historiographical principles on which Schlosser based his work, this book was not mentioned in the first German edition of *Die Kunstliteratur* in 1924. Otto Kurz's addenda to the 1935 Italian translation refer to it as *Historia de la orden de San Jerónimo*, briefly indicating that it is 'important for the history of El Escorial'. An asterisk in that edition directs us to Kurz's final addendum, where he mentions the 1927 Spanish edition and says 'anche separatamente Historia de la Fundación de El Escorial por Felipe II', noting that the part published at that time was the one that describes the founding of the building.[15] When Schlosser's book first appeared in 1924, this section of the history of the Hieronymites in connection with El Escorial had not yet been published separately; moreover, the parts of Sigüenza's book which have art-historical relevance had only appeared one year earlier, in 1923, when Francisco Javier Sánchez Cantón published the first volume of his *Fuentes literarias para el arte español*.

Following Otto Kurz's example, Sigüenza's book was also cited in the Spanish translation of *Die Kunstliteratur* that appeared in 1976 with notes by Antonio Bonet Correa, who added the following sources on El Escorial: the 1975 edition of *Laurentina* by Luis Cabrera de Córdoba; *Las estampas y el sumario de Juan de Herrera* (1959) edited by Luis Cervera Vera; the 1935 edition of *Discurso de la figura cúbica* by Juan de Herrera; and the books on Juan de Herrera by Francisco Iñiguez (1948), Francisco Javier Sánchez Cantón (1941) and René Taylor (1967). In other words, historiographers were focused on El Escorial as architectural discourse and on the figure of Juan de Herrera.[16]

But Sigüenza's text is much more than that, for it offers an interpretation of El Escorial –palace, monastery, library, royal burial..., built by Philip II, starting in 1561, in honour of St. Laurence and remembering the triumph against the French troops in the battle of St. Quentin (1557)–, as the embodiment of the idea of Renaissance art related to the House of Habsburg, applied to a monument of which he takes a holistic view, encompassing its history, symbolism and art.

Sigüenza sees El Escorial, not from the perspective of the history of the monastic Order of Saint Jerome (although this is included), but from that of the reign of Philip II and the king's own person. Consequently, in the first of the two parts devoted to the building, he explains it and its ornamentation by following the historical timeline of its construction. From the search for a place to build it and the reasons it was founded to a description of the death and obsequies of the monarch, Sigüenza consistently gives pride of place to the king and his involvement in the undertaking.

This part, broken down into 22 discourses, is essential for comprehending the ritual and symbolic value of ceremonies, one of the defining traits of the 'Habsburg Renaissance', thus completing the picture from a different point of view than that of Calvete de Estrella's book. It is also essential for explaining the meaning and manner in which Philip used the building and its works of art, as well as the role played by the different actors

---

15 Julius Schlosser Magnino, *La letteratura artistica. Manuale delle fonti della storia dell'arte moderna* (Florence: La Nuova Italia, 1935), 285 and 718.
16 Julius Schlosser, *La literatura artística. Manual de fuentes de la historia moderna del arte. Presentación y adiciones por Antonio Bonet Correa* (Madrid: Cátedra, 1976), 253.

on that stage, such as the Hieronymites, the court and the king himself. All this constituted a system of relations and art patronage unique to the 'Habsburg Renaissance'.

The symbolic intentions of the building are most apparent in the prologue to the first part. Following the biblical culture of his master Arias Montano, Sigüenza compares the building to Noah's Ark, Moses's Tabernacle and the Temple of Solomon, basing El Escorial and even classical architecture itself on parameters that are in fact the opposite of the 'rationalist' premises of Vitruvius who, as we know, believed that the origin of architecture lay in the first habitable structure.

The significance of this book as an art-historical source is even more evident in the second part, 'De las partes del edificio del Monasterio', with 23 discourses on the building's various parts. Numerous of Sigüenza's arguments serve as an indispensable theoretical basis for the 'Habsburg Renaissance': the debate between Vitruvian, Platonic-Augustinian and biblical interpretations of the building's architecture; the discussion of the value and meaning of painted art in the Italian Renaissance as opposed to the Flemish and Spanish versions, for the first time mooting the topic of national schools, pivotal in the geographical and topographical definition of the 'Habsburg Renaissance'; the difficult task, attempted by Sigüenza, of inserting Vasari's historiographical scheme, an idea that failed in both the written text and in the reality of what was painted and exhibited in El Escorial, despite the opposing and complement of Titian and Bosch paintings in that setting, undoubtedly one of the fundamental aesthetic pillars of the 'Habsburg Renaissance' whose basic theoretical features Sigüenza was the first to outline; the role of the arts and sciences in the interpretation of the whole, as well as the connection between humanism, mathematics, geometry and biblical studies found in the library of El Escorial, extensively analysed by Sigüenza; and the importance of religion and its relationship with power. As Maximilian I had done in his project of *Saints Connected with the House of Habsburg*, so Philip II did with the programme of saints' altars in the basilica, their ornament and the holy relics, which Sigüenza discussed at length. Finally, the Hieronymite monk proposed and explained a Renaissance system of visual arts that can be termed Habsburg. This system is present throughout his text, but it crystallises in the second part, specifically in discourses XV devoted to the sacristy and its ornament, XVI on reliquaries, and XVII on painting, which he classifies by geographical provenance: Italy, Flanders and Spain.

Images and texts: Habsburg genealogies

A new type of source, part visual, part literary, and essential for endowing the art of the 'Habsburg Renaissance' with theoretical substance, is the historical and genealogical writings that supported its visual ideology.

Unlike Cosimo I de' Medici, who used the writings of Giorgio Vasari and the works of the Florentine academy to create an ideological and historical foundation for the visual ideology of the Medici dynasty, the House of Habsburg based its ideology on a historiography that glorified the dynastic legitimacy of its power.

The historiographical works that Maximilian I commissioned from Jakob Mennel, Marx Treitzsauerwein, Johannes Stabius, Conrad Celtis and many others constitute the 'scientific' basis of the vast iconography devised by artists such as Albrecht Dürer, Hans Burgkmair, Albrecht Altdorfer and Jörg Kölderer.[17] Rather than the system of intellectual oversight and control that the Florentine academy would adopt soon afterwards, the Habsburgs used that of the *sodalitas* or humanist society, more typical of central Europe. At the same time, the dynastic and heroic nature of Maximilian's enterprises set them apart from the more properly humanistic idea of the gallery of illustrious men proposed by Paolo Giovio in his Como museum and subsequent publication.

Maximilian's influence lasted throughout the sixteenth century and experienced a revival in its final decades, especially at the Tyrolean court of Archduke Ferdinand II and the imperial court of Rudolf II, not to mention its importance for Philip II's library at El Escorial.

Philip gifted to the library the *Historia heráldica y origen de la nobleza de los Austrias* by Hans Tirol, a work in three volumes with 227 miniatures by Jörg Breu the Younger, a follower of Albrecht Dürer. Originally given to Prince Philip by Bishop Otto Truchsess at Augsburg during his *Felicissimo viaje* or 'Happiest Journey', it bridges the gap between Maximilian's genealogical programmes and those of the second half of the sixteenth century.[18] And, of course, we cannot forget the spectacular family tree in scroll form that was offered to Charles V in Rome in 1535, also deposited by Philip at the library he founded.[19]

There are too many printed books to list here, but one should mention *Imagines Gentis Austriacae* (Innsbruck, 1558–1569): five volumes with 74 full-length portraits of the Habsburgs, their wives and their ancestors

---

17 Silver, 37–40, note 5.
18 Elisabeth Scheicher and Julia Hernández Sanz, 'Heráldica y origen de la nobleza de los Austrias en la Biblioteca de El Escorial', *Reales Sitios*, no. 103 (1990), 49–56.
19 *Genealogia illustrissime Domus Austriae que per lineam rectam masculina ab ipso Noe humani generis reparatore usque ad Carolum Regis filium...decepta 1536 mente april*, miniature parchment, Biblioteca Nacional de España, Res, 265.

by Francesco Terzio. These volumes, commissioned by Ferdinand II of Tyrol and each dedicated to a different person—Maximilian II, Archduke Ferdinand II, Archduke Charles II of Inner Austria, Philip II of Spain and Mary of Austria—Maximilian II's wife and Philip's sister—were the basis for the later illustrations of the *Armamentarium Heroicum* and the development of official Habsburg court portraiture.[20]

Between 1600 and 1602, Dominicus Custos published his *Atrium Heroicum* at Augsburg and dedicated it to Archduke Matthias. Divided into four parts and illustrated with 171 engraved portraits of emperors, kings, nobles and clergymen, it is one of the finest and most important Habsburg iconographies, and another seminal resource for understanding the development of court portraiture in the House of Austria.[21] To this we must add the magnificent publications of Jacobius Typotius, who adapted the language of hieroglyphs to devise a total theory and image of Habsburg power; and *Armamentarium Heroicum* by Jacob Schrenck von Notzing, which describes the arms of Ferdinand II of Tyrol and illustrates them with prints by Dominicus Custos based on drawings by Giovanni Battista Fontana.[22]

There are at least three salient themes in this visual culture invented by Maximilian I and his historians and brilliantly continued until the days of Rudolf II. The first is the attempt to give visual entity, whether heraldic or 'real', to the various territories of the empire by means of topographical crests or views of cities. The second is the importance that these publications attach to the idea of dynastic succession in the political and visual justifications for the House of Habsburg, which reached a peak in stunning funerary monuments like the *Hofkirche* of Innsbruck and El Escorial. The third theme is the strong emphasis on the dynasty's heroic deeds, particularly its military feats, reflected in palaces, galleries and funerary monuments.

Conclusion

Among written sources, there is a type whose art-historical point of view gives greater consideration to dynastic identities based on nationalist criteria than to others, and such sources are better able to explain the

---

20 Georg Resch von Geroldshausen and Francesco Terzio, with original drawings by Gaspare Aselli, called Patavinus, *Imagines Gentis Austriacae* (Innsbruck, 1559–1569).
21 Dominicus Custos, *Atrium heroicum, Atrium heroicum Caesarum, regum, [...] imaginibus [...] illustr[atum]. Pars 1–4* (Augsburg: M. Manger, J. Praetorius, 1600–1602).
22 Jacob Schrenk von Notzing, Custos Dominicus, engraver, after drawings by Giovanni Battista Fontana, *Armamentarium heroicum* (Innsbruck, 1601 [Latin edition], 1603 [German edition]).

art produced in the Habsburg world than the canonical succession of artists 'da Cimabue in qua', as Baldinucci said in the seventeenth century,[23] borrowing from Albertian and Vasarian theory. These other theoretical approaches shed the most light on aesthetic and historical foundations of one of the greatest, if not the greatest, commissioners, patrons and collectors of art in sixteenth-century Europe: the House of Habsburg, which extended from Emperor Maximilian I to Emperor Rudolf II, and included such noted collectors as Margaret of Austria, Mary of Hungary and Philip II, in such diverse places as Mechelen, Brussels, Milan, Madrid, El Escorial, Vienna and Prague.

From this historiographical perspective, it is much easier to understand part of the output of several of the most important artists of that time, such as Tiziano (Titian) Vecellio, Leone Leoni and Giuseppe Arcimboldo in Italy (and Vienna); Bosch, Antonis Mor, Vermeyen, Pieter Brueghel the Elder and Bartholomeus Spranger in Flanders; and Juan de Herrera and Alonso Sánchez Coello in Spain, for they all helped define the 'Habsburg Renaissance' of the sixteenth century.

---

23 Filippo Baldinucci, *Notizie de' professori del disegno da Cimabue in qua*, 6 vols (Florence, 1681–1728).

MIGUEL ÁNGEL ZALAMA

Rethinking Vasari

Art and Arts in the Sixteenth Century*

Giorgio Vasari is often credited with being the father of art history, although the same title is not uncommonly ascribed to Johann Winckelmann, who established the guidelines of what we might call modern art history two centuries later. There are even those who believe that the nineteenth century, when the first university chairs dedicated exclusively to the study of the visual arts were established in Berlin and Vienna, marked the true birth of a discipline which has grown exponentially over the last 150 years.

In light of this growth, one might think that the Vasarian postulates are little more than a historical baseline for the evolution of the discipline, a starting point surpassed by later historians which we recall more for precedence than current importance. However, far from losing their interest, the principles set out by Vasari remain relevant today and, in fact, continue to determine the practice of art history. In 1550 Vasari published *Le vite dei più eccellenti architetti, pittori et scultori italiani*, a text which proved so successful that a second expanded and revised edition was released in 1568.[1] In that work, Vasari decreed that the art of his time, the Renaissance, was the finest the world had seen since antiquity, and in fact rivalled the art of the ancients. He established the sequence of phases which we now call styles; he stated that great works of art were entirely indebted to the artist's personality for their greatness; he declared that Italian art—more precisely

---

* The author is member of the University of Valladolid recognized research group and Junta de Castilla y León consolidated research unit, *Art, power and society in the Modern Age*. Also, he is principal investigator, together with Jesús F. Pascual Molina, of the research project ref. PID2021-124832NB-I00 [*Magnifiencia a través de las artes visuales en la familia de los Reyes Católicos. Estudio comparado del patronazfo de ambos géneros*], funded by Spanish government.

1 Giorgio Vasari, *Le vite dei più eccellenti architetti, pittori, et scultori italiani: da Cimabue insino a' tempi nostri* (Florence: Torrentino, 1550). There are several editions, although G. Milanesi's (Florence: Sansoni, 1878–1881) is still fundamental.

Florentine art—was superior to any other; and he identified architecture, painting and sculpture as the three *arti del disegno*, excluding other forms of expression such as precious metalwork, tapestry and inlay, which in many cases were more highly regarded than painting at the time.

Vasari's artistic philosophy: Milestones and historical continuity

Vasari believed that the arts had attained perfection in classical antiquity and that the only way to emulate them was by looking back to the Roman world (Greek civilisation being less familiar and less accessible at the time). The Middle Ages, classified as a dark period by the humanist Flavio Biondo in the fifteenth century,[2] only represented decadence in general, and the rebirth of the arts would not begin until Cimabue, although his successor Giotto was the true agent of change, in Dante's opinion: 'Cimabue thought / To lord it over painting's field; and now / The cry is Giotto's, and his name eclips'd.'[3] Yet that was only the awakening, *i primi lumi*, for it was not until the early-fifteenth century that these achievements became the norm, and their culmination, 'the perfect standard of art' according to Vasari, would not arrive until the dawn of the *Cinquecento* and the rise of artists like Bramante, Da Vinci, Michelangelo and Raphael. Vasari even coined the term 'Renaissance' thanks to his insistence on the rebirth or *rinascita* of the arts. It is hardly necessary to elaborate on the presence and recognition of Renaissance art; although the merits of the artistic manifestations of earlier and later periods have been extolled for some time now, it seems that the primacy of the Renaissance is still indisputable. In this respect, the thesis of the Tuscan painter and architect remains relevant and continues to influence modern assessments of the arts.

This pattern of rebirth (re-nascence) which first saw the light in the *Trecento*, growth in the fifteenth century, and maturity in the *Cinquecento*, which Vasari categorised as ages (styles), has influenced not only our understanding of what constitutes good art—classical art equalled in the Renaissance—but also how we study it, dividing its history into phases. Chronologically and stylistically, Giotto belonged to the medieval world and Gothic art, but scholars insist on his modernity and frequently identify him as the initiator of the Renaissance. This period of early

---

2 Flavio Biondo, *Historiarum ab inclinatione romanorum imperii decades* (Venice: O. Scotus, 1483).
3 'Credette Cimabue nella pittura tener lo campo, ed ora ha Giotto il grido, si che la fama di colui è scura'. Dante Alighieri, *Divine Comedy*, 'Purgatorio', XI, 94–96. English translation by Henry Francis Cary (1785–1802).

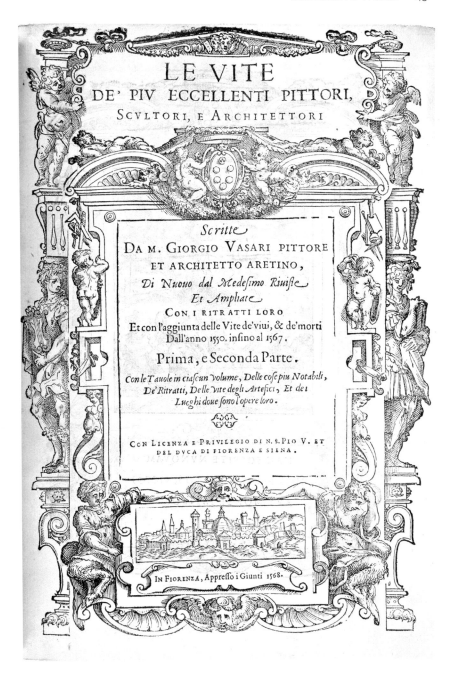

Fig. 3.1. Front page of *Le vite* by Giorgio Vasari, Florence, Giunti, 1568.

achievements was followed by a second phase, *seconda età* or *maniera*, which spans the *Quattrocento*, while the perfect standard of art corresponds to what we call the High Renaissance; furthermore, when Vasari published the second edition of his *Le vite*, he hinted at a *quarta maniera*, which is none other than what we now call Mannerism (even the modern term is Vasarian).

Le vite offers a succession of artists' biographies, for in the author's mind, great works of art owed their existence to great artists. While there is nothing objectionable in this axiom, it is important to note that it is only a partial vision and perhaps the least applicable of Vasari's postulates in our times, although the biographical method has garnered many advocates through the years and still has a following today. Even so, without gainsaying the creator's importance, there are many other factors that have a bearing on works of art—sociocultural, religious, political, propagandistic, financial, technical, patronage—which Vasari ignored because he did not consider them significant. He also attached little importance to artists who were not Italian, and more specifically not Florentine, for even Siena, a city close to Florence, was deemed of little account in the arts—so much so that Duccio merited a mere two pages in comparison to Giotto's twenty. Perhaps the clearest example is Vasari's treatment of Albrecht Dürer, who instead of having his own biography was included in that of Marcantonio Raimondi, undoubtedly a great printmaker but nowhere near as accomplished as the German.

However much it might seem that this notion had fallen out of fashion, and that the idea of judging a work's value based on the artist's affiliation was no longer tenable, the Vasarian paradigm of Italian primacy had a decisive influence on German historiography, which merely reinforced the Italocentric vision of the birth, growth and spread of the Renaissance—a term synonymous with great art. The only question was whether to favour Florence or Rome, which each dominated the arts in the fifteenth and sixteenth centuries respectively, as reflected in the work of two German authors, amongst others: Johann Wolfgang von Goethe and Thomas Mann. In 1786, Goethe travelled to Italy and made a point of exploring the capital of the ancient world, which the Renaissance had revived; and in the early twentieth century, Thomas Mann took a special interest in Florence as the cradle of the Renaissance.[4]

Put simply, it was generally believed that the Renaissance 'gave birth to the central values (rationalism, secularisation, individualism), ideologies (humanism, republicanism) and institutions (capitalism, the centralised nation-state) of modern Europe'.[5] And it was in this context of fascination

---

4 Martin A. Ruehl, *The Italian Renaissance in the German Historical Imagination, 1860–1930* (Cambridge: Cambridge University Press, 2015), 1.
5 Ruehl, *The Italian Renaissance*, 3.

with the Renaissance that Jacob Burckhardt wrote his magnum opus, *The Civilisation of the Renaissance in Italy* (1860), which established the guidelines that would be followed in scholarship for decades and, in many respects, are still applied today. Burckhardt, who shared Vasari's loathing of the Middle Ages, also subscribed to his belief that the Renaissance was the sole intellectual property of Italy. *Italia docet.* This idea led him to treat the art of the Netherlands as a mere substitute, placing it in a passive role, while simultaneously ignoring the importance of the imperial courts, such as Brussels under Charles V and Vienna under Ferdinand I;[6] extraordinary centres like Binche Palace, where Mary of Hungary exercised an incomparable artistic patronage;[7] and Philip II's palace of El Escorial[8]—not to mention the growing importance of collecting in Habsburg circles.[9]

Burckhardt extolled Vasari's Italocentrism to the point that it became an axiom for subsequent generations of historians, effectively settling the North-South debate in favour of the South.[10] During World War I, Burckhardt's theories were emphatically contested by German nationalists. Thus, in 1917, the fourth centenary of Luther's 95 theses, it was claimed that Germanic culture had held itself apart from, and was therefore purer and superior to, Italian culture. It was asserted that this independence instigated a return to the medieval and the spiritual, just as Wilhelm Worringer had proposed in his *Form Problems of the Gothic* in 1912. With Germany's defeat at the end of the conflict, German philosophers and historians like Ernst Cassirer and Erwin Panofsky returned their focus to the Renaissance. Cassirer, in his *Philosophy of Symbolic Forms* (1923–1929), and Panofsky, in his vast work on the visual arts, examined symbolic forms from the perspective of philosophy and the history and theory of art, but in essence neither touched Burckhardt's Italocentric theory.[11]

Panofsky's approach, strongly influenced by idealism, was challenged by another grand master of art history, Ernst Gombrich (1909–2001). Opposed to the notion of human history as a logical, rational process in which spirit and idea were gradually and necessarily revealed through

---

6 See Fernando Checa, ed., *Museo imperial. El coleccionismo artístico de los Austrias en el siglo XVI* (Madrid: Fernando Villaverde, 2013).
7 See Annemarie Jordan Gschwend and Dagmar Eichberger, 'A Discerning Agent with a Vision: Queen Mary of Hungary (1505–1558)', in *Women. The Art of Power*, eds. Sabine Haag, Dagmar Eichberger and Annemarie Jordan Gschwend (Vienna: Kunsthistorisches Museums, 2018), 37–49.
8 Fernando Checa, *Felipe II. Mecenas de las artes* (Madrid: Nerea, 1992).
9 Thomas DaCosta Kaufmann, 'From Treasury to Museum: The Collection of the Austrian Habsburgs', in *The Culture of Collecting*, eds. John Elsner and Roger Cardinal (London: Reaktion Books, 1994), 137–154; Thomas DaCosta Kaufmann, 'The Kunstkammer: Historiography, Acquisition, Display', in *A Arte de Coleccionar. The Art of Collecting*, ed. Hugo Miguel Crespo (Lisbon: Ar/Pab, 2019), 17–33.
10 Ruehl, *The Italian Renaissance*, 22.
11 Ruehl, *The Italian Renaissance*, 30.

the ages (Hegel's omnipresent thesis), the profoundly anti-Hegelian Gombrich—who even confessed he was 'allergic' to Hegel[12]—considered it a blasphemous interpretation or a perversion of the Christian idea of providential history. On this basis, he did not hesitate, following Karl Popper,[13] to compare Panofsky's vision with other providential images from history, whether Marxist or associated with Nazi ideology.

Those theories led to a historicist vision of human evolution, introduced by Leopold von Ranke in his *History of the Latin and Teutonic Nations from 1494 to 1514* (1824) and developed by his school of thought. Although the goal of narrating events 'how it essentially was' might tempt us to view Ranke and historicism as just another chapter of positivism, the true intention of this influential school was to offer a holistic explanation of history.[14] Gombrich was entirely opposed to these historicist theses, which for him constituted a 'fantasy world', a statement that betrays the influence of Schopenhauer's radically anti-Hegelian ideas. In his essay 'In Search of Cultural History' (published in 1979 but reprising a lecture given years earlier), Gombrich recalled how, as early as 1843, Karl Schnaase, in the introduction to his *Geschichte der Bildenden Künste* [*History of the Arts of Design*], tried to insert Hegel's opinions into the art-historical field. Schnaase believed that art belonged to the necessary expressions of mankind, and that the art of each period was the most reliable expression of the national spirit.[15]

Gombrich carefully examined what he considered Burckhardt's Hegelianism before concluding with a consideration of what he called 'Hegelianism without metaphysics', focused on authors such as Heinrich Wölfflin, Alois Riegl, Johan Huizinga and, in certain aspects, even Panofsky, who underscored the existence of periods with a distinctive spirit in his *Renaissance and Renascences in Western Art* (1960).[16] In his essay, Gombrich was less interested in the internal laws of historical progress and its purportedly 'philosophical' rationale, which tried to explain everything with what he called 'exegetic method',[17] than in how events are interconnected. He advocated abandoning Hegelian holism in order to comprehend the fact in itself, examining each event independently rather than as part of a superstructure where everything hinges on the *Zeitgeist*. 'It is this belief in the existence of an independent supra-individual collective

---

12 Ernst H. Gombrich, *Ideals and Idols: Essays on Values in History and Art* (London: Phaidon Press, 1979), 34.
13 See Karl R. Popper, *The Open Society and Its Enemies* (London: Routledge, 1945).
14 See Karl R. Popper, *The Poverty of Historicism* (London: Routledge, 1957).
15 Gombrich, *Ideals and Idols*, 41.
16 Gombrich, *Ideals and Idols*, 50–55; Erwin Panofsky, *Renaissance and Renascences in Western Art* (Stockholm: Almqvist & Wiksell, 1960), 31–32.
17 Gombrich, *Ideals and Idols*, 55.

spirit which seems to me to have blocked the emergence of a true cultural history', concluded Gombrich, whose proposed solution was for history to fix 'its attention firmly on the individual human being'.[18]

Creating a system of the arts

These were great strides forward, no doubt, but they barely modified the Vasarian postulates of Renaissance primacy, a return to classical art, and Italocentrism. Moreover, the system of the arts advocated by Vasari, which remained largely undisputed until recently, is transcendental in the making of art history. If the goal of this discipline is to study visual works of art, the first order of business is to establish what we mean by that term. It is not a question of determining what art is—the unanswerable question which led Benedetto Croce to declare that 'art is what everyone knows it to be'[19]—but rather of clarifying our definition of an artistic object. This task is not an easy one, either, but a survey of history allows us to determine what was considered a work of art at a particular moment in time, and which of those works were the most outstanding.

Vasari declared that there were but three Arts (with a capital A): architecture, painting and sculpture. He called them *arti del disegno* (arts of drawing), for he believed that a mastery of drawing was the foundation on which all great artists rested their work. Although Alberti had already written three treatises on painting, sculpture and architecture one century earlier, it was Vasari who elevated the concept from proposal to standard. Under this system of classification, aesthetic expressions such as precious metalwork, tapestry-making, inlay work and printmaking ceased to be important in theory, if not in practice, although over time their practical relevance also faded. Vasari wrote a fascinating history of the visual arts which, though unrealistic, turned out to be a self-fulfilling prophecy. However, this does not permit the extrapolation of current ideas (and not-so-current, as they originated in the eighteenth century) to the Renaissance, Vasari's time, when the general approach to the visual arts was quite different from what he thought it should be.

Our Vasarian system of the arts became the norm thanks to the most important publication of the Enlightenment, *Encylopédie*, in 1751. In the work's primer, *Discours préliminaire*, co-editor Jean le Rond D'Alembert determined which were the 'Fine Arts': 'Painting, Sculpture, Architecture, Poetry, Music, and their different divisions make up the third general distribution, which is born of imagination and whose parts are comprised under the name of Fine Arts'. He then clarified, 'We can also include them

---

18 Gombrich, *Ideals and Idols*, 59.
19 Benedetto Croce, *Breviario di estetica:* quattro lezioni (Bari: Laterza, 1913), 11.

under the general title of Painting [portrayal], because all the Fine Arts can be reduced to that and differ only by the means which they use'.[20] D'Alembert's classification was largely based on that of Charles Batteux, who five years earlier had already grouped together painting, sculpture and architecture,[21] effectively copying Vasari's system. The title of the first edition of Le vite (1550) clearly indicated that it was about the lives of architects, painters and sculptors. When the second revised edition appeared eighteen years later, Vasari made a seemingly inconsequential change to the title that ultimately proved highly significant: *Le vite dei più eccellenti pittori, scvltori e architettori*. The order had been altered to put painters first (an order apparent even in Vasari's description of himself as a 'painter and architect').[22] In 1568, painting headed up the ranking of the *arti del disegno*, which would become the 'Fine Arts' of the Enlightenment.

Art and arts in the sixteenth century

That the Enlightenment followed Vasari's system of the arts, and that painting was king in the mid-eighteenth century are obvious truths; however, it is a mistake to think that painting was first among the arts in the sixteenth century, a misconception that originated with Vasari. The Tuscan theorist posited that only the *arti del disegno* should be considered arts, and eventually made painting chief among them. The academies that began to proliferate in sixteenth-century Italy, in their zeal to separate purely manual activity (what we would call craft or trade) from creativity (art in modern parlance), followed the example of Vasari, who had promoted the foundation of the Accademia delle Arti del Disegno in Florence in 1563 and placed Michelangelo at its helm.[23] In all of these academies, painting came to be regarded as the greatest of the arts and reached its zenith when the Académie Royale de Peinture et de Sculpture was founded in Paris in 1648, during the reign of the Sun King: in three short years, this academy absorbed the old guilds, thereby setting the standards of *le grand goût*. Louis XIV himself issued a decree in 1667 to

---

20 Jean le Rond d'Alembert, *Preliminary Discourse to the Encyclopedia of Diderot*, trans. Richard N. Schwab with the collaboration of Walter E. Rex (Chicago: The University of Chicago Press, 1995).

21 Charles Batteux, *Les Beaux-Arts réduits à un même principe* (Paris: Durand, 1746). English edition: Charles Batteux, *The Fine Arts Reduced to a Single Principle*, translation, introduction and notes by James O. Young (Oxford: Oxford University Press, 2015).

22 Miguel Ángel Zalama, 'Las artes visuales en la modernidad: reflexiones sobre su consideración', in Matteo Mancini and Álvaro Pascual Chenel, *Imbricaciones. Paradigmas, modelos y materialidad de las artes en la Europa habsbúrgica* (Madrid: Sílex, 2019), 15–44.

23 Nikolaus Pevsner, *Academies of Art: Past and Present* (Cambridge: Cambridge University Press and New York: Macmillan Co., 1940), 42ff.

establish the Manufacture royale des meubles de la Couronne at Gobelins, with Jean-Baptiste Colbert (minister of finance) serving as superintendent and the painter Charles Le Brun as director—the same posts they held at the academy, although the two were separate institutions.[24] If uniting the two had been deemed desirable, the factory would have suffered the same fate as the guilds. However, this was not the case, and the Gobelins Manufactory boasted a staff of 'master high-warp tapestry weavers, gold and silversmiths, metal casters, engravers, stonecutters, ebony and wood cabinetmakers, dyers and other skilled workers....'[25] It also had painters, as someone had to create the designs, but there was a clear distinction between what would later be called Fine Arts and those which over time came to be known as decorative, applied or simply lesser arts (with a lower-case a).

The decree founding the Gobelins Manufactory alluded to an earlier one issued by Henry IV in 1607, but unlike his grandfather, Louis XIV had given precedence to the *arti del disegno* of the academy, which meant relegating all other aesthetic expressions to the background, something that went against the prevailing ideology of half a century earlier and certainly of Vasari's day. During the *Quattrocento*, painting was far from being the greatest of the visual arts. The Medicis preferred to decorate their palaces with Flemish tapestries; there are letters from Giovanni, brother of Piero the Gouty, asking his agents in Bruges to send wall hangings, and Piero's son Lorenzo the Magnificent embellished his study in the palace on Via Larga with tapestries, accumulating approximately 40 by the time of his death.[26] In the sixteenth century, Pope Leo X—who, as the son of Lorenzo the Magnificent, had developed his artistic taste in Florence—commissioned a series of tapestries on the Acts of the Apostles for which Raphael made the cartoons.[27] This series of very rich hangings woven with gold-wrapped threads was intended to adorn the lower walls of none other than the Sistine Chapel; in contrast to the histories painted by the Florentines at the end of the fifteenth century and Michelangelo's ceiling, the first Medici pope chose to introduce tapestries in an obvious attempt to make his mark and outshine the commissions of his predecessors. Of course, his case was not exceptional: the Dukes of Burgundy owned an impressive number of tapestries, most of which are now lost; and hangings were

---

24 Knothe, Florian, *The Manufacture des meubles de la couronne aux Gobelins under Louis XIV: A Social, Political and Cultural History* (Turnhout: Brepols, 2017).

25 Édouard Gerspach, *La manufacture nationale des Gobelins* (Paris: Librairie Ch. Delagrave, 1892), 143: 'maîtres tapissiers de haute lisse, orphèvres, fondeurs, graveurs, lapidaires, menuisiers en ébeine et en bois, teinturiers et autres bons ouvriers...'.

26 Eugène Müntz, *Les précurseurs de la Renaissance* (Paris: Librairie de l'Art, 1882), 161–162 and 194.

27 John Shearman, *Raphael's Cartoons in the Collection of her Majesty the Queen, and the Tapestries for the Sistine Chapel* (London: Phaidon, 1972).

eagerly collected by Matthias Corvinus, King of Hungary, Charles VIII of France, Henry VIII of England; and Sigismund II of Poland (Wawel Castle in Krakow is home to a very important collection). The Medicis were not the only Renaissance Italians to collect tapestries. Others include Federico da Montefeltro, Duke of Urbino; Ferdinand I of Naples; and Ludovico il Moro, Duke of Milan.[28]

In Spain, the auction of the estate of Isabella the Catholic Queen in 1505 clearly proved the pre-eminence of tapestries over paintings. While no buyers could be found for the paintings, even at very low prices, the hangings were quickly purchased for astronomical sums (by way of example, the tapestry *Raising of Lazarus*, now in the Museo de Tapices y Capitular de la Seo in Zaragoza, was valued at 400 ducats, while the 47 panels comprising the so-called *Polyptych of Isabella the Catholic*, attributed to Michel Sittow and Juan de Flandes, were appraised at barely half that amount and still failed to interest potential buyers).[29] The different courts were all of one mind in this matter: for them the arts were more material than aesthetic and had more to do with blatant displays of wealth, understood as munificence, than with spiritual worth. Grandeur and costliness were appreciated more than originality and authorship. And on this scale of values, painting could not hope to compete with items like tapestry.

If there was one court that put a premium on magnificence, it was the fifteenth-century court of Burgundy. Defined by Aristotle in his *Nicomachean Ethics* as an 'excellence' that 'does not, like open-handedness, extend to all actions to do with money, but only to those involving expenditure, and in these it exceeds open-handedness in scale',[30] the concept of munificence or magnificence was highly influential in the 1400s and was present in the courtly ideal of the most illustrious personalities.[31] This magnificence was expressed through Flemish art, the true Northern Renaissance, although the most influential study on the Burgundian court attempted to anchor it in the medieval past. In the 1923 foreword to his

---

28 See Guy Delmarcel, *Flemish Tapestry* (New York: Harry N. Abrams and London: Thames & Hudson, 1999).

29 Miguel Ángel Zalama, 'La infructuosa venta en almoneda de las pinturas de Isabel la Católica', *Boletín del seminario de arte y arqueología. Arte*, LXXIV (2008), 59–62; Miguel Ángel Zalama, 'En torno a la valoración de las artes: tapices y pinturas en el tesoro de Isabel la Católica', in Miguel Ángel Zalama (dir.) and Patricia Andrés González (ed.), *Ellas siempre han estado ahí. Coleccionismo y mujeres* (Madrid: Ediciones Doce Calles, 2020), 15–40.

30 Aristotle, *Nicomachean Ethics*, translation, introduction and commentary by Sarah Broadie and Christopher Rowe (Oxford: Oxford University Press, 1918), Book 4, Chapter 2; Evelyn Welch, 'Public Magnificence and Private Display: Giovanni Pontano's De splendore (1498) and the Domestic Arts', *Journal of Design History*, 15, 4 (2002), 211–221; Antonio Urquízar Herrera, 'Teoría de la magnificencia y teoría de las señales en el pensamiento nobiliario español del siglo XVI', *Ars Longa*, 23 (2014), 93–111.

31 Marina Belozerskaya, *Luxury Arts of the Renaissance* (Los Angeles: The Paul Getty Museum, 2005).

1919 book *The Autumn of the Middle Ages*, Huizinga stated that the leading artists of the Duchy of Burgundy ought to be viewed 'not as initiating and heralding what is to come, but rather as completing the forms of an age in its final stage'.[32] He underscored the quality of magnificence but situated its origins in a medieval world of chivalry which, though still present in his view, was on the verge of disappearing: 'the autumn of the Middle Ages'. His essay, still relevant today, has been criticised for that aspect; while the luxury and ostentation of the court was undeniably important, the truth is that Flanders developed an interest in pictorial realism which banished the International Gothic style. The world of chivalrous knighthood was not quite dead though, as Duke Philip the Good proved in 1430 when he decided to establish the Order of the Golden Fleece, which sought knightly defenders of the Christian faith who were willing to go forth and reconquer the Holy Lands, even though this crusade never actually materialised. However, at the same time Jan van Eyck and Rogier van der Weyden were achieving an unprecedented realism in their paintings, and before them Claus Sluter (d. 1405/1406) had sculpted his *Well of Moses* at the Chartreuse de Champmol in Dijon, with figures so lifelike that they rivalled those of Brunelleschi's *Sacrifice of Isaac*.

One could argue that the appreciation of the arts had changed in the decades since Vasari's words were written; although painting was gradually becoming more important, the fact is that tapestries, as effective displays of their owners' magnificence, retained their primacy in the arts throughout the sixteenth century. Charles V and Philip II enjoyed painting and had painters of the stature of Titian and Antonis Mor in their service, but they continued to commission and spend large sums on tapestries. The emperor acquired series such as *The Honours*, *The Hunts of Maximilian or Charles V* and *The Conquest of Tunis*, and Philip II purchased some of the most important hangings in his father's collection,[33] thanks to a clause in the king's will which stipulated that he could 'tomar[los] en preçio moderado a arbitrio de mis testamentarios' [take them for a modest price at the discretion of my executors].[34] Philip the Prudent acquired so many tapestries in his lifetime that, when his assets were inventoried after his

---

32 Johan Huizinga, *The Autumn of the Middle Ages*, trans. Rodney J. Payton and Ulrich Mammitzsch (Chicago: The University of Chicago Press, 1996), XXI.

33 Guy Delmarcel, *Los Honores. Flemish tapestries for the Emperor Charles V* (Mechelen: SDZ/Pandora, 2000); Fernando Checa, *Tapisseries flamandes. Pour les ducs de Bourgogne, l'empereur Charles Quint et le roi Philippe II* (Brussels: Fons Mercator, 2008), 102–255; Iain Buchanan, *Habsburg Tapestries* (Turnhout: Brepols, 2015).

34 Miguel Ángel Zalama, '"Dejo y mando graciosamente al dicho príncipe todas las tapicerías". Felipe II y su interés por los tapices', in Miguel Ángel Zalama, María José Martínez Ruiz and Jesús F. Pascual Molina, eds., *El legado de las obras de arte. Tapices, pinturas, esculturas... Sus viajes a través de la Historia* (Valladolid: Universidad de Valladolid, 2017), 204.

Fig. 3.2. *The Capture of Tunis* tapestry from *The conquest of Tunis* series, Jan Vermeyen and Pieter Coecke van Aelst, 1543-1548. Madrid, Patrimonio Nacional © Digital image courtesy of the Getty's Open Content Program.

death, he was found to possess more than 700.[35] Some of them were quite extraordinary, like the eight hangings that comprise the *Apocalypse* series woven in 1556 by Willem de Pannemaker, which cost an astonishing 7264 escudos.[36] The king was particularly partial to these tapestries, and when six were lost when the ship carrying them sank at the mouth of Laredo harbour on 9 September 1559, he ordered them remade, despite the great cost.[37] Philip II went even further: in his will, he stipulated that the hangings were to be entailed to the Crown, thereby preventing their sale after his death.[38]

---

35   Guy Delmarcel, 'Le roi Philippe II d'Espagne et la tapisserie. L'inventaire de Madrid de 1598', *Gazette des Beaux-Arts*, CXXXIV (1999), 153–178 (esp. 157); Fernando Checa, ed., *Inventarios de Felipe II. Inventario* post mortem. *Almoneda y Libro de remates. Inventario de tapices / Inventory of Philip II. Post-mortem Inventory. Inventory of sale items and record of sales. Tapestries Inventory* (Madrid: Fernando Villaverde, 2018), 860–866.
36   Zalama, '"Dejo y mando graciosamente…"', 216–217.
37   Louis-Prosper Gachard and Charles Piot, *Collection de voyages des souverains des Pays-Bas*, 4 vols, IV (Brussels: F. Hayez, 1882), 73; Jan Karel Steppe, 'Vlaams tapijtwerk van 16de eeuw in Spaans koninklijk bezit', in *Miscelanea Jozef Duverger*, II (Ghent, 1968), 734–748; Jan Karel Steppe, 'De reis naar Madrid van Willem de Pannemaker, in Augustus-Oktober 1561', *Artes Textiles*, X (1981), 81–124; Iain Buchanan, 'The tapestries acquired by King Philip in the Netherlands in 1549–1550 and 1555–1559: New documentation', *Gazette des Beaux-Arts*, CXXXIV (1999), 131–152 (esp. 134–137).
38   Zalama, '"Dejo y mando graciosamente…"', 204.

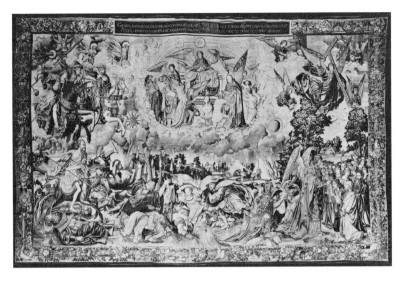

Fig. 3.3. *The revelation of St. John* tapestry from the *Apocalypse* series. Willem de Pannemaker, c. 1550. Madrid, Patrimonio Nacional © Digital image courtesy of the Getty's Open Content Program.

Continuity in the seventeenth century

Philip II was keen to preserve what he considered great works of art, and he gave them pride of place on momentous occasions. For instance, when the ceremony to bestow the chain of the Order of the Golden Fleece was held at the Alcázar in Madrid in 1593, he had the palace decorated with tapestries, even covering up the paintings that hung there.[39] His successors inherited his interest in tapestry, and in the mid-1600s it was still the predominant visual art form. Philip IV, known for his love of painting, bought many tapestry series, some of which were used to decorate the Buen Retiro Palace, like the *Decius Mus* series,[40] which was based on cartoons by Rubens. Infanta Isabel Clara Eugenia, governess of

---

39 Miguel Ángel Zalama, 'The ceremonial decoration of the Alcázar in Madrid: The use of tapestries and paintings in Habsburg festivities' in Fernando Checa and Laura Fernández-González, *Festival Culture in the World of the Spanish Habsburgs* (Farnham: Ashgate, 2015), 41–66.
40 Concha Herrero Carretero, 'Decio Mus consulta el oráculo y La batalla de Veseris y la muerte de Decio Mus', in Thomas Campbell, *Hilos de esplendor. Tapices del Barroco* (Madrid: Patrimonio Nacional, 2008), 95–105.

the Netherlands, commissioned *Triumph of the Eucharist* around 1625, for which Rubens also made the cartoons.[41]

The importance Philip IV attached to tapestries—no different from that exhibited by other powerful figures of the seventeenth century—is clearly illustrated in one of Diego Velázquez's greatest works. In the 1650s, when Velázquez set his sights on becoming a Knight of the Order of Santiago (Saint James), he encountered an obstacle: being engaged in manual trades, including that of painter, made one ineligible for the distinction.[42] Velázquez could not conceal the fact that painting had been his sole activity before arriving at court, so instead he decided to extol the liberality of his art. In *The Spinners, or the Fable of Arachne* he separated manual labour, placed in the shadowy foreground, from the brightly lit scene in the background of richly attired ladies beside a depiction of *The Rape of Europa* (Isabella Stewart Gardner Museum, Boston) by Titian, a painter whom Charles V had ennobled, which was later copied (Museo Nacional del Prado, Madrid) by Rubens, who was a painter and diplomat. The picture clearly alludes to two painters who were also gentlemen. The most striking detail; however, is that, instead of showing a canvas, Velázquez transferred the story told by Ovid in his *Metamorphoses* to a tapestry, the same one woven by the unfortunate Arachne.

If tapestries had not been so prestigious in the reign of Philip IV, who was later instrumental in helping Velázquez to achieve the coveted Cross of Santiago,[43] he would not have included one in his painting. Even in the late-eighteenth century, when the triumph of painting seemed absolute and the Enlightenment had made it clear that the Fine Arts did not include tapestry, Charles IV ordered Francisco Goya to make tapestry cartoons.

---

41 Alejandro Vergara, *Rubens. El Triunfo de la Eucaristía* (Madrid: Museo Nacional del Prado, 2014); Ana García Sanz, 'Un proyecto único para el Monasterio de las Descalzas Reales: la serie de tapices de *El Triunfo de la Eucaristía*', in Fernando Checa, *La otra corte. Mujeres de la Casa de Austria en los Monasterios Reales de las Descalzas y la Encarnación* (Madrid: Patrimonio Nacional, 2019), 338–345.

42 *Regla y establecimientos de la orden y caballería del gloriosso apóstol Santiago, patrón de las Spañas, con la historia del origen y principio de ella*, 1655. Título I. De las calidades. Capítulo V. 'Establecemos, y mandamos, que no se pueda dar el hábito a ninguno que aya sido mercader, o cambiador, o aya tenido oficio vil o mecánico, o sea hijo, o nieto de los que han tenido lo vno o lo otro […] Y oficios viles, y mecánicos se entienden, platero, o pintor, que lo tenga por oficio, bordador, canteros, mesoneros, taberneros, […] o otros oficios semejantes, que viven por el trabajo de sus manos…' [Title I. On qualities. Chapter V. 'We hereby establish and command that the order shall not be bestowed upon anyone who has been a merchant, or money changer, or has had a base or manual trade, or is the son, or grandson of any who have had one or the other… And base and manual trades are understood as those of the silversmith, or painter, who lives by that trade, embroider, stonemasons, innkeepers, publicans… or other similar tradesmen, who live by the work of their hands…'].

43 Jonathan Brown, *Velázquez: Painter and Courtier* (New Haven: Yale University Press, 1986), 251–252.

Goya refused, because he felt that creating cartoons to be transferred to woven cloth was not a suitable task for a painter, and only gave in when the king threatened to take away his stipend.[44] Painting had finally attained the primacy Vasari had wished for it. Although the genre certainly did not have that status when he was writing in the sixteenth century, the Vasarian classification of the arts turned out to be a premonition of things to come.

---

44 Valentín de Sambricio, *Tapices de Goya* (Madrid: Patrimonio Nacional, 1946), docs. 133, 134 and 139.

MATTEO MANCINI

The Antithesis between the Vasarian Canon and the Habsburg Model of the Arts

Defining National Identity in the Italian Risorgimento[*]

Any art historian who has delved into themes characteristic of the sixteenth century or has referred to the so-called *Lives*[1] of Giorgio Vasari (1511–1574) is perfectly aware of the importance of the critical edition produced by Sienese scholar Gaetano Milanesi (1813–1895). Between 1846 and 1855,[2] Milanesi gave the printing presses what was perhaps the most widely read version of the *Lives* for over a century, a work which the same author later republished in the broader context of his edition of Vasari's *Omnia*[3] (vols. I–VII; 1878–1885). Less apparent is the true measure of the magnitude of Milanesi's contribution to shaping what we now define as the 'Vasarian canon'.[4] The subject of his editorial activity has already been amply discussed and needs no further commentary

---

[*] Principal researcher of the project ref. PID2021-124239NB-I00-ART [Miradas Cruzadas. Espacios del coleccionismo habsbúrgico y nobiliario entre España y el Imperio (siglos XVI-XVII)] funded by the Spanish government.

[1] Giorgio Vasari, *Le vite dei più eccellenti architetti, pittori et scultori italiani da Cimabue, insino a' tempi nostri* (Florence: Lorenzo Torrentino, 1550); Giorgio Vasari, *Le vite dei più eccellenti pittori, scultori e architettori italiani da Cimabue, insino a' tempi nostri* (Florence: Giunti, 1568).

[2] Giorgio Vasari, *Le vite dei più eccellenti pittori scultori e architetti di Giorgio Vasari, pubblicate per cura di una Società di Amatori delle Arti Belle*, eds. Vincenzo Marchesi, Carol Pini and Gaetano Milanesi, 13 vols (Florence: Le Monier). The fourteenth volume (indices) was published in 1870.

[3] Giorgio Vasari, *Le opere di Giorgio Vasari, con nuove annotazioni e commenti di Gaetano Milanesi* (Florence: Sansoni, 1878–1885; reprint 1906; facsimile edition, Florence: Le Lettere, 1998).

[4] Fernando Checa Cremades, *Renacimiento Habsbúrgico. Felipe II y las imágenes artísticas* (Valladolid: Universidad de Valladolid, 2018), 21–86.

Matteo Mancini • Complutense University of Madrid

here. Instead, this chapter aims to trace the ideological boundaries of the structures and cultural objectives that Milanesi deployed when composing his commentaries and notes on Vasari's text. The interesting thing about this complex way of conceiving and presenting the fine arts, is how the nineteenth-century ideology and visual approach that Milanesi embodied helped define the way we read Vasari's assertions. Remarkably, during that same period, Milanesi himself played a prominent role in the process that determined the Neoplatonic Renaissance system's interpretation as it unfolded in the Italian *Risorgimento*. That role materialised in his plans for the museographic layout of the Gallerie degli Uffizi in Florence, a museum whose ideological ambitions were (and still are) inextricably interwoven with that conception of the system of arts. A list from May 1889 shows that the paintings were divided into four idealogical categories[5] related to the Vasarian canon of the arts. The arrangement distinguished between paintings worthy of the Galleria; those which ought to occupy the lower levels (in part for conservation reasons); those deemed to have historical or anthropological interest, based on criteria similar to those still used today; and finally, those entirely without merit. Discussing the reasons for these museological decisions would divert us from the aims of this study; however, it is pertinent to note that such approaches to museography did exist and played a relevant and active role in determining the visibility of the works exhibited at the Uffizi (and, obviously, not only at the Florentine picture gallery).

Gaetano Milanesi was a scholar of notable gravitas and influence: having held the post of deputy director since 1856, on 26 February 1861 he was named sole director of the recently-created State Archives of Florence,[6] a post retained throughout the city's brief stint as capital of Italy;[7] from 1889 to 1891 he also served as superintendent of all archives in Tuscany,[8] though his actions as an archivist and his advanced age were quite controversial.[9] At the same time, he was active in some of the most important committees devoted to the promotion and conservation of the fine arts.[10] Looking over the publications and critical volumes he signed

---

5 Paola Barocchi, 'Firenze 1880–1903: cultura figurativa e conservazione', in *Storia dell'arte e politica culturale intorno al 1900. Atti del Convegno*, catalogue of the exhibition held in Florence in 1997 and curated by M. Seidel (Venice: 1999), 297–311, 300–302.
6 Elio Lodolini 'Il personale degli Archivi di Stato in servizio dall'Unità d'Italia alla prima guerra mondiale (1861–1918) e collocato a riposo sino al 1958', in *Repertorio del personale degli Archivi di Stato*, ed. Maurizio Cassetti (Rome: MIBAC, 2008), 3–261, esp. 19.
7 Ugo Pesci, *Firenze Capitale (1865–1870): Dagli appunti di un ex-cronista* (Florence: Bemporad e figlio, 1904).
8 Lodolini, 'Il personale degli Archivi di Stato', 320–321.
9 Lodolini, 'Il personale degli Archivi di Stato', 94–95.
10 Riccardo Dalla Negra, Mario Bencivenni, and Paola Grifoni, *Monumenti e istituzioni, I, La nascita del servizio di tutela dei monumenti in Italia. 1860–1880* (Florence: Alliena, 1987),

individually or to which he contributed, his name was not only linked to the work by Vasari. He was also responsible for one of the most important editions of the hitherto only partially published[11] manuscript of Cennino Cennini,[12] and he played a prominent role in annotating the no less important treatise by Leonardo da Vinci[13] and in publishing Michelangelo's correspondence,[14] a task entrusted to Milanesi by the *Comitato fiorentino per le feste del IV centenario della nascita di Michelangelo* [Florentine Committee for the Fourth Centennial of Michelangelo's Birth].

After the midpoint of the nineteenth century, Milanesi's guiding hand established a Tuscan–Florentine centrality in defining the origins of art history sources. All were essential to laying the foundations of that process, although each had a different prerogative: Cennini was the proto-Renaissance man; Da Vinci was the epitome of the multifaceted genius of the Renaissance artist; and Vasari was the true—and only—lay priest of the faith in the arts and its creators, who had always been Michelangelo's greatest proponent. This system of the arts was manufactured explicitly to identify seminal arguments in historical and literary sources that supported the centrality of Florence and Neoplatonism as the catalyst and epicentre of the *Rinascimento* and, by extension, demonstrated the importance of the *Risorgimento* as a cultural phenomenon that would return the 'Italic genius' to the political, social and cultural spotlight. In Milanesi's annotations on Cennini, Da Vinci and, above all, Vasari and Michelangelo, Florence was once again the centre of the world. It recovered the splendour and brilliance of five centuries previous, of the glorious days of Lorenzo and Cosimo de' Medici. Today we know that many elements of that Florentine-centric model are not supported by historiographical evidence, being part of a topical construct, which occasionally deviates from history to become more akin to a secular hagiography. These are the ideological markers of a complex identity-forging process of far greater magnitude, whose primary purpose was to provide the right cultural

---

ad indicem; Serena Pesenti, *La tutela dei monumenti a Firenze. Le 'Commissioni conservatrici' (1860–1891)*, ad indicem.

11 Prior to Milanesi's edition, the only available (and partial) version of the treatise was Giuseppe Tambroni's edition published in Rome in 1821: Cennino Cennini, *Trattato della pittura messo in luce per la prima volta con annotazioni del Cavaliere Giuseppe Tambroni* (Rome: Paolo Salvucci, 1821).

12 Cennino Cennini, *Il libro dell'arte o Trattato della Pittura di Cennino Cennini di Colle Valdelsa; di nuovo pubblicato, con molte correzioni e coll'aggiunta di più capitolo tratti dai codici fiorentini*, eds. Gaetano and Carlo Milanesi (Florence: Le Monnier, 1859).

13 Leonardo da Vinci, *Trattato della pittura di Leonardo da Vinci. Condotto sul Cod. Vaticano Urbinate 1270 con prefazione di Marco Tabarrini preceduto dalla Vita di Leonardo scritta da Giorgio Vasari con nuove note e commentario di Gaetano Milanesi ed ornato del ritratto autografo di Leonardo e di 265 incisioni* (Rome: Unione Cooperativa Editrice, 1890).

14 Gaetano Milanesi, *Le lettere di Michelangelo Buonarroti: pubblicate coi ricordi ed i contratti artistici* (Florence: Le Monnier, 1875).

framework for establishing Italian identity in both national and nationalistic terms. The Neoplatonism practised and theorised in the Renaissance was not Florentine,[15] or at least not exclusively Florentine; nor was (or is) literary Italian the language of Dante, but a complex, elaborate balancing act between the languages employed by Petrarch and Boccaccio.[16]

It may be necessary to further investigate and expand on Italy's historical context in the mid-nineteenth century to better understand some reasons for the formation of what we now call the Vasarian canon, in which an anti-Habsburg and anti-Spanish idiosyncrasy was undoubtedly taking shape. As in any hagiographic narrative that aspires to be persuasive, a powerful, ruthless antagonist is needed to properly offset and highlight the merits of the protagonist.

This historical dimension is illustrated in *I promessi sposi* (published in English as *The Betrothed*) by Alessandro Manzoni (1785–1873), a foundational text par excellence for the process of defining a patriotic identity and a unified language, the definitive version of which was published between 1840 and 1842,[17] although the first edition appeared in 1827. Besides recounting a dramatic and endearing tale of love and the contrast between the powerful and the weak, this novel was a formidable tool for delineating the defining features of a new, structured Italian identity which saw foreign occupation as the primary and ultimate cause of Italy's subjugation and its chronic lack of national cohesion. In this respect, the Spanish–Habsburg combination lent itself to constructing a vast historical narrative, stretching from the fifteenth century (if not earlier) to the contemporary nineteenth century, when the Austrian Empire's occupation of Milan and northern Italy was perceived as the principal politico-military obstacle to Italian national unity. In the 1800s, anti-Spanish polemic was a highly effective literary strategy used to advocate for the necessity of liberation. Thus, in the guise of a historicist narrative, we can clearly make out traits of the anti-Italian oppressor/invader: the Habsburgs who had ruled Milan for three centuries were Spaniards, although by the nineteenth century they were Austrians; the Bourbons who ruled in the south were also Spaniards, although the dynasty was of French origin and their power a legacy of the

---

15 Carlo Dionisotti, 'Introduzione', in Pietro Bembo, *Prose della volgar lingua, Gli Asolani, Rime* (Turin: Tea, 1989 [1966]); Carlo Dionisotti, *Gli Umanisti e il volgare fra Quattrocento e Cinquecento* (Florence: Le Monnier, 1968); Gianfranco Folena, *Il linguaggio del caos: studi sul plurilinguismo rinascimentale* (Volume 25) (Turin: Bollati Boringhieri, 1991).

16 Alfredo Stussi, 'Storia della lingua italiana: nascita d'una disciplina', in Luca Serianni and Pietro Trifone, eds., *Storia della lingua italiana*, (Turin: Einaudi 1993), 5–27; Claudio Giovanardi, *La teoria cortigiana e il dibattito linguistico nel primo Cinquecento* (Rome: Bulzoni, 1998), 7 and 219–239.

17 Alessandro Manzoni, *I promessi sposi: storia milanese del secolo XVII scoperta e rifatta da Alessandro Manzoni* (Milan: Guglielimi e Redaelli, 1840).

Spanish Habsburgs. In the literary interpretation of the situation in Manzoni's novel, these ideological strands are entwined with attributes of a ruthless power which not only prevents the right and necessary marriage of Renzo and Lucia but also, and more importantly, thwarts Italian ambitions of freedom. The writer provides a detailed ethical, sentimental and passionate profile of each character's personality while describing an atmosphere of stifling oppression where the *gridas*, edicts and laws which different viceroys and governors had unjustly and humiliatingly imposed on Italians, take on a dimension of their own outside the normal narrative structure of a nineteenth-century patriotic novel.[18] To achieve his true objectives, Manzoni resorts to a suitable literary device: he invents names, nicknames, surnames and even noble titles, although sometimes the allusions veer off the course of plausibility and come close to the truth, as when he makes concrete references that set the 'scene' in the plague that swept across Italy between 1629 and 1633.[19] The timeline allows us to conclude that the 'punishing plague' in the novel is the same one Diego Velázquez (1599–1660) encountered and successfully avoided during his first sojourn in Italy.[20] Similarly, the iconographic repertoire that illustrates the 1840–1842 edition of *I promessi sposi* includes certain prints which provide visual imagery that corroborate the definition of that antagonism between the 'Italian' and Habsburg–Spanish identities. While the image of Lucia is close to the iconographic model of the *Immaculate Conception* devised by Velázquez (**Figs. 1–2**), *l'Innominato* is depicted with all the self-assurance, aplomb, poise and arrogance attributed to the Spanish—the same qualities the Sevillian master always conveyed in his portraits, such as that of Juan de Pareja (**Figs. 3–4**). In the emerging Italian culture of the mid-1800s, a repertoire of formal models created an effect that interacted with social types who represented a not-so-distant past, to the point that they were directly associated with Spain, Spanish fashion and Spanish conduct. Manzoni's novel is an accurate literary reflection of a larger cultural substratum that would determine the subsequent dynamics of historiographical development, laying the foundations, to a certain extent, of the Italian version of the Spanish 'black legend'. A case in point is Giuseppe Verdi's opera *Don Carlos*, which premiered at the Ópera de Paris on 11 March 1867 with the Italian version opening at Milan's Teatro alla Scala on 10 January 1884.[21] Although it had an original libretto by François Joseph Méry and Camille

---

18 Ettore Bonora, *Manzoni Conclusioni e proposte* (vol. 264) (Turin: Einaudi, 1976), 27–59.
19 Alfonso Corradi, *Annali delle epidemie occorse in Italia dalle prime memorie fino al 1850, parte terza, 1601–1700* (Bologna, 1870), 63–138, esp. 87–93 for Milan and 101–106 for Venice.
20 Salvador Salort Pons, 'Velázquez a Roma', in *Velázquez a Roma: Velázquez e Roma*, catalogue of the exhibition curated by Anna Coliva in Rome, 17/12/1991–30/01/2000 (Milan: Skira, 1999), 43–50.
21 Two years later, Verdi decided to write a third version which premiered at Modena on 26 December 1886.

Fig. 4.1. Alessandro Manzoni, *I Promessi sposi*, 1840, prints by Francesco Gonin.

Fig. 4.2. Face of Lucia Mondella, print by Francesco Gonin, in Alessandro Manzoni, *I Promessi sposi*, 1840.

Fig. 4.3. *Immaculate Conception* by Diego Velázquez, 1618. © National Gallery of Art, London.

Fig. 4.4. Face of *L'innominato*, print by Francesco Gonin, in Alessandro Manzoni, *I Promessi sposi*, 1840.

du Locle, the structure of the work was based on Friedrich Schiller's dramatic play.[22] The opera is a creative work which, like *I promessi sposi*, highlights and stigmatises the drama of Spanish oppression, though in this case the story is set during the reign of Philip II. It is important to note that Manzoni and Verdi were close friends, and Verdi composed his famous requiem to mark the writer's passing. In ideological terms, the position of both intellectuals was summarised a few decades later by the philosopher and historian Benedetto Croce, who identified the Spanish and French invasions of Italy in the sixteenth century as the principal culprits responsible for disrupting what otherwise would have been the natural course of the Italian Renaissance. However, over the years Croce, who was Italian but of German descent, revised this notion to bring it closer to historical reality, as philosophy historian Fulvio Tessitore recently pointed out.[23] That reality was gradually adjusted to reflect the actual circumstances of a system—the Italian system of the early modern era[24]—where the concept of identity operated via mechanisms structurally unrelated to nineteenth-century efforts to define the nation-state, and whose ambitions and yearnings were expressed in the works of Manzoni and Verdi in the context of Italian cultural output of the 1800s.

The Hispanophobic dynamics described above were intended to construct a narrative for nineteenth-century readers who were on a quest to discover the origins of a common Italian identity, at least in cultural terms. However, these arguments had little basis in the reality of the peninsula in the sixteenth century when, to cite but one example, a prominent literary man like Stefano Guazzo[25] had praised the figure of Philip II, underscoring the supranational value of the courtly system of the arts.[26] This historical context was documented by Benedetto Croce himself over a century ago.[27] And it is in this same light that we must recontextualise the historiographical vision of Spain and the Habsburg dynasty with regard to the creation of art evaluation criteria. The art history views expressed by Manzoni, Verdi and Milanesi contrast sharply with the attitude towards Spanish artists we find in at least part of seventeenth-century Italian art literature.

---

22 Friedrich Schiller, *Dom Karlos, Infant von Spanien* (Leipzig: Georg Joachim Göschen, 1787).
23 Fulvio Tessitore, *La ricerca dello storicismo. Studi su Benedetto Croce* (Bologna: Il Mulino, 2012).
24 Benedetto Croce, *La Spagna nella vita italiana durante la Rinascenza* (Bari: Laterza & Figli, 1917), 262–263.
25 Stefano Guazzo, *Dialoghi piacevoli del Sig. Stefano Guazzo Gentil'huomo di Casale di Monferrato* (Piacenza: Pietro Tini, 1587).
26 Amedeo Quondam, 'La virtù dipinta: noterelle (e divagazioni) guazziane intorno a classicismo e Institutio in Antico Regime', in Giorgio Patrizi, ed., *Stefano Guazzo e la civil conversazione* (Rome: Bulzoni, 1990), 227–395.
27 Croce, 260.

Fig. 4.5. *Portrait of Juan de Pareja* by Diego Velázquez, 1650. ©Metropolitan Museum of Art, New York.

Here we will focus on those authors who identified the positive artistic contributions of some of the greatest Spanish and Habsburgian artists of the seventeenth century, from Rubens (1577–1640) to Velázquez. Chief among these are the Venetians Carlo Ridolfi (1594–1685) and Marco Boschini (1602–1681). We can derive several concepts from the latter, despite his obvious penchant for referencing his native Venice and the undeniable linguistic–idiomatic difficulties (closely linked to his marginality in nineteenth-century historiography) his poems so clearly pose. His references are not, as has occasionally been suggested,[28] localist assertions of a decadent society, much less anecdotal or curious examples; rather, they are significant allusions to ideological contexts essential to understanding the true relevance of the Habsburg model in early modern Italy, or at least the *Serenissima Repubblica di Venezia*. For the insightful reader, *La carta del navegar pitoresco*[29] can be understood not merely as a poetic text about art (which is relevant), but as a treatise offering a veritable compendium of the Venetian art system and ideology of the time. Within that system, two essential concepts determine how to write about art (the prescribed style and language of writing) and the standards by which art and artists should be evaluated and judged. On the first topic, Boschini makes it quite clear that he considers *dialogo* [dialogue] to be the most suitable instrument for the literary expression of the arts, and on the second, that Venice—or more accurately, Venetian art—is the source and 'homeland' of painting and of colour. Art historian Philip Sohm[30] recently clarified and qualified these concepts to offer a better understanding of how they fit into the Venetian context. However, in this contextualising process, we discover there is a very relevant connection—one absent from other European contexts—between these linguistic–semantic categories and those used in literature and Spanish art literature of the seventeenth century:[31] when defining the concepts related to brushwork, certain terms and analogies are used that allude—not incidentally but systematically—to Titian's painting in particular and that of the Venetians in general. This is not simply a question of language; above all, it denotes a different perspective and understanding of the arts. It is the antithesis, at least in certain aspects, of the perspective offered by 'classicist' models of art history, which presumed and projected onto early modern era events the foundational importance

---

28 Marco Boschini, *Descrizione di tutte le pubbliche pitture della città di Venezia e isole circonvicine: a sia Rinnovazione delle Ricche minere di Marco Boschini, colla aggiunta di tutte le opere, che uscirono dal 1674: fino al presente 1733. Con un compendio delle vite, e maniere de'principali pittori* (Venice: Presso Pietro Bassaglia, 1733).

29 Marco Boschini, *La carta del navegar pitoresco: dialogo tra un senator venetian deletante, e un professor de pitura, soto nome d'ecelenza, e de compare; comparti in oto venti* (Venice: Barba, 1660); Marco Boschini, *La carta del navegar pitoresco*, ed. Anna Pallucchini (Venice/Rome: Istituto per la collaborazione culturale, 1966) ['Civiltà veneziana. Fonti e testi', 7, ser. 1, 'Fonti e documenti per la Storia dell'arte veneta']; Eloisa Morra, 'L'arte di descrivere. Su alcuni aspetti della storia della ricezione di Tintoretto tra Cinque e Seicento', in *Italianistica: Rivista di letteratura italiana*, vol. 41, no. 3 (September/December 2012), 94–98.

30 Philip Sohm, *Pittoresco: Marco Boschini, his critics, and their critiques of painterly brushwork in seventeenth- and eighteenth-century Italy* (Cambridge: Cambridge University Press, 1991), 25–62.

31 Javier Portús Pérez, *Pintura y pensamiento en la España de Lope de Vega* (Madrid: Nerea, 1999), 173–188.

of the Vasarian canon for our discipline. In contrast to this viewpoint, encapsulated in Schlosser's *Die Kunstliteratur*, Boschini and other Baroque authors—among whom I include Father Sigüenza and his description of El Escorial[32]—did not adopt an exclusively local perspective. As mentioned above, understanding the importance of those writings has now become essential for assessing and comprehending the complexity of European art circles in the early modern era.[33] The time has come to stop using the conceptual category of 'topographical literature', as Schlosser disparagingly called it, and consider the possibility of a different way of understanding artistic creation, one which may have crystallised a model directly opposed to the Vasarian canon.

Getting to the crux of the matter, we find, for example, that Boschini inserted his laudatory references to Titian in strategic places, not hesitating to describe him as 'God of painting',[34] 'immortal painter'[35] and 'especially celebrated by the world'[36]—by which he meant the courtly world. This approach is particularly relevant in *La carta del navegar pitoresco*, where the royal favours that the emperor bestowed upon his favourite painter —even knighting him based solely on his artistic merits[37]—are systematically and metaphorically celebrated. The painter's association with the Habsburg (but not Spanish) emperor Charles V becomes proof of the magnificence of his art in the service of the greatest rulers of his time. Thus, ideas previously used by painter and art theorist Giovanni Lomazzo were revived.[38] Boschini refers to Titian as the 'Sun' blazing in a firmament of little stars.[39] This bias allows Boschini to compare Titian to the great masters of classical antiquity.[40] Boschini's architecture of the arts rested on two other important pillars. The first is his detailed explanation of the nature and importance of the 'Venetian macchia', a *way* of understanding painting that transcends proper names to become a genuine hallmark of a formal, pictorial and ideological style which thrived thanks to the specific requirements of the local Venetian and, above all, foreign art markets.

---

32 Matteo Mancini, 'De Vasari al padre Sigüenza: El 'Museo Imperial' en los registros ideológicos de la fama escurialense', in Fernando Checa Cremades, ed. *El Museo Imperial: estudios sobre coleccionismo artístico de los Austria en el siglo XVI* (Madrid: Fernando Villaverde Ediciones, 2013), 221–236. Cf. the chapter of Miguel Ángel Zalama in this volume.
33 Sohm, 88–147.
34 Boschini (1660), 15.
35 Boschini (1660), 22.
36 Boschini (1660), 16.
37 Boschini (1660), 10.
38 Giovanni Paolo Lomazzo, *Idea del Tempio della pittura de Gio: Paolo Lomazzo Pittore. Nella qual egli discorre dell'origine, e fondamento delle cose contenute nel suo trattato dell'arte della pittura* (Milan: Paolo Gottardo Ponto, 1590), 150–158.
39 Boschini (1660), 306.
40 Boschini (1660), 17.

Boschini uses the concept of the macchia to exalt the Venetian painter's unique ability to differentiate the volumes of figures by means of colours and their tonalities,[41] relegating drawing to a position of secondary if not negligible importance.

The second pillar is his effusive praise for the gallery of Archduke Leopold of Austria. He considered it a divine creation and showered its owner with courtly compliments, calling him a 'treasurer of painting and of good taste'.[42] In Boschini's eyes, that treasure transcended the series of works printed in David Teniers's *Theatrum Pictorium* to became an essential part of the process of preserving the memory of the visual model of the arts posited by the Habsburgs. In these particular circumstances, it does not seem at all odd that Rubens and Velázquez—or Velázquez and Rubens, according to the chrono-biological order deliberately altered by Boschini—should embody the characteristics and idiosyncrasies of a model of the arts where visual (though not necessarily shallow or superficial) experience was poised to attain its highest expression by means of concrete actions. *Seeing, contemplating, observing and enjoying* displaced the idea of the artist as a *distinguished and exemplary man* established by the Vasarian model, moving towards a model where the artist's genius did not reside in his biographical traits but in his ability to deceive the senses according to the Venetian pictorial method, where empathy and colour were complementary parts of the sensuality of painting.[43]

Diego Velázquez inherited, embodied and projected these models onto the Habsburgian reality of seventeenth-century Spain: his canvases denote the same understanding of Venetian brushwork,[44] and in his work this technique found effective figurative translation beyond the literary ekphrasis of the 'distant macchie' or 'Titianesque patches'. Techniques in this pictorial model took great pains to conceal artistic artifice as a means of visually reinstating nature through colour, to the point of turning painted figures into something which, when seen from a distance, took on the form of a living being.[45] That historiographical account is reflected in Boschini's narrative, which also supplies detailed historical and functional background information on each character mentioned. Thus, Velázquez is presented as court painter to Philip IV, and his courtly responsibilities and distinctions are treated as an integral and substantial part of his own identity. Boschini not only reminds the reader of these attributes but links them to his personality, effectively summing up Velázquez as a 'cavalier che ispirava un gran decoro' [knight who inspired great decorum]; his courtly

---

41 Boschini (1660), 328.
42 Boschini (1660), 39–44.
43 Boschini (1660), 171.
44 Boschini (1660), 55.
45 Miguel Morán Turina, *Estudios sobre Velázquez* (vol. 70) (Madrid: Ediciones AKAL, 2006).

status outweighs his reputation as a painter, and the artist's importance is increased proportionally.[46] Velázquez was a court painter, a painter of colour; he was a knight of great decorum. Therefore, Velázquez was Venetian.

Returning to Manzoni's nineteenth-century literary depiction of the Spaniards who passed through different Italian cities in the first half of the seventeenth century, we discover the existence of at least two antithetical models of the arts rooted in the sixteenth century: an Italocentric model whose defining features are crystallised in the Vasarian canon, and a Eurocentric imperial model which, following Boschini, we might say revolves around the Burgundian legacy of Habsburgian *magnificence*.

In our efforts to understand the nature of this antithesis, we may derive unique insight from an analysis of the characteristic long recognised, positively or negatively, as the distinguishing linguistic and formal peculiarity of Venetian art and later Spanish art, from El Greco to Velázquez, without forgetting the *style* known as Tenebrism. Evidently, that characteristic is colour and its eloquent omission: a systematic process purposely camouflaged to superficially exalt its formal quality and beauty. This is the same process which, for example, has led art history to accept genuine aberrations of visual semantics as 'natural': from the neoclassical reproduction of ancient architecture and sculpture with a rigorous absence of colour or pigment, to assertions which, if carefully examined, verge on the surreal and yet have been enshrined as unquestionable axioms by art critics, despite being consciously or unconsciously functional parts of the mechanisms involved in perpetuating that omission of colour. In this respect, we are inevitably reminded of Erwin Panofsky's strategy of assessing works of art primarily through black-and-white reproductions.[47] The artists of the *Cinquecento* and *Seicento* must not have shared the seminal German art historian's opinion. How else can we logically explain their systematic pursuit, between originals and copies, of perfect accuracy in the reproduction of colours? That quest is often apparent, even to the untrained eye, on the surface of the canvas itself: Rubens's copies of Titian and Van Dyck's famous sketchbook offer more than eloquent proof.[48] The contradiction between the reality of hard facts and the denial or concealment of part of the seminal sources of our discipline rears up once again, like a hydra head, before the scholar's eyes. The heart of the problem does not lie in specifying the idiosyncrasies or qualities of Venetian colour, but in defining

---

46 Boschini (1660), 56.
47 Georges Didi-Huberman, *Confronting images: questioning the ends of a certain history of art*, trans. John Goodman (University Park, PA: Pennsylvania State University Press, 2005), 121–123
48 Giovanni Pietro Bellori, *Vida de pintores*, ed. Miguel Morán Turina (Madrid: Ediciones AKAL, 2005), 150–151.

and comprehending the semantic–ideological substance that resided (and resides) in colour and is manifested solely through colour, ultimately becoming the privileged interpreter of Habsburgian *magnificence*.[49]

The complexity of the question of colour and its semantics must have been understood by the Council fathers who, gathered at Trent in early December 1563, issued a clear and severe warning in their decree on sacred images and relics about the dangers of *colour*, viewed as an essential part of a dialectical path whose opposite pole was *figures*:

> And if at times, when expedient for the unlettered people; it happens that the facts and narratives of sacred Scripture are portrayed and represented; the people shall be taught, that not thereby is the Divinity represented, as though it could be seen by the eyes of the body, or be portrayed by colours or figures.[50]

This ideological–devotional system, besides warning that the divine should not be confused with its figurative representation, emphasises that there are two possible types of interference: iconography (figures) and colour (passions and semantic symbolism). The arguments put forth at Trent imply the existence of a separate horizon for the conception of colour, for its use and purpose in the arts: a horizon diametrically opposed to the scientific perspective argued and debated, for example, in Leonardo da Vinci's *Trattato della Pittura* [*A Treatise on Painting*] annotated by Milanesi. That treatise attempts to establish a perspective that supports knowledge of the uses of colour as essential to the craft or art of any professional painter in the early modern era. This model proved so effective that it became the backbone of the academic establishment and materialised in the seventeenth-century Italo–French model for the proper training of court artists and the creation of the fine arts system as we know it, or at least as it has been told to us.[51]

In the first half of the twentieth century, two periods of artistic production were rooted in a rejection of that orderly, controlled system of the fine arts. These two phenomena, each in their own way, pored over the history of our discipline until they found precedents to support and justify their profoundly anti-academic stance. I am referring to the early avant-garde movements and the nearly contemporary revival of Baroque

---

49 Fernando Checa Cremades, 'El Museo Imperial: estudios sobre el coleccionismo artístico de los Austrias en el siglo XVI', in *El Museo Imperial: el coleccionismo artístico de los Austrias en el siglo XVI*, ed. Fernando Checa Cremades (Madrid: Fernando de Villaverde Ediciones, 2013), 9–14.

50 J. Waterworth, ed./trans., *The canons and decrees of the sacred and oecumenical Council of Trent* (London: Dolman, 1848), 233–236. Translated from *Concilii Tridentini Actorum pars sexta complectens acta post sessionem sextam (XXII) usque ad finem concilli (17 Sept. 1562–4 Dec. 1563). Collegit, edidit, illustravit Stephanus Ehses*, vol. IX (Freiburg, 1929), 1077–1079.

51 Giovanni Previtali, *La periodización del arte italiano* (vol. 21) (Madrid: Akal, 1989).

artists, starting with the demonised figure of Michelangelo Merisi da Caravaggio (1571–1610), dubbed the 'anti-Michelangelo' by Vincenzo Carducci. The muted semantics of colour were resurrected in the explosion of Baroque passions and countless retrospectives that explained and investigated a period hitherto forgotten by historiography and even by the art market. Colour was also the anvil on which the innovative contributions of the avant-garde movements were forged, movements that rejected the academy and its teachings, questioned the function of museums and national identity, and denied the very need for a historical narrative.[52] The gesture, the brushstroke, the macchia, the vagueness of the expressionists or the balanced lines of the neo-plastic functionalists, whose ultimate comprehension was only conclusive thanks to the interaction with colour,[53] returned to the limelight and defined a rhetorical framework of the arts where drawing was on one side and colour—understood as the catalyst of sentiments, passions and powerful semantic meaning—was on the other. Reviving the Tridentine definition of *figures*, these were reduced to a synthetic expression, by means of the iconographic system, of the simplest, most direct aspect of semantic language. The pillars of art history criticism of the day gradually crumbled in academic automatisms. After that point, identifying a national spirit or *essence* in certain artists or works of the past ceased to be an automatic process and became something far more complex, as the investigations of Aby Warburg[54] and Eugenio Battisti[55] proved. Reconstructing another Renaissance whose defining characteristics complement those indicated by the Vasarian canon was, and still is, possible.

---

52 Filippo Tommaso Marinetti, 'Le Futurisme', in *Le Figaro*, Paris (20 February 1909), front page.
53 Els Hoek, 'Piet Mondriaan', in Carel Blotkamp, ed., *De Stijl: Nascita di un movimento* (Milan: Electa, 1989), 92–98; Marijke Küper, 'Gerrit Rietveld', in *Blotkamp*, 424–436.
54 Georges Didi-Huberman, *The Surviving Image: Phantoms of Time and Time of Phantoms: Aby Warburg's History of Art*, trans. Harvey Mendelsohn (University Park, PA: Pennsylvania State University Press, 2016).
55 Eugenio Battisti, *L'antirinascimento* (Milan: Feltrinelli, 1962), 53–66 and 402–424.

JESÚS F. PASCUAL MOLINA

Luxury and Identity in the Sixteenth-Century Habsburg Courts*

> [...] that great is the confusion among lineages, and that only those are seen to be great and illustrious that show themselves so by the virtue, wealth, and generosity of their possessors. I have said virtue, wealth, and generosity, because a great man who is vicious will be a great example of vice, and a rich man who is not generous will be merely a miserly beggar; for the possessor of wealth is not made happy by possessing it, but by spending it, and not by spending as he pleases, but by knowing how to spend it well.
>
> (Miguel de Cervantes, *Don Quijote de La Mancha*, vol. II, Chapter 6)[1]

---

* The author is member of the University of Valladolid recognized research group and Junta de Castilla y León consolidated research unit, Art, power and society in the Modern Age. Also, he is principal investigator, together with Miguel Ángel Zalama, of the research project ref. PID2021-124832NB-I00 [*Magnificencia a través de las artes visuales en la familia de los Reyes Católicos. Estudio comparado del patronazfo de ambos géneros*], funded by Spanish government.

1 Miguel de Cervantes, *Don Quijote de La Mancha*, Instituto Cervantes edition, ed. Francisco Rico (Barcelona: Galaxia Gutenberg, 2004), 737. '[...] es grande la confusión que hay entre los linajes, y que solos aquéllos parecen grandes y ilustres que lo muestran en la virtud y en la riqueza y liberalidad de sus dueños. Dije virtudes, riquezas y liberalidades, porque el grande que fuere vicioso será vicioso grande, y el rico no liberal será un avaro mendigo, que al poseedor de las riquezas no le hace dichoso el tenerlas, sino el gastarlas, y no el gastarlas como quiera, sino el saberlas bien gastar'. *Don Quixote*, trans. John Ormsby (1885).

Jesús F. Pascual Molina • University of Valladolid

Towards a definition of luxury

The concept of luxury is ambivalently associated with power, value and wealth on the one hand and superfluousness, ostentation and extravagance on the other. It has both positive and negative connotations, depending on the context in which it is used.[2] It can be considered an excess—something unnecessary and therefore wrong—a belief that led to passing numerous 'sumptuary laws' against luxury, in an attempt to protect society from wasteful spending and economic ruin.[3] *Lujuria*, the Spanish word for lust (a capital sin from a Catholic perspective) comes from the same root as *lujo* (luxury) and refers to excess and wantonness. Yet, luxury also reflects grandeur and abundance and is related to the image one presents to the world in an effort to stand out. A key component of luxury is distinction: that which differentiates and sets a person apart from the rest.[4]

According to the other perspective, luxury was a virtue based on philosophical doctrines, and in relation to this we can identify three fundamental concepts: magnificence, splendour and ostentation. In Aristotelian philosophy—specifically in *Nicomachean Ethics*[5]—which made no distinction between public and private forms, magnificence or munificence was a virtue associated with lavish spending, indicating that a munificent person is liberal in works that reflect what is good and beautiful. It was also the quality of spending wisely, when necessary and in proportion to available resources. As a virtue, magnificence was associated with the powerful as part of the qualities that indicated their greatness and dignity. In Italian humanism, where Giovanni Pontano's treatise on magnificence (1498) was a key influence, this virtue was primarily exhibited in the public domain and associated with architectural patronage, pomp and spectacle.[6] Pontano also wrote about splendour, which he saw as a personal virtue associated with spending to ensure that a man's goods 'were copious, rare and elegant',[7] and therefore an accurate reflection of his social and financial

---

2 Christopher J. Berry, *The idea of luxury: a conceptual and historical investigation* (vol. 30) (Cambridge: Cambridge University Press, 1994); Jesús de Garay Suárez-Llanos, 'Algunas consideraciones acerca del lujo', *Thémata: Revista de Filosofía*, 10 (1992), 469–499.
3 Juan Vicente García Mansilla, 'El lujo: ¿motor del crecimiento o camino hacia la ruina? Percepciones y actitudes ante el gasto suntuario en la Historia', *Ars & Renovatio*, 7 (2019), 6–26. On sumptuary laws in Spain, see Juan Sempere y Guarinos and Juan Rico Giménez, *Historia del lujo y de las leyes suntuarias en España* (Valencia: Institució Alfons el Magnànim, 2000) [Madrid, 1788].
4 Juan Vicente García Mansilla, 8, quoting Pierre Bourdieu.
5 Sarah Broadie and Christopher Rowe, eds., *Aristotle: Nicomachean Ethics: translation, introduction and commentary* by Sarah Broadie and Christopher Rowe (Oxford: Oxford University Press, 2002), Book 4, Chapter 2.
6 Evelyn Welch, 'Public magnificence and private display: Giovanni Pontano's De splendore (1498) and the domestic arts', *Journal of Design History* 15:4 (2002), 211–221, esp. 214.
7 Welch, 215.

Fig. 5.1. *A goldsmith in his shop*, by Petrus Christus, 1449. © Metropolitan Museum of Art, New York.

status and power. As Pontano wrote regarding ornamental objects, 'The sight of these things brings prestige to the owner of the house' when seen by visitors, and 'should be as magnificent and various as possible, [and] should each be arranged in their own place'.[8] The final purpose of splendour was, therefore, prestige.[9] Finally, ostentation, in one sense of the word, refers to the act of making magnificence visible, a fundamental aspect of luxury from the political perspective that interests us here, as it is associated with the maintenance of power.

---

8 In the 1518 Venice edition of *Opera Omnia* by Pontano, 138.
9 Welch, 215–216.

Enshrined as pillars of moral virtue by various doctrines derived from Aristotelian philosophy which, mixed with Cicero, Christian scholasticism and Renaissance humanism, survived into the early modern era,[10] these concepts also served as a powerful incentive to patronise and collect art and luxury objects, and they helped shape an attitude towards the arts that defined much of the cultural policy of the Ancient Regime.[11] Luxury was justified, not only as something virtuous, but also as serving the greater good.[12] Beautifying cities and buildings, financing architectural works, patronising artists and ornamenting one's person with jewellery and garments were actions that ennobled the patron and displayed their financial solvency and social position—and for sovereigns advertised an economic capacity that would benefit their realms. We can therefore say that luxury and magnificence were, foremost, politics and distinction.

Luxury as identity

The Burgundian court—especially under the dukes Philip the Good and Charles the Bold—has been called the epitome of luxury, and its attitudes were later imitated by other European courts.[13] However, these attitudes towards the arts have often been considered the epilogue of the medieval period, rooted in the past rather than looking to the future novelty of the Renaissance.[14] The eventual predominance of Italian over northern culture, the decline of the House of Burgundy—Duke Charles the Bold died

---

10 Marina Belozerskaya, *Luxury arts of the renaissance* (Los Angeles: Getty Publications, 2005), 2.
11 On the practice of collecting luxury objects in connection with magnificence and the system of the arts, see the chapter by Miguel Ángel Zalama in this volume. See also Miguel Ángel Zalama, 'Las artes visuales en la modernidad: reflexiones sobre su consideración', in *Imbricaciones: paradigmas, modelos y materialidad de las artes en la Europa habsbúrgica*, eds. Matteo Mancini and Álvaro Pascual Chenel (Madrid: Sílex, 2019), 15–43.
12 Antonio Urquízar Herrera, 'Teoría de la magnificencia y teoría de las señales en el pensamiento nobiliario español del siglo XVI', *Ars Longa*, 23 (2014), 96.
13 On the court of Burgundy and the arts, see, among others, Joseph Calmette, *The golden age of Burgundy: the magnificent dukes and their courts* (New York: W. W. Norton, 1962); *Art from the courts of Burgundy: the patronage of Philip the Bold and John the Fearless 1364–1419*, exh. cat. (Paris and Cleveland: Editions de la Réunion des Musées Nationaux and the Cleveland Museum of Art, 2004); *Splendour of the Burgundian court: Charles the Bold (1433–1477)*, eds. Susan Marti, Till-Holger Borchert and Gabrielle Keck, (Brussels: Mercatorfonds, 2009); *Staging the court of Burgundy: proceedings of the conference 'the splendour of Burgundy'*, eds. Wim Blockmans, Till-Holger Borchert, Nele Gabriëls, Johan Oosterman and Anna van Oosterwijk (London: Harvey Miller and Turnhout: Brepols, 2013). On the influence of Burgundian arts in other territories, see Marina Belozerskaya, *Rethinking the renaissance: Burgundian arts across Europe* (Cambridge: Cambridge University Press, 2002).
14 As noted by Huizinga—see Johan Huizinga, *The Autumn of the Middle Ages*, trans. Rodney J. Payton and Ulrich Mammitzsch (Chicago: The University of Chicago Press, 1996)

Fig. 5.2. *Jean Wauquelin presenting his Chroniques de Hainaut to Philip the Good*, frontispiece in miniature from the *Chroniques de Hainaut*, atrib. to Rogier van der Weyden 1448. © Royal Library of Belgium.

in 1477—and the rise of other powers and personalities like Henry VIII, Charles V, Francis I and several influential popes are considered some factors that explain why Burgundian aesthetics became obsolete.

However, it would be more accurate to speak of continuity or evolution rather than obsolescence or obscurity. For instance, in the Habsburg context, Burgundian customs were integrated in the protocol and organisation of the sovereign's household, and therefore remained relevant to a certain extent. When, in 1548, Charles V ordered that the household of Prince Philip should be organised in the Burgundian fashion, he was perpetuating that court's etiquette and traditions.[15] This change, which was also related to Philip's impending European trip, made the household more complex

---

[1923]—whose ideas profoundly influenced subsequent historiography. On this topic, see Belozerskaya, *Rethinking the renaissance: Burgundian arts across Europe*, 1–6 and 40–4.

15 Charles C. Noel, 'La etiqueta borgoñona en la corte de España (1547–1800)', *Manuscrits*, 22 (2004), 143; Santiago Fernández Conti, 'La introducción de la etiqueta borgoñona y el viaje de 1548–1551', in *La corte de Carlos V*, vol. II, ed. José Martínez Millán (Madrid: Sociedad Estatal para la Conmemoración de los centenarios de Felipe II y Carlos V, 2000), 212; *La casa de Borgoña. La casa del rey de España*, eds. José Eloy Hortal Muñoz and Félix Labrador Arroyo (Leuven: Leuven University Press, 2014).

and expensive to maintain, but it also underscored the magnificence surrounding the sovereign, especially in courtly rituals and celebrations.

However, although luxury and magnificence continued to be Habsburg hallmarks following the convergence of Spanish and Flemish-Burgundian traits in the dynasty with Charles V, this attitude stemmed from two sources: on the one hand, the legacy of lavish Burgundy—he was the son of Archduke Philip, whose parents were Emperor Maximilian I and his first wife, Mary of Burgundy, daughter of Charles the Bold—and on the other, the culture of luxury in Spain—on his mother's side, Charles V was descended from the Catholic Monarchs, Isabella and Ferdinand—where it was considered an essential element of exercising power.

In the Spain of the Trastámaras, who sat on the thrones of Castile and Aragon and forged alliances with the most powerful kingdoms in Europe, a very distinctive, almost signature attitude towards luxury was developed by prominent individuals like the monarchs John II of Castile, John II of Aragon and Henry IV of Castile; the constable Álvaro de Luna; and Juana Enríquez, Queen consort of Aragon, to name but a few.[16] Isabella and Ferdinand, the Catholic Monarchs, maintained this attitude and passed it on to their heirs. Though still occasionally repeated, theories about the austerity of the Spanish court—constructs typical of nineteenth-century historiography—should be set aside, having been refuted by period documentation.

Some have noted that the Catholic Monarchs adopted certain aspects of Burgundian fashions to reinforce their role as sovereigns, an attitude that materialised in magnificence and opulence, dynastic monuments and court festivities. The monarchs chose forms imported from Burgundy,

---

16 For example, see José Manuel Calderón Ortega, *Álvaro de Luna: riqueza y poder en la Castilla del siglo XV* (Madrid: Dykinson, 1999); Francisco de Paula Cañas Gálvez, *La cámara real de Juan II de Castilla: cargos, descargos, cuentas e inventarios (1428–1454)* (Madrid: Ediciones de La Ergástula, 2017); Miguel Ángel Ladero Quesada and Margarita Cantera Montenegro, 'El tesoro de Enrique IV en el alcázar de Segovia 1465–1475', *Historia. Instituciones. Documentos*, 31 (2004), 307–352; Miguel Ángel Ladero Quesada, 'Capilla, joyas y armas, tapices y libros de Enrique IV de Castilla', *Acta histórica et archaeologica mediaevalia*, 26 (2005), 851–874; Jesús F. Pascual Molina, 'Juan II de Aragón y las artes suntuarias', *Ars Longa*, 24 (2015), 71–83; *Retórica artística en el tardogótico castellano: la capilla fúnebre de Álvaro de Luna en contexto*, eds. Olga Pérez Monzón, Matilde Miquel Juan and María Martín Gil (Madrid: Sílex, 2018); Jan Karel Steppe, 'Vlaamse kunstwerken in het bezit van doña Juana Enríquez, echtgenote van Jan II van Aragón en moeder van Ferdinand de Katholieke', in *Scrinium Lovaniense: Mélanges historiques Etienne van Cauwenbergh* (Leuven: Université de Louvain, 1961), 301–330; Miguel Ángel Zalama, 'Tapices en los tesoros de Juan II y Enrique IV de Castilla: su fortuna posterior', in *Estudios de historia del arte: homenaje al profesor de la Plaza Santiago*, eds. Jesús María Parrado del Olmo and Fernando Gutiérrez Baños (Valladolid: Universidad de Valladolid), 55–60; Miguel Ángel Zalama and Jesús F. Pascual Molina, *Testamento y codicilos de Juan II de Aragón, y última voluntad de Fernando I: política y artes* (Zaragoza: Institución Fernando el Católico, 2017).

Fig. 5.3. *The Virgin of the Catholic Monarchs*, Master of the Virgin of the Catholic Monarchs, 1491-1493. © Museo Nacional del Prado.

not only because of that court's international reputation for beauty and lavishness, but also because it was held in high esteem by the nobility.[17] However, we must ask ourselves if this was due to the imitation of, and preference for, these forms and customs, or if the Spanish penchant for luxury drew craftsmen from the north who imposed their aesthetics in the south. Those northern artisans were undoubtedly held in high prestige, even in the Italian Renaissance, where Vasari's 'Tuscan-centric' approach was simply one of several coexistent models, among them the highly successful

---

17 Belozerskaya, *Rethinking the renaissance: Burgundian arts across Europe*, 160.

Flemish style.[18] In any case, the abundance of Flemish artists and merchants in Spain denotes a rather complex situation influenced by a number of factors, from economic and tax advantages to flourishing cities and pre-existing trade routes that linked the two regions. These relations intensified when the dynastic ties between Spain and the Holy Roman Empire were reinforced by the double marriage between Prince John and Princess Joanna and Maximilian I's heirs, Margaret and Philip. After that point, the court became an even more powerful magnet for artists and products from different territories and, especially during the reign of Charles, artists from the sovereign's realms flocked to the Spanish court.[19]

Since the Middle Ages, the virtue of magnificence was expressed primarily through architecture, expenditure on feasts and festivities, and richness of attire.[20] Architectural patronage has been studied extensively, but court festivities and the luxury arts still have a lot to offer scholars, especially if they are analysed holistically rather than as unrelated elements. To give just a few examples, some have said that, in Spain, knightly events like jousts and tournaments attempted to emulate the Burgundians, yet chroniclers clarified that there had been a Spanish tradition and even a 'Spanish fashion' of grand spectacles since the days of the Trastámaras which continued throughout the sixteenth century.[21] The same is true of acquiring certain luxury goods, such as Flemish tapestries, which had been significant in Spain since the Middle Ages, pointing to the existence of a 'Spanish style' marked by the use of these textile creations.[22] These Spanish customs also had local idiosyncrasies, such as the Morisco influence, which gave rise to the *juego de cañas* (a sport in which mounted knights attempted to dart each other with a reed or cane) and the ornamental use of rugs and carpets, among other things.

---

18 Bernard Aikema, 'Netherlandish painting and early Renaissance Italy: artistic rapports in a historiographical perspective', *Cultural exchange in early modern Europe, vol. IV: forging European identities, 1400–1700*, ed. Herman Roodenburg (Cambridge: Cambridge University Press, 2007), 100–137.
19 On these economic, social and political matters, see Raymond Fagel, '"As yche othere brothere": The Human Factor within the Hispano-Flemish World', in *Netherlandish Art and Luxury Goods in Renaissance Spain: Studies in Honor of Professor Jan Karel Steppe*, eds. Dann Van Heescg, Robrecht Janssen and Jan Van Der Stock (London/Turnhout: Brepols, 2018), 13–26.
20 Antonio Urquízar Herrera, 97.
21 Jesús F. Pascual Molina, 'La fiesta caballeresca en los orígenes de la Casa de Austria en el tránsito del siglo XV al XVI' (Valencia, 2023) [in press].
22 Jesús F. Pascual Molina, 'Un estilo español: los tapices de la colección real en los actos cortesanos, entre el siglo XVI y el XXI', in *El legado de las obras de arte: Tapices, pinturas, esculturas… Sus viajes a través de la Historia*, eds. Miguel Ángel Zalama, María José Martínez Ruiz and Jesús F. Pascual Molina (Valladolid: Universidad de Valladolid, 2017), 29–40. Other chapters in the present collection also point out the importance of tapestries for Habsburg image-building.

Obviously, interterritorial connections and the movement of people and goods facilitated the spread of Burgundian fashions across Europe, where they mingled with the traditions and customs of each place. Yet the situation was far more complex than that. Historiography uses the term 'hybridisation' to describe combinations and exchanges between different places and traditions, and by now it should be clear that the conventional concept of 'Renaissance' is obsolete.[23] It is not a question of Gothic versus Renaissance, where the former is medieval, northern and rooted, and the latter is a modern phenomenon that emerged in different parts of Italy. When scholars criticise the Burgundian culture of chivalry as medieval and outdated, they neglect to consider that important festivities survived and continued to be celebrated in the sixteenth century across the European continent, often mixed with elements of classical culture and always considered an effective weapon in the game of politics.

Returning to the manifestations of luxury, everything that concerned sovereign representation was associated with magnificence. When the chronicler Fernando del Pulgar spoke of Queen Isabella's virtues, he noted that:

> She was a very ceremonious woman in attire and ornament, and in her daises and seats, and in the service of her person; and she wanted to be served by great and noble men, with great deference and humility. Nowhere have we read of any king of the past who had such great men in his service. However, because of this circumstance she was accused of having some vice, saying that she was overly fond of pomp, but we understand that in this life no ceremony can be deemed too extreme for monarchs, for it is no more than their royal state requires; the monarch being singular and superior in the realms, her ceremony must be great indeed and outshine all other states, for she has divine authority over the lands.[24]

Although Pulgar's statement is well known, it behoves us to reconsider it here. The chronicler not only acknowledges the queen's ostentation but

---

23 See, for example, Peter Burke, *Hybrid renaissance: culture, language, architecture* (Budapest/New York: CEU Press, 2016).

24 Fernando del Pulgar, *Crónica de los Reyes Católicos*, ed. Juan de la Mata Carriazo (Granada: Universidad de Granada, 2008) [Madrid, 1943], 78. 'Era muger muy cerimoniosa en los vestidos e arreos, e en sus estrados e asientos, e en el servicio de su persona; e quería ser servida de omes grandes e nobles, e con grande acatamiento e humiliaçión. No se lee de ningún rey de los pasados que tan grandes omes toviese por ofiçiales. E como quiera que por esta condiçión le era inputado algúnd viçio, diziendo ser pompa demasiada, pero entendemos que ninguna cerimonia en esta vida se puede hacer tan por estremo a los rreyes, que mucho más no rrequiera el estado rreal; el qual así como es uno y superior en los rreynos, así deve mucho estremarse, e rresplandeçer sobre todos los otros estados, pues tiene autoridad divina en las tierras'.

considers it proof of her power. His text subtly touches on the debate between vice and virtue with luxury, concluding that expenditure and pomp are inherent to monarchs. Testimonies like that of the chronicler Antoine de Lalaing, who in 1502 described the Catholic Monarchs as dressing in plain woollen fabrics, have been cited to support the entirely erroneous notion of the Spanish court's austerity.[25] Period accounts are full of details that refute this, corroborated by documentation.[26]

The monarchs prepared their daughters' dowries in keeping with these ideas, demonstrating the importance of luxury objects, particularly jewellery, clothing and tapestries.[27] The chronicles of the day leave us in no doubt as to the image projected by the Spanish infantas. Testimonies repeatedly emphasise the richness of their apartments and their apparel, which reflected on the Spanish court; thus, in Portugal, England and Flanders, the daughters allowed the Catholic Monarchs to display their power through magnificence.

During his first visit to Spain, the future Charles V took great care to show himself before his new subjects with all the pageantry of his ancestors, apparel and court festivities which played an important role in shaping the idea of luxury associated with power. Laurent Vital, who wrote an account of that journey, wrote that he had never seen a better entry than that of Charles into Valladolid in terms of the king's attire, specifying:

> Every time I have seen him entering his various cities, those entries were always gorgeous and triumphant, as were his entries into Ghent, Brussels, Leuven (Louvain), Mechelen (Malines), Antwerp, Bruges and elsewhere; but the magnificence, richness and finery of his apparel at this entry surpassed all others I have seen up to this point.[28]

---

25 Miguel Ángel Zalama, 'Oro, perlas, brocados…: la ostentación en el vestir en la corte de los Reyes Católicos', Revista de Estudios Colombinos, 8 (2012), 13–22.

26 On Queen Isabella's relationship with luxury objects, see Miguel Ángel Zalama, 'Isabel la Católica y las joyas: La custodia de la catedral de Toledo', in El arte en la corte de los Reyes Católicos. Rutas artísticas a principios de la Edad Moderna, eds. Fernando Checa and Bernardo José García García (Madrid: Fundación Carlos de Amberes, 2005), 331–353; Miguel Ángel Zalama, 'Valoración y usos de las artes: Colón y las joyas de Isabel la Católica', in La materia de los sueños: Cristóbal Colón, ed. Fernando Checa (Valladolid: Junta de Castilla y León, 2006), 49–59.

27 Miguel Ángel Zalama, 'Juana I' in Arte, poder y cultura en torno a una reina que no gobernó (Madrid: Centro de Estudios de Europa Hispánica, 2010); Miguel Ángel Zalama, 'Lujo y ostentación: El tesoro de María de Aragón y Castilla, esposa de Manuel I de Portugal', Goya, 358 (2017), 3–19.

28 Louis Prosper Gachard and Charles Piot, eds., Collection des voyages des souverains des Pays-Bas, vol. III (Brussels: F. Hayez, 1874), 150. 'toutesfois si l'ay-je veu en pluisierus entrées de ses villes de par dechà bien gorgias et triumphant, comme à l'entrée de Gand, de Bruxelles, de Louvain, de Malines, d'Anvers, de Bruges et aulleurs; mais la gorgiaseté, richesse et fentillesse de son accoustrement à ceste entrée fut l'oultrepasse de toutes les aultres que j'ay veu jusques à ceste heure'.

Fig. 5.4. *Bust of young Charles V*, anonymous, c. 1520. Valladolid, Museo Nacional de Escultura. © Photo by the author.

Vital—who, as a member of the king's household, was well acquainted with Burgundian luxury and, in his capacity as master of the wardrobe, with the world of fashion and its details—described the king's outfit, saying that nothing like it had ever been seen in Castile, as several locals admitted to him. Such a grand display of luxury was undoubtedly owing to the king's desire to make a good impression on his new subjects: it was his first appearance before them, and he knew that, as a foreigner, some were reluctant to welcome him.

The retinue of the young Charles had to be sumptuous, as befitted his royal dignity, but the Spanish nobles and urban elite who received the sovereign wherever he went were equally determined to put their best foot forward. In his chapter on the proclamation of the king, Vital said the nobles were:

> All richly dressed and robed in cloth of gold, and others in cloth of silver and other rich silks; some of whom had their robes hemmed with

gold plate, and others all covered in beaten gold, some draped in sables, ermines and leopard skins, genets and lambskins from Rommenye, while others were so well wrapped in double furs that none could fail to notice them; all so richly attired that it was indeed a wonder to behold.[29]

A little-known printed document in the British Library corroborates this taste for luxury. The text describes in great detail the apparel of all the nobles who attended Charles V's proclamation as king at Valladolid in February 1518.[30] The author, who signs as Laureus de Garnode, dedicated a substantial portion of his account to the fashions sported by the nobility at that royal event. For instance, he begins by saying:

> First of all, His Grace the Constable of Castile, wearing a robe of cloth of gold lined with the finest marten fur, and a bort, and a tunic of cloth of beaten gold covered with cloth of silver, his mule caparisoned in cloth of gold.[31]

He gives detailed descriptions of other individuals, noting the quality of their garments and the presence of jewellery and precious stones: 'The Marquis of Villena wore a black velvet robe lined with ermine fur, and his hat was weighed down with dangling rubies and pearls' and 'The Count of Benavente [...] the gold chain richly adorned with pendants of diamonds, rubies and enormous pearls'.[32] These chronicles, which read like interminable roll calls packed with detail, not only narrate an event and describe those in attendance; they also conveyed magnificence materialised in those itemised inventories and served as propaganda, confirming the association of luxury with power.

---

29 Gachard and Piot, 224. 'tous richement acoustrés et vestus en drap d'or, les aultres en drap d'argent et aultres riches draps de soyes; de quoy les aulcuns avoient leurs robbes bordées de plates d'or, el les aultres touttes couvertes d'or batu, les aulcunes plaines de sables, d'ermines et liepars, genettes, agneaulx de Rommenye el aultres telz fouraiges et doublés ainsi que chascum l'entendoit, tous si très-richement empoincts que merveille'.
30 [Laureus de Garnode] *Le couronnement du tres puissant et tres redoubé roy catholique Charles...*, 1518. British Library, General Reference Collection C.33.e.24.
31 'Et premierement monseygneur le connetable de Castille, vestu d'une robe de drap dor frize fourre de martes des plus fines, a ung bort de meisme par dehors et a lenuiron dicelle robe de large de demi piet son saion de drap dor batu couuert de drap dargent decoppe, sa mule harnachie de drap dor frize'.
32 'Le marquis de Vellaines vestu d'une robe de vellours noir fouree dermines son bonnet chergie de ballaix, rubís et perles' and 'Le conte de Bonnevente [...] la chaine dor garnie de ballaix deamants rubís e grosses perles bien richement'.

The inheritance of Emperor Charles V

Although he was not a prototypical royal patron or collector when compared with other sovereigns of his time or with some women in his family like Margaret of Austria and Mary of Hungary,[33] Charles V understood the important symbolic value of the arts, a knowledge inherited from his ancestors, especially Maximilian I and the Catholic Monarchs. In addition to carefully cultivating his public image and making propagandistic use of certain artistic creations, such as arms, armour or tapestries, he always made sure that his relatives, particularly those in positions of power, were suitably endowed with important luxury objects.

From the moment the household of Prince Philip was established in 1535, courtiers were assigned to his service and all items needed to adequately represent the crown prince were provided.[34] Tapestries, arms and armour, medals, exotic objects from the Indies, relics, items associated with scientific curiosity and clocks were among Prince Philip's first possessions, which also included luxury fabrics used, among other things, to adorn his chapel.[35] The household had a relatively small budget for the first several years—around three and a half million *maravedís* per annum—commensurate with the needs of a very young prince.[36] If we look at the expenses of Prince Philip's household in the 1540s, when he married for the first time, we see a substantial increase in the funds allotted for his wardrobe, which rose to more than fifteen million *maravedís*.[37] The marriage ceremony itself was celebrated with all the pomp and pageantry that befitted the wedding of the heir to the throne, with ephemeral architecture, tapestries and luxury textiles featured prominently.[38] Exorbitant

---

33 Sabine Haag, Dagmar Eichberger and Annemarie Jordan Gschwend, ed., *Women: The art of power: Three women from the house of Habsburg* (Vienna: Kunsthistorisches Museum, 2018).

34 Fernando Checa, *Felipe II: Mecenas de las artes* (Madrid: Nerea, 1992); José Luis Gonzalo-Sánchez-Molero, 'La formación militar del rey Felipe II', *Militaria: Revista de cultura militar*, 17 (2003), 111–129; José Luis Gonzalo Sánchez-Molero, *Felipe II. La educación de un 'felicísimo príncipe'* (Madrid: CSIC and Polifemo, 2013); Jesús F. Pascual Molina, 'Génesis, uso y destino de la colección de tapices del príncipe Felipe (1527–1548)', in *Magnificencia y arte: devenir de los tapices en la historia*, eds. Miguel Ángel Zalama, María José Martínez Ruiz and Jesús F. Pascual Molina (Gijón: Trea, 2018), 63–80.

35 Archivo General de Simancas (AGS), Casa y sitios reales, leg. 36-8.

36 Santiago Fernández Conti, 'La organización de la casa del príncipe Felipe (1535–1546)', in *La corte de Carlos V, vol. II*, ed. José Martínez Millán (Madrid: Sociedad Estatal para la Conmemoración de los Centenarios de Felipe II y Carlos V, 2000), 101.

37 José Martínez Millán and Santiago Fernández Conti, 'La corte del príncipe Felipe (1535–1556)', in Juan Cristóbal Calvete de Estrella, *El felicísimo viaje del muy alto y muy poderoso príncipe don Phelippe*, ed. Paloma Cuenca (Madrid: Sociedad Estatal para la Conmemoración de los Centenarios de Felipe II y Carlos V, 2001), LX.

38 Jacobo Sanz Hermida, ed., *Recibimiento que se hizo en Salamanca a la princesa doña María de Portugal, viniendo a casarse con el príncipe don Felipe II* (Salamanca: Velociraptor, 2001); Ángela Madruga Real, 'Magnificencia urbana y fiesta real: Salamanca 1543: Elementos

sums were spent on outfitting the contenders in knightly tournaments and festivals during the same period.[39] Expenditures soared with Philip's marriage to Maria Manuela of Portugal in 1543, and this recurred when he married his second wife, Mary Tudor, Queen of England in 1554. Period accounts consistently remark on the luxury and magnificence of Philip II's retinue, where every detail was calculated to present the prince as a worthy representation of the Habsburg lineage—including the emperor's wedding present, the fabulous *Conquest of Tunis* tapestry series.[40]

Philip II was also concerned with the magnificence of his own heir and surrounded him with numerous luxury objects from an early age.[41] At one point, Prince Carlos's household had an annual income in excess of 60,000 ducats,[42] but his expenses were also exorbitant; for example, the prince once paid 25,000 ducats for a diamond, and he spent more than 8 million *maravedís* on a riding harness. Garments of the finest cloth, gold buttons, cameos, antiquities, books, tapestries and luxury armour and arms fill the young prince's inventories, where art played a crucial role in forging an image of the heir that reflected his power—perhaps more figurative than real—as successor to the throne.

While this was standard practice with the direct line of succession, Charles V also took care of other members of his family. For example, in a

---

simbólicos en torno a la figura del príncipe', *Anales de Historia del Arte*, vol. Extraordinario (2008), 103–120; María José Muriel Sánchez, *Ceremonial en los esponsales de Felipe II y María Manuela de Portugal* (Salamanca: Diputación de Salamanca, 2013); Miguel García-Bermejo Giner, 'Carlos V, inspirador e inspiración del programa ideológico tras las celebraciones nupciales salmantinas del príncipe Felipe de 1543', in *Carolus: Homenaje a Friedrich Edelmayer*, ed. Francisco Toro Ceballos (Alcalá la Real: Ayuntamiento de Alcalá la Real, 2017), 103–114.

39 Jesús F. Pascual Molina, 'Magnificencia y poder en los festejos caballerescos de la primera mitad del siglo XVI', in *Visiones de un imperio en fiesta*, eds. Inmaculada Rodríguez Moya and Víctor Mínguez (Madrid: Fundación Carlos de Amberes, 2016), 121–143.

40 Pascual de Gayangos, ed., *Viaje de Felipe II a Inglaterra, por Andrés Muñoz (impreso en Zaragoza en 1554), y relaciones varias relativas al mismo suceso* (vol. 15) (Madrid: Sociedad de Bibliófilos Españoles, 1877); María José Bertomeu Masiá, 'Relaciones de sucesos italianas sobre la boda de Felipe II con María Tudor', *Cartaphilus: Revista de investigación y crítica estética*, 5 (2009), 6–17; José Miguel Morales Folguera, 'El arte al servicio del poder y de la propaganda imperial: la boda del príncipe Felipe con María Tudor en la Catedral de Winchester y la solemne entrada de la pareja real en Londres', *Potestas: Estudios del Mundo Clásico e Historia del Arte*, 2 (2009), 165–190; Jesús F. Pascual Molina, '"Porque vean y sepan cuánto es el poder y grandeza de nuestro príncipe y señor": imagen y poder en el viaje de Felipe II a Inglaterra y su matrimonio con María Tudor', *Reales Sitios*, 197 (2013), 6–25.

41 Jesús F. Pascual Molina, 'Sobre la formación del gusto y la colección del príncipe don Carlos', (Madrid: 2023) [in press]; Miguel Ángel Zalama, 'Don Carlos, príncipe de las Españas, y la tapicería: regalos, adquisiciones, herencia de María de Hungría y su fortuna posterior' (Madrid: 2023) [in press].

42 Fernando Bruquetas and Manuel Lobo, *Don Carlos: Príncipe de las Españas* (Madrid: Cátedra, 2016), 114–115.

document titled *Memorial de lo que Madama suplica a su M. para sus cosas*[43] [Memorial of what Madame requests of H. M. for her things] we can read what was drafted in about 1537 when the emperor was establishing the household for his natural daughter, Margaret, Duchess of Florence and later governess of the Netherlands:

> Will Your Majesty remember to be so kind as to send Madame some jewels. As she wishes to make them of rubies, she has greater need of these than of other thing. Tapestries she has but a few, and not a single piece from Holland. Might Your Majesty order the provision of some such pieces. There being no horses from Spain there, Your Majesty might send her some. And some good driving horses or ponies, as she has nothing good in this line.[44]

This succinct yet illuminating document proves that it was considered customary and normal to have certain luxury items which, regardless of their specific utility (as in the case of driving or riding animals), were deemed indispensable in elite households, especially those of individuals who had to project a certain image because it reflected on their family and gave them legitimacy.

Luxury as an incentive for collectors

In his *Idea del tempio della pittura* (1590), the Milanese painter Giovanni Paolo Lomazzo wrote of the 'great king' Philip II and his possessions:

> His museum, highly celebrated for its paintings and sculptures, books, and arms in such abundance that just looking at them makes our heads reel.[45]

The author links this impressive—in the sense of eliciting admiration—collection with the sovereign's virtue, dignity and immortal fame. In sharp contrast to the myth of the austere king averse to luxury, this statement reminds us that Philip II, like his predecessors, had a strong predilection

---

43 AGS, Patronato Real, leg. 45, doc. 106.
44 'Acuerde v.m. asimismo que aga merced a madama de enbialle alguna joya. Y quisiéndosela hazer de ruuí, tiene más necesidad que de otra cosa. De tapicería tiene poca y no una pieça de Olanda. Podría s.m. mandar prober de algo desto. No abiendo alla cauallos de España, s.m. le podría enbiar algunos. Para carreta algunas acaneas o quartago bueno que no tiene cosa buena de nada desto'.
45 Giovanni Paolo Lomazzo, *Idea del Tempio della Pittura* (Milan: Paolo Gottardo Ponto, 1590), 151. 'Ha dunque questo gran re, oltre il suo museo celebratissimo per l'opere di pittura e scultura, gioie, libri et arme in tanta copia, che solamente a mirarli la mente nostra si confonde'. English translation from *Idea of the Temple of Painting*, trans. Jean Julia Chai (University Park, PA: Pennsylvania State University Press, 2013), 162.

for magnificence and its propagandistic uses. These ideas associated with prestige provided an incentive to collect works of art, making Philip II a paragon among collectors and one of the brightest stars in the Habsburg firmament, for El Escorial is, in one sense, a genuine museum.[46]

The architectural projects undertaken by the king and their decoration, maintenance and growth, his use of the collections of tapestries, luxury objects, arms and armour, the royal library, assorted relics and all the other possessions of Philip II helped materialise an attitude towards the arts that was a defining feature of the House of Austria—the 'Habsburg Renaissance' in the words of Fernando Checa.[47] Historiography has not dealt fairly with the figure of Philip II, tarnished as he and his reign is by the 'Black Legend' and eclipsed by Austrian relatives like Ferdinand II and Emperor Rudolf II, who became model collectors in the late Renaissance.

Until the triumph of painting, luxury—expressed materially, valuing the costly, the modern and the unique in the form of textiles, gold and silver objects, jewellery, books, arms and armour, and exotic items, antiquities or scientific curiosities—constituted a *Wunderkammer*, a reflection of the definition Schlosser gave when referring to the Duke of Berry's cabinet and whose model can be applied to later cabinets.[48] An in-depth analysis of the phenomenon of these collections proves that they were far from being more or less orderly accumulations of objects; their utility went beyond scientific curiosity or art collecting, for they represented the material expression of political and social interests based on self-presentation.[49] In the case of the Habsburgs, that self-presentation took on a dynastic dimension.

A growing number of studies are calling attention to the importance of the so-called 'decorative arts'—a misnomer that implies second-rate status—in this cultural and political context, especially in Spain.[50] Yet historiography, particularly of the generalist variety, continues to overlook this, and neither the Catholic Monarchs nor Charles V nor Philip II are

---

46 Fernando Checa, *Renacimiento Habsbúrgico. Felipe II y las imágenes artísticas* (Valladolid: Universidad de Valladolid, 2018).
47 See his chapter in this volume.
48 Julius von Schlosser, *Die kunst- und wunderkammern der spätrenaissance: ein beitrag zur geschichte des sammelwesens* (Leipzig: Klinckhardt & Biermann, 1908).
49 Hugo Miguel Crespo, 'A Kunstkammer: historiografia, aquisiçao e formas de apresentaçao', in *A arte de coleccionar: Lisboa, a Europa e o Mundo na Época Moderna (1500–1800)*, ed. Hugo Miguel Crespo (Lisbon: ArBap, 2019), 17–31.
50 Belozerskaya, *Luxury arts of the renaissance*; Miguel Ángel Zalama, 'Las artes visuales en la modernidad'; see also Miguel Ángel Zalama's chapter in this volume.

studied in depth in publications on court luxury.[51] Established conceptions need to be questioned, and scholars should further explore the Habsburgs' remarkable contributions to the world of the arts, where luxury was a fundamental element.

---

51 Géza von Habsburg, *Princely Treasures* (London: Thames and Hudson, 1997), 94. This text states that, as far as artistic objects are concerned, the Spanish Habsburgs remain unexplored, although their patronage of painting and sculpture has been studied. See also *Treasures of the Habsburgs*, eds. Sabine Haag and Franz Kirchweger (London: Thames and Hudson, 2013) [2012], where only a short section is devoted to the figure of Emperor Charles V.

VANESSA QUINTANAR CABELLO

Food as a Strategy of Power

The Political Role of Banquets in Prince Philip's Felicissimo Viaje (1548–1551)[*]

Food at the Habsburg court, like so many other fundamental parts of the daily lives of rulers throughout the sixteenth century, was governed by strict rules of etiquette. As Diane Bodart noted, 'this geography of power at the table had a long tradition in the Netherlands, which dates back to the dessert courses at the feasts of the Dukes of Burgundy'.[1] While everyday meals were subject to a variety of rules, public meals were events of great importance, not only for underscoring cordiality and rapport among diners, but also to reinforce the monarch's political role and draw attention to his person. The quantity and quality of the dishes, as well as the structure of the service and seating arrangements, all had to be carefully calculated to convey a consistent, unambiguous message regarding the superiority of the king. As Bodart argued, 'The princely banquet, governed by the rules of etiquette, was one of the most eloquent ways of representing sovereign authority'.[2]

The Spanish monarchs' use of banquets as a political tool, undoubtedly instrumental in shaping the concept of the public banquet among the European courts, was illustrated during the famous journey of Prince

---

[*] This work has been carried out thanks to the funds of the Convocatoria Plurianual para la Recualificación del Sistema Universitario Español 2021-2023 (Margarita Salas contracts) granted by the Complutense University of Madrid and financed by the Ministry of Universities with Next Generation funds from the European Union. This work is also part of the research project *Miradas cruzadas: espacios del coleccionismo habsbúrgico y nobiliario entre España y el Imperio* (PID2021-124239NB-I00-ART).

[1] Diane H. Bodart, 'Le banquet des Habsbourg, ou la politique à table', *Predella- Journal of Visual Arts*, 33 (2014), 63–83, p. 73: 'Cette géographie du pouvoir à table avait dans les Pays-Bas une longue tradition qui remontait aux entremets des festins des ducs de Bourgogne'.

[2] Bodart, 'Le banquet', p. 64: 'Le banquet princier, régi par les codes de l'étiquette, était l'une de formes de représentation les plus éloquentes de l'autorité souveraine'.

Vanessa Quintanar Cabello • Complutense University of Madrid

Fig. 6.1. *Still life of fish and oysters with a cat*, Alexander van Adrianssen, first half of the XVII century. © Museo Nacional del Prado.

Philip (the future Philip II) across a large part of Europe between 1548 and 1551. This royal progress was chronicled in several sources, three of which are particularly noteworthy: *El felicissimo viaje del muy alto y muy poderoso principe don Phelippe* by Juan Cristóbal Calvete de Estrella, the *Relación del camino y buen viaje que hizo el Príncipe de España don Phelipe* by Vicente Álvarez, and part of the *Crónica del Emperador Carlos V* by Alonso de Santa Cruz. Using these three sources, I will attempt to reconstruct the decisive role that banquets played in Prince Philip's European tour and the different purposes they served for the hosts and for the prince himself.

Banquets as political tools during the *Felicissimo Viaje*

In reviewing the accounts of the many meals and banquets given in the prince's honour during his travels, as documented by Calvete de Estrella, Álvarez and Santa Cruz, the first point that strikes the reader is their impressive number. All three chronicles are liberally sprinkled with exhaustive descriptions of food-related events. Many times they are only brief mentions that do not explain the meal or its attendant formalities. At other times, however, the chroniclers take pains to describe the banquets in full detail. I will focus on the latter events to show how both the contents of those meals and the etiquette governing them were used by the future king to impress all Europe with his power and wealth—a strategically significant move, as he would soon inherit the throne—and how his model borrowed elements from other courts and took them to unprecedented heights of sophistication and systematicity.

The Spanish chroniclers who travelled with the prince could not fail to record the importance of these events, although the length and detail of their accounts vary depending on the author and the stage of the journey. For instance, Calvete de Estrella devoted two whole chapters to the banquets at Milan and Binche, but on other occasions Estrella simply alluded to the prince's attendance at constant banquets without specifying their contents, as in the section that describes the prince's stay at Heidelberg. Sometimes food is merely mentioned in passing as a formulaic introduction to the narrative: 'after having heard mass and eaten, he departed from that place' or 'the Prince and Queen having dined, they set sail for Amsterdam'.[3] This formula appears most often in accounts of the prince's travels through the Southern Netherlands, which probably tells us that food was considered to be of secondary importance on those legs of the journey. Bearing these general aspects in mind, what follows is an analyse of the different banquets narrated by the chroniclers who accompanied the prince on his progress and a classification of those banquets according to their primary objectives.

The banquet as a means of confirming loyalty to the future monarch

First, the chronicles offer various examples of banquets used to display the might and wealth of European hosts who honoured the prince, where the acts of hosting and dining were a means of confirming their allegiance to the future king and advertising their affluence in the process. These were special banquets given specifically for the prince or gatherings where he was the guest of honour, and most occurred on the Italian leg of the journey. As Álvarez-Ossorio pointed out, 'Philip's presence in northern Italy was viewed with doubt and misgivings'.[4], so open shows of support and sympathy in the form of convivial meals were especially significant for both the hosts and the prince.

One of the first cities where banquets served this purpose for the hosts was Genoa. As Alonso de Santa Cruz wrote:

---

3 'después de aver oýdo missa y comido, se partió de allí' and 'aviendo comido el Príncipe y Reyna, navegaron para Aemsterdam'.
4 Antonio Álvarez-Ossorio, 'Ver y conocer. El viaje del príncipe Felipe (1548–1549)', in *Congreso Internacional Carlos V y la quiebra del humanismo político en Europa (1530–1558), Madrid, 3–6 de julio de 2000* (Madrid: Sociedad Estatal para la Conmemoración de los Centenarios de Felipe II y Carlos V, 2001), vol. 2, 53–106 (esp. 54): 'la presencia de Felipe en el norte de Italia suscitaba incógnitas y recelos'.

> Throughout the time His Highness spent in Genoa, which was sixteen days, many very great and solemn banquets were given in the city by private citizens, for the grandees of Spain and other lords and noble personages who were at the Court, among those banquets there was one which a citizen gave for all the lords and gentlemen, who were 52 at table, and 31 very lovely ladies who were the wives of the city's leading men, said banquet did cost one thousand ducats, and there was no domesticated meat to be found, only wild game and fowl prepared in every way imaginable.[5]

Calvete de Estrella made special mention of a banquet in Genoa organised by Andrea Doria, underscoring the generosity of the host:

> The greatness and magnificence of Prince Andrea Doria was even more apparent in the great ceremony with which he served and entertained the Prince and gave contentment to his court: and in the good order and decorum he showed in filling His Highness's plate, for he refused to have anything brought to his house except that which he himself had provided with such largesse.[6]

On other occasions, the wealth of the prince's hosts was more evident in the decoration of the rooms and the silver plate used at the table than in the actual dishes of food. A case in point is the banquet that the Duke of Mantua gave for the prince:

> The Duke of Ferrara gave a banquet for His Highness and all the grandees and gentlemen in his retinue that was a sight never seen before, for the tapestries and gold and silver that served the feast (which must have been owned by this Duke) were worth more than

---

5 Alonso de Santa Cruz, *Crónica del emperador Carlos V* ([n.p.], 1920–1925), (Madrid: Imprenta del Patronato de huérfanos de intendencia é intervención militares), V, 2099. 'En todo el discurso de tiempo que estuvo su alteza en Génova, que fueron 16 días, hubo en la ciudad muchos banquetes muy grandes y solemnes que hicieron ciudadanos particulares, así a los grandes de España como a otros señores y personas nobles que había en la Corte, entre los cuales banquetes hubo uno que hizo un ciudadano a todos los señores y caballeros que fueron 52 a la mesa y 31 damas muy hermosas, que eran mujeres de personas principales de la ciudad, el cual banquete costaría obra de mil ducados, y no hubo en él ningún género de carne doméstica, sino todo montesino y caza de aves bravas de todas las maneras que se pudo imaginar'.

6 Juan Cristóbal Calvete de Estrella, *El felicissimo viaje del muy alto y muy poderoso principe don Phelippe* (Madrid: Sociedad Estatal para la Conmemoración de los Centenarios de Felipe II y Carlos V, 2001), 45. 'Mostrávase más la grandeza y magnificencia del Príncipe Andrea Doria en el grande aparato que tenía para servir y recrear al Príncipe y dar contentamiento a su corte; y en la buena orden y concierto que en proveer el plato de su Alteza tenía, porque no consintió que en su casa se traxese cosa alguna, sino lo que él con tanta largueza mandava proveer'.

300,000 ducats, at which the Prince was greatly marvelled and his entire court even more so.[7]

One of the most remarkable banquets in this respect was undoubtedly the one held on New Year's Day 1549 in Milan, organised by Ferrante Gonzaga on the occasion of his daughter's marriage to Fabrizio Colonna, where Ferrante personally 'saw to the installation in his own palace of a canopy over the table where the Prince would dine'.[8] The event is described in great detail in all three sources. Calvete de Estrella remarked on the luxurious details of the table settings—'the napkins were furled with various folds and handiwork, and on each was placed a halberd made of golden wax'[9] —and gave an extraordinary description of the meal's progress, which strictly adhered to the serving methods typical of some European courts. His narrative also points out another important aspect of such events, namely the careful observation of etiquette and the host's acceptance of the established hierarchy, acting more as a servant than a fellow diner. As Calvete de Estrella said:

> There the magnificence and greatness of the Prince Ferrante Gonzaga was truly revealed, for he refused to sit down at the table, though the Prince ordered and pressed him to do so: first he personally saw to the service, and only after the royal dinner had ended did he go to dine with many gentlemen in a room where another table was laid.[10]

Santa Cruz, ever mindful of the cost of such banquets, said of this event:

> the greatness of the banquet defies description, but to give one a general appreciation without reference to further details, I will merely say and aver that the least consequential dish alone, which was the salad, cost 600 escudos.[11]

---

7 Santa Cruz, 2146. 'El Duque de Ferrara hizo un banquete a Su Alteza y a todos los grandes y caballeros que con él iban que fue cosa nunca vista, porque la tapicería y oro y plata que sirvió al banquete (que debían ser de este Duque) valía más de 300,000 ducados, de lo cual quedó el Príncipe muy maravillado y toda su corte mucho más'.
8 Álvarez-Ossorio, 70. 'preocupó de que en su palacio se colocase un dosel sobre la mesa donde debía de cenar el Príncipe'.
9 Calvete de Estrella, 72. 'estavan encrespadas las servilletas de diversos pliegues y lavores, y en cada una d'ellas puesto un alabardero hecho de cera dorado'.
10 Calvete de Estrella, 73. 'Pareció bien en ella la magnificencia y grandeza del Príncipe don Hernando de Gonzaga, el qual no quiso sentarse a la mesa, aviéndoselo el Príncipe mandado y importunado; antes entendió personalmente en el servicio, hasta que después de acaba la real cena se fue a cenar con muchos cavalleros en una pieça donde estaba aparejada otra mesa'.
11 Santa Cruz, 2129–2130. 'la grandeza del banquete no es posible de contarla, pero por que cada uno pueda considerarla sin que aquí se escriba otra particularidad, solamente quiero decir e alegar la menor vianda que fue la ensalada la cual solo costo 600 escudos'.

Vicente Álvarez also mentioned the costly salad, with a striking commentary on the dubious hygiene of the cooks who had prepared it:

> [...] yet for all their politeness and grace, neither Don Lorenço Suárez de Figueroa, nor any other, ate the salads after seeing the hands that prepared them and how they were manhandled.[12]

From these examples, we can see how hosts used these banquets to ingratiate themselves with the prince, assuage any fears of hostility towards him (especially important in the Italian territories) and, at the same time, display a wealth and power to rival the finest European courts.

The banquet as a means of asserting the prince's authority

The hosts were not alone in using these banquets in a political way. The prince, cognizant of the importance of these events, used them with varying degrees of success to consolidate his personal reputation and showcase the hierarchy of power, in which he would soon occupy the highest level. For the prince, therefore, his attendance and behaviour at these banquets was an amenable way to build rapport with his subjects while also clearly reminding them of the rigid political hierarchy that defined their relationship. The prince used two fundamental strategies to achieve this end: he underscored and emphasised differences in rank by employing the strict Burgundian rules of etiquette; or he broke those rules as a sign of his magnanimity and willingness to adapt to local customs. This flexibility, far from diminishing his image, strengthened the bond with his subjects, who were indebted to His Highness for that act of deference.

As an example of the first strategy, sometimes the prince dined alone, despite the friendly and festive atmosphere that surrounded him. The most remarkable instance took place in Mantua where, after a hunt, the party went to dine at a *casa de plazer* or country estate owned by the Duke of Mantua. When they arrived, according to Calvete de Estrella, the guests found:

> a royal banquet laid out, for the Prince and all his courtiers and companions, which was one of the most regal and lavish feasts imaginable, for there was a great variety and abundance of every sort of

---

12 Vicente Álvarez, *Relación del camino y buen viaje que hizo el príncipe de España don Phelipe*, appendix to Juan Calvete de Estrella, *El felicissimo viaje del muy alto y muy poderoso principe don Phelippe* (Madrid: Sociedad Estatal para la Conmemoración de los Centenarios de Felipe II y Carlos V, 2001), 616. 'mas con todos su polideza y gracia no comiera las ensaladas don Lorenço Suárez de Figueroa, ni aun otro ninguno, que veían las manos con que se hazen y cómo son manojeadas'.

victual and delicacy, and so much of everything that it would feed the entire court in the same manner for three or four days.[13]

However:

> The Prince ate alone in one room; he was served with royal ceremony and majesty. The Cardinal of Mantua, the Duke of Ferrara, the Duke of Mantua, Ferrante Gonzaga and the Duke of Alba, and all those grandees, lords and gentlemen ate in a separate hall where a long table was set.[14]

This and several other feasts in Italy aside, some banquets held in the Netherlands were, logically, bound by the strictest rules of etiquette. Members of the Habsburg Courts had to show their power at such events, and the best way to do this was by following Burgundian etiquette, applicable to both the prince and the court of Brussels, to the letter. Perhaps the best example is the dinner hosted by Mary of Hungary in honour of her nephew and her brother, Emperor Charles, at Brussels. Calvete de Estrella's description indicates a strict adherence to etiquette, which stipulated that the highest authorities should be seated at a separate table on a dais:

> The time for dinner having come, the Emperor, the Queens and the Prince and Duchess of Lorraine came away from the windows and entered the hall, where all five dined together at the imperial table on the dais, and the ladies, lords and gentlemen dined at the tables in the hall and chambers. The table was served in great state and majesty, with a great variety and abundance of delicacies and the finest wines, with the very soft music of diverse instruments and singers. The other tables were also served most elegantly with great order, silence and decorum on the part of those who served them.[15]

---

13 Calvete de Estrella, 90. 'un real vanquete, assí para el Príncipe como para quantos venían en su corte y acompañamiento, que fue uno de los más reales y sumptosos que se pueden pensar, porque avía gran diversidad y abundancia de todo género de viandas y delicadeza de manjares, y todas las cosas tan sobradas que bastava para mantenimiento de toda la corte de la misma manera para tres o quatro días'.

14 Calvete de Estrella, 90. 'El Príncipe comió solo en una pieça; fue servido con real cerimonia y magestad. El Cardenal de Mantua, el Duque de Ferrara, el Duque de Mantua, don Hernando de Gonzaga y el Duque de Alva, y todos aquellos grandes, señores y cavalleros comieron aparte en una sala donde estava puesta una mesa a la larga'.

15 Calvete Estrella, 141–142. 'Siendo ya la hora de cenar, el Emperador, las Reynas y el Príncipe y Duquesa de Lorena se retiraron de las ventanas y se entraron a la sala, donde cenaron juntos todos cinco en la mesa imperial que estava en el estrado, y las damas, señores y cavalleros cenaron en las mesas de la sala y cámaras. Fue servida la mesa con gran estado y magestad, con gran diversidad y abundancia de manjares y preciosíssimos vinos, con suavíssima música de diversos instrumentos y cantores. Sirviéronse también las otras mesas altíssimamente con gran orden, silencio y concierto de los que las servían'

In contrast to the strict adherence to Burgundian table etiquette, the prince occasionally broke with protocol during his long European tour to win over his hosts and, with that courteous gesture, place them forever in his debt. The prince sometimes ignored the dictates of etiquette regarding his position at the banquet, his interaction with the other guests, or his consumption of food and drink. We find interesting examples in all three sources, especially in Vicente Álvarez's account.

Álvarez's chronicle seems to suggest this strategy was not improvised, and that the prince knew that breaking with etiquette could be a powerful political tool, because from the first pages we find evidence of this tendency in the description of Philip's attitude. Speaking of the banquet in Barcelona before he departed for Italy, which lasted 'tres oras' [three hours], Álvarez remarked:

> when mass ended, excellent music began to play and a food-taster of the Cardinal entered, followed by twelve gentlemen, each carrying two dishes of food, and placed them on the table of His Highness, who ordered that he should be served not these but those of the Cardinal who ate with him at his table, and that they be served in Teutonic fashion.[16]

Álvarez even indicated that 'His Highness was most delighted and began to partake of the libation somewhat more than was his wont'.[17]

After the preliminaries in Barcelona, his sojourn in Italy was undoubtedly key for putting this strategy to good use.[18] One of the most relevant instances was the banquet to celebrate the nuptials of Ferrante Gonzaga's daughter, where 'from the very first, the Prince was aware that this event presented an opportunity to acquire a reputation in Italy by means of affable gestures'.[19] In the course of the dinner, as both Álvarez and Santa Cruz confirm (Calvete's omission of this fact is significant), the prince refused to sit by himself and ordered the removal of the table reserved for his use:

> For His Highness they had set a small table at the head of the large one, atop a somewhat higher dais so that he could command a view of the large table from end to end, and to do what was fitting in his service

---

16 Álvarez, 604. 'acabada la missa, començóse muy buena música y vino un maestresala del Cardenal, y tras él doze gentileshombres cada uno con dos platos de vianda, y pusiéronlos en la mesa de su Alteza que mandó que no le sirviesen sino los del Cardenal que con él comió en su mesa, y sirviéronlos a la tudesca'.

17 Álvarez, 604. 'su Alteza se regozijó mucho y començóse a hazer al uso del bever un poco más que solía'.

18 On this topic, see the article by Antonio Álvarez-Ossorio, 'Ver y conocer…'.

19 Álvarez-Ossorio. 89. 'desde el primer momento, el Príncipe fue consciente de la oportunidad de aquel evento para adquirir reputación en Italia por medio de gestos afables'.

by giving him the loftiest place. And then His Highness ordered that small table and that dais removed, and taking the bride by the hand, he seated her at the head of the large table in the place reserved for him. And he ordered Fabrizio Colonna to be seated on one side of his wife in an equal place of honour, and he sat on the other side, and he had the Princess, wife of Ferrante Gonzaga, sit alongside him.[20]

Álvarez confirmed this report by briefly stating that 'His Highness did not wish to sit at his table but at the other large one, to which his setting was moved, and he ordered the bride and Ferrante to sit alongside him at its head'.[21]

Days after this event, Álvarez again (unlike Calvete) recorded two eloquent examples of departure from etiquette in Trento:

There was a table on a dais beneath a large cloth-of-gold canopy, with a screen of wooden rods where four settings were laid. In the same room there was a very large table with many places set [...]. His Highness ordered the other table to be brought down and placed crossways to the other, so that on the right hand it was even with that of the ladies, and on the other hand nearly half the table was unoccupied; and His Highness sat in the middle of it, facing the entire table.[22]

On Sunday the Cardinal gave another banquet for His Highness, and the meal went on so long that it was nearly nightfall when they finished, and the tables were placed in the same order as on the other occasion. And so His Highness ordered his table to be moved down beside the other, and he sat and ordered the Cardinal of Augsburg and Duke Maurice to sit, and all the other noblewomen and ladies to sit as they had the other time.[23]

---

20 Santa Cruz, 2128–2129. 'Para su Alteza tenían puesta una mesa pequeña a la cabecera de la grande encima de un estrado algo alto por que pudiese gozar de la vista de cabo a cabo de la mesa grande y para hacer lo que a su servicio se debía en darle el sublime lugar. Y luego su Alteza mandó quitar aquella mesa pequeña y aquel estrado, y tomó a la desposada de la mano, y la hizo sentar a la cabecera de la mesa grande en el lugar que para él estaba dedicado. Y mandó sentar al señor Fabricio Colona a un lado a par de su esposa y él se sentó al otro lado, y a par de sí hizo sentar a la Princesa, mujer de don Hernando de Gonzaga'.
21 Álvarez, 616. 'su Alteza no quiso sentarse en su mesa sino en la otra grande donde le pasaron su servicio, y mandó sentar a la cabecera la desposada suya con don Fernando'.
22 Álvarez, 625. 'Avía una mesa en un estrado debaxo de un gran dosel de tela de oro, con una reja de palo a la redonda en que avía puestos quatro servicios. En la misma sala vía otra muy grande mesa con muchos servicios [...] Su Alteza mandó baxar la otra mesa y ponella atravesada junto con aquella, de manera que por la parte de mano derecha estava ygual con la de las damas y por la otra parte sobrava casi la media mesa; y sentóse su Alteza en medio della, frontero de toda la mesa'.
23 Álvarez, 625. 'El domingo hizo el Cardenal otro banquete a su Alteza, y la comida fue tan larga que era cerca de noche quando acabaron, y por la misma orden que la otra vez estavan puestas las mesas. Y assí mandó su alteza baxar su mesa junto a la otra, y se sentó y mandó

It was undoubtedly during his time in the German lands when Prince Philip manipulated the rules of table etiquette more than ever, adapting to local customs and showing his friendliest side. Once again, we have Álvarez to thank for the knowledge that, at the dinner given by the Duke of Bavaria at Munich ('Menique'), 'there were two tables, a square one just for His Highness and a large one with many settings, and His Highness ordered them to be joined together'.[24] Álvarez's commentary on a dinner at Mehren is revealing, as it suggests that the chronicler was fully aware of the prince's clever strategy:

> And I saw His Highness drink the dregs of others, something so entirely out of character that I realised that many things and everything he did in this way was to please and honour the people against his will, which is astonishing in such a great Prince and of such character and gravity as His Highness has, and dissembling so ably that it seemed perfectly agreeable and natural in him.[25]

In the Habsburg Low Countries, most banquets were marked by strict adherence to etiquette, but we can also find examples of events where the prince dispensed with certain formalities. This was the case of a dinner at Binche and narrated in a similar manner by both Álvarez and Santa Cruz:

> And Our Lord Emperor and the two Queens and His Highness sat at one table, and the ladies and noblewomen and lords and gentlemen sat at another facing it. And as they began to sup, Queen Mary and the Prince rose and moved to the other table, and the Emperor and the Queen of France who had been left alone also rose and sat with them, where they all supped together with great joy.[26]

> As they had begun to dine at one table and the first course had been served at the other, Queen Mary rose from the table and His Highness also, and they went to the other table and sat at it, Queen Mary on one side and His Highness on the other. And His Majesty and the Queen

---

sentar al Cardenal de Augusta y al Duque Mauricio, y todas las otras señoras y damas como la otra vez se avían sentado'.

24 Álvarez, 629. 'avía dos mesas, la una quadrada para solo su Alteza y otra grande con muchos servicios y mándolas su Alteza juntar entrambas'.

25 Álvarez, 630. 'Y vi bever a su Alteza la resta de otros, cosa tan agena de su condición que me dio a entender que muchas cosas y todas las d'esta manera hazía por contentar y cumplir con las gentes contra su voluntad, que es arto para un tan gran Príncipe y de tal ser y tanta gravedad como su alteza tiene, y dissimulallo que parecía serle agradable y cosa natural de su condición'.

26 Álvarez, 653. 'Y se sentaron el Emperador nuestro señor y las dos Reynas y su Alteza a una mesa, y en otra, frontero de aquella, las damas y señoras y señores y cavalleros. Y començando a cenar, alçáronse la Reyna María y el Príncipe y pasáronse a la otra mesa, y el Emperador y la Reyna de Francia que quedavan solos se alçaron también y pasáronse con ellos, donde todos cenaron con muy gran regozijó'.

of France, seeing that Queen Mary and the Prince had sat at the other table, ordered that the food on theirs be taken thence and went to dine with them. The dinner lasted for more than an hour and a half and proceeded with great merriment and joy.[27]

The banquet as a means of displaying Habsburg power and wealth

Although the banquets given in the prince's honour in the Netherlands, organised by his aunt Mary of Hungary and attended by the emperor, had the same objectives as the rest of the festive events celebrated during his European tour, they also had a new and more specific aim: to serve as a political tool by displaying the power, wealth and opulence of the prince, his retinue and the great Habsburg family. By holding lavish banquets dominated by extravagance in equal measure, the Habsburgs sent a message to European courts about their magnificence and might, which was not limited to battlefields and negotiation tables but also extended to daily ceremonies. Veronika Sandbichler summarises it well: by 'Their very nature [banquets] as princely festivities meant that they were events organised for the purpose of showing the magnificence of the ruling dynasty through certain messages intended for contemporary and future audiences'.[28]

We can undoubtedly find the clearest examples in some of the banquets celebrated at Binche, which culminated in the farewell party held in late August 1549. Days before the event that would mark an exceptional moment for festivals throughout Europe, the House of Habsburg had expressed a desire to show its magnificence at the table on the occasion of the prince's visit. During a meal at a *casa de plazer*, usually a more informal affair, Mary of Hungary gave her brother and nephew a banquet with an extraordinarily theatrical *mise en scène*. Though omitted by Calvete de Estrella, Álvarez and Santa Cruz offer us many details about the event. In both accounts, the emphasis was on the guests' attire and the setting of the repast:

---

27 Santa Cruz, 2186. 'Ya que comenzaban a cena en la una mesa y en la otra servido el primer servicio, la Reina María se levantó de la mesa y también Su Alteza y se pasaron a la otra y se asentaron en ella la Reina María a un lado y Su Alteza al otro. Y Su Majestad y la Reina de Francia viendo que se habían sentado la Reina María y El Príncipe en la otra mesa mandaron llevar a ella la vianda que en la suya tenían y fueronse a cenar con ellos. Duró la cena más de una hora y media y fue bien festejada y regocijada'.

28 Veronika Sandbichler, 'Torneos y fiestas de corte de los Habsburgo en los siglos XV y XVI', in *El legado de Borgoña. Fiesta y ceremonia cortesana en la Europa de los Austrias (1454–1648)*, ed. Krista de Jonge et al. (Madrid: Fundación Carlos de Amberes and Marcial Pons, 2010), 607–624 (esp. 609).

Fig. 6.2. *Ceres and two nymphs*, Peter Paul Rubens and Frans Snyders, 1615-1617. © Museo Nacional del Prado.

a table was set with places for Their Majesties and His Highness, where they sat upon arrival and were served by twenty-four ladies, who that day were all lovely and colourfully attired (which is not customary there) [...]: eight of them were dressed as nymphs and another eight as Dianas in hunting costume; and the others as peasant women [...] The first courses were brought by the nymphs, which consisted of fruits and dainty things; the peasants brought the second courses, which were dishes of mutton, kid, suckling pig and hens and all manner of barnyard fowl and meats of tame animals and wild fowl, and of these meat pies and other sorts of delicacies. And later the ladies returned with these courses of other fruits and with each of those courses came two stewards dressed in the manner and costume and colours of the ladies who served [...] The ladies brought all those courses in pairs, carrying gold and silver baskets between them with a handle for each lady, which they then placed on the table.[29]

Santa Cruz's observations are in the same vein, but he added one interesting detail: the elaborately planned costumes and dishes were for a meal that only lasted 'una buena hora' [a good hour].[30]

This extravagant display can therefore be considered a prologue to what would be the highlight of the prince's 'Happiest Journey' in culinary terms: the *sarao* or soirée that marked the end of his stay at Binche and was held in the so-called 'Enchanted Hall' of the palace. The peculiar name of the room and the extraordinary print of the event in a manuscript held at the Bibliothèque royale de Belgique[31] show us the originality of the setting and the atmosphere, 'resulting from the convergence of theatrical, visual and gastronomical space, at once surprising and inviting'.[32]

All of three existing accounts of the banquet are equally useful for reconstructing the events of that evening, as each offers complementary

---

29 Álvarez, 655. 'estava puesta una mesa con servicios para sus Magestades y su Alteza, donde llegados se sentaron y fueron servidos de veynte y quatro damas, que aquel día estavan todas hermosas y avían puesto color (que allá es cosa no usada) [...]: las ocho d'ellas vestidas como nimphas y las otro ocho como Dianas en hábito de caçadoras; y las otras como labradoras [...] Los primeros servicios truxeron las nimphas, que fue de frutas y cosas delicadas; los segundos las labradoras, que fue de cosas de carnero, cabritos, lechones y gallinas y toda aves caseras y carnes de animales mansos y aves montezinas, y d'ello empanadas y otras maneras de manjares. Y a la postre bolvieron las damas con estos servicios de otras frutas y, con cada servicio de aquéllos, venían dos mayordomos vestidos de la manera y hábito y colores de las que servían [...] Todos aquellos servicios trayán las damas en unos cestos de dos assas dorados y plateados de dos en dos, cada una por su assa y assí los ponían sobre la mesa'.
30 Santa Cruz, 2194.
31 For a discussion of this image, see Lisa Minari Hargreaves, 'O espetáculo do açúcar: banquetes, artes e artefatos (século XVI)', PhD thesis, Universidade de Brasília, 2013.
32 Minari, 200. 'configurado a partir do encontro do espaço teatral, visual e gastronômico surpreendente e, ao mesmo tempo, convidativo'.

details that allow us to reconstruct the resources used to stage the event after the farewell banquet on the night of 30 August 1549, which continued into the early hours of the 31st.

Thanks to Santa Cruz's account, the system used to set the stage can be reconstructed, a stage which 'served as both a dining space and an "altar", where spectacle became the driving force of the court's entertainment and the artefacts were truly a sight to behold':[33]

> After the soirée, Queen Mary had set up a collation in another room, the most superb and inventive thing ever seen. When the Emperor and the Queens began to enter this hall, a table started to descend from a ceiling far above, though none could see by what contrivance or artifice, as if it were coming from heaven. The ceiling was strangely painted with signs and planets, sun and moon, and the entire host of other stars: it imitated (as far as possible) the true heavens, for at that hour it shone most beautifully. Every star and each of those celestial figures had real light behind it. And when that table came to rest it appeared to be laden with many flowers and fruits. And when those fruits had been eaten (each of Their Graces taking what pleased them most) the table sank down, and another descended from the ceiling, likewise covered with various fruits, and after eating them this table sank like the other, and His Majesty and the Queens found themselves sitting in their chairs with no table before them. And as they parleyed together, lost in pleasant conversation, suddenly thunder began to rumble and lightning bolts streaked from the ceiling; and when the lightning ceased, there commenced a hailstorm of sweets and a shower of orange-blossom water and a snowfall of sugar.[34]

---

33 Minari, 202. 'funcionava tanto como palco gastronômico quanto como "altar", onde o espetáculo se tornava a força geradora do entretenimento da corte e os artefatos eram verdadeiros objetos de contemplação'.

34 Santa Cruz, 2199–2200. 'Después del sarao tuvo la Reina María aparejada una colación en otra pieza, la cosa más superba y de mejor invención que se había visto. Luego que el Emperador y las Reinas comenzaron a entrar por esta sala comenzó a bajarse una mesa desde un cielo que en lo alto de ella estaba sin que nadie viese con que ingenio ni artificio, sino que venía del cielo. El cielo estaba extrañamente pintado con signos y planetas, sol y luna, y todo el otro ejército de estrellas: imitaba (en cuanto era posible) al verdadero porque a aquella hora resplandecía hermosamente. Tenía cada estrella y cada figura de aquellas celestes verdadera lumbre detrás. Y luego que la dicha mesa se puso en su lugar pareció estar llena de muchas flores y frutas.

Y acabada la comida de aquellas frutas (lo que a cada uno de Sus Altezas más agradaba) se hundió, y luego descendía otra del cielo, llena así mismo de variedad de frutas, y después que comieron de ellas hizo la mesa lo que la pasada y hallóse su Majestad y las Reinas sin mesa ninguna, asentados en sus sillas.

Y estando platicando entresí en buena conversación descuidados comenzó el cielo a tronar y relampaguear mucho; y en cesando los relámpagos comenzó a granizar confites y llover agua de azahar y nevar azúcar'.

Fig. 6.3. *The sense of taste*, Peter Paul Rubens and Jan Brueghel the Elder, 1618. © Museo Nacional del Prado.

As for Calvete de Estrella, his account focused on the contents of the tables, remarking several times on the voracious appetites of the ladies in attendance. Speaking of the first table, he noted:

> adorned with rich cloths, with many and diverse porcelain plates, with all manner of preserves, in every imaginable shape and form, all most excellent and precious.[35]

Resting on the second table:

> many plates and beakers of glass, filled with all sorts of jams, rolled wafers of different colours and a thousand other confections, all white, which after the Emperor, Queens and Prince had tasted it, and the ladies had taken their share, the table then vanished, exciting the admiration of all those present.[36]

Of the third table, Calvete remarked:

> laden with plates, made of sugar, wild game, fowl and fish and salted dishes of the same. And it was a wonder to see a mountain of candy

---

35 Calvete de Estrella, 353. 'adornada de ticas telas, con muchos y diversos platos de porcelana, con todo género de conservas, de quantas maneras ymaginarse podían, todas muy excelentes y preciosas'.

36 Calvete de Estrella, 353. 'muchos platos y taças de vidrio, llenos de todo género de confituras, suplicaciones de diversas colores y otras mil suertes de confecciones, todas blancas, lo qual después de averlo provado el Emperador, Reynas y Príncipe, y tomado las damas su parte d'ello, la mesa con grande admiración de todos desapareció luego'.

sugar most delicately wrought with five laurel trees upon it, which had gold and silver leaves, and filled with fruits of sugar and little flags with the coats of arms of all those states, made of multicoloured silk, and on the one in the middle a live squirrel bound with a small silver chain, which was also set upon by the ladies, along with all the rest.[37]

The importance of sugar on every table, and especially on the third, is remarkable, where sugar was not only a condiment but a material for creating replicas of goblets and other palace objects wares which imitated the ceramic, glass and metal pieces typically found in courtly residences.[38]

Besides the contents of the tables, the chroniclers also highlighted a rock-shaped fountain from which flowed 'superlative wines for those who wished to imbibe, and in great abundance, gushing from a sea crag and rock' with four 'serpents' heads' from which 'white and red hippocras' and 'claret and white wine' flowed.[39] The guests received yet another surprise: throughout the party, 'at times it rained, at times it hailed, and with loud thunder and flashes of lighting inside the same room, artfully contrived yet so natural that it seemed real'.[40]

With such an overwhelming display of theatrical effects and succulent dishes, it is no wonder that the astonished Calvete concluded his account of the festivities at Binche by calling them 'worthy of everlasting fame and remembrance'.[41] The guests and history proved Calvete right. We find evidence of this in various letters written in the weeks that followed by those who had attended the party; for example, an Italian gentlemen wrote on 5 September 1549:

> The feasts held at Binche by Queen Mary for the honour and entertainment of Caesar, and of His Serene Highness the Prince, have

---

37 Calvete de Estrella, 353. 'llena de platos, hechos açúcar, montería, caças sylvestres, aves y pescados y saleros de la misma confección. Y era cosa estraña de ver una peña de açúcar candi sutilíssimamente labrada con cinco árboles de laurel en ella, que tenían las hojas doradas y plateadas, y llenos de frutas de açúcar y de vanderillas con escudos de las armas de todos aquellos estados, hechas de seda de diversa color, y en el de en medio una hardilla biva atada con una cadenilla de plata, la qual también fue saqueada por las damas, con todo lo demás'.

38 Minari, 213.

39 Calvete de Estrella, 353: 'excelentíssimos vinos para quien los quería, y en mucha abundancia, el qual corría de una roca y peña marina'; 'excelentíssimos vinos para quien los quería, y en mucha abundancia, el qual corría de una roca y peña marina', 'hypocrás blanco y tinto', 'vino clarete y blanco'.

40 Álvarez, 616. 'a ratos lluvió, a ratos granizó, y con grandes truenos y relámpagos dentro de la misma pieça artificialmente y tan natural que parecía de veras'.

41 Calvete de Estrella, 353. 'dignas de inmortal fama y memoria'.

been such that everyone who has seen them confesses that they have never seen anything so superb, nor so beautiful, nor so well ordered.[42]

This is also borne out by the description of that grand soirée in Georg Rüxner's *Thurnierbuch*, a seminal reference on the history of tournaments, thanks to which the festivities at Binche became more widely known and admired as the most sensational and marvellous Habsburg celebration of the sixteenth century.[43] Geoffrey Parker corroborated the enduring success of that event and its impact on the future king of Spain, indicating that 'even twenty years later, men still talked about court festivities as being better or worse than "the festivals of Binche". Philip II never forgot them.'[44]

---

42 Samuel Glotz, *De Marie de Hongrie aux Gilles de Binche. Une double réalité, historique et mythique. Introduction critique aux Triomphes de Binche célébrés du 22 au 31 août 1549* (Binche: Société d'archéologie et des amis du Musée de Binche, 1995), 107. 'Le Feste state fatte in Bins dalla Regina Maria per honore et intratenimento di Cesare, e del Serenissimo Prencipe, sono riuscite tali, che ciascuno che le ha vedute confessa di non haverne vedute mai ne di cosi superbe ne cosi belle, ne tanto bene ordinate.'
43 Sandbichler, 611–612.
44 Geoffrey Parker, *Philip II* (Peru, IL: Open Court, 2002), 22.

VÍCTOR MÍNGUEZ

His Polis

The Habsburg Naval Epic in the Mediterranean*

The steel, gold and silver buckler known as the *Parade Shield with the Apotheosis of Charles V* or *Plus Ultra Shield* (c. 1535–1540, Real Armería, Madrid) (Fig. 7.1), commissioned by Charles V from a Mantua workshop, or perhaps given to the emperor by Federico II Gonzaga, was created by a craftsman based on an ink and wash design attributed to Giulio Romano (c. 1535–1540, Teylers Museum, Haarlem).[1] Both the preliminary drawing and the final repoussage show the armour-clad Charles holding a standard topped by an eagle and standing at the prow of a galley. All the elements—armour, standard, bird and galley—evoke classical imagery. They are accompanied by Victory, who crowns him and confirms his destiny, and Fame, who holds a shield embossed with the emperor's motto. Escorting the galley are Neptune with his trident and Hercules hefting his columns. The allegory of a river and a female captive bound to a palm tree recall the military success of the Tunis campaign. This *all'antica* image of the emperor, justified by his identification with the Roman general Scipio Africanus and his victory over nearby Carthage, is interesting because, unlike Charles's other military portraits, it emphasises his dominion over the seas.

In 1535, fifteen years had passed since Charles was elected emperor by the German princes, and five since the pope had crowned him such at Bologna. Until the reign of his predecessor on the imperial throne, his grandfather Maximilian I, the Holy Roman Empire was essentially a land-based military power. In 1519, however, Charles had received oaths

---

* Principal researcher of the project ref. PID2021-127111NB-100 [*La recepción artística de la realeza visigoda en la Monarquía Hispánica (siglos XVI a XIX)*], funded by the Spanish government.

1 Álvaro Soler del Campo, 'Rodela de la Apoteosis de Carlos V o del *Plus Ultra*', in *El arte del poder: la real armería y el retrato de corte*, ed. Álvaro Soler del Campo (Madrid, Museo Nacional del Prado, 2010), 116.

Víctor Mínguez • Jaume I University

Fig. 7.1. *Rodela (shield) of the Apotheosis of Charles V*, anonymous, c. 1535-1540. © Real Armería, Madrid.

of allegiance from the Castilian and Aragonese courts. Those two states were unquestionably maritime powers: Aragon had expanded across the western Mediterranean, southern Italy and even Greece thanks to its war fleet, vying with other maritime states like Genoa and Venice; Castile, after negotiating the division of a still-unknown ocean with Portugal, had embarked on an exploration of the Atlantic that would culminate in Admiral Christopher Columbus's voyages to find a western route to the Indies. The naval enterprises in the Atlantic and the endless wars against African Barbary kingdoms and the Ottoman Empire in the Mediterranean forced Charles, as king of a Spain in the process of unification, to invest heavily in naval expeditions and operations. These efforts were rewarded and in a short time the naval policy of Charles—and later of his son Philip II—caused an Iberian maritime empire larger than any the world had ever known.

John Julius Norwich offered an interesting (yet not entirely unproblematic) interpretation of the consequences of the fall of Constantinople (1453) and Granada (1492), which he defined as cataclysmic events, at either end of the Mediterranean: 'Both led to a proliferation of rootless vagabonds—in the east Christians, in the west Muslims—all of them ruined, disaffected and longing for revenge; and many of them adopted the buccaneering life', turning what had essentially been a relatively peaceful sea of trade routes into a highly perilous maritime scenario. The Christians established their bases in Sicily, Malta and the Dalmatian coast, and the Muslims on the North African coast between Tangier and Algiers.[2] While the Mediterranean was rearmed, other emerging naval theatres also acquired strategic importance, such as the Atlantic (where Spain, Portugal, England and Holland would fight epic battles to rule the waves), the Caribbean (another haven for the international pirates who preyed on the Spanish treasure fleet and wealthy American port towns), and the Indian and Pacific Oceans.

Faced with the growing menace of Ottoman ambition and Barbary and Caribbean piracy, Charles V established large permanent squadrons in the Mediterranean and the near Atlantic to defend coasts and sea routes and facilitate military expeditions.[3] The tonnage and armament of ocean-going vessels increased, and the danger posed by corsairs and long distances, forced maritime trade to be conducted using a system of annual convoys— the Spanish treasure fleet. In the Mediterranean, peril was constant, unpredictable and therefore harder to deal with, although the opposing forces were slightly more evenly matched after Genoese Admiral Andrea Doria crossed to the imperial side in 1528. War fleets had to be organised in both naval theatres on either side of the Strait of Gibraltar: the *Armada de Vizcaya* or Fleet of Biscay and the *Armada de Galeras del Mediterráneo* or Mediterranean Galley Fleet. During the sixteenth century, these were subdivided to form ten fleets: Biscay, Andalusia, Granada, Levante (East Coast), Catalonia, Sardinia, Genoa, Naples, Sicily and America, which were joined by an eleventh, the Lisbon Fleet, after 1580.[4]

It was a herculean effort, but by ensuring its dominion over oceans and seas, Charles's empire extended round the globe and became an even larger political entity given various names: the *Monarchia Universalis*, the Spanish Monarchy, the Spanish Empire or my own proposal, which I believe is a more accurate term for this entity in the second half of

---

2 John Julius Norwich, *The Middle Sea: A History of the Mediterranean* (New York: Random House, 2006), 282.
3 José Manuel Marchena Giménez, *La marina de guerra de los Austrias: una aproximación bibliográfica* (Madrid: Ministerio de Defensa, 2009).
4 Esteban Mira Caballos, *Las armadas imperiales: la guerra en el mar en tiempos de Carlos V y Felipe II* (Madrid: La Esfera de los Libros, 2005).

the sixteenth and all of the seventeenth century: the Double-Headed Habsburg Empire, the first truly global empire in human history. This family empire, if one glosses over the ever present divisions between the Spanish and Austrian branch, which spanned five continents and three oceans and existed from 1555 to 1700, was only possible thanks to its control of the seas, especially during the decades when it included the Kingdom of Portugal. The Habsburg Empire was a thalassocracy, to the extent that it depended entirely on naval supremacy for its survival. This was apparent in the Spanish political ideas of the time, and in the symbolic imagery created by emblematic culture. The 68th device in Diego Saavedra Fajardo's emblem book, *Idea de vn Principe Político Christiano Representada en Cien Empresas* (Munich, 1640), bears the motto *His polis* ('these poles') and the image of two galleon sterns jointly supporting the poles of a globe on which we can make out continents and oceans (Fig. 7.2). In his description of the device, the Murcian diplomat recalled that the first ship in mythology, the *Argo*, brought wealth to Hellas with the Golden Fleece, a mythological metaphor for the abundant fruits of maritime trade. The two galleon sterns symbolise that the Spanish part of the Habsburg Empire rested on its control of the Mediterranean and the Atlantic, and on the superiority of its merchant and war fleets. On the frontispiece of Saavedra's emblem book, above the equestrian portraits of Philip IV and his brother Cardinal-Infante Ferdinand of Austria, we see another globe with the imperial crown and a ship's rudder framed by trophies.

Saavedra Fajardo's allusion to the *Argo* is apropos, for that ship carried the finest heroes of Greece on their quest for the golden fleece under Jason's leadership,[5] and Jason was also the classical inspiration for the Distinguished Order of Knights of the Golden Fleece, founded in 1430 by Philip the Good, Duke of Burgundy, which had been an instrument of Habsburg politics ever since Maximilian I became grand master of the order (an honour later accorded to his heirs Charles V, Philip II and the Spanish Habsburg kings). In the Renaissance courts of Mediterranean maritime states, Jason and other classical heroes like Aeneas and Ulysses, as well as great admirals of antiquity like Caesar and Agrippa, formed a cast of nautical heroes—rediscovered in the works of Homer, Virgil and Plutarch—which European princes sought to emulate and with whom they sought to identify when naval warfare returned to prominence after many centuries of relative tranquillity at sea.

The Habsburgs were quick to grasp the utility of maps for understanding their growing sea empire. Both Emperor Maximilian I and his grandson Charles V—who inherited his grandfather's imperial title the same year Magellan embarked on the first voyage around the globe—had a solid

---

5 Apollonius of Rhodes, *Argonautica*, third century BC; Gaius Valerius Flaccus, *Argonautica*, first century AD.

Fig. 7.2. Imprese 68 *His Polis*, from *Idea de vn Principe político christiano representada en Cien empresas* by Diego Saavedra Fajardo, Munich, 1640.

knowledge of geography, surrounded themselves with learned cosmographers and sponsored the creation of cartographic charts in order to know and manage their vast possessions, and to plan the inevitable military campaigns on land and at sea. In March 1543, Charles V became one of the first to obtain a copy of Nicolaus Copernicus's *De revolutionibus orbium coelestium*, sent by his agent in Nuremberg, Sebastian Kurz.[6] A good example of Charles's cartographic patronage is the *Liber Cosmographicum* by Peter Bennewitz (Antwerp, 1548), which includes a woodcut of a world map over the winds with the figures of the Caesar (Kaiser, emperor) Charles

---

6 He purchased another for Prince Philip the following year. See Mariano Esteban Piñeiro, 'El emperador y la astronomía: el astronómico real del matemático sevillano Alonso de Santa Cruz', in *El Emperador Carlos V y su tiempo* (Madrid: Demos, 2000), 689–697.

and the god Jupiter presiding, each sheathed in a sun.[7] Even when he retired to the Monastery of Yuste, Charles V took numerous geographical maps and star and nautical charts with him to his new residence, including an illustrated copy of Ptolemy's *Geography* (the first printed edition appeared in 1475). The finest atlas ever made for his son Philip II was drawn by the cartographer Christiaan Sgrooten in an illuminated manuscript, *Tabula totius terrae hemisphaerium arcticum* (1568–1592), and although it contains no iconographic references to the monarch, it is undoubtedly a depiction of the 'Philippine' world and was dedicated to him in 1588. Fernando Bouza called it 'the most important of all the cartographic enterprises sponsored by Philip II'.[8]

As for the vessels, the galleys and sailing ships launched in the sixteenth century were designed to be floating palaces as well as war machines, and painters, sculptors, carvers and engineers therefore worked to embellish them, covering the wooden bows and sterns and the sails and standards flying from the masts with elaborate iconographic and heraldic images designed by artists and humanists. Young Charles arrived in Spain in autumn 1517 to take possession of the throne. He headed a forty-ship fleet, and the sails of his carrack were embroidered with images of Christ, Mary and various saints, as well as the Pillars of Hercules with the *Plus Ultra* motto. In 1520, the great sculptor Alonso Berruguete was commissioned to paint the veils and standards of the fleet's flagship that took Charles V from Corunna to Flanders to be proclaimed emperor at Aachen. For his military expedition to Tunis, the emperor commissioned a large quadrireme to serve as the admiral's ship, and those sails also featured a variety of religious and emblematic motifs. Naturally, the same thing occurred in the navies of other European realms. The English vessels *White Bear* (a 40-gun ship built in 1564 and decorated in 1599 with mythological themes and heraldic devices) and *Sovereign of the Seas* (a 102-gun ship ordered by King Charles I from shipwright Phineas Pett, whose iconographic mentors were the writer Thomas Heywood and sculptors John and Mathias Christmas) combined mythology, emblems and heraldry in their decorative programmes.[9]

---

7 The Biblioteca Nacional in Madrid has a copy of the 1575 edition. See *Los Austrias. Grabados de la Biblioteca Nacional* (Madrid: Ministerio de Cultura and Julio Ollero, 1993), 52 and 53.

8 Fernando Bouza, entry 260.2 in the catalogue *Felipe II: un monarca y su época; un príncipe del Renacimiento,* ed. Fernando Checa (Madrid: Museo Nacional del Prado—Sociedad Estatal para la Conmemoración de los Centenarios de Felipe II y Carlos V, 1998), 641–645. The volume is 1020 x 1270 mm and kept in the Biblioteca Nacional, Madrid.

9 Santiago Sebastián, *Emblemática e historia del arte* (Madrid: Cátedra, 1995), 59–61, citing the works of Alan R. Young, 'The emblematic decoration of Queen Elizabeth I's warship the White Bear', *Emblemática*, 3 (1988), 65–77, and Alan R. Young, ed., *His Majesty's Royal Ship: A Critical Edition of Thomas Heywood's 'A True Description of His Majesties Royall Ship'* (New York: AMS Press, 1990).

The symbolic emblematising of warships in their voyages and battles went hand-in-hand with the creation of a whole new visual repertoire of maritime feats, which European princes used to project an alternative image of power from the traditional one based on the medieval culture of chivalry. In this respect, the proliferation of emblems with nautical and geographical motifs beginning in the early sixteenth century is telling. In contrast to the more conventional devices of the Habsburg Maximilian I or Ferdinand II of Aragon, their grandson Charles V and Charles's son and heir Philip II included the mottoes *Plus ultra* [Further Beyond] and *Iam illustrabit omnia* [Now he will illuminate all things]—obvious maritime references—in their respective heraldic badges.[10] In the years that followed, numerous artists used their talents to construct a narrative of Spanish and imperial naval power, such as Giulio Romano who designed the buckler mentioned above. Obviously, the failures were ignored. In the sphere of the Spanish court, we cannot expect to find depictions of the defeat at Preveza in 1538, the 1541 debacle at Algiers, the catastrophic Battle of Djerba in 1560, the disaster of the Spanish Armada in 1588 or the capture of the Spanish treasure fleet in 1628 by the Dutch in Matanzas Bay. Artists in the service of the Habsburgs primarily focused on constructing a visual account of four naval feats: the campaign against Barbarossa at Tunis in 1535; the campaign and Battle of Lepanto in 1571 against the Ottoman Empire; the battle for the Azores archipelago, which pitted the galleons of the newly established Iberian empire against France in 1582–1583; and the naval defence of the Atlantic empire against the aggressions of the Dutch West India Company in the first third of the seventeenth century (particularly the recapture of Salvador da Bahia in 1625, but also other battles like the victories of Gibraltar in 1621 and the Abrolhos in 1631). In this brief survey, I will focus on the two campaigns in the Mediterranean, Tunis and Lepanto, and how a visual narrative was established that turned both battles into effective propaganda tools.

On 16 August 1534, Barbarossa captured the city of Tunis and forced its king, Muley Hassan, to flee. Charles V mounted a counterattack the following year. To prepare for this campaign, the emperor mustered a fleet in the ports of Genoa, Málaga and Barcelona, mostly comprising ships from Spain, Portugal, Genoa, Rome, Naples, Sicily and Malta. The squadrons assembled at Cagliari, waiting until all four hundred vessels had arrived, eighty-two of which were war galleys. The fleet also included the carrack *Santa Anna* of the Knights Hospitaller, the largest ship afloat at the time: launched in 1524, it had four masts, a displacement of three thousand tonnes, two gun decks with fifty heavy cannons and other smaller guns, a metal keel, a hold that could carry provisions for six months and even a

---

10 Víctor Mínguez and Inmaculada Rodríguez Moya, *El tiempo de los Habsburgo: la construcción artística de un linaje imperial en el Renacimiento* (Madrid: Marcial Pons, 2020).

small grove of cypress and orange trees.¹¹ High-ranking Castilian, Italian and Flemish noblemen, thirty thousand regulars from Spain, Italy and Germany, and several thousand soldiers of fortune from across Europe participated in the expedition. Andrea Doria commanded the fleet and the Marquis of Vasto led the army. On 20 June 1535, after the fleet reached the African coast, they laid siege to the fortress of La Goulette, opposite ancient Carthage, which finally fell on 14 July. On the 21st of that same month, after the thousands of Christian slaves being held in Tunis staged an uprising, the city was taken and aggressively sacked for three days. The campaign concluded with no noteworthy field or naval battles but, although Barbarossa escaped to Algiers, King Hasan was restored to the throne, the Barbary fleet was destroyed, and a Spanish garrison was established at La Goulette.

The Tunisian enterprise added a new layer to the emperor's carefully crafted image, identifying Charles V with Scipio Africanus and Saint Louis of France, who also disembarked their armies at Tunis during the Third Punic War and the Eighth Crusade, respectively; in fact, Pope Paul III granted Charles the title of *Africanus*.¹² In this respect, it is interesting to compare the iconographic programmes of the decoration used on the emperor's triumphal tours in Italy, the first in 1529–1530 on the occasion of his papal coronation at Bologna after landing at Genoa, and the second in 1535–1536 after his victorious campaign in Tunis. A surprising number of ephemeral structures were erected for this second triumph in the different cities the emperor visited—Trapani, Monreale, Palermo, Messina, Cosenza, Naples, Rome, Viterbo, Siena, Florence and Lucca—and their iconography betrays the propagandistic intentions behind the celebration of that African victory. Some were the work of renowned artists, such as the triumphal arches designed by Baldassare Peruzzi (Biblioteca Comunale degli Intronati, Siena). On the arches of Messina, the painter Polidoro da Caravaggio had already depicted the emperor as a second Scipio Africanus.¹³

As also discussed in other chapters of this volume on 'Habsburg art', we find visual testimony of the conquest of Tunis in the drawings of Jan Cornelisz Vermeyen—who participated in the African expedition at

---

11 David Nicolle, *Los guerreros de la cruz de Malta* (Barcelona: Osprey-RBA, 2010), 63.
12 María José Rodríguez-Salgado, '¿*Carolus Africanus*? el Emperador y el turco', in *Carlos V y la quiebra del humanismo político en Europa (1530–1558)*, ed. José Martínez Millán, vol. I (Madrid: Sociedad Estatal para la Conmemoración de los Centenarios de Felipe II y Carlos V, 2001), 487–531.
13 André Chastel, 'Les entrées de Charles Quint en Italie', in *Les fêtes de la renaissance II : fêtes et cérémonies au temps de Charles Quint* (Paris: Éditions du Centre National de la Recherche Scientifique, 1975); José Miguel Morales Folguera, *Carlos V. Caesar Imperator: su configuración iconográfica en las entradas triunfales en Italia* (Nordesrstedt: Editorial Académica Española, 2016).

Fig. 7.3. *Capture of La Goleta*, Frans Hogenberg, drawings by Vermeyen, 1540-1590.

the request of Charles V himself, eager to have one of his palace artists by his side—and in various prints produced over the following decades, particularly the series that Frans Hogenberg made between 1555 and 1560 based on Vermeyen's drawings (Fig. 7.3), and the scenes of Tunis in the series of 'Caroline' prints drawn by Maarten van Heemskerck (engraved by Dirck Coornhert, Antwerp, 1556) and Antonio Tempesta (engraved by Matthäus Merian). Besides drawings and prints, various fresco painting cycles were created in Italian and Spanish palaces. The frescoes in Italy were sponsored by Pope Paul III (Taddeo and Federico Zuccaro in the palace at Caprarola and Taddeo again in the Sala Regia at the Vatican) and the Duke of Mantua (in the Gonzaga palace at Marmirolo). In Spain, the frescoes in the Queen's Dressing Room at the Alhambra can still be seen; they were painted by Julio Aquiles and Alejandro Meiner between 1539 and 1544, probably at the behest of the Marquis of Mondéjar, Governor of Granada and a participant in the North African campaign. The eight Tunisian scenes are in the first room and narrate every episode of Charles's expedition, including the assembly of the fleet, the sea voyage to Tunis, and the attack on La Goulette.[14]

Ten years after the Tunis campaign ended, Mary of Hungary, the emperor's sister, commissioned Willem de Pannemaker to create a dozen tapestries after the drawings of Cornelisz–Vermeyen, which Vermeyen himself turned into cartoons with the help of painter and tapestry designer Pieter Coecke van Aelst.[15] Creating a credible representation of the expedition and its different elements—the geography, the fighting, the sacking and various other episodes—was quite a challenge.[16] The inclusion of the painter and the chronicler in some scenes, physically present as eyewitnesses, corroborates the veracity of the images, and the accompanying texts in Castilian Spanish and Latin reinforce and complement the visual message.[17] The tapestries were completed in 1554, and their total cost, paid by the emperor, amounted to the staggering sum of twenty-one thousand Flemish pounds.[18] Several copies were soon ordered for Eleanor of Austria, Mary of Hungary and the Duke of Alba, and more would follow in the seventeenth century. It is significant that Philip II took the *editio princeps* with him to England to adorn Winchester Cathedral on

---

14 Rosa López, 'Las pinturas de la torre de la estufa o del Peinador', in *Carlos V y la Alhambra*, ed. Pedro A. Galera (Granada: Junta de Andalucía-Patronato de la Alhambra y el Generalife, 2000), 109–115.

15 Juan Luis González García, 'Pinturas tejidas: la guerra como arte y el arte de la guerra en torno a la empresa de Túnez (1535)', *Reales Sitios*, vol. XLIV, 17 (2007), 24–47.

16 Fernando Checa has studied the complex, lifelike depiction of Muslim human types in this series. See Fernando Checa Cremades, 'Imágenes hispánicas de otros mundos: turcos y moros en varias series de tapices de la Alta Edad Moderna', in *Arte en los confines del imperio: visiones hispánicas de otros mundos*, eds. Inmaculada Rodríguez and Víctor Mínguez (Castellón: Universitat Jaume I, 2014), 27–47; see also Fernando Checa Cremades, ed., *Tesoros de la corona de España: tapices flamencos en el Siglo de Oro* (Brussels: Fonds Mercator, 2010), 153–179.

17 Antonio Gozalbo has exhaustively studied the written accounts of the campaign on which the tapestries may have been based, seeking the possible inspiration for their images and epigraphic texts in period chronicles, and citing as particularly relevant those of Alonso de Santa Cruz (*Crónica del Emperador Carlos V*), Juan Ginés de Sepúlveda (*De Bello Africo*), Francisco López de Gómara (*Las guerras del mar del Emperador Carlos V*), Gonzalo de Illescas (*Jornada de Carlos V a Túnez*), and Martín García de Cereceda (*Tratado de las campañas y otros acontecimientos de los ejércitos del Emperador Carlos V en Italia, Francia, Austria, Barbería y Grecia desde 1525 hasta 1545*)—especially the first—interpreting tapestries and chronicles as part of a complex system designed to enhance the imperial image. See Antonio Gozalbo Nadal, 'Tapices y crónica, imagen y texto: un entramado persuasivo al servicio de la imagen de Carlos V', *Potestas*, 9 (2016), 109–134.

18 The most comprehensive study to date is that of Hendrik J. Horn, *Jan Cornelisz Vermeyen, painter of Charles V and his conquest of Tunis: paintings, etchings, drawings, cartoons & tapestries*, 2 vols (Doornspijk: Davaco, 1989). See also the exhibition catalogue *Kaiser Karl V erobert Tunis: Dokumentation eines Kriegszuges in Kartons und Tapisserien* (Vienna: Kunsthistorisches Museum Wien, 2013).

the occasion of his marriage to Mary Tudor in 1554, after its first public showing at the Palace of Whitehall. And it was no accident that the tapestries were exhibited at the chapter of the Order of the Golden Fleece assembled in the Cathedral of Antwerp in 1555 or that, after arriving in Spain in 1560 to decorate the royal Alcázar, they were successively displayed at the weddings of Catalina Micaela and Charles Emmanuel I of Savoy (Zaragoza, 1585) and of Philip III and Margaret of Austria (Royal Palace of Valencia, 1599). No other work of art could so eloquently display and impress the cities of Europe with the magnificence, power and strength of the Habsburgs.[19]

In 1568 Philip II named his brother John of Austria, who was just twenty-one years old, captain general of the Mediterranean Fleet, and ordered the Barcelona shipyards to build a royal galley for the new admiral, which may be the best documented example of Habsburg naval art.[20] Once the hull was completed—with a length of 60 metres, a beam of 6.2 metres and 30 oars per bank—the frame was sent to Seville to be decorated by local artists, who created its figurative ornaments under the supervision of Sancho de Leiva, captain general of the galleys of Spain. When he left the city to suppress the Morisco rebellion in the Alpujarras, the responsibility fell to his second-in-command, Francisco Hurtado de Mendoza, Count of Monteagudo. On 30 April 1570, the vessel was admired by Philip II himself when he stopped at Seville on his way to the Kingdom of Granada to celebrate the end of the uprising.[21]

Initially, the iconographic programme of the royal galley was entrusted to Giovanni Battista Castello, known as Il Bergamasco, an architect in the service of Philip II who had been at the Madrid court since 1567 and had drawn up the plans for Álvaro de Bazán's palace in El Viso del Marqués. However, the responsibility fell to Sevillian humanist Juan de Mal Lara when Il Bergamasco died. Mal Lara made changes to Il Bergamasco's programme—although the latter had only had time to design the outer decoration of the stern—and drew on a wide variety of literary sources (mythological, historical, biblical and emblematic), especially the Argonauts' adventures as narrated by Apollonius of Rhodes and Valerius

---

19 José Miguel Morales Folguera, 'El arte al servicio del poder y de la propaganda imperial: la boda del príncipe Felipe con María Tudor en la catedral de Winchester y la solemne entrada de la pareja real en Londres', *Potestas*, 2 (2009), 165–189.
20 In 1971, on the fourth centenary of the Battle of Lepanto, the Museo Marítimo de Barcelona created a full-scale replica of the galley. The museum's director, José María Martínez Hidalgo, spent ten years compiling every source of information he could find on the ship to create that replica. See José María Martínez Hidalgo, *Lepanto: la batalla la galera 'Real': recuerdos, reliquias y trofeos* (Barcelona: Diputación Provincial de Barcelona and Museo Marítimo, 1971).
21 Vicente Lleó Cañal, *Nueva Roma: mitología y humanismo en el Renacimiento sevillano* (Madrid: Centro de Estudios Europa Hispánica, 2012), 78–82.

Flaccus and the emblems of Andrea Alciato.[22] In Mal Lara's own description of the symbolic decoration of the royal gallery, *Descripción de la Galera Real del Sermo: D. Juan de Austria*,[23] he explained a programme that was materialised in structures by the architect Benvenuto Tortello, carvings by the sculptor Juan Bautista Vázquez and his workshop, and paintings by Cristóbal de Casas, Pedro Villegas Marmolejo, Antonio de Alfian and Luis de Valdivieso. The wealth of sources used—Virgil, Ovid, Cicero, Apollodorus, Homer, Pliny, Saint Augustine, Saint Bernard, Pierio Valeriano, Dioscorides, Andrea Alciato, Alessandro Piccolomini and Erasmus of Rotterdam—created a space of humanistic and Christian meditation for the edification of the young admiral who would command the king's navy, a space that also expressed the dream of a universal empire whose authority rested on its dominion over the oceans and seas.[24]

Although John of Austria commanded the Christian navy, the artistic fabrication of the Battle of Lepanto was not an exclusively Habsburgian affair. The great victory over the Ottoman and Barbary fleet off the Greek coast on 7 October 1571 had been achieved by the allied forces of Spain, Venice, Rome and Malta. Many courts had cause to celebrate and commemorate it in visual representations, even realms and republics that did not participate in the Holy League promoted by Pius V. In addition to European states, institutions like the Dominicans and the Society of Jesus helped to ensure the success of the greatest visual artefact of the Counter-Reformation, particularly in the American viceroyalties, far from the Mediterranean, where images of Lepanto are found in great number. While these great artistic programmes were embellishing the palaces of Rome, Venice, Madrid and Genoa, numerous paintings and prints flooded

---

22 Rocío Carande Herrero, *Mal-Lara y Lepanto: Los epigramas latinos de la galera real de Don Juan de Austria* (Seville: Caja San Fernando, 1990), 23.

23 Manuscript in the Biblioteca Colombina, Institución Colombina (Seville): B. 4º 445–441. Edition published in Seville by the Sociedad de Bibliófilos Andaluces, 1876. Reprinted in Manuel Bernal Rodríguez, *Obras completas, II, recebimiento: descripcion de la Galera Real* (ed., Juan de Mal Lara) (Madrid: Biblioteca Castro, 2006).

24 María Dolores Aguilar García, 'La nave como palacio flotante: la galera Real de D. Juan de Austria en Lepanto', in *El barco como metáfora visual y vehículo de transmisión de formas*, ed. Rosario Camacho Martínez (Málaga: Junta de Andalucía, 1987), 339–361; María Dolores Aguilar García, 'El barco como objeto artístico y viaje alegórico: la galera real de Lepanto', *Espacio, tiempo y forma*, 2 (1989), 93–114; Emma Camarero Calandria, 'Nuevos datos sobre pintores españoles y pintura mitológica en el siglo XVI: la galera Real de Don Juan de Austria', *Goya*, 286 (2002), 15–26; Sylvène Édouard, 'Argo, la galera real de Don Juan de Austria en Lepanto', *Reales Sitios*, 172 (2007), 4–26; Elena Postigo Castellanos, '"Capturaré una piel que nos volverá a la Edad de Oro": los duques de Borgoña, la Orden del Toisón de Oro y el "Santo Viaje" (La Jornada de Lepanto de 1571)', in *El legado de Borgoña: fiesta y ceremonia cortesana en la Europa de los Austrias (1454–1648)*, eds. K. de Jonge, B. J. García García and A. Esteban Estríngana (Madrid: Marcial Pons - Fundación Carlos de Amberes, 2010), 399–449; and Rocío Carande, 'Donde las enzinas hablavan: símbolo e ideología en la galera Real de Lepanto', *Acta/Artis: Estudis d'Art Modern*, 1 (2013), 15–27.

chapels and libraries throughout Christendom, popularising the battle's iconography.[25]

At the court of Philip II of Spain, news of the victory at Lepanto was initially disconcerting, for no one had expected it. After the monarch claimed it as his own—the birth of his son Ferdinand a few months later having thwarted his stepbrother's hopes of taking the throne—paintings of Lepanto also filled the court. El Escorial holds a series of six commemorative canvases painted by Luca Cambiaso, although there is no documentary proof that they were commissioned by Philip II. From a bird's-eye view, allegorical and mythological figures (Neptune, Fortune, Bellona, Victory and Fame) narrate the campaign of the Holy League's fleet via explanatory texts in six sequential scenes: *The Holy League Fleet Leaving the Harbour of Messina* (Fig. 7.4), *The Christian Armada Goes Out to Meet the Turkish Fleet, The Ships in Formation Moments before the Fight, The Battle, The Remnants of the Turkish Fleet Retreat as Darkness Falls* and *The Christian Fleet Returns in Triumph to the Harbour of Messina*. Alongside the sequence of military events, the series shows the humanist mythification of this triumph: the sea god witnesses the encounter of the fleets, Fortune presides over the battle and the goddess of war over the boarding, Victory watches the Turkish retreat and Fame contemplates the victors' return. These six canvases reproduce the series of tapestries that Admiral Giovanni Andrea Doria commissioned for the Galleria Aurea of the Prince's Palace in Genoa. The designs, made by Cambiaso himself and Lazzaro Calvi in 1581–1582, were woven later in Brussels and reached their Genoese destination in 1591.[26] These tapestries were intended to glorify Giovanni Andrea Doria, who had commanded the ships on the far right flank of the Christian fleet at Lepanto, which explains why the compositions are framed by allegories and hieroglyphs that proclaim the virtues of the Genoese prince, inspired by Pierio Valeriano's *Hieroglyphica* (Basel, 1567) and Vincenzo Cartari's *Immagini degli Dei de gl'Antichi* (Venice, 1556).[27]

Although many scholars have traditionally believed that Cambiaso's canvases were a royal commission, Rosemarie Mulcahy explained that the six Lepanto paintings were sent by Doria to Antonio Pérez, the Spanish

---

25 Víctor Mínguez, *Infierno y gloria en el mar: los Habsburgo y el imaginario artístico de Lepanto (1430–1700)* (Castellón: Universitat Jaume I, 2019).

26 Laura Stagno and Francesca Cappelletti, *Palazzo del principe; la galleria de Giovanni Andrea Doria* (Genoa: Sagep, 1997); Juan Luis González García, 'Minerva en el telar: iconografía cruzada y tapicerías ricas, de Troya a Lepanto', in *Antemurales de la fe: conflictividad confesional en la Monarquía de los Habsburgo, 1516–1714*, eds. P. García Martín, R. Quirós Rosado and C. Bravo Lozano (Madrid: Universidad Autónoma de Madrid - Ministerio de Defensa, 2015), 59–75.

27 Víctor Mínguez Cornelles, 'Doria y Austria en Lepanto: tapices y pinturas de Luca Cambiaso para una gesta naval', in *Magnificencia y arte: devenir de los tapices en la historia*, ed. Miguel Ángel Zalama (Gijón: Trea, 2018), 81–98.

Fig. 7.4. *Departure of the fleet of the Holy League from the port of Messina*, Luca Cambiaso, 1581-1582, Real Monasterio del Escorial. © Patrimonio Nacional.

Secretary of State for Italy, probably in 1583 when Philip II appointed him admiral of the fleet. Cambiaso arrived at El Escorial that year and probably brought the canvases with him, delivering them to Pérez. When Antonio Pérez's trial began in 1585, his paintings were auctioned, and his property was confiscated by the Crown after he was convicted in 1590. According to Mulcahy, the king acquired the pictures on one of these two occasions.[28] After they reached El Escorial, they were placed in the gallery of the courtyard of the east facade—corresponding to the royal apartments—beside the basilica. José de Sigüenza and Francisco de los Santos mention them as being in the lower East Gallery in their respective works: *Historia de la orden de San Jerónimo* (Madrid, 1605), and *Descripción breve del monasterio de San Lorenzo el Real del Escorial* (Madrid, 1657).[29]

However, Philip II did commission a Lepanto-related painting from Titian, *Philip II Offering the Infante Fernando to Victory* (1573–1575), one

---

28 Rosemarie Mulcahy, 'Celebrar o no celebrar: Felipe II y las representaciones de la Batalla de Lepanto', *Reales Sitios*, 168 (2006), 2–15; A. Delaforce, 'The collection of Antonio Pérez, Secretary of State to Philip II', *The Burlington Magazine*, 124 (1982), 742–752.
29 Bonaventura Bassegoda, *El Escorial como museo: la decoración pictórica mueble en el monasterio de El Escorial desde Diego Velázquez hasta Frédéric Quilliet (1809)* (Barcelona: Universitat Autònoma de Barcelona, 2002), 279 and 280.

of the three paintings sent to the king in 1575 by his ambassador in Venice, Diego Guzmán de Silva.[30] The monarch supervised its creation from a distance, even giving the artist general guidelines for the composition (Fig. 7.5).[31] In it we see the Prudent King holding his naked newborn son and lifting him towards the heavens, where a foreshortened allegory of Victory descends, handing the child a palm leaf of triumph and preparing to crown him with the laurel wreath. A captive Turk sits below, and in the background we see the galley battle. This is a commemorative picture—celebrating the birth of Prince Fernando or Ferdinand, son of Philip II and his fourth wife Anna of Austria, on 4 December 1571—and an allegorical one, as it highlights the glory of the Habsburg dynasty and its triumph in this naval battle. Above all, it reveals Philip II's reconciliation with the victory at Lepanto, which he made his own—his stepbrother John is conspicuously absent from the scene—after the dynastic succession had been secured. The painting was enlarged in 1625 by Vincenzo Carducci to match the measurements of Titian's *Emperor Charles V at Mühlberg*, with which it would form a pair at the Real Alcázar in Madrid, undermining the original perception of the work, which in Checa's view is more a product of the Venetian workshop than of the master's own hand.[32] That Titian's two great battle canvases, Mühlberg and Lepanto, were placed on equal footing, despite the artistic superiority of the former, reveals the degree to which the naval battle had already been integrated in the heroic-military imagery of the Spanish branch of the House of Habsburg in the Spanish Golden Age.

Lepanto was also the theme of another painting, *Religion Succoured by Spain*, sent to Madrid in 1575 from Titian's workshop. This picture portrays the Spanish monarchy as the defender of Catholicism, although it should be noted that the composition was copied from an earlier painting made for Alfonso I d'Este with a different meaning: Virtue and Peace aiding the Duchy of Ferrara against the naval threat of Venice. After the duke's untimely death in 1534, Titian kept the picture and turned it into an allegory of Habsburg might versus the Turkish menace, sending it to Emperor Maximilian II before 1568. Although this first composition was lost, it was copied by the engraver Giulio Fontana (British Museum, London), and in the print we can see Minerva waving the imperial standard

---

30 Matteo Mancini, *Tiziano e le corti d'Asburgo: nei documenti degli archivi spagnoli* (Venice: Istituto veneto di scienze, lettere ed arti, 1998), 422.
31 Juan Miguel Serrera, 'Alonso Sánchez Coello y la mecánica del retrato de corte', in *Alonso Sánchez Coello y el retrato en la corte de Felipe II*, ed. J. M. Serrera (Madrid: Museo del Prado, 1990), 42; Miguel Falomir Faus, 'Tiziano: alegoría, política, religión', in *Tiziano y el legado veneciano*, eds. J. Álvarez Lopera et al. (Galaxia Guttenberg and Círculo de Lectores, 2005), 154–155 and 157.
32 Fernando Checa Cremades, *Tiziano y las cortes del Renacimiento* (Madrid: Marcial Pons, 2013), 475 and 476.

Fig. 7.5. *Philip II offering the infante Fernando to Victory* by Titian, 1573-1575. © Museo Nacional del Prado.

before the Ottoman threat. Titian painted the second version shortly before 1575, turned into a commemoration of Lepanto and sent it to the court of Madrid. And a third, very similar version, though only a workshop copy, belonged to Cardinal Pietro Aldobrandini (Galleria Doria Pamphilj,

Rome).[33] In the second version, the one that arrived in Madrid as *Religion Succouring Spain*, the artist added a Turk driving what had formerly been Neptune's chariot, an allegory of Venice, while Minerva became the Spanish monarchy—holding a shield emblazoned with the arms of Philip II—coming to the aid of threatened Faith (Ferrara in the first version). At the same time, Religion and Minerva establish a gestural dialogue that echoes the compositional typology of an Annunciation scene.[34] The reference to Lepanto in this later version is therefore quite clear, although other interpretations have been suggested by scholars like Rosemarie Mulcahy, who associated it with the crisis of the Catholic faith in the Netherlands.[35] In the year 1600 it was hanging in the royal Alcázar, and in 1636 it was in the lower summer room; in 1661, after Velázquez's death, it is mentioned as being in his workshop, from whence it would be taken to El Escorial.[36] The Spanish Habsburg dynasty thus grasped both the utility and esthetical character of maps and visual arts for fortifying and magnifying their growing sea empire.

---

33 Rudolf Wittkower, 'Titian's allegory of "Religion Succoured by Spain": the change in symbolism', *Journal of the Warburg and Courtauld Institutes*, 3 (1/2) (1939–1940), 138–141; Erwin Panofsky, *Tiziano: problemas de iconografía* (Madrid: Akal, 2003), 183–186. English title: *Problems in Titian, Mostly Iconographic* (New York: New York University Press, 1969), 186–190.
34 Falomir, 'Tiziano', 160.
35 Mulcahy, 'Celebrar o no celebrar', 5.
36 Bassegoda, *El Escorial como museo*, 177 and 178.

ANTONIO GOZALBO NADAL

Habsburg Mars

The House of Austria and the Artistic Representation of Land Warfare

In 1692, King Charles II—who was always hundreds of miles away from the battles fought by the *Tercios* in his service—commissioned Luca Giordano to paint a grand martial composition: the frescoes of the Battle of Saint-Quentin for the main staircase at El Escorial, integrated in the larger programme of the *Glory of the Holy Trinity* on the vaulted ceiling. The pictorial decoration was also complemented on the windows by imitation porphyry medallions representing the victories of Charles V. In this way, the last member of the House of Austria resorted to the image, faith and military glory of his ancestors to create an apotheosis through which the Habsburg lineage might overcome the dismal present and attain eternal glory.

The Habsburgs undeniably knew how to use their overwhelming military might to ensure their political and territorial hegemony, but they also used it as a decisive symbol of prestige when displayed in the arts. Because of the constant wars in which the House of Habsburg found itself embroiled and the need to weave a narrative favourable to their interests, they came to see the visual representation of their victories as a useful tool for designing a family identity and legitimising their ambitions of global dominion. The first to understand the broad persuasive potential of this martial rhetoric was Maximilian I, who appeared as an invincible military man in his autobiographical chivalric novels *Theuerdank, Der Weisskunnig* and *Freydal*, as well as in major artistic commissions like the *Arch of Honour* (Albrecht Dürer and others, 1515–1519; Albertina, Vienna), the *Triumphal Procession* (Albrecht Altdorfer, 1512–1515; Albertina, Vienna)[1]

---

1 Eva Michel and M. Louise Sternath, eds., *Emperor Maximilian I and the age of Dürer* (Munich: Prestel, 2012), ccxxiv–ccxxvii.

Antonio Gozalbo Nadal • Jaume I University

and the reliefs carved by Alexander Collin for his monumental mausoleum in Innsbruck.[2]

As for Charles V, many of his political actions were determined by the constant wars against his powerful enemies of France, the Ottoman Empire and the German Protestant princes. The emperor led a failed Turkish siege of Vienna in 1529, followed by an offensive on the Danube in 1532, then participated in the campaigns of Tunis (1535), Provence (1536), Algiers (1541), Guelders (1543), Germany (1546–1547) and Metz (1552).[3] His court environment favoured the creation of a heroic image of him as the invincible Caesar or Kaiser; for his successors, Charles V was the most prestigious military figure in the Habsburg family.[4]

The first great military success of his reign was the unexpected victory at Pavia (1525), where French troops were utterly crushed and their king, Francis I, was taken prisoner. The news could not have come at a better time for the challenged Charles. Besides his confrontation with the Valois dynasty, he faced a growing Ottoman threat and internal strife in his realms, manifested in the revolts of the Comuneros and of the Brotherhoods (1520–1521) and the Peasants' War in Germany (1524–1525), where the Protestant dispute had also originated. Triumph on the battlefield was a much-needed boost to the young emperor's political prestige, which was further reinforced by an outpouring of visual accolades. In Italy the most remarkable pieces were the crystal intaglios and medal made by Giovanni Bernardi da Castel Bolognese, who recreated the battle in the *all'antica* style typical of the Italian Renaissance (*c.* 1530, Kunsthistorisches Museum, Vienna; *c.* 1530, The Walter Arts Museum, Baltimore; *c.* 1546, Palazzo Venezia, Rome). However, the visual representation of Pavia was much more successful in Germany. Given the tense situation on various fronts, pro-imperial sectors were quick to spread the good news; on the artistic plane, German artists had developed a new and successful way of depicting war, based on the print format and the realistic, first-hand description of a contemporary event. A noteworthy example of this is the large print made by Hans Leonhard Schäufelein (*c.* 1526; Albertina, Vienna), where clashes between combatants are arranged in a conventional space with a high horizon line. Jörg Breu the Elder's magnificent woodcut is more dramatic; the scene unfolds before the walls of Pavia—recreated with topographical accuracy—where the French are powerless to react to the unstoppable tide of Charles V's troops as they sweep across Visconti Park, leaving no doubt as to the might of imperial

---

2 Monica Frenzel, *The cenotaph of Emperor Maximilian I in the Innsbruck Court Church* (Innsbruck: Tiroler Volksunstmuseum, 2003).
3 Wim Blockmans, *Carlos V: La utopía del imperio* (Madrid: Alianza, Madrid, 2000), cclxxxix.
4 Fernando Checa Cremades, *Carlos V y la imagen del héroe en el renacimiento* (Madrid: Taurus, 1987); and *Carlos V: La imagen del poder en el renacimiento* (Madrid: El Viso, 1994).

Fig. 8.1. *Capture of Francis I*, tapestry from the series *Tha Battle of Pavia*, design by Bernard van Orley, manufactured in Bruxelles by William Dermoyen, between 1528-1531. © National Museum of Capodimonte, Naples.

arms (*c.* 1525; British Museum, London). These prints were probably the basis for many paintings, such as the two very similar anonymous panels in Leeds (*c.* 1525–1531; Royal Armouries) and Oxford (*c.* 1525–1528; Ashmolean Museum of Art and Archaeology), the painting by Ruprecht Heller (*c.* 1525; Nationalmuseum, Stockholm) and the anonymous picture in the British Royal Collection (*c.* 1530).

Finer quality works were also of northern origin. The first is the monumental fireplace designed by Lanceloot Blondeel in the Franc de Bruges after the treaties of Madrid and Cambrai, featuring portraits in the round of Charles V and his ancestors, heraldic ornaments and religious scenes (1529–1531).[5] The second and most important visual recreation of the conflict is the tapestry cycle *The Battle of Pavia*, commissioned by the Flemish States General after Mary of Hungary was appointed governess (Bernard van Orley and Willem Dermoyen, *c.* 1528-1531; Museo di Capodimonte, Naples). The spectacular series is a dazzling heroic composition that evinces a selective realism. The chosen settings weave a visual narrative where, in dramatic crescendo, we witness the utter defeat of the French army, the surrender of Francis I, and the consequent achievement of supreme glory by Charles V in his first great military victory.[6]

---

5 Eva Tahon, *Lanceloot Blondel à Bruges* (Bruges: Stichting Kunstboek, 1988), xcii–cxxv.
6 Antonio Gozalbo, 'Pavía (1525), la primera gran victoria de Carlos V', in *La guerra en el arte*, eds. Enrique Martínez, Jesús Cantera and Magdalena De Pazzis (Madrid: Universidad Complutense, 2017), 351–372; Nicola Spinosa et al., *La bataille de Pavie* (Paris: Réunion des Musées Nationaux, 1999).

While the Habsburg-Valois rivalry divided western Europe, the power of a fearsome foe, the Ottoman Empire, inexorably gained ground in the east. Charles V was elected emperor in 1519, and barely one year later Suleiman the Magnificent came to the throne in Istanbul. After that point, the two rulers would be locked in a gargantuan struggle for world domination, noted by contemporaries like Francisco López de Gómara who, in his chronicle, remarked that 'each one strives to become monarch and lord of the world'.[7] The Danube and North Africa were the principal stages on which this grand duel was fought. After the death of Louis II Jagiellon and the defeat of the Kingdom of Hungary at the Battle of Mohács in 1526, nothing stood between the ambitious sultan and the Habsburg residence in central Europe, Vienna. The Ottomans reached the gates of Vienna in the summer of 1529, but adverse weather conditions and the city's seasoned defenders forced Suleiman to lift the siege in mid-October. The resounding defeat of the hitherto invincible sultan inspired many celebratory artworks, with prints as the preferred medium. The most salient example was published by the printer Niklas Meldemann after a drawing by Hans Sebald Beham and is remarkable for its original composition: the woodcut presents a circular aerial view with St. Stephen's Cathedral in the centre and around it the city, the different battle scenes and the Turkish camp (*The Siege of Vienna*, 1529–1530; Wien Museum Karlsplatz, Vienna). Erhard Schön produced another very fine, albeit more conventional, print (*First Siege of Vienna by the Turks*, 1530; Wien Museum Karlsplatz, Vienna). We can also find scenes of the siege in other formats, such as the drawings by Barthel Beham (*Siege of Vienna by the Turks*, 1529; Wien Museum Karlsplatz, Vienna) and Wolfgang Huber (*Siege of Vienna*, 1530; Albertina, Vienna), or the mural paintings at Palazzo Lantieri in Gorizia (Marcello Fogollino: *Siege of Vienna, c.* 1548). Besides these strict recreations of military operations, others captured the fearsome power of the Turks, like the prints published in 1530 by Erhard Schön and Hans Guldenmundt depicting terrible scenes of cruelty. The siege of Vienna was even represented as psychomachia. For instance, a print by Hanns Sebald Lautensack likens the defeat of the Turks to the Old Testament intervention of God when Jerusalem is besieged by the Assyrians (*View of the City of Vienna from the southwest with the Fall of the Assyrian King Sennacherib in front of Jerusalem*, 1559; Wien Museum Karlsplatz, Vienna), and a variety of illustrations in Lutheran Bibles compare the apocalyptic arrival of the nations of Gog and Magog with the Ottoman siege ('Monogrammist AW', 1530; Erhard Altdorfer, 1533–1534; 'Monogrammist MS',1534).

---

7 Francisco López de Gómara, *Crónica de los muy nombrados Oruch y Jaradín Barbarroja (1555–1560)*, Colección *Espejo navegante* (Madrid: Polifemo, 1989), 31: 'cada cual de ellos trabaja por quedar monarca y señor del mundo'.

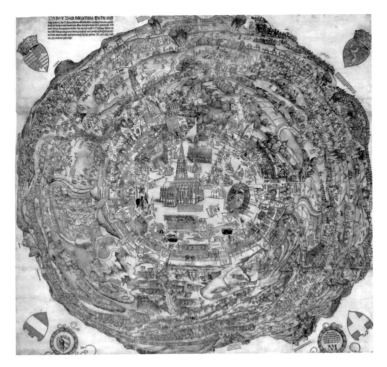

Fig. 8.2. *Panoramic view of Vienna during the first Turkish siege*, by Nikolaus Meldemann, 1530. © Wien Museum.

In 1532, Suleiman the Magnificent was poised to strike another blow against the Habsburg forces and Charles V marched towards the Danube at the head of a mighty army. Yet the long-awaited decisive battle between the two emperors never took place, as the lateness of the season and the stalwart defence of the city of Güns (Kőszeg) led the sultan to retreat. The principal visual account of this operation is found in seven prints that narrate the military actions of Frederick II, Count Palatine of the Rhine, a leading imperial commander during the campaign. In those incredibly detailed woodcuts, Michel Ostendorfer recreated the camp of Charles V at Nussdorf, the army on the march and skirmishes with Ottoman janissaries and *akinji* (1539, in *Warhafftige beschreibung* [...]; Bayerische Staatsbibliothek, Munich).

The next acts in this dramatic duel between the Habsburgs and the Sublime Porte took place in the Mediterranean with the victorious conquest of Tunis and the disastrous invasion of Algiers (1541). In 1535 Charles V took the first of these cities by force, as Hayreddin Barbarossa, a corsair loyal to the Turks, had defeated Mulay Hassan, former *bey* of Tunis and imperial ally, and turned the city into a pirates' den. The Tunis campaign would become the greatest feat represented in Charles V's visual imagery. In representations of the Tunis campaign, he truly fulfilled his imperial duty, leading Christendom to victory against the common heathen enemy. From an artistic viewpoint, the African operation was an important qualitative leap. Here, for the first time, we find evidence of a plan to visually narrate and convey messages about the campaign. Chroniclers and state officials—Felipe de Guevara, Alonso de Santa Cruz, Antoine Perrenin, Francisco de los Cobos y Molina—and artists like Jan Cornelisz Vermeyen were invited to tramp across the Tunisian sands and, under the direct supervision of Luis de Ávila y Zúñiga and Guillaume van Mâle, coordinated their literary and artistic output to produce an 'official truth', as argued elsewhere in this volume as well.[8] In the visual arts, the formerly predominant central European production was overshadowed by a greater number of Italian works, as Italy was the region that most benefited from the conquest. This was a key development, as it consolidated the classical and Renaissance images of Charles introduced in 1530 with his imperial coronation at Bologna. The comparison of Charles's campaign to the Punic Wars also provided the perfect excuse for this antique visual surge, which culminated in Caesar's triumphal entries into various Italian cities upon his victorious return from Africa.

In the following years, this preference for expressions *all'antica* found its way to arms and armour, the most suitable support for projecting a heroic image of the ruler. Thus, we find pieces decorated with mythological and antique themes like the *Plus Ultra Parade Shield* (anonymous Italian artist, c. 1535; Patrimonio Nacional, Madrid), the *Burgonet with Fame and Victory and a Captive Turk* (Filippo and Francesco Negroli, 1545; Patrimonio Nacional, Madrid), or the two versions of the *Medusa Parade Shield* (Filippo and Francesco Negroli, c. 1541; Patrimonio Nacional, Madrid, and Kunsthistorisches Museum, Vienna).[9] Another artistic genre that lent itself to antiquity was medals. Giovanni Bernardi da Castel Bolognese struck a medal on which we see Charles V freeing captives (1535–1540; Kunsthistorisches Museum, Vienna) and produced an excellent engraving that depicts the Tunisian conquest as a classical battle (*The Battle of Tunis*, c. 1544; Metropolitan Museum, New York). In the field of painting, scenes of the African triumph were predominantly frescoes, an ideal medium for monumental narrative compositions. For example, we might mention

---

8 Rubén González Cuerva and Miguel Ángel De Bunes Ibarra, *Túnez 1535: voces de una campaña Europea* (Madrid: Polifemo, 2017), xiv; Juan Luís González Garcia, '"Pinturas tejidas": la guerra como arte y el arte de la guerra en torno a la Empresa de Túnez (1535)', *Reales Sitios*, XLIV, 17, (2007), 24–7; Hendrik J. Horn, *Jan Cornelisz Vermeyen: painter of Charles V and his conquest of Tunis: paintings, etchings, drawings, cartoons & tapestries*. 2 vols (Doornspijk: Davaco, 1989), xv, lxxv and clvii.

9 Álvaro Soler Del Campo, *El arte del poder: la real armería y el retrato de corte* (Madrid: Museo del Prado, 2010).

the cycles painted by the Zuccaros for Pope Paul III or, in Spain, the murals in the Queen's Dressing Room at the Alhambra, which are of great chorographical interest (Julio Aquiles and Alejandro Mayner: *Scenes of the Conquest of Tunis*, 1539–1546). Prints were used to produce cartographic views like those of Agostino de' Musi, aka Agostino Veneziano (*Cavalier Perspective of the City of Tunis*, 1535; Bibliothèque Municipale de le Part-Dieu-Lyon) and brilliant narrative scenes, such as Frans Hogenberg's prints after the cartoons that Jan Cornelisz Vermeyen drew for the tapestries commissioned by the court (1569–1570; Biblioteca Nacional, Madrid).[10] In fact, *The Conquest of Tunis* series, woven in Brussels by Willem de Pannemaker, was undoubtedly the crowning achievement of this great laudatory visual campaign (1548–1554; Patrimonio Nacional, Madrid). Mary of Hungary, at Charles V's behest, entrusted their design to people who had actually witnessed the events in Tunis, such as Jan Cornelisz Vermeyen—who made the cartoons—and quite probably the chronicler and cartographer Alonso de Santa Cruz, whose written account tallies for the most part with the story told on the tapestries.[11] The cycle thus offers a clear and systematic visual narrative of the principal phases of the campaign, making it a perfect iconic pendant to the official chronicles written at the same time.[12] Here, the representation of war according to early modern standards reached definitive formal maturity, establishing an artistic model that would later be widely imitated. Chronologically, the series was woven fifteen years after the event and should therefore be understood in relation to the dynamics of the court and its art commissions after the Schmalkaldic War, when the visual image of Charles V was fully developed.

During the last twenty years of his reign, the emperor's political and military actions were focused on addressing the Protestant problem in central Europe. Increasing political and religious dissent within the Holy Roman Empire eventually led to the creation of the anti-Habsburg Schmalkaldic League in 1531. After years of a containment policy, Charles V finally settled the matter by force of arms. The first stage of the conflict on the Danube in 1546 ended with the unsuccessful Protestant siege of the city of Ingolstadt, as depicted in a fascinating print by Hans Mielich (1549; Germanisches Nationalmuseum, Nuremberg). In 1547 the imperial forces launched a new offensive in the heart of Saxony, the domain of Elector John Frederick I, who was defeated at the Battle of Mühlberg. However,

---

10 Elena Páez, *Los Austrias: grabados de la Biblioteca Nacional*, (Madrid: Biblioteca Nacional, 1993), 86–90.
11 Antonio Gozalbo, 'Tapices y crónica, imagen y texto: un entramado persuasivo al servicio de la imagen de Carlos V', *Potestas*, 9 (2016), 109–134.
12 Fernando Checa, *Tesoros de la corona de España: tapices flamencos en el Siglo de Oro* (Madrid: Fonds Mercator/SEACEX, 2010).

the empire needed to extend that military triumph to the field of visual persuasion. The Lutherans had to be defeated in an 'image war', which they had been winning up to that point. Consequently, the confrontation was recreated in various formats, qualities and visual languages, but always with one goal: to exalt the unquestionable triumph of Charles V. Thus, we find prints like those of Enea Vico, Virgil Solis, Domenico Zenoi, the 'HM Master' and the anonymous images in the chronicle of Ávila y Zúñiga that had such a strong influence on others' works, such as medals by Nickel Milicz, the Leonis and Castel Bolognese; and the pottery of Durantino and Fontana. To all these we must add the grisailles at the Palace of Oriz in Navarre (anonymous, c. 1550; Museo de Navarra, Pamplona) and the commemorative commissions of the Grand Duke of Alba, hero of the conflict, consisting of the mural cycle in the castle of Alba de Tormes (Cristoforo Passini and workshop, 1562–1570) and the series of tapestries now in Liria Palace (Willem de Pannemaker, 1567–1571).[13] At court, Mary of Hungary and Cardinal Granvelle, both great patrons of the arts, backed an ambitious programme extolling the merits of Charles V. An aloof, serious, classical image of the emperor was promoted, portraying him as the guarantor of the new and hegemonic, though short-lived, *Pax Carolina*. Those responsible for its visual materialisation were the Leonis, who produced a series of sculpted portraits of the imperial family, most notably *Charles V and the Fury* (1551–1555; Museo del Prado, Madrid), and Titian. In 1548, Titian moved from his birthplace of Cadore to Augsburg to paint portraits and religious and mythological scenes capable of expressing the dynastic and political values of the House of Austria. The most important was the *Equestrian Portrait of Charles V at Mühlberg* (1548; Museo del Prado, Madrid), a commemorative composition which is more a family icon than a narrative scene.[14] Represented as Ávila y Zúñiga had described him, Charles V looks beyond the picture plane, riding from his historical feat into immortality, the epitome of the *Eroica Maestà* defined by Lodovico Dolce.

This triumphal vision of Charles V was cemented for posterity in two series of ten and eight prints, respectively. The first was designed by Maarten van Heemskerck, published in Antwerp in 1556 and widely circulated (*The Triumphs of Charles V*; Biblioteca Nacional, Madrid). The second, more modest series was based on Caesar's death and created by

---

13 Antonio Gozalbo, '*Veni, vidi, Christus vincit*. Las representaciones de la batalla de Mühlberg (1547) en frescos y tapices', in *Vestir la arquitectura*, eds. René J. Payo et al., 2 vols (Burgos: Universidad de Burgos-CEHA, 2019), 779–784; Gonzalo Redín, 'Los tapices de *Las jornadas de Alemania* del Gran Duque de Alba: del Bombardeo de Ingolstadt a la Batalla de Mühlberg', in *Nobleza y coleccionismo de tapices entre la Edad Moderna y Contemporánea: Las casas de Alba y Denia Lerma* (Madrid: Arco Libros–La Muralla, 2018), 59–83.
14 Fernando Checa, *Carlos V, a caballo, en Mühlberg de Tiziano* (Madrid: TF Editores, 2001).

Fig. 8.3. *Emperor Charles V at Mühlberg*, Titian, 1548. © Museo Nacional del Prado.

the Italian artist Antonio Tempesta (*The Triumphs of Charles V*, 1614; Biblioteca Nacional, Madrid).[15] Together they definitively fixed the image of Charles V as the most outstanding figure of the Habsburg dynasty and, therefore, an example for his successors to follow.

The series that Heemskerck designed was probably commissioned by the emperor's son and successor, Philip II. The new ruler, whose artistic tastes were much more defined, pursued an active policy of patronage as a means of visual legitimisation in which martial imagery figured

---

15 Elena Páez, *Los Austrias: grabados de la Biblioteca Nacional*, 106–115.

prominently. In fact, in several of his first official portraits, the young prince appears clad in armour. This is the case with the canvas painted by Titian at Augsburg in 1551 (Museo del Prado, Madrid), Leoni's sculpture (1551–1553; Museo del Prado, Madrid) and Antonis Mor's portrait after the victory at Saint-Quentin where he is represented as wearing the Burgundy Cross suit of armour (*Philip II on Saint Quentin's Day*, 1560; Patrimonio Nacional, El Escorial). Philip's reign began amid conflict with France; Henry II had come to the French throne in 1547 and immediately broke the truce signed at Crépy-en-Lannois (1544). This marked the beginning of a new period of hostility between the House of Valois and the Habsburgs, although weariness of this war eventually led to the Treaty of Vaucelles in 1556. The very next year, however, saw the flames of rivalry rekindled on Italian soil due to the aggressiveness of Pope Paul IV, who had no love for the House of Habsburg. Philip II sent the Duke of Alba to Naples, where he began an unstoppable march to the very gates of Rome. His actions were visually circulated in prints depicting scenes like the conquest of Ostia (Hieronymus Cock, 1556; Biblioteca Nacional, Madrid)[16] or the French-papal setback during the siege of Civitella del Tronto (anonymous, 1557; Biblioteca del Palacio Real, Madrid).[17]

Philip II waited for news of these events in Flanders, where he planned to attack France on a second front; to this end he assembled a mighty army under the command of Emmanuel Philibert of Savoy and Ferrante Gonzaga, reinforced by English contingents. Imitating his father, he also enlisted the services of an artist, the Flemish painter Anton van den Wyngaerde, to reproduce the events and compose an official graphic record.[18] Thus, in the summer of 1557, Philip's army launched its offensive in Picardy, marching to the strategic town of Saint-Quentin and placing it under siege. The Constable of France, Anne de Montmorency, organised a large relief expedition, but on 10 August the Spanish cavalry crushed his troops in an utter debacle. Given the relevance of this victory, it was immediately depicted in a variety of prints with high chorographical value, including one engraved by Wyngaerde's burin and titled *View of the Battle of Saint-Quentin* (1557; Bibliothèque Nationale de France, Paris). The composition is divided into three scenes/moments, separated by caryatids, that show the dramatic sequence of events: the arrival of French relief forces, the Spaniards pushing the constable into retreat and the final

---

16 Elena Páez, *Los Austrias: grabados de la Biblioteca Nacional*, 156–157.

17 Agustín Bustamante García, 'De las guerras con Francia: Italia y San Quintín (I)', *Anuario del Departamento de Historia y Teoría del Arte*, 21 (2009), 47–68.

18 Montserrat Galera, *Antoon van den Wijngaerde, pintor de ciudades y de hechos de armas en la Europa del Quinientos: cartobibliografía razonada de los dibujos y grabados, y ensayo de reconstrucción documental de la obra pictórica* (Barcelona: Institut Cartogràfic de Catalunya, 1998).

defeat of his troops. Another remarkable print united siege and combat in a single panoramic view (anonymous: *Siege and Battle of Saint-Quentin*, 1557; Biblioteca del Palacio Real, Madrid). This composition, printed in Flanders and Italy, was widely circulated and inspired visions such as that found in the 1578 edition of Sebastian Münster's *Cosmographia* or that offered by Frans Hogenberg in his series of prints.[19]

After taking Châtelet, Philip II did not push through to Paris, giving the French army time to regroup. Henry II took advantage of the situation and responded in 1557 with a terrible counterblow against Calais and Thionville, marching into Flanders to take Dunkirk. The Spanish reaction was forceful and implacable: on 13 July 1558, the squadrons of the Count of Egmont won a clear victory over the French invaders at Gravelines. That triumph was visually documented in an Italian print, a bird's-eye view of great testimonial value (anonymous, 1558; Biblioteca del Palacio Real, Madrid).[20] The Catholic King continued to advance through France and finally met the armies of Henry II between Doullens and Amiens. However, the anticipated battle never materialised, as they entered negotiations that resulted in the Treaty of Cateau-Cambrésis in April 1559. On 10 July the French sovereign died unexpectedly, plunging France into a long period of internal wars that effectively neutralised the Habsburgs' traditional foe.

The successful campaign of 1557–1558 endured as a glorious moment in 'Philippine' imagery and was represented artistically throughout his reign. For instance, it inspired the series of canvases on the war against France painted for the Saint-Quentin Gallery of the Palace of Valsaín, now in El Escorial. Only five of the seven original paintings have survived, sequentially narrating the most important moments in the conflict: *The Battle of Saint-Quentin, Spanish Troops Advance towards Ham, The Surrender of Châtelet, The Burning of the Town of Ham and Taking of Its Castle*, and *Review of the Spanish Troops between Amiens and Doullens*. The two missing pictures therefore must have depicted the conquest of Saint-Quentin and the Battle of Gravelines. Formally, the series is marked by its highly realistic narrative language, recreating the terrain and troop movements against a high horizon. Texts identifying actions and individuals were added to facilitate its interpretation. They therefore have the chorographical style typical of Flemish painting, although their authorship is debated. The works have traditionally been attributed to Rodrigo de Holanda (aka Rodrigo Diriksen), Wyngaerde's son-in-law, who had produced the designs for the Hall of Battles in the Monastery of El Escorial around 1590.[21] The

---

19 Elena Páez, *Los Austrias: grabados de la Biblioteca Nacional*, 158–159.
20 Agustín Bustamante García, 'De las guerras con Francia: Italia y San Quintín (II)', *Anuario del Departamento de Historia y Teoría del Arte*, 22 (2011), 50–62.
21 Carmen García-Frías Checa, 'Las series de batallas del Real Monasterio de San Lorenzo de El Escorial: frescos y pinturas', in *La imagen de la guerra en el arte de los antiguos Países Bajos*,

Fig. 8.4. General view of the Hall of Battles at El Escorial.

high quality and detail of the paintings, as well as heraldic questions, have led Agustín Bustamante García to consider them originals by Wyngaerde and therefore date them to around 1565.[22]

The war against Henry II would also find its place in the Hall of Battles at El Escorial, where the glorification of Philip II's military achievements reached its height.[23] This cycle opens with the large mural of the Battle of La Higueruela, won by John II in 1431 against the Nasrids of Granada. It was painted between 1587 and 1589 by the Genoese artists Niccolò Granello and Fabrizio Castello—who had been working at El Escorial since 1575—and two members of Luca Cambiaso's team, Lazzaro Tavarone and Orazio Cambiaso. The theme is still debated, though it can be linked to the struggle against Islam as a defining trait of the Spanish monarchy. This commitment to fight the infidel had begun in the Middle Ages and was still relevant in Philip's day, as evidenced by the Battle of Lepanto (1571) and the Morisco rebellion in the Alpujarra mountains of Granada (1568–1571). Later, in 1590, Granello, Castello and Tavarone signed a new contract to complete the decoration with views of the campaigns that Philip II was most proud of: the 1557–1558 war against France

---

ed. Bernardo García (Madrid: Fundación Carlos de Amberes/Editorial Complutense, 2006), 148–151.

22 Bustamante García, 'De las guerras con Francia: Italia y San Quintín (II)', 67.
23 Jonathan Brown, *La Sala de Batallas de El Escorial: la obra de arte como artefacto cultural* (Salamanca: Universidad de Salamanca, 1998); Fernando Checa Cremades, *Felipe II: mecenas de las artes* (Madrid: Nerea, 1992), ccclxvi–ccclxvii.

and the annexation of Portugal in 1580. Rather than creating freely, they had to follow the designs prepared by Rodrigo de Holanda who, thanks to his kinship with Wyngaerde, used the older artist's graphic material to assemble an iconic narrative of events. They painted nine murals that show the main actions of the French campaign, including the siege and Battle of Saint-Quentin, the conquests of Châtelet and Ham, the French defeat at Gravelines and the wait for the rival armies at Doullens. The ends of the hall also featured the Battle of Isla Terceira in the context of the naval expeditions led by Álvaro de Bazán in 1582 and 1583 against António of Aviz, Prior of Crato and pretender to the Portuguese throne. Though painted by Italian fresco artists, the murals are defined by a northern visual rhetoric, presumably aseptic in their descriptions of places and events. This formal conception, already used by the court of Charles V in commissions like the *Conquest of Tunis* tapestries, became the 'official' model for displaying the martial glory of the Habsburgs.[24]

The peace treaty with France did not usher in a period of peace for Europe. During the reign of Philip II, Spain maintained its constant struggle with the Ottoman Empire, which came to a head at the Battle of Lepanto; in addition, it annexed Portugal after the Duke of Alba's victory at Alcántara, as depicted in print (anonymous, *c.* 1580; Biblioteca Nacional de Portugal, Lisbon). Philip's reign, and those of his successors, would also be marked by conflict on a new front: the rebellion of the Netherlands. Political and religious dissent in the region was firmly dealt with by the Habsburg monarch, who appointed the Grand Duke of Alba governor in 1567. His harsh measures triggered a widespread revolt, initiating a long, drawn-out conflict that would not be resolved until the mid-seventeenth century. The fight between Alba and the rebels also extended to the visual plane. The Spanish governor commissioned a sculpted portrait from Jacques Jonghelinck to be defiantly displayed in the fortress of Antwerp, and the Protestants responded with satirical visions of his rule.[25] The principal graphic chronicler of these events was Frans Hogenberg, a Flemish printmaker forced by repression to flee to England in 1568. His extensive collection titled *History of the Netherlands, France, Germany and England between 1535 and 1608* depicts with great realism the main historical

---

24 Bustamante García, 'De las guerras con Francia: Italia y San Quintín (II)', 73–77; Francisco Javier Campos and Fernández de Sevilla, 'Los frescos de la Sala de Batallas', in *El monasterio del Escorial y la pintura: actas del Simposium*, ed. Francisco Javier Campos (Madrid: Instituto Escurialense de Investigaciones Históricas y Artísticas, 1999), 165–209; Carmen García Frías Checa, 'Las series de batallas del Real Monasterio de San Lorenzo de El Escorial: frescos y pinturas', 138–143.

25 Fernando Checa, 'Treasures from the House of Alba: 500 years of art and collecting', in *Treasures from the House of Alba: 500 Years of Art and Collecting*, ed. Fernando Checa (Madrid: Ediciones El Viso; Dallas: Meadows Museum, Southern Methodist University, 2016), 74.

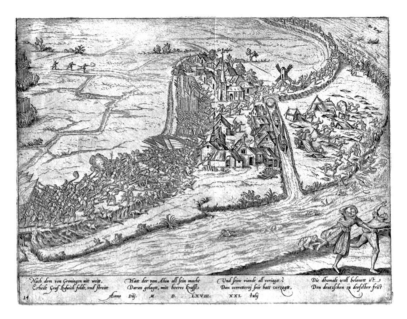

Fig. 8.5. *Jemmingen Battle*, by Franz Hogenberg, 1568. © Biblioteca Nacional de España, Madrid.

developments between 1530 and 1608, devoting nearly two hundred prints to the war in the Netherlands (1569–1631; Biblioteca Nacional, Madrid). Besides political matters, such as Alba's arrival in Brussels or the capture and death of the counts Egmont and Horn, he also represented important military episodes, like the victory of the Habsburg *Tercios* at Jemmingen (1568) and the conquests of Zutphen, Mons and Haarlem. Far from being limited to Álvarez de Toledo's time, the prints also depicted later events like the sack of Antwerp by mutinous Spanish soldiers in 1576, John of Austria's victory at Gembloux, and the numerous military triumphs of Alexander Farnese, Duke of Parma.

In fact, the Duke of Parma's successes were featured in many artworks, and a print by Otto van Veen even portrayed him as Hercules (*c.* 1585; Biblioteca Nacional, Madrid).[26] His numerous victories were included in the aforementioned Hogenberg prints and in two series of paintings that depict military actions in the Netherlands in the final quarter of the sixteenth century, now held in El Escorial. Both series—one consisting of eleven small canvases and the other of six larger paintings—were painted by various unidentified Flemish artists and probably commissioned by

---

26 Elena Páez, *Los Austrias: grabados de la Biblioteca Nacional*, 174.

Archduke Albert of Austria, named governor in 1596. The pictures were sent to Madrid as graphic records of the campaigns, which explains their narrative style and realistic representation of natural features, fortifications and troop movements. The sequence beings with the 1574 victory at Mook (*Battle of Mook*) under the command of Luís de Requesens y Zúñiga and then shows Parma's victories, depicting triumphs over the rebels, mostly Protestants, at the *Siege of Maastricht* (1579), the *Siege of Grave* (1586) and episodes in the French War of Religions such as the *Battle near Ivry*, *The Relief of Paris* and the later *Siege of Paris*. Events that transpired during the governorships of the Count of Fuentes, such as *The Siege of Cambrai* (1595) and Archduke Albert were also included.[27] The Duke of Parma's legend endured long after his death. Even in the late seventeenth century, the prints that Famiano Strada and Guglielmo Dondini included in *Las tres décadas de las guerras de Flandes* depict Parma's feats, albeit using a more pompous language with classical allusions, in keeping with baroque tastes (Juan de Ledesma and Romeyn de Hooghe, 1681–1682; Biblioteca Nacional, Madrid).[28]

The House of Austria saw the imagery of war—whether realistic topographical depictions or complex allegories, simple woodcuts or splendid tapestries—as a decisive means of securing loyalties and assurances for its hegemonic plans. The victorious campaigns of Philip II and, above all, Charles V were instrumental in this sense and became family legends. Visual records of those triumphs served as an inspiration and a model for their heirs, who also pursued ambitious projects like Philip IV's Hall of Realms. The representation of their martial feats was essential to the visual and artistic definition of the Habsburgs, projecting the ultimate image of power of a family with universal aspirations.

---

27 Carmen García-Frías Checa, 'Las series de batallas del Real Monasterio de San Lorenzo de El Escorial: frescos y pinturas', 152–158.
28 Elena Páez, *Los Austrias: grabados de la Biblioteca Nacional*, 188–190.

ANTONIO URQUÍZAR-HERRERA

Sixteenth-Century Notions of *Spolia* and Triumph Representation

> ... and a *Dolle Griet* [sic] carrying away plunder in the face of hell, who looks quite crazy and is weirdly kitted-out in a higgledy-piggledy way. I believe this, as well as some other pieces, to be in the Emperor's palace too.
>
> (Karel Van Mander)[1]

Pieter Bruegel's *Dulle Griet* plundered in the face of hell. At the Museum Van der Bergh in Antwerp we can see the 'Mad Meg' of Flemish folklore represented in Bruegel's painting advancing resolutely through the flames and destruction of battle and accompanied by her army of women. She wears a helmet and a breastplate over her dress, brandishing a sword in her right hand and carrying two baskets and a sack under her left arm, filled with the spoils she has just secured in the fray. Among them is a coffer or strongbox, possibly containing jewellery, a gold chalice, assorted kitchen wares and a frying pan. This pan plundered from the enemy could be an ironic representation of the only weapon of war that traditionally corresponded to women; if so, it is one of the key elements of the fantastic subversion of gender and of class which this painting embodies. The central role of the trophies was probably already acknowledged in the

---

1 Karel Van Mander, *The Lives of the illustrious Netherlandish and German painters, from the first edition of the Schilder-Boeck (1603–1604): preceded by the lineage, circumstances and place of birth, life and works of Karel van Mander, painter and poet, and likewise his death and burial, from the second edition of the Schilder-Boeck (1616–1618)*, ed. Hessel Miedema (Doornspijk: Davaco, 1994), 1, fol. 233v.

Antonio Urquízar-Herrera • National Distance Learning University

Fig. 9.1. *Dulle Griet*, Pieter Bruegel, 1563. © Museum Mayer Van der Bergh (Antwerp).

sixteenth century, when the painting was, as Van Mander believed, in Rudolf II's imperial palace. It is easy to think that the matter did not escape notice when this very painting was looted after the Swedish army conquered Prague in 1648.

The humanistic revival of the classical triumph

The ruins of Rome contained many representations of triumphs, trophies and *spolia*. Some of the best-known visible remains were stone reminders of the triumphs of antiquity, thus made accessible to spectators in the early modern era. In the same way, classical literature (and with it the historical literature read at early modern courts) had repeatedly used their description to highlight the national victories of Rome and the association between its legacy and the family memory of imperial and patrician lineages. In the fifteenth and sixteenth centuries, celebrating victory with a triumph and visually materialising it in the spoils wrested from the enemy after battle was one of 'those things similar to the ancients' which, according to Niccolò Machiavelli (*Dell'arte della guerra*, 1521), the humanists wished to revive from the classical world.² Medieval Europe had never given up the custom of taking and exhibiting trophies. In the fourteenth century, Petrarch turned *I Trionfi* into a valid philosophical framework for any argument. And, as numerous authors have pointed out, from the fifteenth century onwards, the discussion and depiction of classical triumphs became more articulated and habitual in courts across Italy and the rest of Europe.³ In 1586, when triumphs and trophies had already become a customary theme in the visual arts, the painter and writer Giovanni Paolo Lomazzo reviewed the process, identifying the most relevant classical literary sources and contemporary examples that might serve as models, including Andrea Mantegna's *Triumphs* for the Dukes of Mantua and the drawings that Albrecht Dürer made for Emperor Maximilian I.³ Lomazzo also mentioned one of the prime examples of how triumphs had become a standard practice in many palaces, namely the triumphal programme

---

2 In the 1537 Venetian edition: 'COSIMO. Quali sono quelle che voi vorresti introdurre simile all'antiche? FABRITIO. Honorare, & premiare le virtu, non dispregiare la poverta, stimare i modi, & gli ordini della disciplina militare, constringere i Cittadini ad amare l'uno l'altro, à vivere sanza sette, à stimare meno il privato che il publico, & altre simile cose, che facilmente si potrebbono con questi templo accompagnar'. Niccolò Macchiavelli, *Libro dell'arte della guerra* (Venice: Zanetti, 1537), no page. In English: '*Cosimo*: What are those things similar to the ancients that you would introduce? *Fabrizio*: To honour and reward virtue, not to have contempt for poverty, to esteem the modes and orders of military discipline, to constrain citizens to love one another, to live without factions, to esteem less the private than the public good, and other such things which could easily be added in these times'. *The Art of War*, trans. Henry Neville (Mineola, NY: Dover, 2006), 7.

3 See Werner Weisbach, *Trionfi* (Berlin: G. Grote'sche Verlagsbuchhandlung, 1919), 20–58. See also, among others, *Les fêtes de la renaissance*, ed. Jean Jacquot (Paris: CNRS, 1973); Edward Muir, 'Images of power: art and pageantry in renaissance Venice', *The American Historical Review*, 84, 1 (1979), 16–52; Bonner Mitchell, *Italian civic pageantry in the high renaissance: a descriptive bibliography of triumphal entries and selected other festivals for state occasions* (Florence: Leo S. Olschki Editore, 1979); Roy Strong, *Art and power: renaissance festivals, 1450–1650* (Berkeley: University of California Press, 1984); Bonner Mitchell, *The majesty of the state: triumphal progresses of foreign sovereigns in renaissance Italy (1494–1600)* (Florence: Leo S. Olschki Editore, 1986); Barbara Wisch and Susan Scott Munshower, eds., *All the world's a stage…: art and pageantry in the renaissance and baroque* (University Park, PA: Pennsylvania State University Press, 1990), 1; Alfredo Morales, ed., *La fiesta en la Europa de Carlos V* (Madrid: Sociedad Estatal para la Conmemoración de los Centenarios de Felipe II y Carlos V, 2000); Anthony Miller, *Roman triumphs and early modern English culture* (New York: Palgrave, 2001); J. R. Mulryne, Helen Watanabe-O'Kelly and Margaret Shewring, *Europa triumphans: court and civic festivals in early modern Europe* (Aldershot: Ashgate, 2004); Margaret Ann Zaho, *Imago triumphalis: the function and significance of triumphal imagery for Italian renaissance rulers* (New York: Peter Lang, 2004); Randolph Starn, 'Renaissance triumphalism in art', in *The renaissance world*, ed. John Jeffries Martin (Abingdon: Routledge, 2007), 326–345; and *Festival culture in the world of the Spanish Habsburgs*, eds. Fernando Checa Cremades and Laura Fernández-González (Farnham: Ashgate, 2015).

3 Giovanni Paolo Lomazzo, *Trattato dell'arte della pittura, scoltura, et architettura* (Milan: Paolo Gottardo Pontio, 1585), 393–403.

Fig. 9.2. Details of *spolia*, from *Arch of Honor. Triumphal arch* of Maximilian I, various artists, 1515-1518. © Metropolitan Museum of Art, New York.

of the Medicis in Florence, as examined by Randolph Starn and Loren Partridge.[4] In this progression across Europe, the trophies of war printed on paper in Maximilian I's *The Triumphal Arch* became stone reliefs carved on the triumphal gates leading into the palace of his grandson Charles V in Granada. It is safe to say that written or visual depictions of triumphs, trophies and *spolia* were a constant sight during the Renaissance and the entire early modern era. They were reproduced hundreds of times, so often that today it is easy to view them as ornamental devices at risk of losing their original meaning. This may be true to a certain extent, and even Lomazzo advised prudence in their use,[5] but it is hard to deny that the representation of spoils had a symbolic significance related to the reception of classical thought in court settings. Their presence in palaces requires little explanation, but their appearance in religious and other contexts can easily be interpreted as evidence of the appropriation of space by the civil elites.

Literature on Charles V has emphasised the value of triumphs in constructing his imperial image. Fernando Checa analysed the different

---

4 Randolph Starn and Loren Partridge, *Arts of power: three halls of state in Italy, 1300–1600* (Berkeley: University of California Press, 1992), 149–212. See also Mikael Hörnqvist, *Machiavelli and empire* (Cambridge: Cambridge University Press, 2004), 156–193.
5 Lomazzo, *Trattato*, 402–403. See Zaho, *Imago triumphalis*, 120–121.

theoretical sources associated with the conceptualisation of the triumph model in the circle of Charles V—authors like Robertus Valturius, Remy Du Puys and Olivier de la Marche—as well as the principal places where it was exhibited, including Brussels, Bruges, Bologna and Binche.[6] In a particularly interesting way, these 'Caroline' examples of triumphal celebration combined the taste for magnificence, in the sense of a straightforward display of wealth, with the desire to convey a meaning connected with the memory of military victory, which gradually became more relevant. This growing emphasis on martial themes in Charles's triumphs is evident if we compare the narrative of the triumphal entry into Bruges in 1515 with the account of his entry into Bologna for the imperial coronation in 1530. In Bruges, according to Remy Du Puys, the triumphs essentially highlighted wealth and sumptuousness.[7] While magnificence also took precedence over any other semantic sign in descriptions of the Bologna entry, on the Italian peninsula the triumph had a decidedly military air.[8] This is borne out by the numerous accounts of the ceremony that have come down to us, such as the description that Jerónimo de Sempere included in his *Carolea*, which tells us they 'sacavan por valcones la riqueza' [unfurled richness on the balconies] along the emperor's route, but at the same time 'a pies de sus tropheos enxalçados, / están los enemigos de él domados' [at the feet of his exalted trophies / lie his vanquished foes].[9] In the same vein, Paolo Giovio's narrative, and many others, highlighted the tunics, plumes and various colours worn by the military men, as well as the spoils of war and the brightness of the arms and armour, including those of the emperor himself.[10] The classical commemoration of the triumph at Bologna, well

---

6 Fernando Checa Cremades, *Carlos V: la imagen del poder en el renacimiento* (Madrid: Ediciones El Viso, 1999). See also Víctor Mínguez Cornelles and Inmaculada Rodríguez Moya, eds., *Visiones de un imperio en fiesta*, (Madrid: Fundación Carlos de Amberes, 2016).
7 Remy Du Puys, *La triumphante et solemnelle entree… de… Monsieur Charles prince des Espaignes, archiduc d'Austrice… en la ville de Bruges l'an 1515* (Bruges: Société d'Émulation de Bruges, 1839).
8 For an analysis of Charles V's Italian triumphs in a wider context, see Mitchell, *The majesty of state*, 133–179. See also Checa Cremades, *Carlos V*, 140–166; Sylvie Deswarte-Rosa, 'L'expédition de Tunis (1535): images, interprétations, répercussions culturelles', in *Chrétiens et Musulmans à la renaissance*, ed. Bartolomé Benassar (Paris: Honoré Champion, 1988), 73–131; Dolce Maria Luisa Madonna, 'El viaje de Carlos V por Italia después de Túnez: el triunfo clásico y el plan de reconstrucción de las ciudades', in *La fiesta en la Europa de Carlos V*, ed. Morales, 119–153; Marta Carrasco, 'Carlos V en Roma: el triunfo de un nuevo Escipión', in *Carolus*, ed. Fernando Checa (Madrid: SECCFC, 2000), 81–101; and Maria Antonietta Visceglia, 'Il viaggio cerimoniale di Carlo V dopo Tunisi', in *Carlos V y la quiebra del humanismo político en Europa*, ed. J. Martínez (Madrid: Sociedad Estatal para la Conmemoración de los Centenarios de Felipe II y Carlos V, 2000), 2, 133–172.
9 Jerónimo de Sempere, *Primera parte de la Carolea y Segunda parte de la Carolea* (Valencia: Juan de Arcos, 1560), 238. See also Checa Cremades, Carlos V, 147.
10 Paolo Giovio, *Libro de las historias y cosas acontescidas…* (Valencia: Juan Mey, 1562), fol. 39r. For an interpretation of the coronation crown in relation to the insignia, see Girolamo Balbi,

consolidated by this point, included an initial arch dedicated to the Roman emperors on which spoils featured prominently. Many explanations are offered for the differences between these two entries, such as the commercial nature of Bruges versus the academic character of Bologna, the victories that Charles V had won in the interim or the decidedly imperial nature of the second ceremony but, in any case, the changes were marked by a fuller knowledge of the classical triumph and its political implications.[11] Similar to the transformations that transpired between these two entries, as Charles V's reign drew to a close, and especially after it ended, his triumph played an increasingly important role in accounts of his military campaigns and the images in circulation. This was particularly true of texts that aimed for a more epic, rather than descriptive, tone.[12] We see this again in Sempere's *Carolea*,[13] and in numerous images from the second half of the sixteenth century, most notably *The Victories of Emperor Charles V*, a series of prints made by Maarten van Heemskerck at the initiative of Hieronymus Cock.[14]

Most scholarly studies of the modern triumph have focused on incorporating triumphal entries and processions in the ceremonial repertoire of European rulers. The triumph's popularity spread as more people read classical sources and realised its potential political advantages. Many of the most widely read ancient texts in the fifteenth and sixteenth centuries can be understood as a succession of triumphs. This is the case, for instance, of Titus Livius's *Ab Urbe Condita*, where accounts of triumphal celebrations are an important part of the discourse and even the narrative structure of the text.[15] Mikael Hörnqvist noted how Machiavelli himself had recognised the Medicis' efforts to revive the ancient Roman triumphal

---

Hieronymi Balbi episcopi Gurcensis, ad Carolum V impe. de Coronatione (Bologna: Ioannes Baptista Phaellus, 1530), fol. 6v.

11 As Fernando Checa has stated, the image of Charles V as a soldier was mainly an Italian production. Checa Cremades, *Carlos V*, 102.

12 Trophies were not all that common in more descriptive texts, such as Alfonso de Valdés, *Relación de las nuevas de Italia: sacadas de las cartas que los capitanes y comisario del Emperador y Rey nuestro Señor....* ([n.p.], 1525), or Luis de Ávila y Zúñiga, *Comentario ... de la Guerra de Alemaña, hecha de Carlo V Maximo* (Antwerp: Johannes Steelsius, 1550).

13 Bart Rosier, 'The victories of Charles V: A series of prints by Maarten van Heemskerck, 1555–56', *Simiolus: Netherlands Quarterly for the History of Art*, 20, 1 (1990–1991), 24–38. See also Juan Francisco Pardo Molero, 'Los triunfos de Carlos V: transferencias culturales y políticas en la exaltación de la monarquía', in *Las monarquías española y francesa (siglos XVI–XVIII)*, eds. Anne Dubet and José Javier Ruiz Ibáñez (Madrid: Casa de Velázquez, 2012), 17–30.

14 Sempere's description of the imperial tent is a good example. Sempere, *Primera parte*, 315.

15 For a general overview of Roman triumphs, see Gilbert Charles Picard, *Les trophées Romains: contribution à l'histoire de la religion et de l'art triomphal de Rome* (Paris: E. de Boccard, 1957); Hendrik Simon Versnel, ed., *Triumphus: an inquiry into the origin, development, and meaning of the Roman triumph* (Leyden: Brill, 1970); and Mary Beard, *The Roman Triumph* (Cambridge, MA: Harvard University Press, 2009).

processions as a means of legitimising their own political aspirations. On a first level of interpretation, according to Machiavelli, these processions had been useful in Rome because they inspired love of virtue and glory in the Roman people, contributed to keeping private interest subordinated to the common good of the city and fostered a commitment to the city's free, republican way of life. On a second level, Machiavelli contended, triumphs had reinforced the warlike qualities of the Romans by creating a competitive atmosphere where any citizen could aspire to win honour and glory. The fruit of this warring activity was the *spolia*, although access to plunder—and this is an important point—was regulated, in keeping with the idea that such spoils ought to serve the common good of the republic by enriching the state.[16]

The triumph soon escaped the confines of erudite historical exchange and became a useful and influential concept in different spheres of public activity; from politics, as noted by Machiavelli and Francis Bacon at different times, to ancient history itself, as in Flavio Biondo and his *Roma Triumphans*; and religion, as Savonarola stated in his *Triumphus Crucis*.[17] The triumph had made a strong debut as a conversation-enriching novelty in Europe. As Fernando Checa pointed out, Remy Du Puys's narrative of the funeral rites of Ferdinand II of Aragon in Brussels (1515), where Moorish and American spoils were paraded, opens with a section where he explained what triumphs and trophies were.[18] Even in 1571, when Diego Gracián de Alderete translated Plutarch's *Moralia* into Spanish, he felt it necessary to add a side note explaining to readers that a trophy was a memento of some victory consisting of arms and other things'.[19] In 1529, Barthélemy de Chasseneuz had composed an early list of individuals in antiquity who had merited triumphs and statues erected in their honour.[20] In 1540, Pedro Mexía's *Silva de Varia Lección* expressed the triumph in laymen's terms with an entire chapter devoted to explaining it: 'Qué cosa era y cómo se hazían los triumphos en Roma: y por qué cosa se otorgavan, y quantos triumphos uvo en ella, y qué cosa era la ovación' [What were triumphs and how were they made in Rome: and for what were they given,

---

16 Hörnqvist, *Machiavelli*, 162–164.
17 Francis Bacon, 'Of the true Greatnesse of Kingdomes and Estates' in *The Essayes or Counsels, Civill and Morall* (London: John Haviland, 1625), 167–186.
18 Remy Du Puys, *Les exèques et pompe funèbre… don Fernando Roy Catholique… en l'église Saincte Goule à Bruxelles* (Brussels, 1515). Quoted in Checa Cremades, *Carlos V*, 37 and 325.
19 Plutarch, *Morales de Plutarco: traduzidos de lengua griega en castellana*, trans. Diego Gracián (Salamanca: Alexandro de Canova, 1571), fol. 60v: 'tropheo era una memoria que ponían de alguna victoria con armas y otras cosas':
20 Barthélemy de Chasseneuz, *Catalogus gloriae mundi* (Venice: Vincentium Valgrissium, 1569; 1st ed. 1529), 5–7.

and how many triumphs were held there, and what was the ovation].[21] From the 1530s onward, many historical, political and religious texts used the concept of the triumph as a plot device or even as the structural backbone of the entire work. *Los Veinte Triunfos* by Vasco Díaz Tanco de Frexenal (1535), dedicated to twenty Spanish dukes, surveyed the politics of Charles V as a string of victory celebrations.[22]

As is known, the interest in triumphs became even more apparent after the discovery in 1546 of the Capitoline tablets that recorded the *Fasti Triumphales* held to honour Roman victors since the days of Romulus. The impact of the tablets was largely owing to the success of the Latin edition of the inscriptions published by Onofrio Panvinio in 1557; this was followed in 1571 by another edition of the 'De Triumpho' section, translated into Italian and illustrated with a print of a triumphal procession in four parts.[23] Panvinio wanted to clearly convey the connection between the Habsburgs and classical triumphs. Understanding the value of the classical image policy pursued by Charles V, the first edition of 1557, *Fasti et Triumphi Rom: A Romulo Rege Usque ad Carolum V*, portrayed the new emperor as a direct descendant of Romulus via an unbroken succession of Roman triumphs, in which he also shared thanks to his victories in Italy, Germany and Africa. The 1571 edition however, appropriately dedicated to his brother Ferdinand given the date, is especially interesting because of the emphasis on spoils in both the images and the text. The final section of the book is specifically devoted to *spoliis*, reviewing the fundamental classical sources and the most salient episodes of plunder reception in the history of Rome.[24] The prints, which attempted to reconstruct what Roman triumphal processions may have looked like, in the same line as Andrea Mantegna's earlier depictions, emphasised the chariots laden with items plundered after the battle. In keeping with classical sources, some chariots contained arms, breastplates, shields and standards, others carried sculptures and painted panels, and yet others were filled with raw gold and silver. These spoils also included slaves. One decade later, in 1586,

---

21 Pedro de Mexía, *Silva de varia lectión* (Seville: Hernando Díaz, 1570; 1st ed. 1540). For an explanation of the triumphal arch's different sections, see the first illustrations of Juan Calvete de la Estrella, *El felicissimo viaje del muy alto y muy poderoso principe don Phelippe* (Antwerp: Martin Nuyts, 1552), n.p.
22 Vasco Díaz Tanco de Frexenal, *Los veinte triunfos* (Madrid: Junta Técnica de Archivos, Bibliotecas y Museos, 1945).
23 Onofrio Panvinio, *Fasti et triumphi Rom: a Romulo rege usque ad Carolum V* (Venice: Iacobi Strada, 1557); and Onofrio Panvinio, *Comentario dell'vso, et ordine de' trionfi antichi* (Venice: Michele Tramezzino, 1571). On the sources of the prints, see William Stenhouse, 'Panvinio and descriptio: renditions of history and antiquity in the late renaissance', *Papers of the British School at Rome*, 80 (2012), 233–256. See also Jean-Louis Ferrary, *Onofrio Panvinio: et les antiquités romaines* (Rome: École Française de Rome, 1996), 26–38. On Panvinio's reception, see Starn and Partridge, *Arts of Power*, 159–160.
24 Panvinio, *Comentario*, fols. 5v–6r.

Franciscus Modius published his *Pandectae Triumphales*, addressed to the 'ordinem equestrem' of the Germanic empire. This text reinforced the connection between the triumphs of antiquity and the sixteenth-century Habsburgs by creating a compilation of triumphal celebrations from classical, medieval and modern times, which by then had spread to other parts of Europe, and intertwining interesting descriptions of the triumphal arches, columns, obelisks and pyramids of Rome with, for example, an inventory of the *spolia* that accompanied Archbishop Cisneros in his triumphal procession upon returning from Africa or a list of Charles V's various triumphal entries after his conquest of Tunis.[25]

Triumph, trophy and *spolia*

More recent academic literature has primarily assessed the classical *Fasti Triumphales* from the perspective of their impact on public festivities, whereas less attention has been given to the spoils brought to Rome, which were exhibited in these processions and later placed in temples or even the homes of the victors as treasures and mementos of their victory.[26] Yet classical texts and their humanistic reviews always attached great importance to plunder. The accounts of triumphs found in Livy, Plutarch, Varro and other historical sources regularly itemised the arms and riches that arrived with the troops, which were also represented on commemorative reliefs, and usually mentioned their deposit in Rome.[27] The *spolia optima*, the spoils which a Roman general stripped from the body of an enemy leader slain in single combat, was a theme used to legitimise military chiefs in the transition from republic to principate.[28] Pliny the Elder's *Naturalis Historia*

---

25 Franciscus Modius, *Pandectae triumphales, sive pomparum, et festorum ac solennium...* (Frankfurt: Sigismundi Feyerabend, 1586), fols. 26v–31r, 55r, 58v–63v. On Modius's reception, see J. R. Mulryne, 'War and chivalry in plays and shows at the time of Prince Henry Stuart', in *War, literature and the arts in sixteenth-century Europe*, eds. Margaret Shewring and J. R. Mulryne (New York: St. Martin's Press, 1989), 165–190.
26 One example of this trend, among others, can be found in Zaho, *Imago triumphalis*. In this book, spoils are essentially limited to the first chapter, which discusses ancient triumphs, but they are occasionally mentioned in later chapters on the Renaissance re-enactment of triumphs.
27 For an example of the humanistic review of Roman sources on *spolia*, see Robertus Valturius, *De re militari* (Paris: Christianum Wechelum, 1535), 382. See also Versnel, *Triumphus*, 95–96, 304–313; and Beard, *The Roman Triumph*, 175–177.
28 Harriet I. Flower, 'The tradition of the *spolia opima*: M. Claudius Marcellus and Augustus', *Classical Antiquity*, 19, 1 (2000), 36–64; S. J. Harrison, 'Augustus, the poets, and the *spolia opima*', *The Classical Quarterly* 39, 2 (1989), 408–414; and John W. Rich, 'Drusus and the *spolia opima*', *Classical Quarterly*, 49, 2 (1999), 544–555. See also Myrto Garani, 'Propertius' temple of Jupiter Feretrius and the *spolia opima* (4.10): a poem not to be read?', *L'Antiquité Classique*, 76 (2007), 99–117; and Jennifer Ingleheart, 'Propertius 4.10 and the end of the

recorded what happened to those spoils when the celebration ended, both whether they were stored in temples and on the Capitoline or displayed in the atria of noble houses alongside portraits of ancestors.[29] Pliny's words indicate a very telling preoccupation with the potential use of spoils as both social and political symbols.

The revival of these classical narratives about triumph acted on the pre-existing medieval tradition, reinforcing and more fully articulating how *spolia* were exhibited and interpreted. In the context of the war against Muslim enemies, who considered as they were as barbarians were likened to the foreign foes of the Romans, this practice was frequently replicated throughout Europe during the fifteenth, sixteenth and seventeenth centuries.[30] One example is the way in which the Medicis used Ottoman *spolia* in parades, churches and their own armoury.[31] In the particular case of Spain, the late fifteenth-century campaigns in the War of Granada had yielded numerous trophies that ended up in noble residences and many religious establishments.[32] The arrival of Spaniards in the Americas also

---

Aeneid: Augustus, the *spolia opima* and the right to remain silent', Greece & Rome, 54, 1 (2007), 61–81.

29 Pliny the Elder, *The Natural History of Pliny*, Trans. John Bostock and H. T. Riley (London: Henry G. Bohn, 1855), book 25, chapter 2.

30 Rome did not grant triumphs in civil wars. In early modern times, triumphs were awarded in all sorts of conflicts; even so, they were more frequent in wars against foreign enemies, and there was a clear tendency to highlight cultural and religious differences whenever possible. On this tendency, see the English triumphs over the Spanish Armada in Miller, *Roman triumphs*, 62–82.

31 Sean Nelson, 'Relics of Christian victory: the translation of Ottoman *spolia* in Grand Ducal Tuscany', in *The Grand Ducal Medici and the Levant: material culture, diplomacy, and imagery in the early modern Mediterranean*, eds. M. Caroscio and M. Arfaioli (Turnhout: Brepols, 2016), 75–84. On Archduke Ferdinand II's collection of Turkish *spolia*, see Barbara Karl, 'On the crossroads: objects from the Islamic world in Habsburg collections in the late sixteenth and early seventeenth centuries', *Ars Orientalis*, 42 (2012), 114–126 (esp. 122). For another similar example in Eastern Europe at a later date, see Adam Jasienski, 'A savage magnificence: Ottomanizing fashion and the politics of display in early modern East-Central Europe', *Muqarnas Online*, 31, 1 (2014), 173–205 (esp. 187–188). On the Lepanto trophies, see Stephen Hanß, *Lepanto als Ereignis: Dezentrierende Geschichte(n) der Seeschlacht von Lepanto (1571)* (Göttingen: V&R Unipress, 2017), I. See also Robyn Dora Radway, 'Misunderstanding Ottoman Europe: the material culture of the borderlands in renaissance depictions of the Ottoman world', in *Schilde des Spätmittelalters und der Frühen Neuzeit*, eds. Raphael Beuing and Wolfgang Augustyn (Munich: Dietmar Klinger Verlag, 2019), 377–386; Iván Szántó and Eötvös Loránd, 'Ottoman Wars and Safavid Arts in Hungary', in *War-booty: A Common European Heritage*, ed. Sofia Nestor (Stockholm: Royal Armoury, 2009), 127–137; and Matthias Pfaffenbichler, 'Die Türkischen Waffen in der Kunstkammer Rudolfs II', in *Rudolf II, Prague and the World*, eds. Lubomir Konecny et al. (Prague: Artefactum, 1998), 161–165.

32 See José Amador de los Ríos, *Trofeos militares de la Reconquista: estudio acerca de las enseñas musulmanas del Real Monasterio de las Huelgas (Burgos) y de la Catedral de Toledo* (Madrid: Fortanet, 1893). For a recent survey of Islamic trophies in early modern Spain, see Antonio Urquízar-Herrera, 'Islamic objects in the material culture of the Castilian nobility: trophies

Fig. 9.3. Detail of *spolia* (1). Onofrio Panvinio, *Comentario dell'vso, et ordine de' trionfi antichi*, Venice: Michele Tramezzino, 1571.

Fig. 9.4. Detail of *spolia* (2). Onofrio Panvinio, *Comentario dell'vso, et ordine de' trionfi antichi*, Venice: Michele Tramezzino, 1571.

brought new trophies, which were received in the spirit of this tradition, as exemplified by Hernán Cortés's shipments to the Spanish court and various religious establishments.[33] In this respect, analysing the impact of Charles V's European, American and African campaigns is particularly interesting, as it reveals the connection between the scope of the new conquests and the reformulation of classical narratives on *spolia*.[34]

In Maarten van Heemskerck's prints, *The Victories of Emperor Charles V*, spoils are prominently displayed in depictions of the victories over the French at Pavia and the Turks at Vienna, the conquest of Tunis, and the triumph of the Americas where we see, still in indigenous hands, the bows and arrows that would become the archetypical American trophy.[35] In the Vienna print, the image of Turkish weapons scattered on the ground recalls Jerónimo de Sempere's description of that moment: 'The field is strewn with wire shields / With scimitars, spears, precious garments, / With bodies, and heads, all over the ground / Of Turks, with bitter despair'.[36]

In this general context, it behoves us to recall the fact that the numerous objects related to these campaigns in the inventories of Charles V can be considered souvenirs of his victories and analysed in connection with the triumphal iconographic programmes and ceremonies of the court.[37] This relates to how such objects represented the empire's new boundaries and how they overlapped with the old mementos of peninsular history

---

and the negotiation of hybridity', in *Jews and Muslims Made Visible in Christian Iberia and Beyond, 14th to 18th centuries: another image*, eds. Borja Franco Llopis and Antonio Urquízar-Herrera (Leyden: Brill, 2019), 187–212. See also Roberto González Ramos, 'Treasures and collections in the Colegio Mayor de San Ildefonso and University of Alcalá: trophies, *spolia sancta* and museum', *Journal of the History of Collections*, 31, 1 (2019), 111–130 (esp. 114–115); and Borja Franco, 'Images of Islam in the ephemeral art of the Spanish Habsburgs: an initial approach', *Il Capitale Culturale* 6 (2017), 87–116 (esp. 90–93).

33 Hernán Cortés, *Cartas de relación*, ed. Ángel Delgado Gómez (Madrid: Castalia, 1993), 108–110, 128, 132, 138, 140, 149ff, 209–211, 230–233, 259, 429, 438, 458, 649–650. See also Antonio Urquízar-Herrera, 'The meaning of objects from the indies in early sixteenth-century Castilian households', in *Materiality: Making Spanish America*, ed. Jorge Rivas (Denver: Denver Art Museum, 2020).

34 Renate Pieper, *Die Vermittlung einer neuen Welt. Amerika Im Nachrichtennetz Des Habsburgischen Imperiums 1493–1598* (Mainz: Von Zabern, 2000).

35 See Urquízar-Herrera, 'The meaning of objects from the indies…'.

36 Sempere, *Primera parte*, Canto IV. 'Sembrado está de Escudos de arambre / De alfanges, lanças, ropas preciosas, / De cuerpos, y cabeças, todo el suelo / De Turcos, con amargo desconsuelo'.

37 See, for instance, Checa Cremades and others, eds., 'Los inventarios de Carlos V y la familia imperial' (Madrid: Fernando Villaverde Ediciones, 2010), I, 267–279, 314–317, 320–323, 328, 341 and 353. One particular example could be the trophies taken by Charles V from John Frederick I of Saxony and shared with the Duke of Alba, who participated in the elector's capture. See Stephen V. Grancsay, 'A Parade Shield of Charles V', *The Metropolitan Museum of Art Bulletin*, 8, 4 (1949), 122–132 (esp. 123).

that also appear in the inventories.³⁸ This overlap is evident, for instance, in literary accounts of the conquest of Tunis, where descriptions of taking spoils are a central element. We find this, for example, in Alonso de Sanabria's chronicle, which is particularly interesting because he took care to note that the sacking also recovered Christian plunder previously carried off by the Tunisians. There were trophies won from the French king, Saint Louis, and from the Spaniards at the Battle of Djerba, like the armour belonging to the Duke of Alba's father, which he claimed to have recovered upon entering Tunis with Charles V.³⁹

Another particularly interesting question related to 'Caroline' spoils is how the trophy-taking tradition established a framework of interpretation for new objects that arrived from the Americas. Documentation reveals that the idea of plunder, and especially the 'fifth part', a 20% tax due to Charles V, was one of Hernán Cortés's primary concerns during the conquest of Mexico. In Cortés's *Relaciones* and the earliest accounts of the conquest, the classical notion of the trophy was the best way to visibly convey the magnitude of the victory and formulate a solution to the unstable situation of Spanish commanders in the Americas. This circumstance made it necessary to construct narratives that would garner more support from the Crown and keep the memory of his achievements alive.⁴⁰ Finally, it is worth reflecting on the location of Charles V's American trophies during the interesting interval between his abdication and his death. On the one hand, there were those objects that the emperor took with him to Yuste, among them several feather bed covers; and on the other hand, there were the no-less-significant items that Philip II bought at the auction of his father's goods with the idea of eventually making them Crown property. These goods also included several of those feather bed covers from the Indies.⁴¹ A trophy's value lay in it's ability to endure as a physical reminder of the past. Decades after these events, about 1630–1640, the *Allegory on the Abdication of Emperor Charles V in Brussels* by Frans Francken II showed American feathers still serving that purpose, accompanied by other *spolia* intended to illustrate how the feats of Charles V were passed on to his successors.⁴²

---

38 See, for instance, the swords of Ferdinand III and the Catholic Monarchs and the so-called saddle of El Cid. Fernando Checa Cremades and others, eds., *Los inventarios*, 314–330.

39 See Alonso de Sanabria, *Comentarios y Guerra de Túnez*, Biblioteca Nacional de España, Mss 1937 (1535), fols. 156v–157r and 170r–173r. See also Gonzalo de Illescas, *Jornada de Carlos V a Túnez* (Madrid: Real Academia Española, 1804), 37; Duque de Berwick y de Alba, *Discursos leídos ante la Real Academia de la Historia en la recepción pública del...* (Madrid: Imprenta de Blass, 1919), 39; Checa Cremades, *Carlos V*, 190–193.

40 See Urquízar-Herrera, 'The meaning of objects from the indies...'.

41 Checa Cremades and others, eds., *Los inventarios*, 285, 314, 364, and 501–502.

42 Rijksmuseum, SK-A-112. See Víctor Mínguez, 'Sine fine: Dios, los Habsburgo y el traspaso de las insignias del poder en el Quinientos', *Libros de la Corte*, 1 (2014), 163–185.

In connection with these practices, it is interesting to note how sixteenth-century authors tried to distinguish between triumph, trophy and *spolia*, based on the idea that these three concepts, though related to each other and often used rather ambiguously, had different implications. For instance, the latter two, trophy and *spolia*, were material in nature and expected to stand the test of time. Something similar occurred when the term was applied to architectural elements seized from the vanquished and reused in the constructions of the victors, best exemplified by the Egyptian obelisks brought to classical Rome and given a Christian reinterpretation in the Renaissance.[43] Some texts, such as Robertus Valturius's military treatise,[44] were especially concerned with the value of trophies as permanent reminders, in contrast to the ephemeral nature of the pomp of triumphs, and told stories that identified the custom of exhibiting *spolia* in tree branches on the battlefield as the origin of the first trophies, which enjoyed enduring popularity in humanist literature and even found their way into early art theory.[45] The same idea was echoed in the dictionaries of various languages of the time, wherein the trophy was defined as a permanent memorial erected after a battle, from that improvised tree display to stone monuments or the emblems of victory placed at the feet of representations of the powerful.[46]

The distinctions between triumph, trophy and *spolia* were based on classical sources, but they also concerned what happened in the fifteenth and sixteenth centuries. A triumph typically entailed the display of trophies and spoils, but trophies and *spolia* could exist without a triumph. Trophies were normally based on *spolia* taken from the enemy, but they could also be arms, armour or jewellery which, again following the example of classical texts, the sovereign gave to his worthiest commanders. This was common practice in the sixteenth century. Charles V, according to his eulogist Francesco Sansovino, was generous to the captains who

---

43 Among the extensive literature on monumental *spolia*, see, for instance, Jaś Elsner, 'From the culture of *spolia* to the cult of relics: the arch of Constantine and the genesis of late antique forms', *Papers of the British School at Rome*, 68 (2000), 149–182. See also Valturius, De re militari, 372–376.
44 Valturius, *De re militari*, 351–383.
45 A few examples are found in Sempere, *Primera parte*, fol. 138r; and Leon Battista Alberti, *Los diez libros de Arquitectura de León Baptista Alberto* (Madrid: Alonso Gómez, 1582), 25–26. It is interesting to note that Sempere's commentaries on Charles V's triumphal arches at Aachen make a distinction between *trofeos* (trophies) and *despojos* (spoils). Sempere, Primera parte, Canto X.
46 See Francesco Alunno da Ferrara, *Le osservationi di .... sopra il Petrarca* (Venice: Paolo Gherardo, 1550), fols. 446v and 282r–482r; Sebastián de Covarrubias, *Tesoro de la lengua castellana, o española* (Madrid: Luis Sánchez, 1611), fols. 312v and II, 55r–v; and Aimar de Ranconnet, *Thresor de la langue Françoyse, tant ancienne que moderne* (Paris: David Douceur, 1606), 199, 644, 646.

had served him in war,[47] and historical sources, French-language ones included, recall the gold chains he presented to his subordinates as a classical token of victory on the battlefield.[48] Even his own arms and armour could be exhibited 'puestas como tropheos' [placed as trophies], as Calvete de Estrella described the military accoutrements of Charles V displayed on his catafalque in Valladolid.[49] Shields played a very important part in this tradition. Pliny identified the representations painted on the shields of victors, later exhibited as trophies, as one of the earliest instances of painting.[50] To a certain extent, this idea survived into the sixteenth century,[51] and as a result it became customary to produce parade shields with allegorical representations commemorating a victory. Several of these shields were directly related to Charles V, such as those in the Royal Armoury of Madrid known as the shields of the conquest of the Americas and the conquest of Africa, gifts from the Duke of Mantua after the conquest of Tunis; or the shield commemorating the triumph at Mühlberg, now in the Metropolitan Museum in New York, formerly owned by the German House of Waldburg, who likely received it as a gift from the Habsburgs.[52] This custom of exhibiting the arms and armour of a victor as a sign of martial virtue became an archetype imitated in numerous representations and, over time, practically an ornamental pattern. Archduke Ferdinand II's *Heldenrüstkammer* in the Schloss Ambras armoury, with its collection of portraits of great generals of his time with their arms and armour, is a quintessential example.[53] The publication of prints with images and objects from this armoury, amid ornamental decorations of *spolia*, was rooted in the commemorative traditions that the Habsburgs had been forging since the days of Maximilian I, which linked triumphs

---

47 'Era largo co Capitani che lo avecano servito alla guerra'. *Francesco Sansovino, Il simolacro di Carlo Quinto Imperadore* (Venice: Francesco Franceschini, 1567), fol. 24v.

48 See, for instance, the chains presented to the Hungarian captains in Luis de Ávila y Zúñiga, *Comentario...*, fol. 100v. See also François de la Noue, *Discours politiques et militaires* ([n.p.], 1612), 302–303.

49 Juan Cristóbal Calvete de la Estrella, *El tumulo Imperial: adornado de historias y letreros y epitaphios en prosa y verso Latino* (Valladolid: Francisco Fernandez de Cordova, 1559), fol. 3v. See also the *spolia* on the Mexican funerary monument in Francisco Cervantes de Salazar, *Túmulo imperial de la gran ciudad de México* (Mexico City: Antonio de Espinosa, 1560). See also Checa Cremades, *Carlos V*, 307–338.

50 Pliny, *The Natural History*, book 35, chapter 3.

51 See, among many others, David du Rivault de Flurance, *Les états, esquels ils est discorou du prince, du noble, et du tiers estat* (Lyon: B. Rigaud, 1596), 300; and Nikolaus Reusner, *Icones sive imagines vivae, literis Cl. Virorum, Italiae, Graeciae, Germaniae, Galliae, Angliae, Ungariae* (Basel: Conr. Valdkrich, 1589), n.p. (preface).

52 Grancsay, 'A Parade Shield', 127–131.

53 See Elisabeth Scheicher, 'Historiography and display: the Heldenrüstkammer of Archduke Ferdinand II in Schloss Ambras', *Journal of the History of Collections* 2, 1 (1990), 69–79.

with arms and armour.⁵⁴ Ferdinand II revised these traditions, applying a more classical perspective. The wider impact of this collection and its publication is evidenced by the fact that, for the families included, having ancestors whose arms and armour appeared among the trophies in that gallery was a badge of honour.⁵⁵

Taking trophies and *spolia* was an act associated not only with political legitimisation but also with the justification of social distinction and the display of symbols of recognition. This is confirmed by the fact that the classical conception of *spolia*—particularly Pliny's emphasis on their conservation in temples and private atria—had a significant impact on debates around social theory. Treatises on nobility and texts for the education of nobles provide clear proof of the link between lineage and the Plinian veneration for 'spoils of the enemy' interspersed with family portraits.⁵⁶

For example, in the *Memorial de Cosas Notables* written by Íñigo López de Mendoza, Duke of El Infantado, the remembrance of Rome's victories was a matter of state (pertaining to the temple of Jupiter), but it also had to do with the public visibility of noble families which, like his in Castile, had personified the military experience of the republic, the empire or, in his case, the Crown.⁵⁷ The ornamental programme in the hall of ancestors at his Guadalajara palace, on the first floor beside the entrance, was not far removed from the spirit of Pliny's atria. As the Count of Tendilla's explanation of the hall in Luis Zapata's *Carlo Famoso* clarified, the coats of

---

54 Larry Silver, *Marketing Maximilian: the visual ideology of a holy Roman emperor* (Princeton, NJ: Princeton University Press, 2008), 98–100 and 147–168. See also Chassica Kirchhoff, 'Memories in steel and paper: a spectacular armor and its depictions in early modern Augsburg', *MEMO: Medieval & Early Modern Material Culture Online*, 4 (2019), 26–57 (esp. 47–50). On the connections between Maximilian I's publications and Charles V's print and paper programmes, see Jesús F. Pascual 'Propaganda de papel: libros, dibujos y estampas de Maximiliano I a Carlos V', in *Imbricaciones: paradigmas, modelos y materialidad de las artes en la Europa Habsbúrgica*, eds. Matteo Mancini and Álvaro Pascual (Madrid: Sílex, 2019), 190–198.
55 'Ferdinand Archiduc d'Austriche, fils de l'Empereur Ferdinand I, conserve soigneusement en son Arsenal non seulement le Pourtrait, mais le Heaume, la Cuirace, les Brassards, & Gantelets, & l'Espée mesme du Colonel de Tassis'. [Ferdinand Archduke of Austria, son of Emperor Ferdinand I, carefully preserves in his armoury not only the portrait but also the helm, breastplate, vambraces & gauntlets & even the sword of the Colonel of Tassis.] Jules Chifflet, *Les marques d'honneur de la maison de Tassis* (Antwerp: Balthasar Moretus, 1645), 145.
56 Pliny, *The Natural History*, book 35, chapter 2. See also Antonio Urquízar-Herrera, 'Teoría de la magnificencia y teoría de las señales en el pensamiento nobiliario español del siglo XVI', *Ars Longa*, 23 (2014), 93–112; and Antonio Urquízar-Herrera; 'Making invisible things visible and palpable: visual marks of nobility in early modern French social theory and the embodiment of social estates in collections, 1550–1650', *Word & Image*, 31, 3 (2015), 386–397.
57 Íñigo López de Mendoza, Duke of El Infantado, *Memorial de cosas notables* (Guadalajara: Pedro de Robles and Francisco de Cormellas, 1564), 35.

Fig. 9.5. Portrait of *Johann Baptista de Tassis* from Jakob Schrenck von Notzing, *Augustissimorum Imperatorum ... verissimae imagines ... quorum arma, aut integra, aut horum partes ... heroica facinora patrarunt ...*, Innsbruck: Johannes Agricola, 1601.

arms of the Castilian nobility that decorated it were viewed as narratives of martial events and collections of *spolia*.[58] This relationship between spoils, their representation and the origin of coats of arms is an interesting line of rescarch that brings us closer to the field of emblem studies.[59]

Throughout Europe, the debate on whether nobility was linked to blood and personal virtue found a fundamental argument in the display of trophies and *spolia*.[60] The point of departure was Pliny's texts, which allowed François de L'Alouëte, like many other authors, to conclude that the nobility most worthy of respect and honour was that which, 'chargée de vieux trophees' [laden with old trophies], maintained its own virtues.[61] Trophies educated descendants and thus ensured the continuation of the family's splendour. This idea is expressed in the dedication of the print series *The Victories of Emperor Charles V* to Philip II,[62] and was repeated throughout the sixteenth century in all manner of family histories and aristocratic biographies, which persistently emphasised the value of the old spoils won in battles, and of their depictions in portraits, tombs and paintings to be emulated by future generations. Juan Calvete de Estrella's description of trophies in his encomium of the Duke of Alba, though too long to include here, is well worth reading. The flags and arms won from the enemy and taken to his palace in Alba de Tormes were interpreted

---

58 Luis de Zapata, *Carlo Famoso* (Valencia: Juan Mey, 1566), fol. 136r y. See also Jesús Carrillo and Felipe Pereda Espeso, 'El caballero: identidad e imagen en la España imperial' in *Carlos V. Las armas y las letras*, eds. Fernando Marías and Felipe Pereda (Madrid: Sociedad Estatal para la Conmemoración de los Centenarios de Felipe II y Carlos V, 2000), 183–200 (esp. 193).

59 Hans Belting has highlighted the relationship between coats of arms and portraits as means of representing the genealogical body of a noble lineage. According to him, the advent of the modern portrait introduced a new function of representation of the body that had to be understood in relation to the tradition of symbols of the body which coats of arms had long incorporated. This heraldic interpretation of portraits was characteristic of the nobility, from which the bourgeois portrait would gradually detach itself. Hans Belting, *An anthropology of images: picture, medium, body* (Princeton, NJ: Princeton University Press, 2011), 62–83. See also Mason Tung, 'From heraldry to emblem: a study of Peacham's use of heraldic arms in Minerva Britanna', *Word & Image*, 3, 1 (1987), 86–93. For an interesting example of the survival into the early modern era of the connection between the classical narrative of *spolia* and coats of arms, see Marc de Vulson de la Colombiére, *La science heroique, traitant de la noblesse, et de l'origine des armes, de leurs blasons, et symboles...* (Paris: Sebastien Cramoisy, 1649), 13–24.

60 See, among others, Du Rivault de Flurance, *Les états*, 267, and 296–297; Giovambattista Nenna, *Il Nennio: nel quale si ragiona di nobiltá* (Venice: Andrea Valvassore & Fratello, 1542), 102; Fray Juan Benito Guardiola, *Tratado de nobleza, y de los títulos y ditados que oy día tienen los varones claros y grandes de España* (Madrid: Viuda de Alonso Gomez, 1591), fol. 48r, 103v; Francisco de Rades y Andrada, *Tratado qué cossa es nobleça, hijo Dalgo, Ynfançon y cavallero*, Biblioteca Nacional, Mss. 8631 (16th century), fol. 93r.

61 François de L'Alouëte, *Traité des nobles et des vertus dont ils sont formés...* (Paris: Robert le Manier, 1597), fols. 48v–49r.

62 See Rosier, 'The Victories of Charles V...', 24.

in light of his lineage and personal virtues, proving that the duke had managed to surpass the deeds of his forebears.⁶³

The notion of the two versions of the classical trophy—as plunder taken from the enemy and as a memento or token of victory bestowed by a sovereign—is an important framework of interpretation that contributes to a much better understanding of objects like chains, rings and, more obviously, arms and armour⁶⁴ which appear in depictions, literary descriptions and inventories of assets from the early modern era. We also cannot forget that enslaving people, and listing 'slaves' as portable assets in inventories, had been among the most visible spoils since antiquity. Many texts read at court, from chivalric literature to historical accounts, confirmed that objects could be read as insignia of the victors. Valturius, for example, devoted a chapter of his treatise to 'triumphantium insignia & ornatus', and explained that these tokens of triumph could be public or private and passed down from generation to generation.⁶⁵ In this context, the fact that Gonzalo Fernández de Córdoba was habitually depicted with a chain on his chest can be linked to Paolo Giovio's account of the moment this token was handed over by the defeated Louis XII of France, and to the abundant classical references about the significance of such gifts.⁶⁶ In another field, it is also interesting to note the influence of the theoretical framework of

---

63 Juan Cristóbal Calvete de Estrella, Encomium *ad excellentissimum at magnanimum principem Ferdinandum Alvarum de Toletum Albae ducem* (Antwerp: Christophe Plantin, 1573), 20–23. On this text, see Manuel Antonio Díaz Gito, 'El *encomio del duque de Alba* de Calvete de Estrella: entre la apología y el desagravio', *Criticón*, 132 (2018), 33–49. See also Antonio Sánchez Jiménez, 'La Arcadia (1598) de Lope de Vega y los frescos del palacio del Gran Duque de Alba', in *El duque de Medina Sidonia: mecenazgo y renovación estética*, eds. José Manuel Rico García and Pedro Ruiz Pérez (Huelva: Universidad de Huelva, 2015), 179–188; and Checa Cremades, *Carlos V*, 263–269. See also Paolo Giovio, *Elogios o vidas breves, de los caballeros antiguos y modernos, illustres en valor de guerra que estan al vivo pintados en el Museo de Paulo Iovio* (Granada: Hugo de Mena, 1568), fol. 216r. On the fifteenth-century trophies of the House of Alba, see Joaquín Yarza Luaces, *La nobleza ante el rey: los grandes linajes castellanos y el arte en el siglo XV* (Madrid: Ediciones El Viso, 2003).

64 Among the many sources on the early modern symbolic interpretation of weapons, chivalric literature is particularly interesting. In connection with the court of Charles V, see, for instance, Olivier de la Marche, *El cavallero determinado*, trans. Hernando de Acuña (Antwerp: 1555), fol. 81v. The poem entitled *La contienda de Áyax Telamonio y de Ulises sobre las armas de Aquiles*, also by Hernando de Acuña, is quite illustrative. See Ramón Mateo Mateo, 'Sobre el tema de las armas y las letras en la poesía narrativa de Hernando de Acuña', *Castilla: Estudios de literatura*, 6–7 (1983–1984), 73–100; and Checa Cremades, *Carlos V*, 20. Trophy narratives were also constructed around artillery seized from the enemy. On the German artillery pieces placed in the castle of Pavia as trophies ('en señal de enterna memoria de la victoria y triumpho' [as an eternal reminder of victory and triumph]), see Calvete de la Estrella, *El felicissimo viaje...*, fol. 20r. See also Juan Cristóbal Calvete de Estrella, *De aphrodisio expugnato, quod vulgo Aphricam vocant, commentarius* (Antwerp: Martinum Nutium, 1551), fols.

65 Valturius, *De re militari*, 355–356. See also 365–369.

66 Giovio, *Elogios o vidas breves...*, fol. 120r.

the trophy on the perception of works of art. Classical sources had already highlighted that the *spolia* paraded in Rome included 'many images of metal and marble, and painted panels' and, in the sixteenth century, Panvinio's book included chariots of loot containing sculptures and paintings taken from the holy places of the vanquished to become ornaments and tokens of victory in Roman temples and private residences.[67] This idea, already present in Renaissance campaigns,[68] permeated the entire early modern era reaching its peak in the nineteenth century when Napoleonic troops carried the art they had plundered from Italy and Spain to Paris. This event, normally viewed as signalling the dawn of the contemporary era, is also a summary of the two ideas of the artwork and the trophy, ideas that were defined in the age of humanism.[69]

---

67 Lucius Annaeus Florus, *Compendio de las catorze décadas de Tito Livio Paduano…* (Argentina: Agustín Frisio, 1550), decade 6, book 9, fol. 90r–v. Panvinio, Comentario, n.p. See also Emily Gowers, 'Augustus and "Syracuse"', *The Journal of Roman Studies*, 100 (2010), 69–87 (esp. 80).

68 See, for instance, Jerónimo de Sempere's description of the statues in the castle of Milan. Sempere, Primera parte, fol. 20r.

69 See Cecil Gould, *Trophy of conquest: The Musée Napoléon and the creation of the Louvre* (London: Faber and Faber, 1965). See also Antonio Urquízar-Herrera, 'El coleccionismo en la formación de la conciencia moderna del arte: perspectivas metodológicas', in *Conflictes bèl·lics, espoliacions, col·leccions*, ed. Inmaculada Socías Batet (Barcelona: Universitat de Barcelona, 2009), 169–182.

CHRISTIAN BEAUFORT-SPONTIN

The *Armamentarium Heroicum* of Archduke Ferdinand of Tyrol

Archduke Ferdinand of Tyrol stands out among the great European collectors of the sixteenth and seventeenth centuries for his love of experimentation and, above all, his originality. He left behind collections that remain invaluable for historical research to this day, even aside from their aesthetic appeal.[1]

Collections were ravenously compiled at nearly every royal court in Europe in the sixteenth century. Collecting had become vogue, and the genteel man did so out of personal pleasure and to entertain educated and sensible guests. Cabinets of art and curiosities were more popular north of the Alps, but libraries were amassed, and coins, paintings and sculptures collected everywhere. Archduke Ferdinand (1529–1595), second son of Emperor Ferdinand I and nephew of Emperor Charles V, left behind a collection of considerable quality and quantity, which was certainly above average yet still overshadowed by truly large collections. The Archduke must have known this, given his knowledge of the rich collections held by his relatives—for example, those of Emperor Rudolf II, King Philip II of Spain, the Duke of Bavaria, the Houses of Gonzaga, d'Este, Medici, and so on—who collected paintings by great masters. He did not, however, strive to create such a gallery of works. Perhaps he preferred to allocate available funds for collecting in the areas of his initial interests, primarily the worship and commemoration of famous individuals.[2]

---

1 Thomas, Bruno (ed.), *Die Heldenrüstkammer (Armamentarium Heroicum) Erzherzog Ferdinands II auf Schloß Ambras bei Innsbruck: Faksimiledruck der lateinischen und der deutschen Ausgabe des Kupferstich Bildinventars von 1601 bzw. 1603* [Facsimile of the Latin and German editions of the collection of copper engravings from 1601 and 1603 respectively] (Osnabrück, 1981).

2 Hirn, Joseph, *Erzherzog Ferdinand II von Tirol: Geschichte seiner Regierung und seiner Länder*, vol. II, (Innsbruck, 1888); Beaufort-Spontin, Christian, 'Die "Ehrliche Gesellschaft"

Christian Beaufort-Spontin • Kunsthistorisches Museum, Vienna

This choice secured his place as a collector of great renown who tapped into an entirely new field of collecting with his 'Heroes' Armoury', the *Atrium Heroicum*, which contained the armour and weapons of all those monarchs and men of war who had performed particularly special feats during wartime in the Archduke's century and the century prior. The eligible armour and equipment, in memoriam of their wearers, were worn during great historical events. The Archduke also planned for a monumental publication, the *Armamentarium Heroicum*, to serve as an eternal memorial to the honourable men acknowledged in his collection.

Mounted atop life-size figures, the armour stood close together in a row on wooden pedestals in timbered niches. These armoured 'heroes' thus looked down at the viewer with an eerie sense of being alive. The pedestals supported small portraits with inscriptions which documented the lives of the portraits' models. The name given these portraits by the Archduke reflects how he perceived them to be an 'the Honourable Society', 'genteel' in the understanding of the time.

The earliest and most informative record of this collection comes from the report of Venetian messengers Zuan Michiel and Lunardo Donado, who visited Archduke Ferdinand on 11 September 1577 to pay him the republic's respects on the passing of Emperor Maximilian II (10 December 1576), the Archduke's older brother. During the messengers' visit to Schloss Ambras, they wrote:

> two beautiful collections of weaponry, one of which can arm 1000 men if needed and is very well preserved; the other of which only serves as adornment and compiles the personal armour and weaponry of various kings, princes, or distinguished figures who fought on land or sea during wartime. Therefore, that of Your Majesty was coveted, as well as those of the two senators Barbarigo and Bragadin which will be shown in this hall together with the other suits of armour, like trophies and with their eulogy below. A book about them is to be composed and printed. This work (please excuse me, illustrious sirs) could also provide a great impetus to honour our meritorious citizens and prevent that they remain without a public recognition and fall into oblivion, because if foreign rulers, to which these citizens are not connected, are

---

erzherzog Ferdinands von Österreich: Die originellste Sammlung des 16. Jahrhunderts?', in: Hans Ottomeyer (ed.), *Das Exponat als historisches Zeugnis: Präsentationsformen politischer Ikonographie*, Deutsches Historisches Museum Berlin, (Dresden, 2010), 121–130; Gamber, Ortwin, 'Erzherzog Ferdinand und die Ambraser Rüstkammer', in: E. Scheicher (ed.), *Führer durch das Kunsthistorische Museum: Die Rüstkammern, Sammlungen Schloß Ambras*, 30 (Wien, 1981), 24–32.

honoured and immortalised with texts and statues, what shouldn't we do?[3]

Ferdinand's collection in 1577 must have been sufficiently impressive for the two Venetian diplomats to be overwhelmingly impressed by it, as this report recounts. They were also impressed by the Archduke's plan to announce his collection in an illustrated catalogue.

The Archduke's personal secretary, Jakob Schrenk von Notzing, oversaw the preparation of the catalogue. Notzing's letter of 7 October 1591, written to the renowned humanist Heinrich von Rantzau, clarifies the motivations and intents of this highly unusual field of collection. Notzing writes that, fourteen years prior, in 1577, the Archduke embarked on a new and previously unattempted undertaking of such a manner that he would have no competition among the great collectors of Europe. He wished to collect weaponry that monarchs and men of war had taken into battle, and only those who achieved fame as model rulers would be included in the collection. Two years later, in 1579, the Archduke appointed Notzing to compile and arrange this collection. Ferdinand must have begun his collection earlier, perhaps as early as during his governorship of the Lands of the Bohemian Crown (1547–1567), but certainly by 1575, when he asked his brother-in-law Francesco de Medici for the armour of Cosimo I. He had conducted the acquisition correspondence with agents and owners or their heirs, dispersed across the continent from Spain and Portugal to Turkey, from France to Lithuania, from Denmark to southern Italy. In addition, he commissioned images and biographies for each set of armour.

The sole requirement to be eligible for the *Atrium Heroicum* was to have provided outstanding services, meaning the wearers of the armour had been 'heroes'—from the Emperor down to people of the most modest means who became militarily significant commanders and men of war, regardless of whether or not their prowess had been directed in the service of, or against, the royal house.

The 'collection catalogue' contains 125 full-body images of heroes. These are primarily friends and foes from the Habsburgs' conquests, both

---

3 Beaufort-Spontin, 121–130. '… Hai doi bellissime armarie; l'una per utilità, da poter armare in un bisogno, mille homeni, et più, molto ben tenuta; l'altra per ornamento; nella quale procura di hauere l'armature proprie di qualunque Rè, ò principe, ò persone più segnalate, che sian state nelle guerre, et trouatisi nelle giornate ò maritime, ò terrestre; come ne ricerò quelle di V. Serta, et di quelli doi senatori, Barbarigo, et Bragadino, che scriuessimo, per dricciarle in quella sala, insieme con le altre, come trofei, con li suoi elogii, sotto ciascuna; delle quali ne fà un libro, da esser poi messo alla stampa. Quello, che (perdoninmi questi signori IIImi.) doueria esser loro un gran stimolo, di no permetter, che resti senza alcuna publica dimo-stratione, come morta, et estinta la memoria di cosi ualorosi, et benemeriti suoi cittadini, che se principi esterni, à quali essi cittadini non appartengono, procurano et con scritti, et con statue, non solo d'illustrarli, ma mantenerli eterni, et immortali, che doueressimo far noi?…'

in the Archduke's time and the preceding century: against France, against Turkey, Tunis, and Algiers, against the Netherlands and the Protestants (the Schmalkaldic War in particular). Also included were persons involved in battles for supremacy in the Italian territories—Milan, Savoy, Mantua, Parma, Tuscany, Naples, Sicily, and Venice and the Papal States among them.[4] The heroes were arranged by social rank, starting with emperors and kings, to princes, archdukes, lords and knights.[5]

It was not always easy to obtain the desired armour and weapons. In some cases, such as the 'Skanderbeg relics', the correspondence detailing the hoped-for acquisition of the collection lasted 10 years. Diplomatic representatives, agents and mediators across Europe were involved in the Archduke's project. Ferdinand ordered one delegate, sent to Muscovy, not to spare any expense in acquiring the armour of the Grand Dukes of Moscow, as he assumed that a high price could be expected from 'this barbaric, greedy people'. Requests to descendants were often successful as it gradually became more honourable to be represented in the *Atrium Heroicum*. Also, the Archduke promised two copies of the future *Armamentarium Heroicum* to his donors.

Ferdinand worked especially hard to obtain a particular set of Habsburg armour, namely that of Charles V from the victorious Battle of Mühlberg, but his son Philip II refused out of respect and piety and did not give the armour away. Instead, in 1585, Ferdinand obtained the cuirassier's armour that Charles V wore in the campaign against Wilhelm of Jülich, Kleve, and Berg (today in Vienna, KHM, HJRK A 546). In March 1572, Philip II donated his magnificent knight's armour (Vienna, KHM, HJRK A 547) 'decorated with broad lines of engravings' (*de sus anchas fajas*), the main component of which is located in the Real Armeria (A 189 – A 216). In 1576 the imperial delegate in Madrid, Hans Khevenhüller, received the cuirassier's armour of the Duke of Alba (Vienna, KHM, HJRK A 420), worn in the Schmalkaldic War in 1546/47. Other Spanish heroes are also represented in the *Atrium Heroicum*, including King Ferdinand of Aragon (Vienna, KHM, HJRK A 5), Antonio de Leyva, Prince of Ascoli (Vienna, KHM, HJRK A 500), Don Juan de Austria (Vienna, KHM, HJRK A 1048), and Alessandro Farnese (Vienna, KHM, HJRK A 1117).[6]

A particularly obvious example of the collection's criteria can be found in the acquisition of the cuirassier's armour of Alessandro Farnese, Duke

---

4 Fiedler, Joseph von, ed., *Fontes rerum Austriacarum, II: Relationen venezianischer Botschafter über Deutschland und Österreich im 16. Jahrhundert*, (Vienna: Hof- und Staatsdruckerei, 1870).

5 Auer Alfred, 'Das Inventarium der Ambraser Sammlungen aus dem Jahre 1621, I. Teil: Die Rüstkammern', in: *Jahrbuch der Kunsthistorischen Sammlungen in Wien*, 80 (1984), I–CXXI.

6 Küster, Thomas, 'Dieses heroische Theatrum: Die Heldenrüstkammer von Schloß Ambras', in: Sabine Haag and Veronika Sandbichler (eds.) *Ferdinand II: 450 Jahre Tiroler Landesfürst* (Innsbruck, 2017), 83–87, 234–237.

of Parma and Piacenza (1545–1592), a modest set of functional armour found on plate 59 of the catalogue. Ferdinand had tried since 1578 to obtain the armour and a portrait of the famous commander and when he finally received it in 1590, he expressed his gratitude in writing. Along with the simple cuirassier's armour, Farnese also promised to send Ferdinand a set of decorative armour for man and horse. He later did so, but it was not admitted into the *Atrium Heroicum*, as it was a precious set of ornamental armour (Vienna, KHM, HJRK A 1132, A 1153). Of course, the *Armamentarium* could not want for Ferdinand's own representation.[7] In commemoration of his greatest heroic feat, he selected a modest set of armour that he had worn in the successful campaign against the Ottomans in Hungary in 1556 (Vienna, KHM, HJRK A 767). On plate 47, he is positioned in the printed copperplate work between Cosimo I Medici (plate 46) and Ottavio Farnese (plate 48).

Raised in line with the ideal of a *uomo perfetto* [perfect man], Archduke Ferdinand was undoubtedly a highly cultured man with a wealth of contemporary knowledge. His interest in extraordinary people was entirely due to the humanistic perspective adopted by the educated class during the Renaissance.[8] The outstanding enterprise or special intellectual feat achieved through this new and modern sentiment, by which the armoured hero could be compared to the saints and martyrs, was important. The memento of a hero—a celebrity—could thus be honoured as if it were a saint's relic. This form of royal hero worship was by no means new, although previously, as with Emperor Maximilian I, it had always taken a dynastic and genealogical approach, constantly striving to emphasise the splendour and size of each hero's house.

From his youth, Ferdinand had a great interest in portraits of historically significant people, well beyond the interest in his own dynasty. He collected the portraits of all the houses ruling in Europe at that time, including the Turkish sultans and dignitaries of the Catholic Church. His systematically-arranged portrait gallery of famous people was based on similar models found in Italy. Series of images representing 'Neuf Preux' [Nine Worthies] like the *uomini illustri* [illustrious men], including ancient heroes and genealogical ancestral halls, had been popular in Italy since the early Renaissance, but always represented in a two-dimensional form, either painting, graphic art or, ideally, coins and medallions. Ferdinand's interest in the *viri illustres* [illustrious men] may thus have begun with his acquisition of a painted portrait. In any event, the Archduke already possessed a great number of portraits, certainly not limited to commanders,

---

7 Lhotsky, Alphons, *Festschrift des Kunsthistorischen Museums zur Feier des fünfzigjährigen Bestandes*, vol. 1 (Vienna, 1941–1945), 179–202.
8 Luchner, Laurin, *Denkmal eines Renaissancefürsten: Versuch einer Rekonstruktion des Ambraser Museums von 1583* (Wien, 1958).

before finally settling in Tyrol in 1567. This small, straightforward, manageable gallery of paintings, the formats of which were reduced multiple times for space reasons, until he ultimately decided on a size approaching that of a postcard (13.5 x 10.5 cm), a size which still remains a highly important iconographic source for identifying portraits. To his petitions to copy portraits inaccessible to him, he attached postcard-sized sheets of paper as a template. The Archduke strove to obtain these portraits with the same energy he invested in acquiring suits of armour. He often wished to obtain both the portrait and armour, though it was easier to get the portraits, since these were primarily copies. Among the artists he commissioned for this purpose were Lukas Cranach the Younger, who copied portraits of members of the Saxon Dynasty; Caio Cesare Curzio, who worked for the Archduke in Genoa; Giovanni Battista Cavagna in Rome; the younger Bronzino in Urbino; and Hans Schöpfer in Bavaria. His personal royal artists Francesco Terzio, Pietro Rosa, Heinrich Teufl, Anton Waiss and others also painted portraits. As occurred with the armour, everyone who could help in this endeavour did so: relatives, diplomats, officials and others were all engaged in building the collection. Even the imperial tax collector Zacharias Geizkofler in Augsburg provided the Archduke with portraits of women.[9]

Ferdinand was influenced by Maximilian I to take a dynastic approach to Habsburg portraits and in this way he contributed to the largest possible collection of portraits of that house. There was also a very rich collection of portraits of the vast dynasty of the House of Gonzaga of Mantua, to whom the Habsburgs were related by marriage. Ferdinand's interest concentrated on individuals. He limited himself to the direct line of the Saxon ruling monarchs, and his collection of portraits of the Ottoman sultans is particularly notable. He collected monarchs and commanders of every class who had performed considerable feats in any given field. When acquiring portraits of contemporaries, the Archduke highly valued iconographical integrity and sought out certified examples from historical individuals. Undoubtedly the most famous source was the portrait collection of Paolo Giovio (1483–1552). The great historian and humanist started compiling this collection in 1536 and exhibited it in his palace on Lake Como. Nearly 400 portraits of statesmen, commanders, jurists, scholars, literati and artists were represented in it. Ferdinand verifiably had some portraits copied from Giovio's paintings. The resulting collection in Schloss Ambras ultimately contained 1,077 portraits that varied widely in quality. Some of these small portraits remain to this day as the only preserved—or the only

---

9 Ladner, Gerhart B., *Die Porträtsammlung des Erzherzogs Ferdinand von Tirol*, (Kunsthistorisches Museum, Wien, 1932); Schütz, Karl, 'Die Portraitsammlung Erzherzog Ferdinands von Tirol und ihr Verhältnis zu Paolo Giovio: Ein Berich zur Forschungslage', in: *Il Ritratto Antico Illustrato: Rivista di Documentazione e Critica*, I, 1984, 54–61.

reliable—visual record of their sitters. England is not represented in the collection, although France was, until Napoleon removed the portraits and armour of Frenchmen and took them to France.

Paolo Giovio would also play an important role in the *Atrium Heroicum*; he dedicated the *Elogia Virorum Bellica Virtute Illustrium*, published in 1551, to the Archduke's father, King Ferdinand I. This undoubtedly provided a model concerning the selection of the heroes, their portraits and the events of their lives, which Notzing added to the illustrations in his catalogue. Von Notzing also referred to other publications of this type, such as Francesco Sansovino's *L'historia di Casa Orsina*.[10] Indeed, there was an immediate predecessor with regard to the content of the *Atrium Heroicum*. The scholar Heinrich von Rantzau (1526–1598) assembled a series of portraits of significant commanders at his Breitenburg Castle, and each painting bore a distich with a brief explanation. The sets of armour of some renowned lords were to be seen in Rantzau's armoury, as recounted in Georg Kruse's description of the castle from 1569. By 1593, the *Atrium Heroicum* contained 119 important names, which Ferdinand published in a printed *Verzaichnuß* [Index].[11] He thus documented the successful development of his project, how he encouraged donors, and how the publication of his volume of plates was prepared.

There was apparently great urgency to accomplish the catalogue project upon the Archduke's death. The admission of 28 eligible heroes into the work was declined in the first illustrated edition.[12] The question arises as to whether Ferdinand may have attached portrait busts to the figures wearing the armour, either cut from wood or modelled out of papier-mâché, as described in the inventory of the sets of armour in his other armouries and of which three have even been preserved.

As if in a museum, Ferdinand's numerous, at times quite valuable, sets of armour and weaponry from his illustrious governorship in Bohemia, were installed in the 'Full-body Armoury' in an adjacent hall. Here the armour for men and steeds were arranged in two rows on naturalistic figures of men and horses. These included luxuriously sewn festival attire, as well as tournament and wartime armour. Hanging from the ceiling were flags, colourful attire for horses and glorious textiles. Ferdinand presented

---

10 Sansovino, Francesco, *L'Historia di Casa Orsina . . . . Con quattro libri degli uomini illustri dagla famiglia del Cardinale...* (Venice, 1565).
11 *Verzaichnuß der Roemischen Kayser, Koenig, Fürsten, Graffen, Herren und vom Adel, wellicher Leibharnisch unnd Rüstungen, zum thail ganz, und zum. thail Stuckweiß, so wider den Feind gebraucht, inn des ....Herrn Ferdinanden, Ertzhertzogen zu Osterreich ...in Schloß Ombraß bey Innßprugg, zu ainer ewigen Gedaechtnuß, auff behalten und gesehen werden. Biß auf den vierdten September, Anno M.D.XCIII. Gerruckt zu Ynßprugg bey Joanni Paur*
12 Schrenck von Notzing, Jacob, *Der aller Durchleuchtigsten und Grossmächtigen Kaiser... Köningen und Ertzhertzogen ... Fürststen warhafftige Bildnussen und kurtze Beschriebungen* (Innsbruck, 1603).

himself here as a regent, monarch, and knight in a colourful and theatrical display, unlike the depiction in the *Atrium Heroicum,* in which he was made to appear solemn, stern and imposing.

There was more. Ferdinand filled the front area of a large, bisected hall with objects more akin to a chamber of art and natural curiosities. This contained all those weapons and sets of armour that did not fit in the two preceding collections for reasons of formality or character. Among these were his exotic and Turkish artefacts, his curiosities—such as the armour of the 2.4 metre-tall court giant Giovanni Bona and that of the court dwarf—as well as inherited or foreign sets of armour, and similar items.

This section also included the three original figures, those of the court giant and two pages. All figures were equipped with a mechanical system that allowed for positioning of the arms, heads and hips. All have customised faces; the giant has portrait features, and the pages even have real hair glued onto them. The two halves of the room served as a sports depot in which the jousting and racing gear of Archduke Siegmund and Emperor Maximilian I were stored. At the time they were already old, but still usable, and Ferdinand continued to use them.[13]

Ferdinand's hope for a male heir from his second marriage in 1582 to Caterina Gonzaga of Mantua remained unfulfilled. He had two sons from his first, secret marriage with the commoner Philippine Welser (died 1580)—the first sentimental *mesaillance* in the House of Habsburg. He granted the cardinalate to the oldest of the two, Andreas of Austria. To the younger, Karl von Burgau, he bequeathed Schloss Ambras and the associated collections. In his last will and testament drafted in 1594, Ferdinand implored his son to preserve the collections after his death (in 1595) and to expand them in his memory. Karl von Burgau did add some heroes to the 'Honourable Society', the acquisitions of which may have been initiated by his father. He also included himself and his brother Cardinal Andreas of Austria in the *viri illustres.*

The release of the catalogue in Latin in 1601 and in German in 1603 may also have had a mercantile purpose for the heir: both editions were dedicated to Emperor Rudolf II and King Philip III of Spain, likely with the idea of gaining them as potential buyers. Rudolf II ultimately purchased the castle and the collections in 1607 for 170,000 guilders, securing the primogeniture of the House of Habsburg as an entailed estate.

The *Armamentarium Heroicum,* advanced by Ferdinand but only published posthumously, was the first printed and illustrated collection catalogue and is extraordinarily significance in the context of collection history. Although it was only released after his death, the Archduke had a clear concept of the document he planned to create. He was a manic collector

---

13 Schrenck von Notzing, Jacob, *Augustissimorum Imperatorum serenissimorum regum atque archiducum ... imagines* (Innsbruck, 1601).

Fig. 10.1. Frontpage of the *Armamentarium Heroicum*, Dominicus Custos after Giovanni Battista Fontana, 1601.

and would likely never have finished the project, as there were always new *viri illustres* to include. He knew of many engravings and in 1593 the collection numbered 119 heroes. An incompletely preserved draft of the *Armamentarium* is stored in the royal hunting chamber and armoury. Of the 125 plates in the final draft, 70 are included, but that version also contains 49 hand-written biographies that often deviate considerably from the printed edition.

The complete *Armamentarium Heroicum* comprises splendid copper engravings of 125 heroes, and Jakob Schrenk von Notzing is considered the author responsible. The engraver Dominicus Custos (born after 1550, Antwerp; died 1612, Augsburg) based his work on prior illustrations by Giovanni Battista (born 1524, Verona; died 1587, Innsbruck), Simon Gartner (died 1611, Innsbruck) and, presumably, the royal painter Francesco Terzio (1523–1591).[14]

Following the title page in the Latin edition from 1601 (see Appendix) is the dedication to Emperor Rudolf II, succeeded by commemorative poems, and then the portrait of an imperious Archduke in a medallion copper engraving below his coat of arms. Thereafter follows a litany of allegorical references to his rank and claim to rule, a list of his military endeavours from 1556 to 1566 and, finally, a description of the scientific nature of the work. The copper engraving is signed 'Joha(nnes) Battista Fon(tana) delj(neavit) Anno 1582 und Dominicus Custodis (recte Custos)....Oeniponti schabit (recte scalpsit)'. These prefaces are followed by the 125 plates of 'heroes', although there are 128 plates in two subsequent editions.

Eventually, the inventory from Ambras was united with Rudolf II's collections in Prague, otherwise the collection would have fallen into the hands of the Swedes in 1648.[15] Ambras thus remained largely untouched, managed by subsequent territorial princes and supplemented by their weaponry. As of 1615, the castle and its collections could be viewed by interested visitors for a fee. The Schloss Ambras collections—largely unscathed—was largely forgotten until the early nineteenth century, when Napoleon ordered that the 10 'French heroes' be delivered to France, while the officers commissioned with this task helped themselves to the rest of the collection's rich inventory. The Kunsthistorisches Museum [Art History Museum] of the Imperial Palace opened in 1891, combining the Ambras collections with the imperial armoury—which had always been housed in the palace—with the royal hunting chamber, resulting in the world's most significant collection of this kind.[16]

---

14 Thomas (ed.).
15 Auer, I-CXXI.
16 Beaufort-Spontin, 121–130.

THE *ARMAMENTARIUM HEROICUM* OF ARCHDUKE FERDINAND OF TYROL[17]

Augustissimorum Imperatorum, Serenissimorum Regime, Atque Archiducum, Illustrissimorum, Principum, necnon Comitum, Baronum, Nobilium, aliorumq: clarissimorum virorum, qui aut ipsi cum imperio bellorum Duces fuerunt, aut in ijsdem praefecturis insignioribus laudabiliter functi sunt, verissimae imagines, &rerum ab ipsis domi, forisq; gestarum succinctae descriptiones.

Quorum Arma, Aut Integra, Aut Horum Partes, Quibus Induti, Usi'que Adversus Hostem Heroica Facinora Patrarunt, Aut Quorum Auspiciis tam prospera quam adversa gestae sunt, a Serenissimo Principe Ferdinando, Archiduce Austriae, Duce Burgundiae, Comite Habspurgi & Tyrolis &c.

Exomnibus fere orbis terrarum Provinciis partim ab illorum haeredibus& successoribus transmissa, in celebri Ambrosianae arcis Armamentario, a sua Serenitate non procul civitate Oenipontana extructo, conspiciuntur.

Opus Praelibati Serenissimi Archiducis iussu in vita inchoatum, & ab eiusdem Serenitatis consiliario & Secretario Iacobo Schrenckhio a Notzingen continuatum & absolutum.

Oeniponti, Excudebat Ioannes Agricola, M.DC.I

Cum Privilegio Caesareo.

---

17 Title page of Jacob Schrenck von Notzing, *Augustissimorum Imperatorum*... (Innsbruck, J. Agricola, 1601).

PATRICIA ANDRÉS GONZÁLEZ

The Habsburg Dynasty and Emblematic Literature

A Historiographical Assessment*

> Let us return for a bit to the main subject, for I feel that I have neglected to say as much as I should on the matter of mottoes and devices, of which there are a great many at this moment, and which provide grace and ornament, and it is almost as the same as putting up the coat of arms or the insignia of a prince who is hosting a party or in whose honour the party is given, but with more grace and a certain ingenious courtesy; such as, when instead of putting up the coats of arms of Emperor Charles V, they sometimes put up the *Plus ultra* [Further beyond] device; and in London, in place of the arms of King Philip, they occasional display the motto *Nec spe nec metu* [(By) neither hope nor fear]; and the arches of King Henry sometimes bear the royal coat of arms of France, and sometimes bear his Moon device.[1]

---

* The author is member of the University of Valladolid recognized research group and Junta de Castilla y León consolidated research unit, *Art, power and society in the Modern Age*. She is member of the research project ref. PID2021-124832NB-I00 [*Magnifiencia a través de las artes visuales en la familia de los Reyes Católicos. Estudio comparado del patronazfo de ambos géneros*], funded by Spanish government.

1 'E ritornando un poco alla materia principale, perche mi pare aver lasciato di parlare quanto conveniva della materia dei motti e delle imprese, che sono di momento pur assai, e danno grazia ed ornamento, ed equasi come mettere armi o insegna del príncipe che fa o per chi si fa la festa, ma con più grazia e con una certa gentilezza ingegnosa; come in cambio di metter l'arme di Carlo V imperadore, mettevano talvolta l'impresa del PLUS ULTRA; ed a Londra come per un arme del Re Filippo, missono qualche volta il motto: NEC SPE NEC METU: e negli archi del Re Enrico talvolta l'arme reale di Francia, talvolta l'impresa sua

---

| **Patricia Andrés González** • University of Valladolid

Ars Habsburgica, ed. by Fernando Checa & Miguel Ángel Zalama, Habsburg Worlds, 6 (Turnhout: Brepols, 2023), pp. 177–198

With these words, the Benedictine monk Vincenzo Borghini advised Cosimo I de' Medici that, on the 1565 occasion of his son Francesco's marriage to Joanna of Habsburg-Jagiellon, daughter of the Holy Roman Emperor, he should display devices instead of using the prince's arms, as these were more graceful and decorative. To justify this recommendation, he cited several examples related to the House of Austria.

The use and presence of emblematic literature was increasingly evident in every sphere starting in the late fifteenth century and throughout the sixteenth. Its Italian origins have been studied thoroughly, but assessments of its impact in the Habsburg universe are quite sparse. For years, emblematic literature has been an essential source for all historians, from modernists to scholars of the history of law, politics and music, to name but a few. It is also a subject of study for historians and for those who investigate matters pertaining to literature and languages, both classical and modern. Art history has not overlooked it either, as emblematic forms—emblems, *imprese*, hieroglyphs, devices—lend themselves to formalist, authorial, iconographic, iconological and other methods of analysis because they have a visual component (the *pictura* or the fact that they are graven images). Therefore, emblematic literature is both a subject and source for art-historical research.

Yet there are many aspects of emblematica that have yet to be analysed—some ideas for which this text attempts to sketch and underline, such as the diverse media on which emblems and their variants were used, from books and ephemeral architecture to precious metalwork and tapestries:[2]

> The emblematic projection of art was adapted in each country to the art forms of each region when it came to designing emblematic public or private spaces: from emblems embroidered on tapestries (in Flanders and especially England) and palatial series of fresco paintings (in Spain, Austria and Bohemia) to court portraits on canvas (at

---

della Luna'. Giovanni Gaetano Bottari and Stefano Ticozzi, *Raccolta di lettere sulla pittura, scultura ed architettura scritte da'piu celebri personaggi dei secoli XV, XVI e XVII*, 8 vols (Milan: G. Silvestri, 1822; repr. Hildesheim/New York, 1976), vol. l, 63.

2 The presence of emblems on different supports has been analysed in several studies. By way of example, devices on clothing are discussed in José Julio García Arranz, 'Emblemas portátiles: el empleo de divisas metálicas como adorno de sombrero y vestimenta, y su función en el origen del género emblemático', *IMAGO: Revista de Emblemática y Cultura Visual*, 7 (2015), 7–23. DOI: https://doi.org/10.7203/imago.7.4289; emblems on precious metalwork in Patricia Andrés González, *Arte, fiesta e iconografía en torno a la eucaristía. Juan de Arfe y su obra: la custodia monumental de Valladolid* (Valladolid: Ayuntamiento de Valladolid and Instituto Universitario de Historia 'Simancas', 2010); and on tapestries in Patricia Andrés González, 'Sobre la presencia de la emblemática en los tapices: la serie de triunfos del Archiduque Alberto', in *El Sol de Occidente: Textos, imágenes simbólicas e interculturalidad* (Santiago de Compostela: Andavira, 2020), 421–438.

the French and Spanish courts) and textile devices that completed gentlemanly apparel (in all of Europe), the possibilities of emblematic art are myriad.[3]

The time has come to formulate general visions that can lead to conclusions about the influence of the Habsburg dynasty on this literary genre.

The first observation is logical. A royal house like this, which attained tremendous size and power, was not above using emblematic literature to express its authority, create its image and tell its history. This artistic-literary genre and the different branches of the Habsburg family intertwined throughout an array of circumstances, revealing a dynasty that promoted new forms and concepts, which prompted the novel artistic manifestations that appeared in the late fifteenth century and gradually spread throughout the sixteenth, seventeenth and part of the eighteenth century.

Between device and emblem: Formal diversity

The complexity of the emblematic genre is derived, first, from the diverse forms it encompasses. The emblem triplex created by Andrea Alciato (1492–1550) in 1531,[4] the same year the first edition of the *Emblematum liber* was published at Augsburg, is often considered canonical and pioneering. However, other forms included in the emblem genre, such as the hieroglyph, device and *impresa*,[5] had already been developing over the course of the fifteenth century. As Giuseppina Ledda noted, 'La

---

[3] Víctor Mínguez et al., eds., *La fiesta barroca: los virreinatos Americanos (1560–1808): triunfos barrocos* (Castelló de la Plana: Publicacions de la Universitat Jaume I, 2012). 'La proyección emblemática del arte se adaptó en cada país a las formas artísticas de cada región, a la hora de configurar espacios emblemáticos, públicos o privados: de los emblemas bordados en tapices –en Flandes, y sobre todo en Inglaterra–, a las series palaciegas pintadas al fresco –en España, Austria y Bohemia–, pasando por retratos áulicos sobre lienzos –en las cortes francesa y española–, a las divisas textiles que completaba el atavío caballeresco –en toda Europa–, las posibilidades del arte emblemático son multiples'.

[4] Andrea Alciati, *Viri clarissimi D. Andreae Alciati Iurisconsultiss. Mediol. Ad D. Chonradum Peutingerum Augustanum, Iurisconsultum Emblematum Liber* (Augsburg: Heinrich Steyner, 1531). Two editions were actually published that year, and the same printer published a third in 1534. That same year it was published under the title *Emblematum libellus* (Paris: Chrestien Wechel, 1534). After that edition, the *Emblematum liber* was published in Paris for over thirty years. The Alciato editions can be consulted on the website of the University of Glasgow project 'Alciato at Glasgow': http://www.emblems.arts.gla.ac.uk/alciato/index.php.

[5] The difference and use of these two terms is derived from the French tradition, in the case of device, and the Italian tradition, in the case of *impresa*. In Spain and in England, the two were used interchangeably. Anne Rolet, 'Aux sources de l'emblème: blasons et devises', *Littérature* 145, 1 (2007), 53–78. https://www.cairn.info/revue–litterature–2007–1–page–53.htm

producción de Alciato fomentó, en realidad, un nuevo medio de expresión más que crearlo' [Alciato's production actually promoted, rather than created, a new expressive medium].[6]

Hardly any emblematists distinguished between the different types. Even in the early-seventeenth century, Sebastián de Covarrubias defined the word *emblema* in his *Tesoro de la lengua castellana, o española*:

> *Emblem* comes from a Greek word meaning entertainment, or the interlacing of different small stones or enamels of various colours to form flowers, animals and various figures: on pavements of different marbles [...] Alciato in the preface to his emblems
> [says they are] made by the distinguished hand of craftsmen:
> Just as one affixes trimmings to clothes and badges to hats
> So it behoves every one of us to write in silent marks.
> Metaphorically, emblems also describe verses attached to some painting or carving, with which we signify some concept of war, morality, love or in another way, helping to declare the intention of the emblem and of its author. This term is often confused with that of symbol, hieroglyph, pegma, impresa, insignia, enigma, etc. You shall refer to my brother the Bishop of Guadix, in the first book of his emblems, where all is explained at great length, with erudition and distinction.[7]

It is usually said that emblematica originated in medieval times, having some things in common with heraldry and other expressions of the chivalric world, but it is undoubtedly related to an older symbolic tradition that

---

6 Giuseppina Ledda, 'Emblemas y configuraciones emblemáticas en la literatura religiosa y moral del siglo XVII', in *Actas del IV Congreso Internacional de la Asociación Internacional Siglo de Oro (AISO), (Alcalá de Henares, 22–27 de julio de 1996)*, 2 vols, eds. María Cruz García de Enterría and Alicia Cordón Mesa (Alcalá de Henares: Universidad de Alcalá, 1998), 1, 45–74.

7 Sebastián de Covarrubias Orozco, *Tesoro de la Lengua Castellana, o Española* (Madrid: Luis Sánchez, 1611), fol. 342v. 'Emblema es nombre Griego, significa entretenimiento, o enlaçamiento de diferentes pedrecitas, o esmaltes de varias colores de que formauan flores, animales y varias figuras: en los enlosados de diferentes marmores [...] Alciato en el principio de sus emblemas
Artificium illustri signaque fact maru:
Vestibus ut torulos petassis ut figere parmas
Er valeat tacitus seribere quisque notis
Metaforicamente se llaman emblemas los versos que se subscriuen a alguna pintura, o talla, con que significamos algún concepto belico, moral, amoroso, ó en otra manera, ayudando a declarar el intento del emblema y de su autor. Este nombre se suele confundir con el de símbolo, hieroglifico, pegma, empresa, insigna, enigma, etc. Verás al Obispo de Guadix mi hermano, en el primer libro de sus emblemas, a donde está todo muy a la larga dicho, con erudición y distinción'.

began in classical antiquity and remained a steady undercurrent throughout the Middle Ages.

'Proto-emblematic' forms have received less scholarly attention, though lately this field is proving quite fertile, primarily thanks to a research project by Laurent Hablot at the Université de Poitiers[8] and another by Sagrario López Poza at the Universidad de La Coruña.[9] Their use is documented from the early-fourteenth century, while hieroglyphs spread over the course of the fifteenth century. Both reveal a gradual evolution of these symbolic forms towards what would become a widely circulated literary genre in the sixteenth and seventeenth centuries, distributed via the printing press and other channels.

An example from this early period is the device created for Queen Catherine of Lancaster (1373–1418), wife of Henry III of Castile, which appeared on many works she patronised, such as the monastery of Santa María la Real de Nieva in Segovia and the Church of Santa María de Arbás in Mayorga, Valladolid. The device featured a pinecone, symbolising the fruits of virtuous living,[10] which would be used some years later by the Dutch physician and humanist Hadrianus Junius (1511–1575).[11]

The House of Trastámara, among others, used these devices to highlight their virtues. Besides heraldic crests that connected and acknowledged a family and its members, they also felt the need for personal symbols that announced the ambitions or summarised the virtues of each individual—although occasionally these did become inherited signs, as happened when the pomegranate became an identifying symbol from the moment Henry IV (1425–1475) adopted it with the motto *Agro dulce*.[12] We later find it associated with close relatives like the Catholic Monarchs

---

8 Laurent Hablot, *Devise : emblématique et héraldique à la fin du Moyen-Âge*, Centre d'Etudes Supérieures de Civilisation Médiévale, Université de Poitiers [online], http://base-devise.edel.univ-poitiers.fr/index.php.

9 Sagrario López Poza and Nieves Pena Sueiro, *Symbola: divisas o empresas históricas*, BIDISO database (*Biblioteca Digital Siglo de Oro*), A Coruña [online], https://www.bidiso.es/Symbola/.

10 Álvaro Fernández de Córdova Miralles, 'El cordón y la piña: signos emblemáticos y devociones religiosas de Enrique III y Catalina de Lancaster (1390–1418)', *Archivo Español de Arte*, LXXXIX, 354 (April–June 2016), 113–130. It is interesting that after 1412 and the decree of Catherine of Lancaster which triggered the destruction of synagogues in Castile and other Iberian kingdoms, the pinecone of Catherine came to be used on these buildings as they were claimed for Christendom: Muñoz-Garrido, Daniel. 'The Medieval Synagogue of Molina De Aragón: Architecture and Decoration'. *Arts* 9.1 (2020) DOI: https://doi.org/10.3390/arts9010009.

11 Emblem 37, with a pinecone motif and the motto: *Virtus difficilis, sed fructuosa*. Adriano Junio, *Emblemas*, ed. Beatriz Antón (Zaragoza: Libros Pórtico, 2013).

12 Sagrario López Poza, 'La divisa de las granadas del rey Enrique IV de Castilla y su estela posterior', *IMAGO Revista de Emblemática y Cultura Visual*, 6 (2014), 81–95, DOI: https://doi.org/10.7203/imago.6.4131.

Fig. 11.1. Recto of a Sheet with Maximilian, from *The Genealogy of Emperor Maximilian* I, Hans Burgkmair, 1509-1512. © Metropolitan Museum of New York.

and their daughter Catherine of Aragon (1485–1536), Queen consort of England, and more distant relations like Maximilian I (1459–1519), whose device was a six-spoked wheel (the wheel of fortune) with an imperial orb above and a pomegranate below, beside the motto *Per tot discrimina*.[13] (Fig. 11.1)

Devices were very successful in Spain from an early date, as Paolo Giovio noted in his *Dialogo dell'imprese militari et amorose*, written in 1551 and published posthumously in 1555. In the House of Aviz, somewhat later, we find an interesting device that Charles V (1500–1558) ordered

---

13 Motto inspired by the *Aeneid* (I, 204–205): *per tot discrimina rerum / tendimus in Latium…*

for his wife, Isabella of Portugal (1503–1539), which pictures the three Graces of classical mythology, Aglaia, Euphrosyne and Thalia, the divine incarnations of beauty, love and fertility, accompanied by the motto *Has habet et superat*.[14] Ten years after Isabella's death in 1539, it was included on a silver medal commissioned from Leone Leoni (now at the Museu Casa do Moeda in Lisbon).

Francis I of France (1494–1547) had a very famous device whose *pictura* featured a salamander, while the motto read *Nutrisco et extingo* (I nourish and I extinguish);[15] equally renowned were the *imprese* of Charles V, who used as many as six, from that with the *Nondum* [Not yet] legend and the *pictura* of a sun rising through the zodiac constellations and passing over Cancer but not yet at the zenith; to the famous paired columns and *Plus ultra* [Further beyond] motto.[16] In addition to this early use of devices and hieroglyphs, the Habsburgs also employed emblems, especially in a later period and in books, which reveal the members of this dynasty as both protectors and patrons of the new literary genre.

Patrons, Sponsors and Clients

In a Burgundian tradition, the Habsburgs sponsored the efforts of certain emblematists. For instance, Juan de Borja, the first to write an emblem book in Spain, published his *Empresas morales* in 1581 thanks to the patronage of Rudolf II of Austria (1552–1612), secured during his time in Prague as ambassador of Philip II (1527–1598).[17]

---

14 Francisco Gómez de la Reguera y Serna, *Empresas de los Reyes de Castilla*, ed. Nieves Pena Sueiro (A Coruña: SIELAE and Sociedad de Cultura Valle Inclán, 2011), 203; José María González de Zárate, 'Rubens. Pensamiento estoico y pintura poética. El juicio de Paris. Una alegoría del mal gobierno. Las tres gracias. Imagen de la liberalidad', Potestas, 5 (2012), 107–132; Nieves Pena Sueiro, 'Las Empresas de las reinas de Castilla (1504–1611)', in *Emblemática trascendente: hermenéutica de la imagen, iconología del texto*, eds. Rafael Zafra Molina and José Javier Azanza López (Pamplona: Universidad de Navarra, 2011), 639–649 and 580–581; See also the database directed by Dr Sagrario López Poza, *Symbola*: https://www.bidiso.es/Symbola/divisa/184

15 Sagrario López Poza, 'Empresas, emblemas, jeroglíficos: agudezas simbólicas y comunicación conceptual', in *La aparición del periodismo en Europa: comunicación y propaganda en el barroco*, eds. Roger Chartier and Carmen Espejo (Madrid: Marcial Pons Historia, 2012), 37–85: http://hdl.handle.net/2183/14765

16 Earl E. Rosenthal, '*Plus Ultra, Non Plus Ultra*, and the columnar device of Emperor Charles V', *Journal of the Warburg and Courtauld Institutes*, XXXIV (1971), 204–228; Earl E. Rosenthal, 'The invention of the columnar device of Emperor Charles V at the Court of Burgundy in Flanders in 1516', *Journal of the Warburg and Courtauld Institutes*, XXXVI (1973), 222–223.

17 Rafael García Mahiques, *Empresas morales de Juan de Borja: imagen y palabra para una iconología* (Valencia: Ayuntamiento de Valencia, 1998).

Yet there is evidence that the Habsburgs had embraced and promoted the use of emblems long before this. There are many examples, but a particularly interesting case is that of Jacopo Nizzola da Trezzo (c. 1514–1589), who entered Prince Philip's service in 1554. Working in Brussels, he created several important *imprese*, such as the two conceived and engraved for the prince's marriage to Mary I of England (1516–1558) in 1554. On the reverse of the future king's device, we find the image of Apollo driving a *quadriga* that leaps over the sea between two promontories, with the motto *Iam illustrabit omnia* [Now he will illuminate all things].[18] It appears to have formed a pair with his wife's device, which represents Mary as the queen who would bring peace to the persecuted Christians of her realm. As a symbol of the stability she would bring, she is seated on a throne over a cubic stone engraved with two clasped hands and a balance, and she is dressed as a matron, crowned and holding an olive branch and a palm leaf in her hand. Her motto reads *Caecis visus timidis quies* [Sight for the blind, comfort for the frightful].[19] (Fig. 11.2)

---

18 Pedro Galera, 'Un emblema solar para Felipe II', *Actas de I Simposio Internacional de Emblemática, Teruel, 1 y 2 de octubre de 1991* (Teruel: Instituto de Estudios Turolenses, 1994), 457–472; Virgilio Bermejo Vega, 'Princeps ut Apolo. Mitología y alegoría solar en los Austrias hispanos', *Actas de I Simposio Internacional de Emblemática, Teruel, 1 y 2 de octubre de 1991* (Teruel: Instituto de Estudios Turolenses, 1994), 473–492; Almudena Pérez de Tudela Gabaldón, 'Algunas precisiones sobre la imagen de Felipe II en las medallas', *Madrid: Revista de arte, geografía e historia*, 1 (1998), 241–272; Víctor Mínguez Cornelles, *Los reyes solares: iconografía astral de la Monarquía Hispánica* (Castelló de la Plana: Publicacions de la Universitat Jaume I, 2001); Sagrario López Poza, '"Nec spe nec metu" y otras empresas o divisas de Felipe II', in *Emblemática Trascendente: hermenéutica de la imagen, iconología del texto*, eds. Rafael Zafra Molina and José Javier Azanza López (Pamplona: Sociedad Española de Emblemática–Universidad de Navarra, 2011), 435–456; Sagrario López Poza, 'Iam illustrabit omnia', in *Symbola: divisas o empresas históricas – BIDISO (Biblioteca Digital Siglo de Oro)*, A Coruña, Spain [online]. Posted: 30-08-2017. Updated: 30-03-2019. https://www.bidiso.es/Symbola/divisa/163 [accessed 11-04-2023].

19 The *impresa* appeared in several emblem books, albeit with some variations, such as those of Gómez de la Reguera and Sadeler. Donald Gordon, '"Veritas filia temporis": Hadrianus Junius and Geoffrey Whitney', *Journal of the Warburg and Courtauld Institutes*, 3, 3/4 (Apr.–Jul., 1940), 228–240; Mason Tung, *Impresa index to the collections of Paradin, Giovio, Simeoni, Pittoni, Ruscelli, Contile, Camilli, Capaccio, Bargagli, and Typotius* (New York: AMS Press, 2006); María Jesús Pérez Martín, *María Tudor: la gran reina desconocida* (Madrid: Ediciones Rialp, 2008, repr. 2012); Nieves Pena Sueiro, 'Las Empresas de las reinas de Castilla (1504–1611)', in *Emblemática trascendente: hermenéutica de la imagen, iconología del texto*, eds. Rafael Zafra Molina and José Javier Azanza López (Pamplona; Universidad de Navarra, 2011), 639–649; Andrea Maceiras Lafuente, Empresas o divisas históricas: un catálogo basado en fuentes de 1511 a 1629 (A Coruña: SIELAE & The Society for Emblem Studies, 2017); Carlota Fernández Travieso, Nieves Pena Sueiro and Sagrario López Poza, 'Caecis visus timidis quies', in *Symbola: divisas o empresas históricas – BIDISO (Biblioteca Digital Siglo de Oro)*, A Coruña, Spain [online]. Posted: 02-09-2018. Updated: 02-09-2018. https://www.bidiso.es/Symbola/divisa/101 [accessed 11-04-2023].

Fig. 11.2. Medals of *Philip II and Mary I of England*, Jacopo da Trezzo, 1555. © National Archaeological Museum, Madrid.

All the leading emblematists, at one point or another, had a connection with the Habsburg dynasty. This was never truer than in the second half of the sixteenth century, when the popularity of emblem books and the use of emblems in all sorts of celebrations was at its height. The close nature of the relationship is illustrated by several highly significant examples. One is Johannes Sambucus (aka János Zsámboky), whose involvement with the court began in 1557 when he was appointed librarian at the imperial library of Ferdinand I in Vienna. In 1565 he became imperial historiographer to the court of Maximilian II, and in 1567 he was named court physician and *comes palatinus*. Approximately two years later, he was awarded the post of *consiliarius aulae*, but his greatest ambition, to be appointed to the position of *praefectus bibliothecae*, was never fulfilled. He published several books, including his *Emblemata* (Antwerp, printed by Christophe Plantin) in 1564. Among scholars, it is generally believed that he intended this book as a commendation of his colleagues and, in fact, one third of the emblems are dedicated to them. Above all, the collection was dedicated to Maximilian II, from whom he hoped to obtain the coveted post.

Politics, festivities and education

Having seen that emblems adopted various forms—devices, *imprese*, emblems and hieroglyphs—and were commissioned for the Habsburgs' own purposes or because of their capacity as patrons of emblematists, we must also consider the reasons that inspired the cultivation of emblematic literature. In such a wide field, these reasons are logically as varied as the media on which those emblems were represented.

Emblems were present on occasions that might not seem particularly significant, such as those related to war. For instance, the hulls of warships—which Santiago Sebastián called 'floating palaces'[20]—were decorated with allegorical and symbolic motifs, including emblems, which aimed to show the heroic ideal or political or religious reasons behind those battles. John of Austria commanded from a galley at the Battle of Lepanto, which was built at the Barcelona shipyards in 1548 and then sailed to Seville to be embellished with paintings. The art followed an iconographic programme designed by Juan de Mal Lara and based on Alciato's emblems, of which he even wrote a description: *Descripción de la Galera Real del Sermo. Sr. D. Juan de Austria*.[21]

There are three essential emblematic functions that should be highlighted, which reflect the diverse interests of this dynasty: political propaganda, festive pomp and texts associated with the education of princes and, in some cases, princesses. Regarding the first, there is ample evidence that practically every dynasty used images to give the people an idea of its policies—in other words, for propagandistic purposes. This was certainly the case with members of the Habsburg dynasty from Maximilian I onwards,

---

20 Santiago Sebastián, *Emblemática e historia del arte* (Madrid: Cátedra, 1995), 59–61, citing the works of Alan R. Young, 'The emblematic decoration of Queen Elizabeth I's warship the White Bear', *Emblemática*, 3 (1988), 65–77, and Alan R. Young, ed., *His Majesty's Royal Ship: A Critical Edition of Thomas Heywood's 'A True Description of His Majesties Royall Ship'* (New York: AMS Press, 1990).
21 Karl Ludwig Selig, 'The commentary of Juan de Mal Lara to Alciato's emblemata', *Hispanic Review*, 24, 1 (1956), 26–41; María Dolores Aguilar García, 'El barco como objeto artístico y viaje alegórico: la Galera Real de Lepanto', *Espacio, Tiempo y Forma*, 2 (1989), 93–114; Rocío Carande Herrero, *Mal-Lara y Lepanto* (Seville: Caja de Ahorros San Fernando, 1990), 23; Víctor Mínguez Cornelles, 'Iconografía de Lepanto: arte, propaganda y representación simbólica de una monarquía universal y católica', *Obradoiro de Historia Moderna*, 20 (2011), 251–280; Víctor Mínguez Cornelles, *Infierno y gloria en el mar: Los Habsburgo y el imaginario artístico de Lepanto (1430–1700)* (Castelló de la Plana: Universitat Jaume I, Servei de Comunicació i Publicacions), 2017.

and especially with Charles V and Philip II. The timeline is longer, but this use of emblems is most evident during their reigns, and undoubtedly more consolidated in Philip's day. Writers and artists helped to create and circulate that image, often through emblematic literature. The literature about the monarchs of the House of Habsburg and their relationship with emblematica is extensive,[22] but further study is warranted in the case of Charles V, because his role as promoter of the propagandistic use of emblems is particularly interesting given the chronology of his rule.

Maximilian I was a genuine master of personal promotion, for which he resorted to the newly invented printing press.[23] He is considered one of the first European rulers to use this new tool for propagandistic purposes. He commissioned several 'pseudo-biographical' epic narratives starring his three alter egos: *Freydal, Der Weisskunig* and *Theuerdank*,[24] and these works portrayed the Austrian archduke as a knight, pious crusader and leader, respectively. Alongside these works, the *Triumph* series of miniature paintings and the *Arch of Honour* woodcut engraving series were undoubtedly the finest examples of his efforts to construct that image with the help of printed texts and pictures.[25]

There can be no doubt as to the symbolic nature of these three books, with their abundant and interesting illustrations. Thus far, scholarship has not extensively explored the occasional use or clear influence of emblematic forms in these books. Their use in relation to the world of chivalrous heraldry[26] denotes an unprecedented openness to new forms of language—emblematic language that pursues a personal agenda, primarily through devices and *imprese*.

---

22 One of the editors of this book, Fernando Checa Cremades, has written prolifically on this topic in connection with both Charles V and Philip II. His scholarly contributions include, among other works: Fernando Checa Cremades, *Carlos V y la imagen del héroe en el renacimiento* (Madrid: Taurus, 1987); Fernando Checa Cremades, *Felipe II, mecenas de las artes* (Madrid: Nerea, 1992); Fernando Checa Cremades, *Carlos V, la imagen del poder en el Renacimiento* (Madrid: Ediciones El Viso and Iberdrola, 1999); Fernando Checa, *Renacimiento habsbúrgico: Felipe II y las imágenes artísticas* (Valladolid: Ediciones de la Universidad de Valladolid, 2018).
23 Larry Silver, *Marketing Maximilian: the visual ideology of a Holy Roman Emperor* (Princeton, NJ: Princeton University Press, 2008).
24 Paul van Dyke, 'The Literary Activity of the Emperor Maximilian I', *The American Historical Review*, 11, 1 (Oct. 1905), 16–28.
25 On the use of the book as a propaganda tool, see the recent work by Jesús Félix Pascual Molina, 'Propaganda de papel: libros, dibujos y estampas de Maximiliano I a Carlos V', in *Imbricaciones: paradigmas, modelos y materialidad de las artes en la Europa Habsbúrgica*, eds. Matteo Mancini and Álvaro Pascual Chenel (Madrid: Sílex, 2019), 179–204.
26 Robert Jones, *Bloodied banners: martial display on the medieval battlefield* (Woodbridge: Boydell, 2010).

Let us examine the first and most extensively studied of them: *Freydal* (1512–1515).[27] This book about tournaments and jousts is similar to other tomes sponsored by the emperor himself or produced in similar settings, such as the Turnierbuch manuscript with the *Triumph* series of prints by Hans Burgkmair the Younger, now in Munich.[28] The book contains 250 miniatures enhanced in silver and gold depicting 64 tournaments that show the rules of this knightly game in all its diversity; the emperor himself, well acquainted with the sport, is a participant in practically every scene. The text is an epic allegory that tells the story of the intrepid hero, Freydal (Maximilian), proving his love for a princess (Mary of Burgundy) until they are finally married at Ghent in 1477. Sources indicate that the work must have been taken to the printer and reproduced by means of woodblocks, although no examples have survived other than the five woodcuts by Dürer that reproduce the same number of miniatures.[29]

The works of Alan R. Young are seminal references on the use of emblems in tournaments,[30] although the theme has been approached from different angles by earlier authors like Ceballos and Rico.[31] However, considering the specific world of knightly tournaments in the days of Maximilian and the different books published on this topic,[32] further study from an emblematic perspective seems increasingly imperative:

---

27 Christian Beaufort Spontin, 'El Freydal y la cultura del torneo en la corte de Maximiliano I', in *El siglo de Durero: problemas historiográficos: symposium, 16 y 17 de noviembre de 2007*, eds. Fernando Checa Cremades, María del Mar Borobia Guerrero and Dolores Delgado (Madrid: Museo Thyssen-Bornemisza, 2008), 221–234; Stefan Krause, 'The Freydal miniatures in Vienna', in *The last knight: the art, armor, and ambition of Maximilian I*, exh. cat. The Metropolitan Museum of Art, ed. Pierre Terjanian (New York: Metropolitan Museum of Art, 2019), 120–122; Stefan Krause, 'The Freydal sketches in Washington, DC', in *The Last Knight: The Art, Armor, and Ambition of Maximilian I*, exh. cat. The Metropolitan Museum of Art, ed. Pierre Terjanian (New York: Metropolitan Museum of Art, 2019), 123–125; Stefan Krause, Freydal. *Medieval games. The tournament book of Emperor Maximilian I* (Cologne: Taschen, 2019).

28 Bayerische Staatsbibliothek in Munich, *cod. Icon. 403*, Hans Burgkmair, 'The Younger', Turnierbuch, c. 1540.

29 Stefan Krause, 'The Freydal woodblock prints', in *The last knight: the art, armor, and ambition of Maximilian I*, exh. cat. The Metropolitan Museum of Art, ed. Pierre Terjanian (New York: Metropolitan Museum of Art, 2019), 127–129.

30 Alan R. Young, 'The emblem in tournaments', in *Companion to emblem studies*, ed. Peter Daly (New York: AMS Press, 2008), 477–487; Alan R. Young, *Tudor and Jacobean tournaments* (London: George Philip, 1987).

31 Francisco Rico, 'Un penacho de penas: de algunas invenciones y letras de caballeros', in *Texto y contextos: estudios sobre la poesía Española del siglo XV* (Barcelona: Crítica, 1990), 189–230; Alfonso Ceballos Escalera, 'Las divisas en la heráldica castellana del siglo XV', *Hidalguía*, XXXIII, 192 (1985), 665–688 (esp. 666).

32 Stefan Krause and Matthias Pfaffenbichler, eds., *Turnier: 1000 Ritterspiele* (Vienna: KHM / Munich: Hirmer Verlag, 2017); Robert Coltman Clephan, *The mediaeval tournament* (1st ed. London: 1919; New York: Dover Publications, 1995).

In addition to their distinctness from the realm of heraldic studies, the use of imagery in tournaments, particularly those held in Maximilian's time, should also be held as apart from the field of emblem and impresa studies. While this has been touched on briefly in wider scholarship, the depths of tournament imagery in connection to emblems is far from fully explored.[33]

The colours of the garments, the motifs on the shields and banners and the crests on the helmets are just some of the details that take on emblematic significance in the highly symbolic text and miniatures sponsored by the Holy Roman Emperor; some of them even function as personal devices or *imprese* that could identify an individual.[34] Maximilian's alter ego Freydal, for example, can be recognised by the large plume of feathers he wears like a crest, sometimes rising from the centre of a crown, while his opponents bear a short inscription with their names. Their crests, and occasionally the emperor's, are quite varied. Some feature familiar elements from the field of heraldry such as lions, griffins or dragons, while others have an obvious iconographic meaning and perhaps even a symbolic intention, becoming a device or *impresa*, as in the miniature of Freydal and Anton van Yvan (fol. 101), where the latter's crest is the wheel of fortune that later became one of the emperor's devices.[35] We see this same *impresa* on the clothing worn by Ernhold, the faithful squire in *Theuerdank*, a continuation of *Freydal's* tale. (Fig. 11.3)

A horse's caparison was also frequently used to display personal *imprese* or devices. We see this, for example, in the Turnierbuch woodcuts,[36] which feature emblematic elements on symbolic crests and horses. Specifically, plate number six shows a rider with a windmill crest within a laurel wreath whose horse bears the image of a winged boy on a toy horse carrying a spear tipped with a windmill, copying the method by which young children learned. This same model of boys learning the art of jousting was depicted by Albrecht Altdorfer in Maximilian's *Book of Hours*, now at the Bibliothèque Municipale de Besançon.[37] Aside from the possible existence of a favourite iconographic type, which also might explain its

---

33 Natalie Margaret Anderson, The tournament and its role in the court culture of Emperor Maximilian I (1459–1519), PhD thesis, University of Leeds, 2017, 168, http://etheses.whiterose.ac.uk/id/eprint/18205.
34 For a magnificent article on the iconography of Charles V on flags and banners, see Jesús Félix Pascual Molina, 'La iconografía de las banderas de Carlos V: ejemplos y noticias documentales', *Archivo Español de Arte*, 90, 357 (2017), 31–48.
35 Carles Sánchez Márquez, '"Fortuna velut luna": iconografía de la rueda de la Fortuna en la Edad Media y el Renacimiento', *eHumanista: Journal of Iberian Studies*, 17 (2011), 230.
36 Heinrich Pallmann, ed., *Hans Burgkmair des Jüngeren: Turnierbuch von 1529* (Leipzig: Hiersemann, 1910), plate 6.
37 Walter L. Strauss, ed., *Book of hours of the emperor Maximilian the First* (New York: Abaris Books Inc., 1974), 298, folio 149v.

Fig. 11.3. Left: *Freydal, The Book of Jousts and Tournament of Emperor Maximilian I: Combats on Horseback*, Plate 79, c. 1515. © National Gallery of Art, Washington; Right: 'Theuerdank Nearly Shoots Himself with a Crossbow', from *Theuerdank*, Hans Burgkmair, 1517. © Metropolitan Museum of Art, New York.

repetition, the windmill takes on the value of an *impresa* or device related to the training of knights from infancy when united with that laurel wreath: through regular practice and a knowledge of the arts of the joust and knightly tournaments, fame can be achieved.

We find another example in the motifs used by Gašper Lamberger (Caspar von Lamberg), a knight who regularly participated in Maximilian's tournaments and even had a similar book made.[38] Lamberger's personal *impresa* is emblazoned on his horse's caparison and his own breast: a porcupine, two interlocking Cs and a heart. (Fig. 11.4)

The presence of emblems in books and for other propagandistic purpose should not surprise us, but this literary and artistic genre also found an outlet for expression of the monarch's image in ephemeral architecture and festive events.[39] Public celebrations in which kings, queens, princes

---

38 Alan Duff, Trans., *The tournament book of Gašper Lamberger* (Kunsthistorisches Museum, Vienna, Codex A 2290) [Ljubljana: Viharnik, 1997].

39 Élie Konigson and Jean Jacquot, eds., *Fêtes de la Renaissance*, 3 vols (Paris: CNRS, 1956–75); Veronika Sandbichler, 'Elements of power in court festivals of Habsburg Emperors in the sixteenth century', in J. R. Mulryne, Maria Ines Aliverti and Anna Maria Testaverde, *Ceremonial entries in early modern Europe: The iconography of power* (London: Ashgate Publishing Ltd, 2016).

Fig. 11.4. *Turnierbuch. Ritterspiele gehalten von Kaiser Friedrich III und Kaiser Maximilian I in den Jahren 1489–1511*. Hans Burgkmair, the younger. © Bayerische Staatsbibliothek.

and other leading personalities participated directly or indirectly—as was the case of every festival in the Spanish American colonies,[40] where their presence was always visible even though they were far away and never attended in person—became opportunities to publicise their images and pay them homage.[41] Logically, most of these creations have not survived, but we do have descriptions and detailed accounts, published for the same

---

40 Inmaculada Rodríguez Moya and Víctor Mínguez Cornelles, eds., *Visiones de un imperio en fiesta* (Madrid: Fundación Carlos de Amberes, 2016); Víctor Mínguez Cornelles, 'Jeroglíficos para un imperio: la cultura emblemática en el virreinato de la Nueva España', *Quiroga: Revista de Patrimonio Iberoamericano*, 11 (Jan.–June 2017), 56–68.

41 On the use of emblems in these kinds of celebrations, see Rafael Tovar, Gerardo Estrada and Jaime Cuadriello, eds., *Juegos de ingenio y agudeza: la pintura emblemática de la Nueva España* (Mexico City: Museo Nacional de Arte, 1994); Víctor Mínguez Cornelles, *Los reyes solares*; Juan Chiva Beltrán, *El triunfo del virrey. Glorias novohispanas: origen, apogeo y ocaso de la entrada virreinal* (Castelló de la Plana: Universitat Jaume I, 2012); Víctor Mínguez Cornelles et al., eds., *La fiesta barroca: los virreinatos americanos (1560–1808)*, Colección Triunfos barrocos, vol. 2 (Castelló de la Plana: Universidad de Las Palmas de Gran Canaria and Universitat Jaume I, 2012); Víctor Mínguez Cornelles, 'Jeroglíficos para un Imperio'.

purposes, that comment on them and in some cases even include prints illustrating those visual tributes.[42]

When an *impresa* or device was applied to ephemeral architecture, it was called an 'invention', and in many cases it consisted of a hieroglyph.[43] Most celebrations—births, deaths,[44] weddings, coronations, visits to cities —followed two models: the triumphal entry of Charles V into Burgos in 1520[45] and Philip II's progress through the Netherlands and Italy between 1548 and 1551, as well as his various stops along the way, narrated by Juan Calvete de Estrella. However, these were not the first such uses. The general opinion among historiographers, at least until now, has been that the original model was the triumphal entry of Alfonso V the Magnanimous, King of Aragon, into Castel Nuovo in 1443,[46] and the earliest royal entry described in a book is that of Ferdinand the Catholic King's entry into Seville in 1508.[47]

The text written by Juan Cristóbal Calvete de Estrella (c. 1510–1593), published in 1552 as *El felicissimo viaje del muy alto y muy poderoso principe don Phelippe*, is fundamental for understanding the use of emblems in this festive context.[48] It describes their use in every city through which

---

42 *Las relaciones de sucesos en España (1500–1750): actas del primer Coloquio Internacional (Alcalá de Henares, 8–10 de junio de 1995)* (Paris: Publications de la Sorbonne / Alcalá de Henares: Universidad de Alcalá, 1996).
43 López Poza, *Empresas*, 37–85.
44 M.ª Adelaida Allo Manero, 'Origen, desarrollo y significado de las decoraciones fúnebres: la aportación española', *Ephialte: Lecturas de Historia del Arte*, 1 (1989), 89–104; Javier Varela, *La muerte del Rey: el ceremonial funerario de la Monarquía Española (1500–1885)* (Madrid: Turner, 1990).
45 Jenaro Alenda y Mira, *Relaciones de solemnidades y fiestas públicas de España* (Madrid, 1903); Domingo Hergueta Martín, 'Entrada solemne en Burgos de Carlos I el domingo 19 de febrero de 1520', *Boletín de la Comisión Provincial de Monumentos Históricos y Artísticos de Burgos*, 5 (1924), 141–149; Luis Huidobro, 'Fiestas en Burgos en 1520', *Boletín de la Comisión Provincial de Monumentos*, 56 (1939), 222–224; Miguel Ojeda Gonzalo, 'Carlos I de España y V de Alemania en burgos y provincia', *Boletín de la Institución Fernán González*, 146 (1st quarter 1959), 502–513.
46 Isabel Sánchez Gil, *El arco del Castelnuovo de Nápoles y su relación con la introducción del lenguaje renacentista en Castilla*, (unpublished PhD thesis, Universidad Complutense de Madrid, 2015), 61–85.
47 Andrés Bernáldez, Manuel Gómez-Moreno and Juan de Mata Carriazo Arroquia, eds., *Memorias del Reinado de los Reyes Católicos* (Madrid: Real Academia de la Historia, 1962); Vicente Lleó Cañal, 'Recibimiento en Sevilla del Rey Fernando el Católico (1508)', *Archivo Hispalense Sevilla*, 61, 188 (1978), 9–23; Miguel Falomir Faus, 'Entradas triunfales de Fernando el Católico en España tras la conquista de Nápoles', in *La Visión del Mundo Clásico en el arte Español: VI Jornadas de Arte, CSIC* (Madrid: Alpuerto, 1993), 49–55; José Nieto Soria, *Ceremonias de la realeza: propaganda y legitimación en la Castilla Trastámara* (Madrid: Nerea, 1993).
48 Juan Cristóbal Calvete de Estrella, *El felicissimo viaje del muy alto y muy poderoso principe don Phelippe* (Antwerp: Martin Nuyts, 1552); José Luis Gonzalo Sánchez-Molero, José Martínez Millán, Santiago Fernández Conti, Antonio Álvarez-Ossorio Alvariño and Fernando Checa

the Spanish prince passed, and it had a proven influence on the spread and circulation of *imprese*, hieroglyphs, emblems and other iconographic elements in Spain. It was the first Spanish text to describe hieroglyphs on ephemeral architecture,[49] and after its publication these began to figure in both iconographic programmes and 'chronicles of events'. Calvete was also one of the prince's tutors, and from 1541 to 1547 he was responsible for acquiring the bulk of the books that initially comprised his private library. One of them may have been Horopollo's *Hieroglyphica*, listed in the catalogue from 1530,[50] which could have been partly responsible for the popularisation of hieroglyphs in the Spanish context.

Without going into the details of each festivity, it is worthwhile to comment on a particular type of celebration, which can be extrapolated to others, in connection with the presence of emblems and how different Habsburg houses helped to popularise them. Emblems were regularly present in the royal entries made by Habsburg monarchs and emperors while travelling through their realms and at celebrations embellished by more or less complex ephemeral creations. As Daniel Russell rightly points out, 'the origins of the emblem are inseparably bound up with space and movement, both of these constitutive elements of a royal entry'.[51]

The literature on this subject is abundant, from analyses of entries into specific cities to studies of entire journeys that discuss all the attendant pomp, as well as the presence and the sources of emblems.[52] Births, coronations,[53] marriages and deaths were celebrated in a similar manner, although here we will only comment on royal obsequies.

The first accounts of funeral rites were commissioned in Flanders in 1506, France in 1512 and at the court of Vienna in 1519. They appeared somewhat later in Spain; although small pamphlets were published in

---

Cremades, eds., *El felicissimo viaje del muy alto y muy poderoso principe don Phelippe* (Madrid: Sociedad Estatal para la para la Conmemoración de los Centenarios de Felipe II y Carlos V, 2001).

49 Pedro Germano Leal, 'On the origins of Spanish hieroglyphs (I)', *IMAGO: Revista de Emblemática y Cultura Visual*, 6 (2014), 27–38. DOI: http://dx.doi.org/10.7203/imago.6.4234.

50 Real Biblioteca del Monasterio del Escorial, sign. 16–V–22: Bernardino Trebazio Horopollo, *Orus Apollo Niliacus de hieroglyphicis notis, à Bernardino Trebatio Vicentino latinítate donatus* (Estienne, 1530). Recorded as 'ene/jul–1543 De jeroglificos de Horus'.

51 Jacek Żukowksi, 'Ephemeral architecture in the service of Vladislaus IV Vasa', in Mulryne, Aliverti and Testaverde, *Ceremonial entries in early modern Europe*, quoting Daniel S. Russell, 'Emblems and hieroglyphics: some observations on the beginnings and the nature of emblematic forms', *Emblematica: An Interdisciplinary Journal for Emblem Studies*, 1, 2 (1986), 227–244.

52 Silke Knippschild, Víctor Mínguez Cornelles and Heinz–Dieter Heimann, eds., *Ceremoniales, ritos y representación del poder* (Castelló de la Plana: Universitat Jaume I, 2004).

53 Víctor Mínguez Cornelles, 'Sine fine: Dios, los Habsburgo y el traspaso de las insignias de poder en el Quinientos', *Libros de la Corte*, extra issue 1 (2014), 163–185.

1506, 1539 and 1545, they cannot be properly considered 'chronicles of events', as the genre did not really take hold there until the death of Charles V and the corresponding obsequies in 1558.[54] From that moment on, they were widely used throughout the empire:

> In imperial Spain, as in imperial Rome, the funerary rites of each monarch became a grand ceremony in the spectacle of the representation of power, especially considering that this was a hereditary system. Every death of a king meant the ascent to the throne of another member of the dynasty. To ensure a smooth transition from one king to the next and the loyalty of every kingdom, city and town in the empire to the crown prince, an enormous propaganda machine was set in motion after every royal death. The primary elements of this machine were funerary rites, architectural catafalques and the iconographic programmes that adorned ephemeral structures and spaces of mourning at each of the thousands of obsequies held in every church across the empire.[55]

These ceremonies featured an increasing abundance of devices, *imprese*, hieroglyphs and emblems, which at the time were generically referred to as 'hieroglyphs':

> For people living in those days, hieroglyphs were the most surprising and entertaining part of obsequies: they were painted on large sheets of paper and hung on cords around the catafalque, or hung from the catafalque itself. The public vied for the privilege of tearing them down, and guards were posted day and night for as long as the mourning rituals lasted; universities or city councils would

---

54 M.ª Adelaida Allo Manero, 'Las exequias reales de la casa de Austria y el arte efímero Español: estado de la cuestión', in *La fiesta cortesana en la época de los Austrias*, eds. María Luisa Lobato and Bernardo J. García (Valladolid: Junta de Castilla y León, 2003), 117–135.

55 Víctor Mínguez Cornelles, 'Tumbas vacías y cadáveres pintados, el cuerpo muerto del rey en los jeroglíficos novohispanos, siglos XVII y XVIII', *e-Spania: Revue interdisciplinaire d'études hispaniques médiévales et modernes*, 17 [online] (1 February 2014), accessed 11 April 2023. DOI: https://doi.org/10.4000/e-spania.23282. 'En la España imperial, como en la Roma imperial, las honras fúnebres de cada monarca devinieron en una ceremonia capital en el espectáculo de la representación del poder, y aun más tratándose de un sistema hereditario. Cada fallecimiento de un rey implicaba la subida al trono de otro miembro de la dinastía. Para garantizar que la transición de uno al otro en el trono se efectuaba sin dificultades y que la lealtad de todos los reinos, ciudades y villas del imperio al príncipe heredero no corría peligro, un enorme aparato de propaganda se ponía en marcha en cada ocasión, siendo sus principales elementos los ritos funerarios, los túmulos arquitectónicos y los programas iconográficos que decoraban espacios y estructuras efímeras luctuosas, en cada una de las miles de exequias que se organizaban en todos los templos del imperio'.

organise competitions, and only the winning and approved designs were displayed.[56]

Another genre that is also quite interesting due to the dual nature of emblems as both subject of, and source for, scholarship, as noted at the beginning of the text, is their presence in 'mirrors for princes'.[57] This time-honoured literary subgenre experienced one of its most glorious moments under the Habsburgs. *Institutio Principis Christiani*,[58] a text written by Erasmus of Rotterdam (1469–1536) and dedicated to the very young Duke of Burgundy, the future emperor, would shape imperial policy, distinguishing between the Christian ruler and the Machiavellian prince who, in his abusive pursuit of national interest, exercised a cunning, amoral, pessimistic style of political leadership. Erasmus's Christian prince was echoed in several texts and even expressed through emblems, as in Diego de Saavedra Fajardo's famous *Idea de un príncipe político cristiano*.[59] (Fig. 11.5)

This work, dedicated to the ill-fated Prince Balthasar Charles (1629–1646), set a new standard for political emblematica, especially in Spain, as the political concerns of the time are revealed throughout the text. Besides outlining the instruction and conduct of the future king at different stages of his life, it also defines a *raison d'état*. And all this was achieved in a literary genre that had already been producing great titles under Habsburg patronage for the previous one hundred years:

> I propose to Your Highness the *Idea of a Christian Political Prince*, represented with the burin and the quill so that, by way of the eyes and

---

56 María Adelaida Allo Manero and Juan Francisco Esteban Lorente, 'El estudio de las exequias reales de la monarquía Hispana: siglos XVI, XVII y XVIII', *Artigrama: Revista del Departamento de Historia del Arte de la Universidad de Zaragoza*, 19 (2004), 86. 'el mundo de la época consideró a los jeroglíficos como la parte más sorprendente y entretenida de las exequias; se pintaban en grandes pliegos de papel que se colgaban en cuerdas en torno al túmulo o pendientes del propio túmulo, el público se los disputaba y arrancaba, y se ponían guardias durante el día y la noche para que duraran los días de las celebraciones; la universidad o los ayuntamientos convocaban los concursos para su ejecución y sólo se exhibían los premiados y aceptados'. On this subject, see also María Adelaida Allo Manero, 'Líneas de investigación sobre el lenguaje emblemático del arte efímero: las composiciones simbólicas para las exequias reales de la Casa de Austria', *Boletín del Museo e Instituto Camón Aznar*, LXXXV (2001), 5–12.

57 Víctor Mínguez Cornelles, *Las virtudes emblemáticas del príncipe: arte e ideología durante el reinado de los últimos Austrias* (València: Universitat de València, 1990).

58 Erasmus, *Institutio Principis Christiani* (1516).

59 Diego de Saavedra Fajardo, *Idea de un príncipe político christiano, representada en cien empresas* (Munich: 1640; 2nd ed. Milan: 1642).

Fig. 11.5. Frontpage of *Idea de vn principe politico christiano*, by Diego de Saavedra Fajardo. © Biblioteca Nacional de España, Madrid.

ears—instruments of knowledge—the spirit of Your Highness may be better instructed in the science of ruling and the figures may serve as an ingenious reminder.[60]

---

60 Propongo a V. A. la *Idea de un príncipe político cristiano*, representada con el buril y con la pluma para que por los ojos y por los oídos —instrumentos del saber— quede más informado el ánimo de V. A. en la sciencia del reinar y sirvan las figuras de memoria artificiosa.

Concluding remarks

The foregoing evidence supports the hypothesis that further scholarship in the field of emblematic literature will corroborate the idea that the early modern era and its changes were connected to the development of such cultural manifestations. Using emblematic literature, and its consequent circulation via the different Habsburg branches, is precisely what made it so important.

The idea of emblems was an entirely humanistic one. They invented a new language by looking to the past. That combination of images and words was inspired by classical antiquity, its mythology and its coins, among other elements. It also drew on the medieval world and its symbolism, including the culture of knightly devices, as the break with the Middle Ages was not all that radical. Emblematic literature gave birth to a novel language with evident didactic intentions, providing instruction on doctrinal and moral matters but also, from an early date, illustrating a political idea for propagandistic purposes as only the House of Habsburg could.

JOSÉ LUIS GONZALO SÁNCHEZ-MOLERO

Books and Libraries in the Construction of the Habsburg Dynasty's Image During the Sixteenth Century

When Konrad Celtis dedicated his *Rhapsody* to Emperor Maximilian I in 1505, the humanist counted among the emperor's merits the organisation of the *Bibliotheca Regia*:

> I have busily carried out, with all the diligence and attention I am capable of, Your noble intentions and orders and established the royal library, which although it is still small in scale, is well endowed with Greek, Latin, and exotic authors; the scientific books recently purchased by Your Majesty, together with the larger globes and maps that depict the skies and those that depict the earth have been integrated systematically.[1]

Celtis's words constitute one of the earliest records of what we might call *Bibliophilia Austriaca*, employing the formula of the more familiar term *Pietas Austriaca*. After Maximilian I, several of his descendants—including Margaret of Austria; Charles V and his brother, Emperor Ferdinand I; Mary of Hungary; Philip II; Maximilian II; and Rudolf II—helped to establish the great libraries of Brussels, El Escorial and Vienna over the course of the sixteenth century, giving full meaning to that bibliophilia. Since the Late Middle Ages, the European courts had gradually developed a greater appreciation for reading, and the knowledge gleaned from it was considered a royal and noble virtue. In the fifteenth century, monarchs like

---

1 Celtis personally presented the monarch with a copy: J. Rest, 'Das Dedikationsexemplar der Rhapsodie des Conrad Celtes für König Maximilian I', *Zeitschrift für die Geschichte des Oberrheins*, 158 (2010), 159–173. English translation from the website of the Österreichische Nationalbibliothek, https://www.onb.ac.at/en/about-us/650th-anniversary/timeline/1500-emperor-maximilian-i-and-the-origins-of-the-bibliotheca-regia.

José Luis Gonzalo Sánchez-Molero • Complutense University of Madrid

Alfonso V in Naples and Matthias Corvinus in Hungary, and great noblemen such as Philip the Good in Burgundy and Federico da Montefeltro in Urbino, became renowned for their libraries.[2] The founding of the Vatican Library (1448) revived the idea of the universal library that Alexandria had represented in antiquity. Another influential factor in this process was the new 'court civilisation', to use the term coined by Norbert Elias.[3] The courtly setting had been created and constructed to ensure that greater, like lesser, rulers of the day were surrounded by a suitable blend of practical service, regal acclaim and social control over the nobility. In this respect, the court was instrumental in establishing a remarkable trend of palatine bibliophilia over the course of the sixteenth century.

The Habsburgs were by no means oblivious to this cultural process. It is fascinating to study their bibliophilia in the sixteenth century, not only because of the importance of the people who had a hand in its configuration, but also because of the volumes they collected and the relevance of that heritage today. We should not forget that, from the time of Emperor Maximilian I, several of his descendants, such as Philip II in Brussels and San Lorenzo de El Escorial, or Ferdinand I and his son Maximilian II in Vienna, founded important public libraries. The efforts of these monarchs to amass large collections of ancient manuscripts and printed books were not merely driven by personal interest; rather, they were part of a calculated cultural policy in which books came to symbolise the greatness of the dynasty and its roles, first as the guardian of Renaissance humanism and later as defender of the Catholic faith. Although scholars have paid more attention to the art patronage of the House of Habsburg, one of the most important in modern Europe,[4] it should not be forgotten that members of both branches of this dynasty were also unstinting in their efforts to fill other rooms in their palaces: the libraries.[5]

---

2 For just a few examples of the extensive literature on this subject, see Hanno Wijsman, 'Bibliothèques princières entre Moyen Age et humanisme. A propos des livres de Philippe le Bon et Mathias Corvin et de l'interprétation du XVe siècle', in *Mathias Corvin, les bibliothèques princières et la genèse de l'État moderne*, eds. Jean-François Maillard, István Monok and Donatella Nebbiai (Budapest: Országos Széchényi Könyvtár, 2009), 121–134; Marcella Peruzzi, *Cultura, potere, immagine: La biblioteca di Federico di Montefeltro* (vol. 20) (Urbino: Accademia Raffaello, 2004); Camille Gaspar and Frédéric Lyna, *Philippe le Bon et ses beaux libres* (Brussels: Éditions du Cercle d'art, 1944).

3 Norbert Elias, *The Civilizing Process* (Oxford: Blackwell, 2000).

4 As this artistic patronage is discussed by other authors in their respective contributions to this volume, there is no need to provide an extensive list of references here. I will merely mention the well-known essay by Hugh Trevor-Roper, *Princes and Artists: Patronage and Ideology at Four Habsburg Courts, 1517–1633* (New York: Harper & Row, 1976); and Fernando Checa Cremades, *Felipe II: mecenas de las artes* (Madrid: Editorial Nerea, 1992).

5 The Spanish case has been studied by Fernando Bouza Álvarez, 'Leer en palacio: de "aula gigantium" a museo de reyes sabios', in *El libro en Palacio y otros estudios bibliográficos*, eds. Pedro Manuel Cátedra García and María Luisa López-Vidriero Abello (Salamanca:

Fig. 12.1. *Portrait of Charles V* by Cristoph Amberger, c. 1532.
© Staatliche Museen zu Berlin, Gemaldegalerie.

Habsburg bibliophilia began with Maximilian I (1459–1519), 'builder' of the subsequent fortune of the dynastic image of the House of Austria. According to Larry Silver, Maximilian was the first ruler to exploit the propagandistic power of printed images and text. Silver believes that the emperor's preference for the language of propaganda was due to his lack of stable territorial authority. This prompted him to undertake expensive

Fig. 12.2. *The librarian*, painting by Arcimboldo, *c.* 1566. © Skokloster Castle, Sweden.

'visual-media' campaigns to forward his claims to imperial rank. He patronised and even personally supervised and collaborated with the best printers, craftsmen and artists of his time to produce illustrated books, prints, medals and armour.⁶ This resulted in an ambitious programme of initiatives, two of which are noteworthy: the monarch's personal library and the publishing projects he financed. In both cases, the book was treated as a highly useful cultural object for improving the Habsburg dynasty's image. Although Maximilian's enterprises did not materialise in a large public library, they did produce an imperial *studiolo* and a 'paper library' where tomes and prints displayed the history, grandeur and power of the House of Austria. The true 'stone libraries' founded by his descendants later served the same purpose.

The emperor's choice of Konrad Celtis to organise his library around 1497 has been viewed as the most direct antecedent to the *Hofbibliothek* or Imperial Library in Vienna, founded by Maximilian II in 1575. When the emperor called Celtis into his service, he had just inherited a notable library of manuscripts from his father, Frederick III († 1493), which included items acquired by various ancestors and relatives from Duke Albert III of Austria to King Wenceslaus I of Bohemia, as well as a little over one hundred of his progenitor's own books.⁷ As the husband and widower of Mary of Burgundy, Maximilian was acquainted with the library of the Dukes of Burgundy and probably thought that the imperial library had to be just as great, if not greater. Consequently, he strove to enrich his own library, trying to make it a symbol of Habsburg antiquity and grandeur. He pursued this goal with the inestimable assistance of Celtis, a humanist from Nuremberg who had studied in Italy under Giovanni Battista Guarino, Marcus Musurus and Julius Pomponius Laetus. Celtis had the books of Emperor Frederick III moved from his palace in Wiener Neustadt to Ambras Castle near Innsbruck, where Maximilian preferred to live, and advised the emperor on book acquisitions. We know, for instance, that the emperor tried to secure the magnificent library of King Matthias Corvinus († 1490) without success, although he did gradually acquire other libraries like that of his cousin Ladislaus the Posthumous (1440–1457), Duke of Austria and King of Hungary and Bohemia.

Ediciones Universidad de Salamanca, 1996), 29–42; 'Reyes sabios: la majestad, los libros y la educación de los príncipes', in *Biblioteca Nacional de España, La Real Biblioteca Pública, 1711–1760, de Felipe V a Fernando VI, Madrid, 2 de junio–19 de septiembre, 2004* (Madrid: Biblioteca Nacional, 2004), 165–174; and *El libro y el cetro: la biblioteca de Felipe IV en la Torre Alta del Alcázar de Madrid* (Salamanca: Instituto de Historia del Libro y de la Lectura, 2005).

6 Larry Silver, *Marketing Maximilian: the visual ideology of a Holy Roman Emperor* (Princeton, NJ/Oxford: Princeton University Press, 2008).

7 Alphons Lhotsky, 'Die Bibliothek Kaiser Friedrichs III', *Mitteilungen des Instituts für Österreichische Geschichtsforschung*, 58 (1950), 124–135; Franz Unterkircher, 'Die Bibliothek Friedrichs III', in *Ausstellung: Friedrich III: Kaiserresidenz Wiener Neustadt* (Wiener Neustadt: Friedrich Jasper, 1966), 218–225.

However, there is no evidence this *bibliotheca* was organised like an Italian-style *studiolo*. Maximilian's books were kept in leather-bound chests that accompanied him on his travels through Germany or to his summer residences. This suggests that it was a portable library rather than a fixed architectural space, perhaps because the books had to adapt to their master's itinerant style of rule. Yet Maximilian I did introduce, as an innovative alternative, a 'paper library' by publishing a series of 'autobiographical' works that extolled the House of Habsburg. These volumes were printed to be distributed, not to enlarge his library. Works such as *Theuerdank, Der Weisskunig* and the prayer book for the Order of Saint George, or the collections of prints for the *Saints Connected with the House of Habsburg, Arch of Honour* and *Triumphal Procession* series were part of this revolutionary typographic project. Obviously, using books as a propaganda tool was nothing new. The emperor's initiative was novel because he realised that the printing press and woodcuts, skilfully combined with the new political, literary and aesthetic ideas of the Renaissance, could spectacularly magnify public perception of the Habsburgs.[8] Maximilian's publishing projects were so ambitious and meticulous that he could not complete them all. Some, like *Freydal*, never made it past the manuscript stage. However, a luxury edition of *Theuerdank* was printed and published by Johannes Schönsperger at Augsburg (1517). That same year, the emperor also saw the 182 prints of the *Arch of Honour* series published (1517–1518), but the *Triumphal Procession* woodcuts were not printed until 1526.[9]

Maximilian's daughter Margaret proved to be an efficient collaborator on his projects. Their correspondence hints at other examples of this collusion. In 1510, for example, he asked his daughter to send him a recently printed genealogy of the kings of France and a copy of Valera's short history of Spain, *Crónica de España abreviada*,[10] and in February 1518 he sent Margaret the very first prints of the *Arch of Honour* series.[11]

---

8 For a recent analysis of the subject, see *The book triumphant: print in transition in the sixteenth and seventeenth centuries*, eds. Malcolm Walsby and Graeme Kemp (Leiden/Boston: Brill, 2011); Apparently, it was Peutinger who advised the emperor to publish the books of his autobiography: Karl Schütz, 'Maximiliano y el Arte', in *Reyes y Mecenas: Los Reyes Católicos, Maximiliano I y los inicios de la Casa de Austria en España*, catálogo exposición *Museo de Santa Cruz, Toledo, marzo–mayo 1992* (Madrid: Ministerio de Cultura/Patrimonio Nacional/JCCM, 1992), 237.
9 Stanley Appelbaum, trans., *The triumph of Maximilian I: 137 woodcuts by Hans Burgkmair and others* (New York: Dover, 1964).
10 Letters from Maximilian I to Margaret of Austria (Villingen, 27 Oct. 1510, and Freiburg, 31 Dec. 1510). Published in Andre Joseph Ghislain Le Glay, *Correspondance de l'empereur Maximilien Ier et de Marguerite d'Autriche, sa fille, Gouvernante des Pays Bas, de 1507 à 1519. Publiée d'après les Manuscrits originaux* (Paris: Jules Renouard & Cia, 1839), vol. I, 344 and 368.
11 Dagmar Eichberger and Lisa Beaven, 'Family Members and Political Allies: The portrait collection of Margaret of Austria', *The Art Bulletin*, 77, 2 (1995), 225–248 (esp. 247).

Fig. 12.3. *The young White King learns black magic*, from the *Weisskunig*, woodcut by Hans Burgkmair, 1516.

It is therefore hardly surprising that his daughter cemented the dynasty's bibliophile tendencies. Educated in the Netherlands, France and Germany, betrothed to King Charles VIII of France and twice married and widowed (to John, Prince of Asturias and Philibert, Duke of Savoy), in 1506 Margaret returned to the land of her birth, where she governed the Netherlands as regent on behalf of her under-age nephew Charles after the death of his father, Philip the Fair. Philip should have been the protagonist of these lines, but his untimely demise at Burgos (1506) prevented him from playing a relevant role in Habsburg bibliophilia.[12] Fortunately, his sister shouldered that responsibility with brilliant success. By the end of Margaret's life, the library contained approximately 400 volumes, mostly manuscripts,[13] which reflected not only the history of Burgundy and the Franco-Flemish culture of the day, but also a powerful awareness of female readership that had been growing steadily in Central Europe since the fifteenth century.[14]

Although Margaret acquired several important manuscripts in France, Castile and Savoy and inherited books from deceased relatives like her step-grandmother Margaret of York,[15] it was not until she was widowed for a second time that she showed signs of wanting to create a large library. Her goal was to restore Burgundy's former glory through books. The archduchess knew that after her grandfather Charles the Bold died at the Battle of Nancy (1477), the ducal library had been plundered or pawned, and one of her aims was to make up for those losses. After taking possession of her dead brother Philip's estate (including his library), she bought codices from the libraries of Netherlandish nobles known for their love of books and beautiful manuscripts,[16] like Charles de Croÿ, Prince of Chimay (1511) and Jean de Wavrin.[17] Margaret's efforts to rebuild the old library of the Dukes of Burgundy were undoubtedly connected to what her father was doing concomitantly in Germany with a similar aim: assembling the books of his Germanic ancestors.

However, Margaret's bibliophilia was also innovative in several respects. Unlike Maximilian I, who stored his books in chests, when

---

12 However, this does not mean that he did not have his own library. See Hanno Wijsman, 'Philippe le Beau et les livres: rencontré entre une époque et une personnalité', in Hanno Wijsman, ed., *Books in transition at the time of Philip the Fair: manuscripts and printed books in the late fifteenth and early sixteenth century Low Countries*, Burgundica 15 (2010), 17–91.

13 Ghislaine De Boom, 'La librairie de Marguerite d'Autriche', *Revue de l'Université de Bruxelles*, I (1926), 1–40; Marguerite Debae, *La librairie de Marguerite d'Autriche: exposition Europalia 87 Österreich: Bibliothèque Royale Albert I*^{er}*, Chapelle de Nassau: du 18 septembre au 5 décembre 1987. Catalogue par Marguerite Debae* (Brussels: Bibliothèque Royale Albert Ier, 1987); and by the same author, Marguerite Debae, *La Bibliothèque de Marguerite d'Autriche: essai de reconstitution d'après l'inventaire de 1523–1524* (Louvain/Paris: Editions Peeters, 1995).

14 Dagmar Eichberger, Anne-Marie Legaré and Wim Hüsken, *Women at the Burgundian court: presence and influence / Femmes à la cour de Bourgogne: présence et influence*, Burgundica 17 (Turnhout: Brepols, 2010).

15 On the bibliophilia of this duchess of Burgundy, see Georges Dogaer, 'Margareta van York, bibliofiele', in *Handelingen van de Koninklijke Kring voor Oudheidkunde, letteren en kunst van Mechelen*, 79 (1975), 99–111; L. M. J. Delaisse, 'Marguerite d'York et ses livres', in *Marguerite d'York et son temps* (British Week in Brussels, 29 Sept.–7 Oct. 1967) (Brussels: Banque de Bruxelles, 1967), 13–14; and *Charles le Téméraire : exposition organisée à l'occasion du cinquième centenaire de sa mort* (Brussels: Bibliothèque Royal, 1977), 17–19 and 96–100.

16 Thomas Kren and Scot McKendrick, eds., *Illuminating the renaissance: the triumph of Flemish manuscript painting in Europe* (Los Angeles: Getty Museum/Royal Academy of Arts, 2003).

17 Debae, *La librairie de Marguerite d'Autriche*, XVII.

Margaret moved her books to the palace at Mechelen, she placed the volumes in dedicated rooms with special furniture to shelve them.[18] The library of 'Madame' was hardly portable (according to an inventory from 1523–1524, it contained 386 books), which explains the need for a specific room to store the volumes. In that space, already known as *la Librairie*, the carefully numbered books were arranged on lecterns or desks. The different cases were not classified by content, but the people responsible for this library created a simple topographical catalogue system to make works easier to find. The permanent location of the books and the use of an organisational system were both significant developments. Although the library was still conceived as a late medieval 'book-hoard', its custodians were applying certain innovative library science methods typical of the public libraries of the day. However, Margaret never believed her *librairie* should be open to the public. She simply felt that, given the palatial setting and the money spent to acquire those books, the library should be a courtly showcase that offered visitors an image of magnificence and displayed the universal power of the House of Habsburg. It is therefore not surprising that her library contained a portrait gallery picturing members of her dynasty and family and other illustrious figures like Charlemagne, Charles VIII of France and a Turkish sultan.[19] In 1523, Margaret added new ornaments to her *librairie*; the family portraits were joined by paintings of religious themes and battles and an exotic collection of objects

---

18 As deduced from the inventories of her assets at the Palace of Savoy, first published by Henri Victor Michelant, 'Inventaire des vaisselles, joyaux, tapisseries, peintures, manuscrits, etc. de Marguerite d'Autriche, régente et gouvernante des Pays-Bas, dressé en son palais de Malines, le 9 juillet 1523', *Académie Royale des Sciences des Lettres et des Beaux-Arts de Belgique, Bulletin de la Commission royale d'histoire*, 128, ser. 3, no. 12 (Brussels, 1871), 5–78 and 83–136; H. Zimmerman, 'Inventoire des parties des meubles estans es cabinetz de Madame en sa Ville de Malines', *Jahrbuch der Kunsthistorischen Sammlungen des Allerhöchsten Kaiserhauses*, 3, 2 (1885), 93–123. The inventories were also transcribed by Eleanor E. Tremayne, *The first governess of the Netherlands: Margaret of Austria* (London: Methuen, 1908), and finally by Fernando Checa Cremades et al., eds., *Los inventarios de Carlos V y la familia imperial*, 3 vols (Madrid: Fernando Villaverde, 2010). The latter is currently the most accessible and error-free record of these inventories. The third volume also includes an introduction to the archduchess's inventories by Dagmar Eichberger, 'Margaret of Austria and the documentation of her collection in Mechelen', 2351–2363.

19 Listed in 1516 under the heading *Les painctures estans en la librayre de Madame*. On the functions of Margaret's portrait collection at Mechelen, see Dagmar Eichberger and Lisa Beaven, 'Family members and political allies; the portrait collection of Margaret of Austria', *The Art Bulletin* 77, 2 (1995), 225–248; and Dagmar Eichberger, 'Margaret of Austria's treasures: an early Habsburg collection in the Burgundian Netherlands', in *Museo imperial: el coleccionismo artístico de los Austrias en el siglo XVI*, eds. Fernando Checa Cremades, Elena Vázquez Dueñas and Santiago Arroyo Esteban (Madrid: Fernando Villaverde Ediciones, 2013), 71–80.

from the Americas given to her by Charles V.[20] Most were pieces crafted with precious metals and feathers, but there were also some rare mounted animals.[21]

With such sumptuous decoration—which allows us to identify her library as a forerunner of the *Kunst- und Wunderkammern* so dear to later Habsburgs—it is easy to understand why Margaret liked to receive distinguished guests in this room. Some visitors to this *librairie* at Mechelen left us testimonies of the impression it made on them. Around 1518, Erasmus of Rotterdam was permitted to consult the rich *Evangeliary* in the archduchess's possession (now known as the *Codex Aureus Escurialensis*, copied for Emperor Henry III in 1046),[22] and the humanist recalled that it was always presented to him with great ceremony amid blazing torches.[23] In all likelihood, given its great age the archduchess regarded it almost as a holy relic. In his *Diary*, Albrecht Dürer also recounted his interview with Margaret at Mechelen in June 1521, praising her library and picture gallery. He said that she showed him a little book on the proportions of the human body by Venetian painter Jacopo de' Barbari. Dürer begged her to give it to him, but the archduchess regretfully declined, saying she had promised it to Bernard van Orley.[24]

---

20 Deanna MacDonald, 'Collecting a new world: the ethnographic collections of Margaret of Austria', *The Sixteenth Century Journal*, 33, 3 (2002), 649–663; Paul Vandenbroeck, 'Amerindian art and ornamental objects in royal collections: Brussels, Mechelen, Duurstede, 1520–1530', in *America: Bride of the Sun: 500 Years Latin America and the Low Countries* (Antwerp: Royal Museum of Fine Arts, 1991), 99–119; and Dagmar Eichberger, 'Naturalia and artefacta: Dürer's nature drawings and early collecting', in *Dürer and His Culture*, eds. Dagmar Eichberger and Charles Zika (Cambridge: Cambridge University Press, 1998), 24–25.

21 Checa Cremades, *Los inventarios*, 2403.

22 Pieter F. Hovingh, 'Erasmus and the "Codex Aureus"', *Quaerendo*, 19, 4 (1989), 308–313.

23 In the early seventeenth century, Fray José de Sigüenza reported the flattering testimony of the Dutch humanist: 'Erasmo Roterodamo celebró mucho este libro en las anotaciones al Nuevo Testamento, y le llama el códice áureo, y sacó de él algunas buenas y germanas lecciones que no halló en otros originales. Encarece la solemnidad con que se lo mostraron, y se mostraba siempre encendiendo antorchas y otras ceremonias santas como debidas a joya tan preciosa. Dice lo vio la primera vez en poder de la Princesa Margarita, hija de Maximiliano, mujer del malogrado Príncipe don Juan. Después dice que lo tenía la Reina María, hermana del Emperador Carlos V'. [Erasmus Roterodamus highly praised this book in his commentaries on the New Testament and called it the golden codex, and drew from it good and germane lessons which he did not find in other originals. He extolled the solemnity with which it was shown to him, and it was always shown lighting torches and performing other holy ceremonies as befitted such a precious gem. He said that he first saw it in the possession of Princess Margaret, daughter of Maximilian and wife of the ill-fated Prince John. Later he said that Queen Mary, sister of Emperor Charles V, had it.] José de Sigüenza, *La fundación del monasterio de El Escorial* (Madrid: Aguilar, 1963), 433–434.

24 Albrecht Dürer, *Sketchbook of His Journey to the Netherlands 1520–1521* (New York: Praeger, 1971), 44.

Emperor Charles V might have carried on the bibliophilic tradition of his aunt and paternal grandfather. When Margaret died in 1530, her nephew was declared the principal heir to her assets, but the monarch did not want the books, preferring to let his sister Mary have use of them. She, rather than her powerful brother, is the next important character in our retrospective survey of Habsburg bibliophilia. Mary of Austria (1505–1558), Dowager Queen of Hungary and Governess of the Netherlands, had been educated by Margaret herself at her Mechelen palace, until she left for Vienna in 1514 to continue her education beside her grandfather Maximilian while awaiting her marriage to Louis Jagiellon, heir to the Hungarian throne.[25] In that realm, she would discover the magnificent Bibliotheca Corvinian in Buda. After Hungary was invaded by the Ottoman army (1526), Mary saved some codices kept there, including the splendid *Missal of Matthias Corvinus* and an evangeliarium in Greek believed to be an autographed work by Saint John Chrysostom. Yet even at this early stage, it seems Mary was more interested in the heated religious debates that divided Europe in those days than in ancient manuscripts. Mary was an avid reader of Erasmus and Luther's works, Charles V himself cautioned her not to take such a benevolent view of Lutheranism.[26] This may explain why, when Mary returned to the Netherlands to rule as governess (1531), she had no desire to merely follow in her Aunt Margaret's bibliophilic footsteps. She left Mechelen and settled in Brussels, at Coudenberg Palace,[27] bringing the books with her to join the codices of the Dukes of Burgundy already there. She placed the volumes in a specific room of the palace, the upper *Salle*, where they were inventoried in 1536.[28] The collection then

---

25 Gernot Heiss, *Köningin Maria von Ungarn und Böhmen: ihr leben und ihre wirtschaflichen Interessen in Österreich, Ungarn und Böhmen*, 2 vols (Vienna: Phil. Diss., 1971).
26 Bart Jan Spruyt, 'Verdacht van Lutherse Sympathieën: Maria van Hongarije en de religieuze controversen van haar tijd', in Boogert, Kerkhoff and Koldeweij, *Maria van Hongarije: koningin tussen keizers en kunstenaars 1505–1558* (Zwolle: Waanders, 1993), 87–103; On the Erasmian leanings at her court, see Katherine J. Walsh and Alfred A. Strnad, 'Eine Erasmianerin im hause Habsburg: Königin Maria von Ungarn (1505–1558) und die anfänge der evangelischen bewegung', *Historisches Jahrbuch*, 118 (1998), 40–85.
27 Krista de Jonge, 'Le palais de Charles-Quint à Bruxelles: ses dispositions intérieures aux XVe et XVIe siècles et le cérémonial de Bourgogne', in *Architecture et la vie sociale: l'organisation intérieure des grandes demeures à la fin du Moyen Âge et à la Renaissance*, ed. Jean Guillaume (Paris: Picard, 1994), 107–126; and Bob van den Boogert, Jacqueline Kerkhoff and A. M. Koldeweij, *Maria van Hongarije: koningin tussen keizers en kunstenaars, 1505–1558* (Zwolle: Waanders, 1993).
28 Henri Victor Michelant, 'Inventaire des joyaux, ornements d'église, vaisselles, tapisseries, livres, tableaux, etc., de Charles-Quint, dressé à Bruxelles au mois de mai 1536', *Compte-rendu des séances de la Commission Royale d'Histoire ou recueil de ses bulletins*, 3rd series, vol. XIII, II bulletin (1871), 199, 217–218, 236, 256–329; Brief references to this inventory in Par Robert Wellens, 'L'intérêt des inventaires des joyaux, vaisselles et effets des souverains des Pays-Bas pour l'histoire de la cartographie sous le règne de Charles Quint', *Imago Mundi*, 26, 1 (1972), 27–30.

doubled in number to six hundred tomes. Mary created the great dynastic library at Coudenberg, the 'library of Burgundy', although she merely preserved its holdings and made no effort to enlarge the collection. Remember that the books belonged not to her but to her brother Charles V, who had merely given her the right to use and enjoy them.

After 1540, Mary showed interest in having a library for her own private use.[29] She never owned many volumes, but the personal nature of her book collection is revealed by manuscript bookplates ('*Ce liure apartient &. La Royne*' [This book belongs [to] The Queen]) and woodcut bookplates with her coloured coat of arms. Using these marks of ownership is interesting, as it indicates the adoption of a custom typical of Renaissance bibliophiles and humanists, and a desire to personalise the books and identify them as belonging to a separate collection. A chance to create such a collection finally presented itself in 1545 when construction began on her palace at Binche, considered the finest example of her art patronage.[30] This great project encouraged the sovereign to enlarge her library, acquiring parts of the libraries of Netherlandish nobles like Anne de Croÿ, Princess of Chimay († 1539), and her husband Philippe de Croÿ (1496–1549). She also purchased a very old manuscript of *De Baptismo* by Saint Augustine, believed to be written in the saint's own hand, from the Benedictine monks of Werden Abbey, who had fled to the Netherlands after Protestants ousted them from their monastery in Germany.[31] This

---

29 On her library, see Louis Prosper Gachard, 'Notice sur la librairie de la reine Marie de Hongrie, sœur de Charles Quint, régente des Pays-Bas', *Compte-rendu des séances de la commission royale d'histoire, ou recueil de ses bulletins*, 10, 10 (1845), 224–246; Claudine Lemaire, 'De librije van Maria van Hongarije', in Bob van den Boogert, Jacqueline Kerkhoff and A. M. Koldeweij, *Maria van Hongarije tussen keizers en kunstenaars van Hongarije 1505–1558* (Zwolle: Waanders Uitgevers, 1993), 179–188; and Claudine Lemaire, 'La bibliothèque des imprimés de la reine Marie de Hongrie régente des Pays-Bas, 1505–1558', *Bibliothèque d'Humanisme et Renaissance: Travaux et Documents*, 58, 1 (1996), 119–139; José Luis Gonzalo Sánchez-Molero, *Regia Bibliotheca: el libro en la Corte española de Carlos V*, 2 vols (Mérida: Editora Regional de Extremadura, 2005), I, 339–446; José Luis Gonzalo Sánchez-Molero, 'La biblioteca de María de Hungría y la bibliofilia de Felipe II', in *Marie de Hongrie: politique et culture sous la Renaissance aux Pays-Bas: actes du colloque tenu au Musée royal de Mariemont les 11 et 12 novembre 2005*, eds. Bertrand Federinov and Gilles Docquier, Monographie du Musée Royal de Mariemont, 17 (Morlanwelz-Mariemont: Musée Royal de Mariemont, 2009), 156–173; and José Luis Gonzalo Sánchez-Molero, 'Mary of Hungary (1505–1556): Female reading and dynastic bibliophilia on Mary of Hungary', in *Mary of Hungary, Renaissance patron and collector: gender, rat and culture*, ed. Noelia García Pérez (Turnhout: Brepols, 2020).

30 Krista De Jonge, 'Marie de Hongrie, maître d'ouvrage (1531–1555)', in *Marie de Hongrie: politique et culture sous la Renaissance aux Pays-Bas: actes du colloque tenu au Musée royal de Mariemont les 11 et 12 novembre 2005*, eds. Bertrand Federinov and Gilles Docquier, Monographie du Musée royal de Mariemont, 17 (Morlanwelz-Mariemont: Musée Royal de Mariemont, 2008), 124–139.

31 Gonzalo, *Regia Bibliotheca*, II, 242, 2.

and other rare books were probably added to the *Kunstkammer* that Mary created at Binche. However, unlike the *librairie* at Mechelen, here books were not the main attraction. The new Mannerist fashion for these rooms was to collect items such as statues of emperors, gods and heroes, assorted portraits, coins, minerals, stuffed animals and fossils. In one of his letters, Ferdinand of Austria praised his sister's cabinet of curiosities, filled with examples of both *naturalia* and *artificialia*.[32] The destruction and looting of Binche Palace by French troops in 1554 put an end to the queen's project.

However, at practically the same time, Mary made two important decisions about her books. Both were motivated by her desire to step down as governess of Flanders and retire to Spain with her siblings Charles and Eleanor of Austria. The queen realised, logically, that she would have no use for the Burgundian codices received from her Aunt Margaret and had them removed to Turnhout Castle; their rightful place was in the Netherlands, as dynastic property that should not leave the country. Simultaneously, she assembled a new library of books easy to carry and read, something to fill her hours of leisure and reading with her ladies in Castile. She purchased approximately three hundred volumes in French, all printed between 1550 and 1556. The subjects varied widely, including theology, spirituality, history, moral philosophy, natural philosophy, poetry, history and music, revealing palace reading material that contrasted with the ascetic choices of Charles V for his retreat at Yuste. In Castile, these books were joined by those from the library of her physician, Daniël van Vlierden (1557), with which Mary hoped to endow the library of a university school she wished to found at Zorita de los Canes in Guadalajara. Her death in 1558 prevented this idea from becoming a reality, but it was an interesting new development in Habsburg patronage.[33]

For most of his reign, Charles V monarch was not concerned with creating an imperial library or continuing the project begun by Maximilian I. His reading preferences were highly personal and far removed from the bibliophilic tastes of other family members.[34] However, for a few short years the emperor did show a willingness to establish a public imperial library. The idea had been put to him in 1537 by Hernando Colón, who

---

[32] We know that her brother King Ferdinand gave Mary several such items between 1548 and 1550, including a stag antler, pieces of copper and silver dross shaped like fish, and a substantial collection of old coins. Hans von Voltelini, 'Urkunden und regesten aus dem K. u. K. Haus-, Hof- und Staats-Archiv', *Jahrbuch der kunsthistorischen Sammlungen des allerhöchsten Kaiserhauses*, XV (1894), entries 6400, 6401 and 6402.

[33] Gonzalo, *Regia Bibliotheca*, I, 430–433.

[34] José Luis Gonzalo Sánchez-Molero, 'La biblioteca postrimera de Carlos V en España: las lecturas del emperador', *Hispania: Revista Española de Historia*, 206 (2000), 911–943; Gonzalo, *Regia Bibliotheca*, 2 vols; and by the same author, *El César y los libros: un viaje a través de las lecturas del emperador desde Gante a Yuste* (Yuste: Fundación Academia Europea de Yuste, 2008).

offered him the vast collection of books he owned in Seville for the purpose of founding a royal library open to the public. Canon of the Cathedral of Seville, Colón's only heir was his feckless nephew Luis Colón de Toledo, so he probably thought that seeking imperial protection was the best way to ensure the survival of his library. Yet he never received a reply, and after his death in 1539 Colón's library went to the Cathedral of Seville.[35] Then, the emperor had a sudden change of heart. In late 1539 his former rival, Francis I, invited him to travel across France, and on the way Charles V stopped at Fontainebleau, where the French king had a famous library. The shelves were stocked with the medieval illuminated codices of his ancestors and Greek and Latin manuscripts which the humanists at his court consulted to prepare critical editions then sold across Europe, imprinted as *Ex Bibliotheca Regia Francorum* [From the Library of the Royal Franks].[36] Charles V did not have such a library, and he had never promoted such an ambitious humanistic publishing project. These comparative shortcomings were compounded by a political 'insult': Francis I owned many codices from the former royal library in Naples, which Charles VIII had plundered and taken to France in 1493, while the true sovereign of Naples, the emperor, had none.

Understandably, as soon as he arrived in the Netherlands, Charles V appointed Pieter Coecke van Aelst as *libraire de son Imperialle Maiste* (1540), believing that a library could prove highly useful for boosting his political reputation. However, realising these cultural plans was no easy task. Given the vastness of the Caroline empire, it was difficult to decide where this library should be located, and even harder to choose a model to be emulated. Should it imitate the French library at Fontainebleau or the Roman library at the Vatican? Settling these matters was further complicated by the pressing political problems he faced, but in 1542 Charles V decided. He deposited the bulk of his portable library at the Castle of Simancas in the province of Valladolid, recently established as the home of the new royal archive of Castile. He never specified the library's intended purpose, nor did he complete it, for in 1543 the monarch left Spain and did not return until 1556, after his abdication. In any case, it

---

35 Klaus Wagner, 'Hernando Colón y la Biblioteca Colombina', in *Sevilla en el imperio de Carlos V: encrucijada entre dos mundos y dos épocas. Actas del simposio internacional celebrado en la Facultad de Filosofía y Letras de la Universidad de Colonia (23–25 de junio de 1988)*, eds. Pedro M. Piñero Ramírez and Christian Wentzlaff-Eggebert (Seville: Universidad de Sevilla and Universität zu Köln, 1991), 77–85; and by the same author, 'La biblioteca colombina en tiempos de Hernando Colón', *Historia. Instituciones. Documentos*, 19 (1992), 485–495.

36 Ursula Baurmeister and Marie-Pierre Laffitte, *Des livres et des rois: la Bibliothèque royale de Blois, catalogue d'exposition. Blois, château royal/ Paris, BN* (Paris: Bibliothèque nationale, 1992); and Christine Bénévent, Anne Charon, Isabelle Diu and Magali Vène, eds., *Passeurs de textes: Imprimeurs et libraires à l'âge de l'humanisme*, Études et rencontres, 37 (Paris: Publications de l'École nationale des chartes, 2012).

does not seem that he intended to make it a public library, in the spirit of humanism; instead, he rather favoured a dynastic model inspired by the old *Hofbibliothek* of his grandfather, Maximilian I, an idea borne out by the fact that Charles V left his finest pieces of armour at the castle along with his books. This motley assortment of books, armour, spoils from his North African campaigns and historical documents allows us to associate the Simancas project with the idea of the *Wunderkammer*, conceived as a 'shrine to Caesar's fame'.[37] All the materials were sent to Simancas, but the emperor's plans for them never materialised. When he died in 1558, his chests of books and his armour were sent to Madrid, leaving only the vast archives of the monarchy at the Castle of Simancas.

Of all the Habsburg monarchs, it fell to Philip II to complete the transition from the book-hoard/cabinet of curiosities concept to fully-fledged royal public library. The son and heir of Charles V, Philip had received a markedly humanistic education, and one consequence was a precocious love of books. By 1553, he already had more than eight hundred volumes in his personal library. Later known as the *librería rica* or 'rich library', its contents had been acquired between 1541 and 1547 with the goal of creating a compendium of all knowledge, in the Renaissance spirit of Conrad Gesner's *Bibliotheca Universalis*.[38] The books were also bound in Salamanca, following a strict heraldic model. This novel attempt at formal homogeneity, and the elevated cost of creating this rich princely library, cannot be entirely explained by the bibliophilic tastes of the young Philip II. In 1546 his books, stored in chest-desks, were taken from Valladolid to the Real Alcázar in Madrid. Although the reason was not specified, Philip probably already had it in mind to establish a royal library.

Between 1548 and 1556 the young Philip II also had the opportunity to see numerous European libraries during his 'Happiest Journey' and his brief English reign. There are very few references to these visits, but without them it would be hard to explain the monarch's favourable reception of the memorial presented to him by Juan Páez de Castro in Brussels, proposing the foundation of a royal library (1555). Although this text has been interpreted as being at the inception of the library at El Escorial, in reality its primary aim was to reactivate the plan for the Castle of Simancas, adapting it to new Renaissance models (which the humanist had seen in Venice and Rome). Páez therefore advised that the books be moved from the castle to the city of Valladolid, where the court was then installed, and that the library be 'converted' into a centre of reading and cultural dissemination, purchasing books in the classical and eastern languages to later be printed and circulated. What he proposed was essentially a public library

---

37 Gonzalo, *Regia Bibliotheca*, I, 264–294; Gonzalo, *El César y los libros*, 218–252.
38 José Luis Gonzalo Sánchez-Molero, *La 'Librería rica' de Felipe II. Estudio histórico y catalogación* (San Lorenzo de El Escorial, Madrid: Ediciones Escurialenses, 1998).

under royal patronage rather than another *studiolo* or *Wunderkammer*. This model was not initially implemented in Spain but in Brussels, where in 1559 Philip II decided to found a royal library, combining the books he had inherited from Margaret of Austria, still at Turnhout Castle, with the collection of the former Dukes of Burgundy in Coudenberg Palace. The king's decision to create this library had great political significance, presenting him as a sovereign protector of the Burgundian dynastic tradition and the 'national' identities of the Netherlands.[39] He placed this library in the hands of the Frisian jurist Viglius Zuichemus ab Aytta' (Wigle van Aytta vanZuychem), who managed it superbly[40] until the religious and political conflicts that sparked the Eighty Years' War brought his work to a halt. Although Brussels was controlled by the Dutch rebels for a short time, in 1585 Governor Alexander Farnese informed the king he had found the royal library and the rest of Coudenberg Palace 'tout en meilleur ordre que je ne pensais' [all in better order than I thought].[41]

Amid the work in Brussels, Philip II returned to Spain in 1559, where he also had to make a decision about his personal library. He had inherited books a year earlier from Joanna the Mad, Charles V and Mary of Hungary, who died in quick succession, and added them to the volumes in his already extensive 'rich library'. The monarch owned nearly two thousand printed or manuscript works; his library was far larger than the one in Brussels, and its dynastic origin and symbolism were just as relevant. However, his plan to establish a royal library in Spain had to be postponed when a serious religious situation arose: groups of Protestants had been discovered in his own country and were targeted by the Inquisition in 1558 and 1559. Philip II had to settle for moving all the books to the high tower of the Alcázar in Madrid, the city where he permanently settled his court in 1561, while he waited for the best time to create the library and to work out a plan that would be viable in Spain. The model of the royal library in Brussels was too closely linked to Netherlandish culture, and Páez de Castro's project for remodelling the library-archive at Simancas had become obsolete.

Constructing the Monastery of El Escorial gave Philip II the chance to design a new kind of royal library, more in keeping with Spanish traditions

---

39 Willy Vanderpijpen, 'Koninklijke Bibliotheek (1559–1794)', in *De Centrale Overheidsinstellingen van de Habsburgese Neederlanden (1482–1795)*, ed. Erik Aerts, 2 vols (Brussels: Algemeen Rijksarchief, 1994), 2, 921–930; Claudine Lemaire and Marguerite Debae, 'Esquisse historique 1559–1837', in *Bibliothèque royale, Mémorial 1559–1969* (Brussels: Bibliothèque royale Albert Ier, 1969), 3–83; and Margot Thøfner, 'Princely pieties: the 1598–1617 accessions of the royal library in Brussels', *Quaerendo* 30, 2 (2000), 130–153.
40 Jules Lambert, 'La Bibliothèque royale de 1559 et son conservateur Viglius van Aytta', *Archives, Bibliothèques et Musées de Belgique*, XXX (1959), 235–256.
41 Vanderpijpen, 'Koninklijke Bibliotheek', 922 (n. 3).

and the monarch's confessional politics. Initially, the king had not considered that the building should have a magnificent library, but in 1564 the planners discussed the need to establish a college at the monastery, with its own library—the perfect chance to resume his royal library project. After obtaining the Hieronymite community's approval, the king's books were moved from the Alcázar in Madrid to El Escorial between 1566 and 1569. Right around the same time, Juan de Herrera modified the monastery's initial layout, designed by Juan Bautista de Toledo, and placed the new royal library at the front of the building, in the most public and easily accessible part of the monastery. The Prudent King wanted it to be a new 'universal' library for public use.[42] In fact, the king's secretary Antonio Gracián Dantisco referred to it as a public library in his *Declaración de las Armas de S. Lorenzo el Real*:

> Esta obra nos ha traído el glorioso santo Lorenzo, don de su Majestad, pública librería tanto mayor y más preciosa que las pasadas cuanto que su poder se aventaja a los que le hicieron. Para este efecto ha hecho recoger todo lo que de los infortunios pasados en el reino se ha conservado.[43]

To achieve this goal, around 1570 Philip embarked on an ambitious campaign to acquire ancient Greek, Hebrew and Latin manuscripts in Spain and the rest of Europe.[44] The results were spectacular: in 1576 the monastery's magnificent library comprising 4,546 volumes, printed and manuscript, received nearly two thousand books that Diego Hurtado de Mendoza had gifted to the king[45] and several curious books owned by Carlos, Prince of Asturias.[46] After Benito Arias Montano organised and

---

42 José Luis Gonzalo Sánchez-Molero, 'Felipe II y los orígenes de la biblioteca humanística de Escorial', in *La Biblioteca Ambrosiana tra Roma, Milano e L'Europa. Atti delle giornate di studio 25–27 novembre 2004*, eds. Franco Buzzi and Roberta Ferro, Studia Borromaica, 19 (2005), 139–190.
43 Gonzalo, *Regia Bibliotheca*, I, 16: 'The glorious Saint Lawrence has brought us this work, a gift of His Majesty, a public library greater and more precious than any of its precedents, surpassing them to the same extent that his power exceeds that of those who made them. To this end he has mandated the compilation of all surviving records of past misfortunes in the realm'.
44 José Luis Gonzalo Sánchez-Molero, 'La Real Biblioteca de El Escorial: El "Arca de Noé" de la bibliofilia renacentista española', in *Bibliofilias: Exposición con motivo de 38º Congreso Internacional y 21ª Feria Internacional de la ILAB* (Madrid: Fundación Lázaro Galdiano, 2008), 87–95.
45 Gregorio de Andrés Martínez, 'Entrega de la librería real de Felipe II (1576)', in *Documentos para la Historia del Monasterio de San Lorenzo el Real de El Escorial*, vol. VII (Madrid: Imp. Helénica, 1964), 5–233.
46 Don Carlos tried to compete with his father in this matter, amassing a large library in his apartments, as well as a portrait gallery and a collection of *naturalia*. José Luis Gonzalo Sánchez-Molero, 'Lectura y bibliofilia en el príncipe don Carlos (1545–1568), o la alucinada búsqueda de la "sabiduría"', in *La memoria de los libros: estudios sobre la historia del escrito y de*

Fig. 12.4. Façade of El Escorial, detail of the situation of the Royal Library. © Photo by the author.

catalogued all the books, he was given the post of librarian at El Escorial and the library opened in 1583. Pellegrino Tibaldi's decorative programme for the library's Hall of Frescoes, painted between 1590 and 1592, did much to enhance its contents.[47]

While the Spanish king was busy displaying his power and cultural leadership skills by founding the royal libraries of Brussels and El Escorial,[48] his Austrian relatives in Vienna were not to be outdone. The learned Emperor Ferdinand I (1503–1564), brother of Charles V, had inherited the library of Maximilian I, who bequeathed ten or so books to his Spanish

---

    la lectura en Europa y América, eds. Pedro M. Cátedra and María Luisa López-Vidriero, 2 vols (Salamanca: Instituto de la Historia del Libro y de la Lectura, 2004), I, 705–734.

47 Fernando Bouza Álvarez, 'La biblioteca de El Escorial y el orden de los saberes en el siglo XVI', in *El Escorial. Arte, poder y cultura en la corte de Felipe II*, ed. Fernando Checa Cremades (Madrid: Cursos de Verano de El Escorial, 1988), 81–99; Checa Cremades, *Felipe II: mecenas de las artes*, 384; and Selina Blasco Castiñeyra, 'La descripción de El Escorial de fray José de Sigüenza: Reflexiones en torno a la transmisión literaria de la fama de los edificios', in *El Escorial: Arte, poder y cultura en la corte de Felipe II*, 37–62.

48 See the works of Fernando Bouza Álvarez compiled in *Imagen y propaganda: capítulos de la historia cultural del reinado de Felipe II* (Madrid: Akal, 1998).

grandson.⁴⁹ Later, as ruler of the dynasty's Austrian territories, Ferdinand came into possession of the bulk of Maximilian's *Hofbibliothek*.⁵⁰ Thanks to his excellent humanistic education, he immediately grasped the importance of the library his grandfather had assembled. He kept it safe and, after being elected King of the Romans, he revived some projects that Maximilian I had left unfinished upon his death, such as the publication of the *Triumphal Procession* (1526). As King of the Romans and of Hungary, subordinate to his brother and with a very complicated state of internal affairs in his hereditary lands, Ferdinand had little time to add to his library. However, after consolidating his power as the new Holy Roman Emperor in 1558, the *Hofbibliothek* became one of his main concerns. At this time, his goal was to adapt the contents of the new imperial library—as his nephew Philip was doing in Brussels and El Escorial—to Renaissance models. To achieve this, he enlisted the aid of several learned men, including Wolfgang Lazius and Augier Ghislain de Busbecq. The former visited German libraries and archives to research the history of the dynasty and its hereditary lands. When he returned, he brought back a large consignment of books for the emperor's library. Busbecq, whom Ferdinand I sent to Istanbul as his ambassador (in 1554 and 1556), purchased valuable Greek manuscripts in the Ottoman Empire, more than 270 of which ended up in the imperial library, among them the famous fourth-century *Codex Vindobonensis* manuscript by Dioscorides.⁵¹

When Ferdinand I died, he was succeeded by his son Maximilian II (1564–1575), a man whose religious convictions were close to Protestantism and who preferred to support other cultural and artistic activities. In contrast, Archdukes Charles and Ferdinand, rulers of Styria, were more interested in enriching their libraries and the famous Schloss Ambras *Wunderkammer* which, in addition to a spectacular art collection, housed part of Maximilian I's old book collection and nearly 7,000 books (1596).⁵² However, at the Viennese court, it was not until 1575 that Maximilian II made the unexpected decision to name Dutch scholar Hugo Blotius his

---

49 Theodor Gottlieb, *Die ambraser handschriften: beitrag zur geschichte der Wiener hofbibliothek (band 1): Büchersammlung Kaiser Maximilians I. mit einer Einleitung über älteren Bücherbesitz im Hause Habsburg* (Leipzig: Spirgatis, 1900), 48.
50 Josef Stummvoll, *Die Österreichische nationalbibliothek: festschrift herausgegeben zum 25 jährigen dienst Jubiläum des Generaldirektors Univ.-Prof. Dr. Josef Bick* (Vienna: H. Bauer Verlag, 1948).
51 Gábor Almási, *The uses of humanism: Johannes Sambucus (1531–1584), Andreas Dudith (1533–1589), and the Republic of Letters in East Central Europe*, Brill's Studies in Intellectual History, vol. 185 (Leiden/Boston: Brill, 2009).
52 According to the exhibition catalogue *Ambraser kunst-und wunderkammer: die bibliothek. Katalog der Ausstellung im Prunksaal 28. Mai bis 30. September 1965* (Vienna: Österreichische Nationalbibliothek, 1965); and to Elisabeth Scheicher, *Schloß Ambras, Innsbruck/Tirol: Schloß Ambras und seine sammlungen* (Munich: Schnell & Steiner, 1981).

Fig. 12.5. Portrait of *Philip II*, Juan Pantoja de la Cruz, c. 1590, Library of El Escorial. © Patrimonio Nacional.

librarian.⁵³ The *Hofbibliothek* had rarely been used in the years prior to his appointment, but Blotius was still shocked to find the books in such a woeful state of neglect. They had been tucked away in dark rooms, covered with dust and cobwebs, and in some cases even damaged by moths and worms.⁵⁴ Blotius had the rooms cleaned and he catalogued their contents. In 1576, the library consisted of approximately 7,400 manuscripts and rare books containing more than 20,000 separate works. That same year, Rudolf II succeeded his father Maximilian II to the throne. The new monarch had received an excellent education at both the Austrian and Spanish courts, giving him first-hand knowledge of the projects of his uncle, Philip II, and an impressive personal library.⁵⁵ Consequently, Rudolf II strove to make the old imperial library inherited from his ancestors at least as splendid as its Spanish counterpart. He commenced on an extensive campaign to acquire ancient manuscripts and even entire libraries from contemporary bibliophiles like Jacopo Strada⁵⁶ and Johannes Sambucus, who, for example, sold the emperor five hundred Latin and Greek manuscripts from his own collection.⁵⁷ With Rudolf's support, Blotius did not hesitate to make ambitious plans for the *Hofbibliothek*; he envisioned it as a future 'library of humanity' which, in its contents and exemplary organisation, would surpass the greatest libraries of the day, including that of the Bibliotheca Apostolica Vaticana in Rome. By the time Blotius died in 1608, the *Hofbibliothek* held 11,000 volumes.

By the early 1600s, the Habsburg family could proudly claim to be patrons of several of Europe's largest libraries. They had managed to accumulate a vast store of bibliographic wealth at their palaces in Madrid, Brussels, Ambras, Prague and Vienna, riches which King Philip IV in Spain and Emperor Leopold I in Austria both helped to enlarge over the course of the seventeenth century. Thanks to the solidity of their projects, today, centuries later, the contents of those same libraries are available to readers, researchers and society in general. These books offer valuable insight into the cultural patronage of the Habsburgs and the role that libraries played

---

53 Henry Carrington Bolton, *A model librarian three hundred years ago: on the work of Hugo Blotius as librarian of the imperial library* (Washington: 1899); and Hermann Menhardt, *Das älteste handschriftenverzeichnis der Wiener hofbibliothek von Hugo Blothius 1576* (Vienna: Österreichische Akademie der Wissenschaften, 1957).
54 Stuart A. P. Murray, *The library: an illustrated history* (New York: Skyhorse, 2012), 241.
55 R. Bauer and H. Haupt, 'Das Kunstkammerinventar Kaiser Rudolfs II: ein inventar aus den jahren 1607–1611', *Jahrbuch der kunsthistorischen Sammlungen in Wien*, 72 (1976), 1–191; Thomas DaCosta Kaufmann, 'Remarks on the collections of Rudolf II: the kunstkammer as a form of representation', Art Journal, 38, 1 (1978), 22–28.
56 Dirk Jacob Jansen, *Jacopo Strada and cultural patronage at the imperial court: the antique as innovation*, 2 vols (Leiden/Boston: Brill, 2019).
57 Gábor Almási, *The Uses of Humanism: Johannes Sambucus (1531–1584), Andreas Dudith (1533–1589), and the republic of letters in East Central Europe*, Brill's Studies in Intellectual History, vol. 185 (Leiden/Boston: Brill, 2010).

in promoting a certain image of their dynasty. If we wish to find a visual representation of this vibrant *Bibliophilia Austriaca* in the art of that time, we might look to one of Giuseppe Arcimboldo's best-known paintings: *The Librarian* (1566). With his customary skill and inventiveness, the Italian painter composed a human bust constructed of books and other objects: bookmarks suggesting fingers, bookcase keys instead of eyes, and animal-tail dusters to simulate a beard. This is undoubtedly one of his most famous 'composite heads', but we should not forget that this figure made of books also represents a librarian in the service of the Habsburgs.[58]

---

58 K. C. Elhard, 'Reopening the book on Arcimboldo's "Librarian"', Libraries & Culture, 40, 2 (2005), 115–127.

MARÍA JOSÉ VEGA

Epic and Truth

Writing for the Habsburgs in Sixteenth-Century Spain

Writing for the Habsburgs

The epic is the literary genre most closely associated with representation of sovereign image and power, legitimisation of the imperial enterprise and construction of legendary and historical genealogies of ruling houses. In the sixteenth century it was considered the most excellent and perfect genre, as it dealt with the loftiest subjects (the valiant deeds of warriors and princes, the founding of nations and empires, the victories of the faith), had an unbroken tradition of critical reflection and commentary, and was the backbone of the European literary canon. The epic was, foremost, the genre of the *Aeneid*, which narrated the founding of Rome by the survivors of the Trojan War and the construction of an empire *sine fine* that culminated in the greatness of Augustus. In the sixteenth century, Europe's ruling dynasties looked to epic models to shape their public images and link their mythical and historical genealogies to Troy and Rome. The Habsburg poets showed a clear predilection for this eminently political and panegyric genre of poetry, so much so that, in the second half of the sixteenth century, not a single year passed without the publication, translation or reprinting of a heroic poem in Castilian Spanish.[1] This exaggerated heroic output, unrivalled in other European literary contexts, was undoubtedly linked to the need to represent power. Many of the works were about the campaigns of Charles V, from Pavia to Mühlberg; the most salient battles and sieges of Philip's reign, such as

---

1 For an overview of Spanish epic literature in the sixteenth century, see Frank Pierce, *La poesía épica del Siglo de Oro* (Madrid: Gredos, 1968); Frank Pierce, 'La Poesía Épica Española del Siglo de Oro', *Edad de Oro*, IV (1985), 87–105 (1985); Lara Vilà, 'La épica española del renacimiento (1540–1605): propuestas para una revisión', *Boletín de la Real Academia Española*, 83/287 (2003), 137–150.

María José Vega • Autonomous University of Barcelona

Saint-Quentin, Malta and Lepanto; the conflicts in the Netherlands; or the empire's expansion in the Americas, from New Spain to the southernmost tip of the Arauco region. Even epic texts on medieval themes (El Cid, Bernardo del Carpio, Roncesvalles, etc.) were useful for representing the Habsburg Empire in Virgilian fashion—that is, through prophecies and visions, and particularly through the ekphrasis of imaginary works of art (tapestries, shields, statues) that told future generations the history of the nation or the genealogy of its monarchs.

The metatextual commentaries of authors and editors allow us to identify the core concepts on which the theory and practice of the epic were based in sixteenth-century Spain.[2] The most widely shared definition of epic poetry describes it as an improved version of history, more memorable and emphatic, but also as a tool for shoring up dynastic legitimacy and constructing the political memory of the present for posterity. Its founding ideas, therefore, have to do with truth, morality and memory. Epic poetry is objectively necessary for realms and rulers for both political and poetic reasons, which makes the composition of such texts an extension of service to the monarch. In Spain and Portugal, reflection and writing were determined by the belief that an *epic of the present* and an *epic of truth* were possible. The technical aspects of Italian neo-Aristotelian poetics (how to construct a fable, attain verisimilitude or perfect imitation, etc.) were therefore less important than the political needs of the empire and the perceived existence of a 'poeticisable' history that was *already* heroic before being told. Unlike Italian poetic theory that focused on imitation and fable, and in contrast to the 'miserable nation' of Italy (the adjective is Guicciardini's) that offered no foundation for a heroic present, Spanish authors claimed to be convinced that they were living in an exceptional age which rivalled the splendour of the Augustan empire. The contrast is striking. Italian poetry regulated epic practice by renouncing recent history which, in the words of Torquato Tasso, curtailed invention and bound poets to the truth:

> The poet who sought to describe the exploits of Charles V was far too bold in his retelling of events which many who are still alive today witnessed and endured. No man can suffer being deceived in things

---

2 On epic paratexts in the Renaissance, see Giovanni Caravaggi, *Studi sull'epica ispanica del rinascimento* (Pisa: Università di Pisa, 1974), 169–209; Denis Bjaï, *La Franciade sur le métier Ronsard et la pratique du poème héroïque* (Geneva: Droz, 2001), 56ff.; María José Vega, 'Idea de la épica en la España del quinientos', in *La teoría de la épica en el siglo XVI*, eds. M. J. Vega and L. Vilà (Barcelona: Academia del Hispanismo, 2010), 103–136; Lara Vilà and María José Vega, 'La teoría de la épica en España: quince prólogos de poemas épicos españoles (1566–1607)', in *La teoría de la épica en el siglo XVI*, eds. M. J. Vega and L. Vilà (Barcelona: Academia del Hispanismo, 2010), 271–312.

they know of first-hand or of which they have had reliable reports from their Fathers and Grandfathers.³

The situation was reversed in the territories of the Spanish monarchy. The Habsburgs had built an empire—in Flanders, Lombardy, the Mediterranean, the Americas—that was symbolically viewed as heir to the Roman Empire of Augustus, which it had undeniably surpassed.⁴ Virgil's *Aeneid*, which explained the present of Rome from the past of Aeneas, provided a suitable ideological model for the representation of the empire.⁵ The same was true, for various reasons, of Lucan's *Pharsalia*, appreciated in Spanish circles for the very reason it was rejected by Italian treatise writers—namely, that it narrated true events so recent that readers could still remember them. Alonso de Ercilla and Jerónimo Corte Real, for example, based their Lepanto narrative on Virgil's account of the Battle of Actium in the eighth book of the *Aeneid*, a dual strategy of recognition and innovation that established a political affiliation (and comparison) between the Spanish monarchy and the Augustan empire.⁶ This was also an act of continuity and spatial appropriation, as Lepanto and Actium were fought in the same waters. Similarly, the crossing of the River Elbe where Charles V began his Mühlberg campaign (1547) was ideologically (re)worked from the classical episode of Julius Caesar crossing the Rubicon, which informed the emperor's image in both chronicles and poetry.⁷ The epic of antiquity was thus reused to serve present needs. This was not an exclusively literary phenomenon or an exercise in erudition or style, for it determined a large part of the monarchy's cultural representation in writing, painting, arms and armour, and the ephemeral arts.

In this chapter, I aim to analyse some of the common ideas of Spanish authors on the political function and value of the epic written in the time of the Habsburgs and for the Habsburg dynasty, and subsequently

---

3 'Di troppo sfacciata audacia parrebbe quel poeta che l'imprese di Carlo Quinto volesse descrivere altrimenti di quello che molti, ch'oggi vivono, l'hanno viste e maneggiate. Non possono soffrire gli uomini di essere ingannati in qulle cose che o per se medesimi sanno, o per certa relazione dei Padri, e degli Avi ne sono informati'. Torquato Tasso, *Discorsi dell'arte poetica*, in *Scritti sull'arte poetica*, ed. Ettore Mazzali (Turin: Einaudi, 1959), I, 12.
4 See Marie Tanner, *The last descendants of Aeneas: the Habsburgs and the mythic image of the emperor* (New Haven: Yale University Press, 1993), passim; Elizabeth B. Davis, *Myth and identity in the epic of imperial Spain* (Columbia: University of Missouri Press, 2000), 12ff.; Lara Vilà, *Épica e imperio: imitación virgiliana y propaganda política en la épica española del siglo XVI* (Bellaterra: Universitat Autònoma de Barcelona, 2001).
5 Frank Pierce, *La poesía épica*; Giovanni Caravaggi, *Studi sull'epica ispanica*; José Lara Garrido, *Los mejores plectros: teoría y práctica de la épica culta en el Siglo de Oro*, Appendix XXIII (Málaga: Analecta Malacitana, 1999). Elizabeth Davis (*Myth and identity*) and Lara Vilà (*Épica e imperio*) facilitate a political reading of Spanish epic poetry.
6 David Quint, *Epic and empire* (Princeton: Princeton University Press, 1993), 25–32.
7 María José Vega, 'The prodigies over Mühlberg and the construction of history in the sixteenth century', *Euphorion: Zeitschrift für Literaturgeschichte*, 108/1 (2015), 69–90.

compare them with the theory and practice of epic literature in Italy. This analysis will be based on a review of twenty heroic Spanish poems from the second half of the sixteenth century and a careful reading of instances of self-reference—those in which the poet, like the offeror of devout images, represents himself, his writing and his intended audience within his own work.

Writing the Truth?

In sixteenth-century Spain, the authors of 'political epics' presented their poems as *true* works, and therefore as a form of history, if not the most exemplary kind. This shared idea contrasted with the principles governing thoughts about the epic in contemporary Italian culture, which were closely inspired by the reading and adaptation of Aristotle's *Poetics*. As is well known, Aristotle's *Poetics* declared poetry to be superior to history, because poetry is not bound by real-life events or facts but represents what is possible and necessary in accordance with plausibility and imitation. Spanish epic theory, on the other hand, rested on the moral and ontological superiority of truth over pretence and was based on the humanistic idea that history is not merely an account of facts or *memoria gestarum* but a source of experience and morality, a compendium of political knowledge and sum of *exempla, consilia* and *sententia*.

The texts are unambiguous: Luis de Zapata, when dedicating his *Carlo Famoso*, claims to write 'con toda verdad' [with all truth] so that no prose historian would have an advantage over him;[8] in *La Carolea*, Jerónimo de Sempere 'lleva cuenta más con la verdad de la Historia que con el Poético estilo' [attends more to the truth of History than to Poetic style];[9] Pedro de la Vecilla Castellanos aspired to be a 'humilde historiador poético' [humble poetic historian] or 'poeta histórico' [historical poet];[10] Joan Pujol says that he attempted, insofar as it was possible, to 'narrar vera historia' [tell true history];[11] Agustín Alonso avers that the magnitude of the 'true' facts narrated in his poem makes it unnecessary to 'fingir otras

---

8 Luis de Zapata, 'A la Cesárea real majestad del rey Don Felipe Segundo nuestro señor', in *Carlo Famoso* (1566) (Valencia: Juan de Mey, 1566; fac. ed. Barcelona/Gerona: Seminario de Poética del Renacimiento/Instituto Lucio Anneo Séneca de la Universidad Carlos III de Madrid, 2009), n.p.
9 Jerónimo de Sempere, 'Argumento de la obra', in *La Carolea* (Valencia: Juan de Arcos, 1560), n.p.
10 Pedro de la Vecilla Castellanos, *Primera y segunda parte de el León de España* (Salamanca: Casa de Juan Fernández, 1586), Prologue, n.p.
11 Joan Pujol, *Dedicatoria*, in *La singular y admirable victòria que, per gràcia de nostre senyor Déu, obtingué el sereníssim senyor don Joan d'Àustria de la potentíssima armada turquesca* (1574; fac. ed. Barcelona: Diputación de Barcelona, 1971); See C. Esteve, A. Moll, 'Ficción épica

caballerías' [invent other chivalrous deeds];[12] Baltasar Escobar admired the *Monserrate* by Cristóbal de Virués because the plot was based on 'cosa verdadera' [true thing];[13] Lasso de la Vega maintains 'el rigor que pide la historia' [the rigour that history demands], even eschewing the use of hyperbole to exalt the intellect and deeds of Hernán Cortés, and Jerónimo Rodríguez appreciated his *Mexicana* because it gave a 'noticia cierta' [true report] of things in the New World;[14] in *La Austríada*, Juan Rufo claims to 'estar en lo cierto' [be in the right] as his subject was not invented but a 'true' and 'modern' history;[15] and Antonio de Saavedra y Guzmán was concerned not only with 'true' history but also with the linguistic accuracy of the names he used in his poem and the veracity of geographical reports.[16] Epic authors laid claim to the prestige of history as a discipline and to its protocols of investigation and writing, to its method of acquiring knowledge and conferring testimony, and to its use of documentary sources and witness interviews—in short, to the concept of historical truth as a product of method and study. Zapata says that he cited 'relaciones, papeles y memoriales' [reports, papers and memorials]; Agustín Alonso visited bookshops and diligently searched for facts; Rufo says he omitted only those events for which he lacked documentary sources; Joan Pujol, for his *Victoria*, claims to have gathered information from the soldiers who fought in the Battle of Lepanto;[17] in the *Segundo Cerco*, Corte Real strove 'por saber' [to know] as a historian, seeking eyewitnesses to the narrated events, and in the letter to Philip II prefacing his *Felicísima Victoria de Lepanto*, states that he sought 'the truest information it was possible for me to obtain, taking the substance of those reports which, though coming to me from various quarters, were finally reduced to the most common opinion'.[18] Many poets actually participated in the events they narrated.

---

y verdad histórica: el poema sobre Lepanto de Joan Pujol', *e-Spania*, 27 (2017), https://journals.openedition.org/e-spania/26717.

12 Agustín Alonso, *Historia de las hazañas y hechos del invencible caballero Bernardo del Carpio* (Toledo: López de Haro, 1585), 'Dedicatoria', n.p.

13 Prefatory letter (1602) by Baltasar de Escobar in Cristóbal de Virués, *El Monserrate segundo*, ed. M. Fitts Finch (Valencia/Chapel Hill: Albatros Hispanofilia Ediciones, 1984).

14 Jerónimo Ramírez, 'Prólogo al discreto lector', in Gabriel Lobo Lasso de la Vega, *Mexicana* (1594), ed. José Amor y Vázquez (Madrid: Atlas, 1970).

15 Juan Rufo, Dedication of *La Austríada de Juan Rufo* (Madrid: Casa de Alonso Gómez, 1584), n.p.

16 Antonio de Saavedra y Guzmán, *El peregrino indiano* (Madrid: Pedro de Madrigal, 1599), n.p.

17 Luis de Zapata, *Carlo Famoso*; Agustín Alonso, *Historia de las hazañas*; Joan Pujol, *La singular y admirable victòria*, n.p.

18 'las más verdaderas informaciones que me fueron posibles, tomando la substancia de aquellas que aunque de varias partes me fueron traídas al fin se reducían a la más común opinión': Jerónimo de Corte Real, 'Prólogo a la Magestad del Rey Philippe', in *Espantosa y felicísima Victoria concedida del cielo al señor don Juan de Austria, en el golfo de Lepanto de*

Perhaps the most famous case is that of Alonso de Ercilla, eyewitness, chronicler, author and character in his own poem, the *Araucana*, 'tan cierto y verdadero' [so accurate and true] that it was written on the battlefield itself as events unfolded, turning not only the present but the very moment into an epic as he witnessed history in the making:

> [what little time] I was able to steal I spent on this book which, to make it more accurate and true, was written in the midst of the war and in the same passages and places, often writing on leather for lack of paper, and on scraps of letters, some so small they could barely hold six lines, which gave me no small work putting them together later.[19]

Nineteenth-century critics censured Spanish epic authors for their strict reliance on historiographical sources, not understanding the legitimacy and added value this reliance gave to their poetic discourse. This interest in corroborating facts also left obvious marks on the course of the poems, the arrangement of their subject matter, and even on their typesetting. Luis Zapata, for instance, placed an asterisk beside the octaves of his poem *Carlo Famoso* in which he waxed inventive to distinguish them from the rest, which were to be taken as gospel truth. In Canto V he refers to the emperor's chroniclers and historians to whom he turned for corroboration (Sepúlveda, Zurita, Pedro Mejía, Busto, Santa Cruz), predicts their future celebrity and presents them as unimpeachable witnesses who verify the truth of the poem because they first participated in the events they later narrated as historians. Among them, he highlights Luis de Ávila y Zúñiga, whose *Comentarios de la guerra de Alemaña* (1548–1549) recorded Charles V's campaigns against the Protestant princes of the Schmalkaldic League (1546–1547).[20] The poem refers to Luis de Ávila when, in the chronology of the narrated events, he had not yet written the *Comentarios* which Zapata used as a source:

> He shall write, and not as a seer
> but what he himself saw, and in which he had a great part.

---

la poderosa armada otomana... (Lisbon: António Ribeiro, 1575); See Hélio Alves, *Camões, Corte-Real e o sistema da epopeia quinhentista* (Coimbra: Universidade de Coimbra, 2001), 257 and 297.

19 Alonso de Ercilla y Zúñiga, *La Araucana*, eds. Marcos A. Morínigo and Isaías Lerner (Madrid: Castalia, 1990), I, 121. '[el poco tiempo que] pude hurtar le gasté en este libro, el cual, porque fuese más cierto y verdadero, se hizo en la misma guerra y en los mismos pasos y sitios, escribiendo muchas veces en cuero por falta de papel, y en pedazos de cartas, algunos tan pequeños que apenas cabían seis versos, que no me costó después poco trabajo juntarlos'.

20 Luis de Ávila y Zúñiga, *Comentario de la guerra de Alemania hecha por Carlos V, máximo emperador romano, rey de España, en el año de 1546 y 1547* (Antwerp: Johannes Steelsius, 1549).

And he himself shall write the same history...[21]

In a kind of *mise en abyme*, the poet predicts his source, cites the authority of a third-party chronicle in his verses and incorporates as a character the historian who verifies the 'truth' of his lines.[22] *Carlo Famoso* at once foretells and rewrites Luis de Ávila's *Comentarios*, which are then presented as a reflection of things seen and experienced.

However, it is not just the epic poet who assimilates the chronicle; the historian and witness to the war, Luis de Ávila, also refers to his text as a kind of baseline, a 'free and plain' account that would allow future poems to be written in a loftier style more suited to the greatness of the narrated events.[23] Therefore Ávila, too, seems to regard epic literature as a continuation of history by other means, or as a mould capable of giving readers a more exalted, grandiose, and intense vision of the truth. A poem, unlike a chronicle, could offer a more vivid, ingenious account with a certain latitude in details and a more decisive moral and providential interpretation of the facts. The epic is thus a palimpsest of history that simultaneously gives the narrative a monumental dimension.

However, it would be reductive to view the epic of the 1500s as a mere 'reflection' or reworking of history. It is more like an active agent of representation that aspires to intervene in the construction of official memory and influence political action. It does not refer to the past or the immediate present; rather, it possesses a future tension because it creates convictions, spurs action, legitimises war, ratifies international policy decisions, strengthens bonds between the military and the crown and the sense of identity and belonging of religious orders.

War

Miguel Martínez and Elizabeth Davis have pointed out that a remarkable number of Spanish epic literature authors came from the ranks of soldiers, captains, nobles and gentlemen who not only narrated war but also had

---

21 Luis Zapata, *Carlo Famoso*, V, 25v. 'Escribirá él y no como adivino / mas lo que él mismo vio, y do fue gran parte. / Y él mismo escribirá la misma historia...'

22 Or, to paraphrase Lucien Dällenbach, the authority of the source is the authority in the source; see Lucien Dällenbach, *Le récit spéculaire: Essai sur le mise en abyss* (Paris, 1977), p. 119 – writing about another text, Dällenbach writes that the story of the novel is the story in the novel.

23 See Cesc Esteve, 'La victoria más grande de Carlos V. Historia, épica y propaganda de la Guerra de Alemania', in *Épica y conflicto religioso en el siglo XVI: anglicanismo y luteranismo desde el imaginario hispánico*, eds. J. Burguillo and M. J. Vega (London: Boydell and Brewer, 2021).

first-hand knowledge of it.²⁴ Alonso de Ercilla, Juan Rufo, Cristóbal de Virués, Jerónimo de Urrea, Diego Jiménez de Ayllón, Francisco Garrido de Villena, Nicolás Espinosa and Gaspar Pérez de Villagrá were all soldiers. Davis understood that soldier-writers constructed a military identity in their poems, which was also a projection of their own image, and the epic actively promoted an ostensibly aristocratic group ethos. In this light, the Habsburg epic is another of the genres favoured by veterans, who wrote memorials, chronicles, accounts, dialogues and manuals on military arts and were prolific in the second half of the sixteenth century in Spain.²⁵ There are also many ideological and conceptual elements that the Habsburg epic and military arts have in common. Both genres purport to be a product of the union of arms and letters, or they present writing as a continuation of or substitute for service in the field. In the prologue to *Carlo Famoso*, Luis Zapata, who was in the emperor's service for twenty-one years, claims to continue that service with his pen, 'como quien desde la niñez no sabe otro viaje' [as he who from childhood has known no other path] and speaks of his poem as a 'servicio pequeño' [small service].²⁶ In *Los famosos y heroicos hechos del Cid*, Jiménez de Ayllón also writes that 'a la edad de diez y ocho años comencé a servir a su Majestad Católica en el hábito militar, en cuyo servicio he permanecido hasta el día de hoy' [at age eighteen I began to serve His Catholic Majesty in military uniform, in whose service I have remained until today] and can therefore 'mostrar por verdadera información y conocimiento' [show with true information and knowledge] the lives of soldiers.²⁷ The situation is repeated in the poems, dedicatory epistles and prologues of Alonso, Ercilla, Vecilla, Pedro de Oña, Saavedra y Guzmán, Francisco Mosquera de Barnuevo, and in works on the military arts like Bernardo de Vargas Machuca's *Milicia y descripción de las Indias*.²⁸

---

24 Maxime Chevalier, *Lectura y lectores en la España del siglo XVI y XVII* (Madrid: Turner, 1976), 122ff.; Davis, *Myth and identity*, 332ff.; Miguel Martínez, *Front lines: soldier's writing in the early modern Spanish world* (Philadelphia: University of Pennsylvania Press, 2016), *passim*.
25 See Mario Rizzo and Giuseppe Mazzocchi, eds., *La espada y la pluma: il mondo militare nella Lombardia spagnola cinquecentesca*, Atti del Convegno Internazionale di Pavia, 16–18 October 1997 (Lucca: Mauro Baroni, Università di Pavia, 2000), 11–34; Raffaele Puddu, *El soldado gentilhombre, autorretrato de una sociedad guerrera: la España del siglo XVI* (Barcelona: Argos Vergara, 1984); Antonio Espino López, *Guerra y cultura en la época moderna* (Madrid: Ministerio de Defensa, 2001); Miguel Martínez, *Front lines*, *passim*.
26 Luis de Zapata, 'Dedicatoria', *Carlo Famoso*, n.p.
27 Diego Jiménez de Ayllón, 'A los lectores', in *Los famosos y heroicos hechos del invencible y esforzado caballero, honra y flor de las Españas, el Cid Ruy Díaz de Vivar* (Antwerp: Juan Lacio, 1568), n.p.
28 Agustín Alonso, *Historia de las hazañas*, 'Dedicatoria'; Alonso de Ercilla y Zúñiga, *La Araucana*, I, 121–122; Vecilla, *El León de España*, Prologue, n.p.; Pedro de Oña, *Primera parte del Arauco domado* (Ciudad de los Reyes [Lima]: Antonio Ricardo de Turin, 1596), 'Prólogo al lector', n.p.; Antonio de Saavedra y Guzmán, *El peregrino indiano* (Madrid: Casa de Pedro

The intense production of epic poems and military treatises and works seemed to go hand-in-hand in the second half of the sixteenth century; the two phenomena were concurrent and singular. As Fernando González de León has noted, there were more military treatises in the days of Philip II than in those of Charles V, but both reigns produced a remarkable quantity and quality of such texts, which were editorial successes and internationally circulated. The war in Flanders inspired the most modern treatises, written by more experienced officers, but the total number of works on martial and military arts written by Spanish officers and soldiers is unparalleled in the rest of Europe.[29] These were not mere manuals on strategy, for they also addressed matters of politics, morality and conduct. In addition to discussing tactical questions, such as how to sustain a siege, repel ambushes and transport artillery, they also celebrated the deeds, valour and effort that conferred true nobility, equal if not greater to that derived from inheritance or blood.[30] Military virtue already played a prominent role in the honourable warfare described by Juan López de Palacios Rubios in his *Tratado del esfuerzo bélico heroico*,[31] and the emphasis seemed to grow in later works. Bernardino de Escalante's *Diálogos del arte militar*

Madrigal, 1599), Dedication, n.p.; Francisco Mosquera de Barnuevo, *La Numantina: dirigida a la nobilissima ciudad de soria y a sus doze linages y casas a ellos aggregadas* (Seville: Luis Estupiñán, 1612), Dedication, n.p.; Bernardo de Vargas Machuca, *Milicia y descripción de las Indias* (Madrid: Casa de Pedro Madrigal, 1599), 'Prólogo del autor', n.p.

29 See F. González de León, '"Doctors of the military discipline": technical expertise and the paradigm of the Spanish soldier in the early modern period', *Sixteenth Century Journal*, 27/1 (1996), 61–87; John Rigby Hale, 'Printing and military culture in renaissance Venice', *Medievalia et Humanistica*, 8 (1977), 21–62; Antonio Espino López, *Guerra y cultura*; Esther Merino Peral, *El arte militar en la época moderna: los tratados 'de re militari' en el renacimiento: aspectos de un arte español* (Madrid: Ministerio de Defensa, 2002). For a comparison of Spanish military arts and the antiquity of the few such works produced in Italy, cf. Frédérique Verrier, *Les armes de Minerve : l'humanisme militaire dans l'Italie du XVIᵉ siècle* (Paris: Presses de l'Université de Paris-Sorbonne, 1997), 115ff.

30 Military or political nobility was deemed more relevant than hereditary or court nobility, as war ennobled those who waged it with virtue, generosity and boldness. This idea has been studied in detail by Puddu (*El soldado gentilhombre*, 74ff.), who noted that military service or 'nobility of arms' was the most recognised form of upward social mobility in the sixteenth century, particularly in Flanders, where the Duke of Alba actively favoured the promotion and ennoblement of those who demonstrated great courage and integrity. This is a recurrent idea in period literature. In his *Crónica llamada las dos conquistas del Reyno de Nápoles* (1559), Hernán Pérez del Pulgar reminded readers that 'la nobleza y alto nascimiento' [nobility and high birth] of a man is not as important as his 'natural virtud' [natural virtue], which cannot be inherited from one's ancestors but can only be earned by deeds. Bernardo de Vargas Machuca likewise affirmed this in *Milicia y descripción de las Indias* (1599), which not only discusses the 'modo de hacer soldados' [way of making soldiers] but also notes how 'la milicia ennoblecce al que viene de baja estirpe' [military service ennobles one who comes from humble stock].

31 Juan López de Palacios Rubios, *Tratado del esfuerzo belico heroico compuesto por Palacios Ruvios, del Consejo Real de la Reyna Doña Juana y del Emperador Carlos su hijo... a ruego de*

described an officer who was a model of integrity and heroism with vast historical knowledge.[32] Diego de Álava believed that virtue was the principal attribute of an officer in war. The 'perfect captain' in the title of his treatise was a paragon of stoic virtues (strength, constancy, temperance), but he also had to be well-versed in philosophy and understand the causes of war; in history, to know the great battles and lives of generals past; in rhetoric, to rouse and inspire his men with conviction and eloquence; and in medicine, to heal injuries on the battlefield. He also had to be a master of military strategy and excel at arithmetic and geometry, the foundations of artillery and fortification.[33]

The soldierly virtues in military treatises coincide with those of captains in the historical epic: courage, prudence, liberality, honour, tenacity, civility, greatness of mind, mercy to the vanquished and exemplary conduct in the field. Epic poems also portrayed the erudition, eloquence, history and understanding of war that treatise writers demanded of the perfect captain. They include classical examples, rousing speeches, descriptions of places and campaigns, accounts of past battles, reflections on justice or the necessity of war, on its ultimate purposes or on its relevance to the present moment. They feature valiant soldiers and captains like Hernán Cortés, Diego Álvarez de Toledo and Diego García de Paredes, who were also exemplary in the arts of war.[34] Such poems were widely popular, although they were intended for young men, military officers and aristocrats.[35] The printer of *Carlo Famoso* believed that readers would find in the poem 'todo cuanto complace' [all things pleasing], to wit: 'batallas, heroísmo, ejemplos de príncipes' [battles, heroism, exemplary princes] and 'navegaciones, combates, contiendas, guerras y batallas' [sea voyages, combats, contests, wars and battles]. Jerónimo Ramírez praised the *Mexicana* because it combined 'avisos de graves sentencias, descripciones de muchos lugares, dichos de soldados, razonamientos de capitanes' [notices of grave utterances, descriptions of many places, sayings of soldiers and reasoning of captains] and painted a vibrant picture of 'crueles batallas,

---

Gonçalo Pérez de Bivero, su hijo primogenito (Salamanca: A Expensas de Gaspar de Rostiñolis, 1524).

32 Bernardino de Escalante *Diálogos del arte militar, dirigidos a Don Rodrigo de Castro* (Seville: Andrea Pescioni, 1583).

33 Diego de Álava y Viamont, *El perfeto capitán instruido: en la disciplina militar, y nueva ciencia de la artilleria* (Madrid: Pedro Madrigal, 1590); See F. González de León, '"Doctors of the military discipline"', 70.

34 Mariarosa Scaramuzza Vidona, 'Le armi al servizio della pace: gli storici di Carlo V presentano le imprese dei soldati spagnoli in Lombardia', in *La espada y la pluma: il mondo militare nella Lombardia spagnola cinquecentesca: atti del Convegno Internazionale di Pavia, October 16–18 (1997)*, 106.

35 On the readers of sixteenth-century Spanish epics and the presence of epic literature in library inventories, see María José Vega, 'Idea de la épica', 122–129.

muertes violentas, sucesos repentinos' [cruel battles, violent deaths and sudden events], and Alonso de Ercilla understood that his poem was about 'cosas de guerra' [things of war] which have 'muchos aficionados' [many enthusiasts].[36]

War was undoubtedly a constant in the first half of the sixteenth century during the reign of Charles V, and the reign of Philip II was marked by battles of tremendous literary and historical impact like Lepanto, which inspired its own epic cycle. Understanding the ethics and representation of war is therefore essential to comprehending the culture of the 1500s, everyday ways of life and even the expectations of upward social mobility harboured by a large part of the male population. Many sixteenth-century heroic poems revolve around a crucial battle (or one painted as crucial, such as the Battle of Lepanto), a siege (Malta), a string of victories (from Pavia to Mühlberg, for instance) or campaigns (as in the American poems), or else they incorporate prophetic visions of future battles (Saint-Quentin in La Araucana), relive past battles (Covadonga, Clavijo, Navas de Tolosa) or reinterpret them as foreshadowing present victories (Roncesvalles as a prefiguration of the French-Spanish wars and the defeat of Francis I). If we read the epic in a non-literary context—as a discourse contiguous with military treatises and chronicles—we can see how the Habsburg poets constructed the celebration of war (in contrast to the irenicism of spiritual writers), extolled the magnanimity and clemency of the sovereign and his captains and painted a virtuous picture of the military profession, which conferred nobility and dignity on those who exercised it generously and fearlessly.

In addition, the war epic can be understood as a written creation of space, for it reshaped the idea of Europe and brought order to the world by symbolically appropriating it (in the Americas, Asia or Africa), describing it as an extension of acts of power, authority and warfare, or glorifying the dynasty in its inseparable bond with its territories. The Habsburg epic proposes a *spatial understanding* of the empire and the boundaries of the Spanish monarchy. It parcelled and described a multi-centric Europe in the context of great campaigns, reorganised the Mediterranean and the relationship with the Turks and ultimately charted a heroic geography of conquest in Mexico, Chile, Peru and, later, Argentina. The epic is therefore an instrument of domestication or symbolic appropriation. This poetic (and political) cartography is equally significant for its highlights and

---

36 Juan Mey, 'El Impressor al Lector', in Zapata, *Carlo Famoso*, n.p.; Jerónimo Ramírez, 'Carta al discreto lector', in Gabriel Lasso de la Vega, *La Mexicana*, n.p.; Ercilla y Zúñiga, *La Araucana*, I, 121.

shadows, ennobling and underscoring the crown's relationship with the defence of Catholicism. The limits (and cause) of the empire and religion are often blurred.[37]

Building Fame

One common factor in the dedications, liminal poems and prologues of epic poems from the latter half of the sixteenth century is their celebration of the glory and fame that the heroic poet and the historian bestow upon illustrious men and kings—chief among them Charles and Philip—for the imperishable was not heroism or virtue but the eloquent word. This established topos, rewritten often in European literature, presents certain variants specific to Castilian literature. Many classical texts refer to the power of letters to grant man immortality,[38] but one in particular—Cicero's oration in defence of the poet Archias—contains a reflection on the posterity of writing to which epic authors frequently turned. In his speech, Cicero observed that great men supported writers so they would record their deeds and call on the power of the written word to bestow fame. The wisest voices and the most exemplary lives would lie buried in darkness if they were not set down in writing and upheld for our imitation and motivation.[39] At that point, Cicero told a memorable anecdote: Alexander the Great, he said, stood before the grave of Achilles and called him happy and fortunate, because his virtue had been proclaimed in the hexameters of Homer. If the *Iliad* had not been written, the tomb and the body it covered would have remained nameless: 'Nam nisi Ilias illa exstitisset, idem tumulus qui corpus eius contexerat nomen etiam obruisset'. It was Homer who had saved Achilles from oblivion; and it is literature, and literature alone, that preserves memory, for the hero, though reduced to ashes, will live forever in a handful of hexameters.

Knowledge of the *Pro Archia* in early modern Europe is usually dated to the fourteenth century. From that moment on, the passage and anecdote about Alexander, hitherto rarely read, became the shared property of every educated man and a frequent prefatory motif in literary compositions. Fifteenth-century Spanish humanism is riddled with reminders of the *Pro*

---

37 Katharina N. Piechocki, *Cartographic Humanism: The Making of Early Modern Europe*, (Oxford: OUP, 2019).
38 See María Rosa Lida, *La idea de la fama en la edad media castellana* (Mexico City: Fondo De Cultura Economica, 1952), 17, 21–24, 30–31; See Cicero, De finibus, 3.17.57; Tusc. 1.45.109; De resp., 5.7; Pro Caelio, 73 and 76; In Pisonem, 82; Pro Sestio, 138; Cato, 82; De oratore, 2.225; See Horace, Od., 2.2., 3.11, 4.3, 4.9; See Ovid, Met., 15. 871–872 and 12.615–619; Amores, 1.3.
39 'Sed pleni sunt omnes libri, plenae sapientium voces, plena exemplorum vestustas: quae iacerent in tenebris omnia, nisi litterarum nomen accederet'. Cicero, Pro Archia, 6.14.

Archia, especially in the prologues to the first romance versions of the *Iliad* and *Aeneid*. The common ground of fame through literature was frequently applied to the Castilian situation, embroiled in wars of conquest. Fernán Pérez de Guzmán, at the beginning of *Generaciones y semblanzas* and in his *Loores de los Claros Varones de España*, assigned historians and poets the responsibility of preserving the deeds of great gentlemen for posterity. He asserted that Spain had little glory for this reason because, though rich in heroes, it was poor in writers: 'Spain did not remain silent / and mute in histories / for lack of victories, / or dearth of virtues, / but for want of a great herald / like Homer was of Greece / in the famous Iliad'.[40] The verses allude to the anecdote in the *Pro Archia*, and Íñigo López de Mendoza, the Marquis of Santillana, did the same in his *Diálogo de Bías contra Fortuna*,[41] albeit in the form of a lament over the Spanish situation, which was not found in other versions. This idea that Spain had an abundance of heroes but a shortage of poets was frequently repeated. Even the prologue to the fabulous *Amadís of Gaul* opened with a reminder of Sallust's warning that the greatness of deeds depends on the greatness of the writers who proclaim them, imagining what might have happened if 'acaesciera aquella santa conquista que el nuestro muy esforçado Rey hizo del reino de Granada' [that holy conquest which our most valiant King made of the kingdom of Granada] had occurred in classical antiquity.[42]

This idea was extraordinarily widespread. We find it, for example in Fernando de Herrera's *Anotaciones* to Garcilaso's poetry, where he states that the neglect of literature in the previous century was due to the military urgency of the Reconquest, and it was a common theme in history books

---

40 'No quedó España callada / e muda en las istorias / por defectos de victorias, / nin de virtudes menguada, / mas porque non fue dotada / de tan alto pregonero / como fue Grecia de Omero / en la famosa Iliada'. He later wrote: 'España non caresció / de quien vertudes usase / mas menguó et fallesció / en ella quien las notase; / para que bien se igualasen / debían ser los caballeros / de España, e los Omeros / de Grecia que los loasen' [Spain had no shortage / of men of virtue / but it suffered for want / of men to take note of it; / for there to be an equality among / the great gentlemen of Spain, and the Homers / of Greece to praise them]. Lida, *La idea de la fama*, 23; Diego Enríquez's prologue to the Crónica del Rey Enrique el quarto is quite similar, admitting that the Spaniards 'fatigaron más sus manos en el uso de las armas' [tired their hands more in the use of arms] and consequently 'adurmieron sus memorias' [let their memories slumber]: Diego Enríquez del Castillo, Diego, *Crónica del Rey D. Enrique el Quarto de este nombre, por su capellán y cronista Diego Enríquez del Castillo* (Madrid: Antonio de Sancha, 1787), 'Prólogo', 1.
41 See Lida, *La idea de la fama*, 276–277; Juan de Mena (*El laberinto de fortuna o las Trescientas*, iv) also refers to the darkness in which the fame of Spanish feats lies, 'dañada de olvido por falta de autores' [doomed to oblivion for lack of authors].
42 Garci Rodríguez de Montalvo, *Amadís de Gaula*, ed. Manuel Cacho Blecua (Madrid: Cátedra, 1987), 219–220; Sallust, *De conjuratione Catilinae*, 8.2–3.

like those of Sebastian Fox Morillo or Juan de Mariana.[43] In *Democritus Primus*, Juan Ginés de Sepúlveda noted that the long period of peace provided by the Catholic Monarchs would give young noblemen sufficient leisure to engage in the literary pursuits they had formerly neglected *propter bella*; and in the dialogue on glory, *Gonsalus Sive de Appetenda Gloria*, he bemoaned the fact that the many bellicose enterprises of the Castilian nobility had adversely affected the writing of history and poetry, explicitly referencing the *Pro Archia*.[44] The topos survived in epic prologues of the second half of the sixteenth century. Agustín Alonso, for instance, recalled the 'tight' times which 'no dieron lugar a que en nuestra España hubiese escritores, porque ninguno tenía tal espacio' [made it impossible for our Spain to have writers, there being no room for them]. And Vecilla acknowledged that Spaniards 'fueron siempre más aplicados al ejercicio militar de las armas que a la quietud y sosiego de las letras' [had always applied themselves more to the military exercise of arms than to the calmness and serenity of letters], even though both were equally necessary for the preservation of republics.

This widely held conviction makes it easier to understand one of the recurring ideas in Spanish epic literature: the claim that epic poems somehow repaid or settled the ancient debt of letters to arms. On the one hand, we find frequent allusions to the *Pro Archia* anecdote, as the feats of Charles V (or of Hernán Cortés) surpassed those of Achilles and therefore required epic poetry and a history that would do justice to their greatness.[45] On the other, the idea of epic writing as a form of remembrance, a way of 'avenging from oblivion' the deeds of past and present

---

43 Lida, *La idea de la fama*, 272; Baltasar Cuart, 'La larga marcha hacia las historias e España en el siglo XVI', in Ricardo García Cárcel, *La construcción de las historias de España* (Madrid: Fundación Carolina/Marcial Pons, 2004), 66.

44 'At vero id quam longe abhorreat a summorum imperatorum institutis, nemo valeat dubitare, qui meminerit Alexander Macedo, cum in Sigaeum venisset ad Achillis sepulchrum, quibus verbis honorem habuerit Homero'.: Juan Ginés de Sepúlveda, *Dialogus de appetenda gloria qui inscribitur Gonsalus* (Rome, 1523), Giv vº. On the *Gonsalus sive de appendenda gloria*, see A. Espigares Pinilla, *La cuestión del honor y la gloria en el humanismo del siglo XVI a través del estudio del Gonsalus de Ginés de Sepúlveda y del honore de Fox Morcillo*, PhD thesis, Madrid: Universidad Complutense, 1992, 51ff.

45 See the prefatory texts by Juan Despuig in Nicolás Espinosa, *La segunda parte del Orlando con el verdadero sucesso de la famosa batalla de Roncesvalles* (Antwerp: Martin Nuyts, 1556); Jeronimo Oliver and Jorge de Montemayor in Sempere's *Carolea*; Hipólito Sans in *La Maltea*; Gaspar López in Pedro Mejía, *Historia imperial y cesárea*; By way of example, I will cite the preface to the *Lyra Heroica* by Francisco Núñez de Oria: 'Nisi enim Homerus superstes foret, Achillis gesta perpetuis tenebris delitescerent: & nisi Maronis Augustus meminisset Aeneae gesta sepulta iacerent. Omitto hic referre quamplurima exempla Chronographorum, Poetarum, videlicet Lucani, Titolivii, Suetonii, Plutarchi, Tucididis, quorum scribendi solertia, & amoenissimo stylo, maximorum regum & clarissimorum ducum trophaea perpetua fama claruerunt. Tandem nullus rex, nullus princeps gloria & excellentia splenduit, qui non aliquem insignem scriptorem aut Poëtam, qui eorum facinora

Spaniards, was also a common factor. Zapata, for instance, claims to write for his homeland, so that 'tantos hombres como en España ha habido señalados' [the many distinguished men there have been in Spain] would not languish 'in oblivion', because doing deeds worth writing about is just as commendable as writing deeds worth praising;[46] Núñez de Oria wanted to proclaim the triumphs of Charles V and Philip II and the excellent heroes of Spain;[47] Vecilla proposed to 'dar nueva vida a los que ha sepultado el olvido' [give new life to those whom oblivion has buried], 'resucitar memorias muertas' [resurrect dead memories] and 'vengar del olvido las antiguas hazañas de sus pasados' [avenge from oblivion of the old deeds of bygone days];[48] Ercilla wrote to remedy the wrong of such feats lingering 'en perpetuo silencio, faltando quien las escriba' [in perpetual silence, having none to write of them];[49] and even Nicolás Espinosa revived the deeds of the Peers of France from a Spanish perspective because 'estaban sepultados en el olvido nuestros Españoles, que a estos y muchos más en la nombrada lid de Roncesvalles vencieron y sobraron' [our Spaniards were buried in oblivion, they who defeated and overcame these and many more in the renowned battle of Roncesvalles].[50] The need for feats of arms to be immortalised by the pens of heroic poets makes it easy to understand why the authors of epics claimed to 'serve their homeland' through writing, a service no less important than that provided in the past or present by others on the field of battle.[51]

& trophaea memorie traderet, penes se haberet'.: Francisco Núñez de Oria, *Lyrae Heroicae Libri XIV*, Dedication, n.p.
46 Zapata, 'A la Cesárea real Majestad del rey don Felipe Segundo Nuestro Señor', in *Carlo Famoso*, n.p.
47 Luis de Zapata, *Carlo Famoso*, Dedication, n.p.; Núñez de Oria, *Lyrae Heroica*..., Dedication, n.p.
48 Pedro de la Vecilla Castellanos, *Primera y segunda parte de El León de España* (Salamanca: Casa de Juan Fernández, 1586), Prologue, n.p.
49 Ercilla y Zúñiga, *La Araucana*, I, 121–122.
50 Nicolás Espinosa, 'Información de lo que ha de tratar la presente historia', in *La segunda parte del Orlando con el verdadero sucesso de la famosa batalla de Roncesvalles* (Antwerp: Martin Nuyts, 1556), n.p.
51 Vecilla claims to be settling a 'deuda con la patria' [debt with his homeland] (*El León de España*, n.p.); Baltasar de Escobar understands that writing an epic poem is a way of 'de cumplir el precepto de Platón de que *nacemos para nuestra patria*' [fulfilling Plato's precept that *we are born for our homeland*] ('Carta', in Virués, *Monserrate*, n.p.). And Cristóbal de Mesa confesses that 'por la deuda natural *que deben los hombres a sus patrias*, por no ser miembro manco de una República tan sabia y poderosa como España, he querido hacerle esta oferta de mi talento' [given the natural *debt which all men owe to their homelands*, not wishing to be a faulty member of a Republic as wise and powerful as Spain, I have decided to make this offering of my talent]: Cristóbal de Mesa, 'A los Lectores', in *Las Navas de Tolosa* (Madrid: Viuda de Madrigal, 1594), n.p. This persistent idea can be traced back to the poetry of the fifteenth century. In his commentary on Mena's *Las Trescientas*, Hernán Núñez recalled 'aquella notable sentencia de Platón, el qual en la Nona Epístola... dize ninguno

Thus, according to the theory implicit in Renaissance poems written in Habsburg Europe, the epic is a form of history and a school of ethical, political and military virtues. It provides an understanding of war, educates young men and instructs them in past and present history, favours the imitation of the noblest figures, strengthens ties of allegiance to the sovereign and reinforces dynastic legitimacy, promotes a bond among men and shows how nobility can be earned through prowess at arms. The epic teaches—like the military treatises and dialogues of honour—principles of good conduct in the peculiar courtesy of war, which are those ideally embodied by the noble captains of the *Tercios* of old; and it sheds light on the new forms of warfare in the Indies. This literature represents the most perfect marriage of arms and letters—the dual honour, as Zapata would say, of doing deeds worth writing about and of writing deeds worth praising—to the point that authors describe their writing as a personal act of service to their homeland and to their lords and kings. In the Spain of Philip II, the theory of epic literature is therefore very close to the humanistic theory of history but has little to do with Italian neo-Aristotelian poetics, not only because it eschews its conditions and concepts, but also because it implicitly challenges its principles.

---

de nosotros ser nascido para sí solo, antes ha de dar parte de sus acciones a sus padres, parte a sus amgios *e parte a su patria*' [that notable statement of Plato's, who in the Ninth Epistle... says that none of us being born solely for ourselves, man must first devote part of his actions to his parents, part to his friends and part to his homeland]: Hernán Núñez de Toledo, *Glosas sobre las 'Trezientas' del famoso poeta Juan de Mena* (1499), eds. Julian Weiss and Antonio Cortijo Ocaña (Madrid: Polifemo, 2015), Prologue, 3; Mena's epitaph refers to this very act of patriotic service: 'Patria feliz, dicha buena, / escondrijo de la muerte / pues que te cupo por suerte / el poeta Juan de Mena' [Happy homeland, blessed fortune, / death's hiding place / for luckily you had room / for the poet Juan de Mena]. Francisco Sánchez de las Brozas, *Las obras del poeta Juan de Mena nuevamente corregidas y declaradas* (1582), in *Opera Omnia* (Geneva: Fratres de Tournes, 1766), 220.

LARA VILÀ

Philip II as *Rex Pacificus*

Belligerence and Pacifism in Epic Versions of the Battle of Saint-Quentin (1557)

While staying at Augsburg in the winter of 1548, Charles V summoned Titian and requested him to paint a canvas commemorating his recent victory over the princes of the Schmalkaldic League at Mühlberg. In what was destined to be one of his most famous portraits, Charles is depicted as a victorious warrior whose likeness combines the Roman imperial legacy and the chivalrous image of a soldier of the faith.[1] Yet the man painted by Titian is not shown in the heat of battle; the serene countenance is that of a stoic and virtuous emperor, defender of the faith and of peace.[2] A similar interpretation can be made of the speech that Charles gave on the occasion of his abdication in October 1555, in which he told the story of a life marked by campaigns that his enemies, he claimed, had forced upon him, though he had never aspired to anything but peace.[3] However, the words used to describe his victories clearly convey the pride of the Burgundian nobleman for whom the exercise of power was inseparable from the cult of belligerence in which he had been raised. This was associated with a glorious perception of war, understandable in a culture where military prowess was considered a sign of virtue and nobility. Viewed in

---

1 See F. Checa Cremades, *Carlos V y la imagen del héroe en el renacimiento* (Madrid: Taurus, 1987), 124–114.
2 See F. Checa Cremades, 'Imágemes para un cambio de reinado: Tiziano, Leoni y el *Viaje* de Calvete de Estrella', in *El felicissimo viaje del muy alto y muy poderoso principe don Phelippe*, ed. P. Cuenca (Madrid: Sociedad Estatal para la Conmemoración de los Centenarios de Felipe II y Carlos V, 2001), 163–178.
3 'La mitad del tiempo tuve grandes y peligrosas guerras, de las cuales puedo decir con verdad que las hice más por fuerza y contra mi voluntad que buscándolas ni dando ocasión para ellas'. [Half the time I had great and perilous wars, which I can honestly say I fought more by force and against my will than by actively seeking or giving cause for them.] In Prudencio de Sandoval, *Historia de la vida y hechos del emperador Carlos V*, XXXII, 34, ed. Carlos Seco Serrano (Madrid: Atlas, 1956), 481.

Lara Vilà • University of Girona

perspective, Charles's iconography presents a very precise notion of the imperial figure, whose extensively-studied symbolic construction revolves around war. For the emperor, the resounding triumph over the German princes—actually a civil war in the guise of a fight against heresy—was in some respect a highlight of his career; this partly explains the particular importance he attached to that campaign, the memory of which dictated the official interpretation of events.[4]

The triumphant light in which the arts and letters cast the end of the conflict in Germany and the Caesar's retirement from public life glossed over the political, military and personal setbacks of his final years, which led to the downfall of the imperial utopia. Charles had confronted his brother Ferdinand in a conflict only partly resolved by the accession agreement of 1551. One year later, his former ally Maurice of Saxony humiliated him at Innsbruck and the French defeated him at Metz, forcing him to grudgingly accept the Peace of Augsburg (1555), which Ferdinand negotiated, and later the Treaty of Vaucelles (1556). During those years, his health had deteriorated noticeably and he suffered frequent bouts of melancholy, which only grew worse after the death of his mother, Queen Joanna, in April 1555, sending Charles into a deep depression. In contrast to the victorious image he strove to leave for posterity, the mistakes made at the end of his reign—particularly his unwillingness to admit defeat, his refusal to accept the Peace of Augsburg until the very end, and his stubborn insistence on clinging to power—painted a negative picture of him which his enemies did not hesitate to spread and exaggerate. In part of Europe, Charles would be remembered as an ambitious, irascible, bellicose man ultimately responsible for the conflicts that ravaged Christendom during his imperial reign.

The emperor's belligerence would become a heavy burden for his son and heir to the Spanish throne. Charles's brother Ferdinand warned him of this in a letter written in July 1555, reproaching him for creating a conflict with France that his son would inherit.[5] Yet the character of the

---

4 J. L. Gonzalo Sánchez-Molero, *El César y los libros: un viaje a través de las lecturas del Emperador desde Gante a Yuste* (Yuste: Fundación Academia Europea de Yuste, 2008), 269–302. This author associates the text of the *Memorias*, intended to convey the emperor's personal vision of the campaign, with a written history of his reign that never materialised. On the subject of the Memorias as a diary of the German campaign, see K. Brandi, *Carlos V: vida y fortuna de una personalidad y de un imperio mundial* (Madrid: Editora Nacional, 1943), 487–488, and M. Fernández Álvarez, *Corpus documental de Carlos V* (Salamanca: Universidad de Salamanca, 1975–1979), IV, 461–481.

5 '[…] partant v.m. sans faire aucune paix, elle peult considerer, en quelle perplexite se trouveront ses pays de par dela pour les inconveniens et dommaiges irreparables qui sen suiveroient. […] Je ne lui veut ausi en ce donner ordre, saichant, que comme prudent prince et preveant toutes choses icelle y scaura mettre ordre par provisions considerables au bien communde tous affaires de la chrestiente'. […Your Majesty leaving without making any peace, you must consider the perplexing situation in which this puts your realms, past a

prince, who had received a fine humanistic education, suggested that he would be a more moderate, peaceful ruler, and the two had more than a few disagreements during Philip's regency and early years on the throne.[6] According to the evidence of several letters, the writings of Erasmus as recommended by two of Philip's humanist tutors, Juan Cristóbal Calvete de Estrella and Honorato Juan, appear to have made a stronger impression on the prince than the military treatises supplied by Juan Ginés de Sepúlveda, another of the instructors appointed by Charles V to oversee Philip's education.[7] Father and son had different attitudes to war, and this difference would prove crucial in shaping the public perception of the new king, a task further complicated by the need to refute rumours that had been circulating in the European courts for some time. The emperor had kept a close eye on his son's rule until 1556, and as a result Philip

---

point of no return given the inconveniences and irreparable damage they would suffer. [...] I do not want to give you orders, knowing full well that, as a prudent prince who foresees all these things, you will arrange and make considerable provisions for the common good of all the affairs of Christendom.] In *Correspondenz des Kaisers Karl V*, ed. Carl Lanz (Leipzig: Brockhaus, 1844–1846), III, 666.

6 On this subject, see J. L. Gonzalo Sánchez-Molero, 'El príncipe Felipe en el proyecto imperial carolino: su aprendizaje político"' in J. L. Castellano & F. Sánchez-Montes González, *Carlos V. Europeísmo y universalidad*, 2 (Madrid: Sociedad Estatal para la Conmemoración de los Centenarios de Felipe II y Carlos V, 2001), II, 313–338; On this period, see M. J. Rodríguez-Salgado, *Un imperio en transición. Carlos V, Felipe II y su mundo, 1551–1559* (Barcelona: Crítica, 1992).

7 In a letter sent in February 1544, for example, Philip asked Charles to negotiate a truce with France, arguing that it would be to his advantage. However, the most interesting thing is how his words convey the irenicist ideas about the evils of war that he had gleaned from his extensive reading: 'Y así yo, conosciendo lo mismo que ello y el affectión y celo con que mueven [los consejeros de Estado], de su parte y de la mía, lo suplico a V. M. cuan encarescidamente puedo, y que tome esto que aquí digo con la intención y la sinceridad de ánimo que se escribe. Lo cual no se hace por poner estorbo a V. M. en sus grandes pensamientos, los cuales son de su imperial valor, sino por traerle a la memoria la cualidad de los tiempos, la miseria en que está la república cristiana, las necesidades de sus Reinos, los daños que de tan grandes guerras se siguen por más justas que sean, y el peligro en que están por estar las armadas enemigas tan cerca, y la poca forma que hay para resistir y proveer en tantas partes, para que mirándolo todo con su grandísimo juicio tome en ello la resolución que viere más convenir.' [And so I, knowing the same as that and the affection and zeal that motivates them [the counsellors of state], on their behalf and my own, do beg Your Majesty as earnestly as I can, and hope that what I say will be received with the same intention and sincerity of spirit in which it is written. I say this not to thwart Your Majesty in your lofty thoughts, which are of imperial valour, but rather to remind you of the quality of the times, the misery in which the Christian republic finds itself, the needs of your Realms, the harm that ensues from such great wars, however just they may be, and the imminent peril they face from the enemy fleets so nearby, and the little means available to resist and provide in so many quarters, so that in seeing all this with your most excellent judgement you may take the decision you deem most convenient.] Letter from Philip to Charles, Cigales, 4 February 1544. In M. Fernández Álvarez., *Corpus documental...*, II, 192, apud. J. L. Gonzalo Sánchez-Molero, 'El príncipe Felipe en el proyecto imperial carolino...', 327.

was perceived as a weak and indecisive man who did not share Charles's taste for war.⁸ Philip and his advisers knew that he had to distance himself from the bellicose tendencies that much of Europe attributed to the emperor, but they also realised he could not renounce the spirit of military honour essential to all monarchs and associated with the formidable figure of his warrior-father. Philip's public image had to convey firmness and rectitude, making it clear that he would use force when necessary while also cultivating a pacifist attitude.⁹ The events that transpired in the 1550s would be instrumental in forming this ambivalent image, which retained elements of his father's reputation while also communicating new traits that emphasised Philip's nature as a sovereign who favoured peacekeeping over warmongering.

This image, which in time would find a more flattering expression in the epithet of the 'Prudent King', was forged during this period and rests on the gradual linking of Philip's irenicism with the Solomonic ideal that played such a relevant role in the project of the Monastery of El Escorial.¹⁰ The earliest evidence of this association is found in connection with the prince's famous progress through northern Italy, Germany and the Netherlands in 1548–1549. Part of an ambitious plan to cement dynastic succession, the *Felicissimo viaje* or 'Happiest Journey' was designed to present Philip as Charles's heir in Germany and the Low Countries. To this end, the iconography of many of the triumphal entries in different

---

8   This idea of Philip's distaste for war would not change over time. In a report sent to the Doge and the Senate in 1559, Venetian ambassador Michiel Surian wrote that '[...] although he resembles his father in his features, in his mode of speech, in his observance of religion, and in his kindness and good faith, he is dissimilar in many other respects [...]. The Emperor delighted in all that pertained to war, but his Majesty has neither knowledge of warlike matters, nor delight in them. The Emperor undertook great expeditions, but these the King avoids'. Report concerning King Philip of Spain, presented by Michiel Soriano (Surian) to the Doge and the Senate, c. 1559. In *Calendar of State Papers Relating to English Affairs in the Archives of Venice*, vol. 7, 1558–1580 (London: Her Majesty's Stationery Office, 1890), entry 274. Hereafter *CSPV*.

9   As he wrote to his father in 1554, 'Yo querría mucho justificar mis actiones para con el mundo, de no pretender estados agenos pero tambien querria que se entendiesse de mi que he de defender aquello que V. Magd. me ha hecho merced'. [I would dearly love to justify my actions to the world, explaining that I have no designs on foreign states, but I would also wish it to be understood of me that I must defend that which Your Majesty has bestowed upon me.] Letter from Philip to Charles, 16 November 1554. Archivo General de Simancas (hereafter AGS) E, Leg. 808, folio 54. See also M. J. Rodríguez-Salgado, *Un imperio en transcición*, 56.

10 See J. L. Gonzalo-Sánchez-Molero, 'Los orígenes de la imagen salomónica del Real Monasterio de San Lorenzo del Escorial', *Literatura e imagen en El Escorial. Actas del Simposium, 1–4 de septiembre de 1996*, eds. F. J. Campos and Fernández de Sevilla (El Escorial: Real Centro Universitario Escorial-María Cristina, 1996), 251–294; and J. R. de la Cuadra Blanco, *Arquitectura e historia sagrada: nuevas consideraciones sobre la idea de El Escorial y el Templo de Jerusalén*, Cuadernos de Arte e Iconografía, XXII(43), 2013.

Fig. 14.1. Woodcut from *Le triomphe d'Anvers faict en la susception du Prince Philips, Prince d'Espaign[e]* written by Cornelius Grapheus, Page Liiii recto, by Pieter Coecke van Aelst, 1550. © Metropolitan Museum, New York.

cities along the way resorted to comparisons with other royal fathers and sons, among them David and Solomon.[11] This metaphorical connection also suggested that Philip shared the biblical king's virtues of wisdom, prudence and pacifism, which over time would extend to the idea of his political practice. One of the most significant moments of this process was England's return to Catholicism, which Mary Tudor and Philip, in his role as king-consort, tried to achieve by conciliatory means. In the ceremony to mark this great event, held at the English Parliament in Whitehall in November 1554, we find an early example of the gradual public affiliation of Solomonic virtues with Philip's policies (as many chapters in this volume argue). In his speech, the papal legate Cardinal Reginald Pole drew a comparison that caught the attention of those in attendance, likening Philip II to Solomon as *Rex Pacificus*, the one chosen by God to build his temple and complete the work begun by his father, King David, whom Pole identified with the emperor:

> I can wel compare hym to David, whiche, thoughe he were a manne elected of God, yet, for that he was contaminate with bloode and war, coulde not builde the temple of Jerusalem, but lefte the finishynge thereof to Salomon, whiche was *Rex pacificus*. So may it be thoughte, that the appeasing of controversies of religion in Christianity, is not appoynted to this emperor, but rather to his sonne, who shal perfourme the buildyng that his father hath begun.[12]

---

11 Specifically in Brussels, Leuven, Ghent, Bruges, Ypres, Lille, Tornay, Arras, The Hague, Leyden, Haarlem and Amsterdam. See P. Cuenca, ed., *El felicissimo viaje del muy alto y muy poderoso príncipe don Pheplippe*, 129, 160–161, 187, 189, 213–214, 229, 244, 245, 269–270, 293, 474, 477–478, 484.

12 As recorded by John Elder, a Scot residing at the court, in J. G. Nichols, *The Chronicle of Queen Jane, and of Two Years of Queen Mary, and especially of the Rebellion of Sir Thomas Wyatt* (London: J. B. Nichols, 1850), 158. There is also a version in Spanish, printed in Seville in 1555 and included in Andrés Muñoz's *Viaje de Felipe Segundo a Inglaterra*, ed. P. de Gayangos (Madrid: Sociedad de Bibliófilos Españoles, 1877), 135: '[…] dixo al Rey que en su primera salida auia hecho tan gran servicio á Dios de conuertir y reducir este reyno á la verdadera y cathólica religión: y que aunque el Emperador, como christianísimo príncipe, auia trabajado en juntar materiales y querer edificar el templo, que nuestro señor no auia permitido sino que lo edificasse y acabasse su hijo: como acaesció á David y Salomón: y así se ha visto, pues en breues días aurá acabado un edificio tan grande, y no de materiales como el Salomon, sino de ánimas que tan perdidas estauan por mal exemplo y doctrina'. [… told the King that on his first foray he had served God so well by converting and subjecting this kingdom to the true and Catholic religion; and that although the Emperor, as a most Christian prince, had worked to assemble materials and wanted to build the temple, Our Lord had instead disposed that it would be built and finished by his son: just as happened to David and Solomon: and so we have seen, for in a few short days he will have completed a great edifice, made not of materials like Solomon's, but of souls led so far astray by bad example and doctrine.] See J. Solís de los Santos, 'Relaciones de sucesos de Inglaterra en el reinado de Carlos V', *Testigo del tiempo, memoria del universo: cultura escrita y sociedad en el mundo ibérico*

Cardinal Pole's words, inspired by the Old Testament, made a distinction between Solomon, a king of peace, and his father David, a more bellicose ruler, and likened building the temple to the restoration of a united Christendom which the emperor had been unable to complete.[13] Philip's willingness to embrace this Solomonic allegory at that time and in those terms is clear from the speech he gave before parliament in 1555 and the donation that the English sovereigns made to the Sint Jan church in Gouda, part of Habsburg Holland, two years later to commemorate Philip's victory at Saint-Quentin.[14] The stained-glass 'King's Window', created by Dirck Crabeth, depicts the Dedication of King Solomon's Temple above and the Last Supper below, where we can see the praying figures of Philip and Mary.[15] Barely two years later, in 1559, Philip was overtly identified with the biblical king in the picture painted by Lucas de Heere for the choir of Saint Bavo's Cathedral in Ghent. It represents the moment when Solomon, whose features are those of Philip, receives the Queen of Sheba, an allegory of the Netherlands offering the monarch all its wealth in exchange for his wise rule.

The Solomonic image adopted by Philip II during his time in England and the Netherlands in that pivotal decade established a continuity with his father's work and simultaneously distanced him from the accusations of belligerence levelled at the emperor. Without forsaking his heritage, Philip crafted his own image, emphasising the peaceful personality of a king whose political mission was to achieve the unity of Christendom. To cement his reputation as a peace-loving yet strong and resolute monarch, he still lacked one thing: the crown of military victory that every proper sovereign needed to earn at the beginning of his reign. The war with France would help him to finish the task. After months of doubt and hesitation, Philip found himself against the ropes and responded to the fierce anti-Habsburg propaganda campaign instigated by France and the

---

(*siglos XV-XVIII*), eds. M. Fernández et al. (Mexico City: Rubeo, 2009), 668–669, to whom I am indebted for the report, and G. Parker, *Felipe II* (Barcelona: Planeta, 2010), 131.

13 'Then he called for Solomon his son, and charged him to build a house for the Lord, the God of Israel. David said to Solomon, "My son, I had it in my heart to build a house to the name of the Lord my God. But the word of the Lord came to me, saying, 'You have shed much blood and have waged great wars; you shall not build a house to my name, because you have shed so much blood before me upon the earth. Behold, a son shall be born to you; he shall be a man of peace. I will give him peace from all his enemies round about; for his name shall be Solomon, and I will give peace and quiet to Israel in his days'"'. I Chronicles 22: 6–9 (RSVCE).

14 On the king's speech, see J. L. Gonzalo Sánchez-Molero, 'Los orígenes de la imagen salomónica...', 739–740.

15 See R. de la Cuadra Blanco, 'King Philip of Spain as Solomon the Second: the origins of Solomonism of The Escorial in the Netherlands', *The Seventh Window: The King's Window Donated by Philip II and Mary Tudor to Sint Janskerk in Gouda (1557)*, ed. Wim de Groot (Hilversum: Verloren Publishers, 2005), 169–180.

Fig. 14.2. *The Queen of Sheba visits King Solomon*, painting by Lucas de Heere, Ghent Saint Bavo Cathedral. © Photo by Pol Mayer.

pope by taking up arms against both to defend his honour, as the Venetian ambassador Michiel Surian informed the Doge and Senate in a report dated June 1557.[16] Once he had gone to war, and knowing he had to impress the world with a display of his supremacy, he felt that the only way to achieve this was by taking to the battlefield himself.[17] We see this in Philip's repeated missives to the general in command of his forces, Emmanuel Philibert of Savoy, insisting he not engage in battle until the king came to lead the troops.[18] The delayed arrival of English reinforcements prevented

---

16 '[…] and as the dignity and repute of princes is of no less importance to them than their states, he for his honour had been compelled to make war'. Michiel Surian to the Doge and Senate, 7 June 1557. *CSPV*, vol. 6, 1143.

17 F. Checa Cremades, *Carlos V y la imagen del héroe en el Renacimiento*, 125; speaking of the victory at Mühlberg, this author writes that it 'definitively established the image of the heroic warrior who directly participated in military actions'.

18 The record of campaign communiqués between Philip and the Duke of Savoy on the French front leaves no doubt as to this resolve. In several letters sent between 6 and 9 August, we read: 'I am extremely displeased at not being able to come nor is it possible to come soon, for the English have written that they will not arrive here until Tuesday, although I have urged them to hurry up. […] I am quite desperate. […] Touching your point about engaging in battle in the event that they provoke it, what I can say is that the first concern must be to take care that they do not relieve the town. Unless absolutely necessary to prevent them relieving it, you must avoid engaging in battle until I arrive. […] If there is no way

Fig. 14.3. *The Last Supper*. Detail from the stained-glass window number 7 in the Sint Janskerk at Gouda, Netherlands, by Dirk Crabeth, 1557. © Photo by Rolf Kranz.

Philip from being on the front line during the battle that broke Saint-Quentin, but he arrived in time to enter the city with his army. Against all odds, Philip prevailed over his two bitterest foes, although the outcome was more a product of luck and the miscalculations of his enemies, who never imagined that the king whom they had taken for a weak, spineless man could be so bold.

This military triumph gave Philip the image he so fervently desired, that of the sovereign victorious on the field of battle. His honour had been defended and his person publicly and magnificently displayed. The Battle of Saint-Quentin therefore proved decisive and did much to cement the new image of the monarch which, by showing clemency to his two adversaries after the victory, further emphasised the Solomonism exploited during those years. While this triumph seemed to confirm Philip as a new Charles, the king soon made it clear that he was a very different sort of ruler. Though energetic like his father when necessary, he remained even-tempered, peaceful and true to himself. He made peace with the pope in September 1557 at a very high cost, thereby refuting the rumours that the Holy See had spread about him. The Treaty of Cateau-Cambrésis signed with France in April 1559 was welcomed with great relief in Europe. The victory at Saint-Quentin helped Philip forge a public image in which war and peace found the balance this sovereign sought.[19]

In the following years, this image was also clearly established in Spain, as the great project of El Escorial attests. Poetry is one field in which we find evidence of this consolidation, as María José Vega discusses in her contribution to this volume.[20] The following paragraphs will focus on how different epic poets described the Saint-Quentin episode in the years after the battle, and specifically how their verses convey the Solomonic image of this new king of peace. The selected texts, published between 1566 and 1578, show how epic poetry incorporated the same imagery projected by regal magnificence, underscoring the values of wisdom, justice and mercy. Besides portraying Philip as a virtuous prince during his regency and a pious monarch who ruled justly and wisely, their version of what happened at Saint-Quentin paints the picture of a king who put an end to armed violence and was merciful to his enemies. As we shall see, the poets emphasise his restraint in waging war, viewed as a necessary evil in order to bring peace and unity to Christendom and whose fury is checked by the sovereign.

---

to avoid an engagement before I arrive, I cannot enjoin you too strongly to inform me post haste, so as to give me the means and opportunity to arrive in time. Since I know that you desire my company in such an eventuality, I do not wish to press you further, but I beg you to have spare horses waiting day and night to be able to inform me'. From Philip II to Emmanuel Philibert, Duke of Savoy, August 1557. *Letters of Philip II of Spain, to Emmanuel Philibert, Duke of Savoy*; 4 May 1557–1513 Aug. 1558, BL MS Add, 28264, ff. 19, 26–27. Quoted in Henry Kamen, *Philip of Spain* (New Haven/London: Yale University Press, 1997), 68.

19 On this topic, see the interesting study by B. Haan, 'Mostrando su persona: el combate de Felipe II por su reputación en su advenimiento al trono', *e-Spania: Revue interdisciplinaire d'études hispaniques médiévales et modernes*, 24 (15 June 2016), accessed 12 March 2020. URL: http://journals.openedition.org/e-spania/25674. DOI: https://doi.org/10.4000/e-spania.25674.

20 Cf. María José Vega, 'Epic and Truth: Writing for the Habsburgs in Sixteenth-Century Spain', in this volume.

The earliest example is found in one of the many prophetic passages of Luis Zapata's lengthy poem *Carlo famoso*, possibly completed in early 1565 and published in 1566, which poetically narrates the life and deeds of Emperor Charles V.[21] Canto XXXV describes the defence of Vienna from Ottoman attackers, led by Charles and his brother Ferdinand. For the occasion, Charles ordered Luis de Ávila to go to Augsburg and order new armour on his behalf from a descendent of Vulcan named Colman. He was said to be none other than Desiderius Kolman Helmschmied, His Majesty's armourer and one of the most renowned smiths in Europe at the time, as well as a wise man with the gift of prophecy. Like the god Vulcan, Colman forged images of the life and future victories of Philip II on Charles's armour, a prophetic ekphrasis echoing that of Aeneas's shield in the eighth book of the *Aeneid*. I would like to highlight two passages here. In the first, Zapata describes Philip as regent of Spain, noting the wisdom with which the prince has managed the affairs of the realm:

> Somewhere else he saw a King who, leaving the realm to tend to other affairs, appoints a man not yet fully made (though well-made and handsome was he) to take charge of his kingdoms. This young man gives all and sundry their due and rules the nations wisely, his counsels being better than the those of sage old men.[22]

The second excerpt reproduces two of the octaves devoted to describing the victory at Saint-Quentin. In the first, the triumphant Philip appears among his men, overcoming the town's resistance; in the second, which concerns the subsequent siege of Châtelet, Zapata notes that the city surrenders to his mercy more than to his power. Though victorious like his father, in Zapata's version Philip is portrayed as a king wise in politics and merciful in war.

> And behold, in the fire etched in fine gold, the King, not tired of war, in his glorious victory, driving a people from their city. And accompanied by his brave warriors, who followed him in the previous fierce strife, he stormed by force the place named Saint-Quentin in the engraving. // From there, the King, who shall be renowned a thousand centuries for his thousand exploits, one great feat not keeping him from another, sends his companies to Châtelet. Châtelet, hearing his feared name and

---

21 The authorisation of the poem was signed by Juan de Robles on 8 March 1565.
22 Luis Zapata, *Carlo famoso* (Valencia: Ioan Mey, 1566), XXXV, 11. 'En otra parte vio que aun no bien hecho / hombre (aunque muy bien hecho y hermoso era) / de sus reynos le encarga todo el hecho / un Rey, que a otros negocios se iba fuera. / Él da a aquestos y aquellos su derecho / y gobierna las gentes de manera / quentre otros muy expertos sabios viejos / siempre eran los mejores sus consejos'.

seeing strange arms all around, surrenders to one whose great power, though mighty indeed, is exceeded by his great mercy.[23]

The next example is far more telling. We find it in Book IV of *El victorioso Carlos V* by Jerónimo Jiménez de Urrea, a narrative poem that recounts the war against the Schmalkaldic League. Though finished before 1572, it was never published and has survived in the form of two manuscripts, now kept at the Biblioteca Nacional de España and the Hispanic Society of America in New York.[24] The context of the chosen passage is, as in the case of Zapata's poem, one of poetic ekphrasis. One of Charles's allies, Albert, Margrave of Brandenburg, is being feted at Rochlitz Castle, taken by imperial forces in February 1547 and governed by Princess Elisabeth von Rochlitz, a leading figure in the Protestant Reformation. The lady holds a banquet in his honour, hoping to detain him while she secretly informs her brother, Philip of Hesse, that the emperor's men have arrived. The feast is spread out on a lovely ivory table, crafted by the divine metalsmith who forged the armour that Charles V would wear on that glorious day by the River Elbe, decorated with different war scenes of the 'future' reign of Philip II. The verses below narrate events related to the Battle of Saint-Quentin, which the king 'takes swiftly by force of arms' (IV, v. 699). The interesting thing about this excerpt is that Urrea only spends a few lines describing the victory itself, preferring to dwell on the consequences of this triumph and the one achieved in Italy over the pope which, according to the poet, ushered in a new era of lasting peace that pleased God:

> Behold the August and venerable image of the great Charles V in his son. His mettle, his courage and his alacrity, his invincible spirit and long-suffering, his gallantry at arms, his fine bearing, his divine art and providence observe, his grave demeanour and pleasant countenance, goodness, truth, honesty, modesty and all the greatness of his works. […] and Philip brings peace to all Italy, solid and enduring for many

---

23 Luis Zapata, *Carlo famoso*, XXXV, 21-22. 'Y aquel Rey no hartarse en tal estado, / con aquel tan glorioso vencimiento, / el fuego de oro fino iluminado / se vía, y batir un pueblo de su asiento. / Y de su brava gente acompañado, / antes seguido aquel con fiero intento, / expugnar el lugar a fuerza pura / que San Quintín decía la entalladura. // A dond'estando aquel, qu'esclarecido / en mil siglos será por mil hazañas, / de un gran negocio a otros no impedido, / desde allí a Xatelete enviar compañas. / Xatelete, qu'el nombre tan temido / de aquel oye y ve'entorno armas estrañas, / se da a quien, aunqu'es tanta su potencia / es más qu'el gran poder su gran clemencia'.

24 The copy at the Biblioteca Nacional de España (BNE Ms. 1469) must be the one prepared for the printing press. The preliminary folios of the manuscript bear the date 1584 and the approval of Alonso de Ercilla. At the bottom of each page is a signature affixed by the censor Fray Franscisco Mansilla, who authorised the manuscript in 1579. The copy owned by the Hispanic Society of America (Ms. CLXVII) is incomplete.

a year, bringing back that Octavian age which is a clearer victory and more eternal triumph than that achieved by arms, pleasing to men and to the heavens.[25]

In the verses that follow the triumph at Saint-Quentin, Philip is likened to his father in having won a military victory, for Urrea presents Philip as the new Charles in war. A few lines down, this image is qualified by the distinctive personal attributes of the new sovereign. Thanks to him, Italy would have 'solid and enduring' peace, a reference to the treaties with the pope and the French, which the poet considers favourable to Philip's interests, not only in the political sphere but also with regard to his honour and public image. For our purposes, the most interesting aspect of this passage is the idea that the conquest of peace was a greater victory than that achieved by force of arms. These lines paint a much more polished picture of Philip as a victorious and peaceful king than Zapata's verses.

The following excerpt from the poem *Felicísima victoria concedida al cielo al señor don Juan de Austria en el golfo de Lepanto*—written by the Portuguese author Jerónimo Corte-Real in 1575 and published and dedicated to Philip II in 1578—is particularly interesting. Once again, the verses devoted to the Battle of Saint-Quentin are a prophetic ekphrasis of a suit of armour, this time forged by Vulcan himself. The armour belongs not to Charles V but to his illegitimate son John of Austria, presented by Venus to her young protégé before the battle commences. John sees the feats of his father and brother depicted on the shield, allowing the poet to establish a continuity between the emperor and his two sons. The most outstanding paternal feats are those in which he participated, the siege of Vienna and the victory over the Schmalkaldic League, which closes the ekphratic part dedicated to Charles's successes, making no mention of the failures that followed. The section devoted to Philip opens with an apotheosis of the king and continues with verses about the Battle of Saint-Quentin. As in Urrea's poem, Corte-Real offers a brief account of the battle, only mentioning the cruellest and bloodiest aspects. The entire episode revolves around the description of the king as a powerful figure sheathed in his armour and mounted on his steed. But while Corte-Real describes Charles as wielding weapons at Vienna, Philip only holds the staff of command and his horse's reins in his hands, indicating that his is a different sort of power.

---

25 Jerónimo Jiménez de Urrea, *El victorioso Carlos V*, IV, vv.705–713, vv. 723–728. 'Mira la Augusta y venerable imagen / de Carlo Quinto Máximo en su hijo. / Su brío, su valor y su presteza, / su ánimo invencible y sufrimiento, / su gallardía en armas, su buen aire, / su divino arte ver y providencia, / su grave aspecto y agradable rostro, / bondad, verdad, honestidad, modestia / y toda la grandeza de sus obras. / [...] / y pone luenga paz en toda Italia, / firme por mucho tiempo y duradera, / tornando aquella edad de Octaviano / que es más clara victoria y triunfo aeterno / que aquella por las armas alcanzada, / agradable a los hombres y a los cielos'.

While Charles's head was protected by a German morion, Philip wears a sallet adorned with pearls and plumes. The vigorous military spirit of the entire scene is concentrated in the image of his white horse, which fiercely stamps the ground and fretfully champs at the bit with which the rider holds it back:

> There was the powerful king, mighty at arms, in strong armour all encased. His pristine sallet bedecked with gold and pearls and rich plumes, sitting astride a white Spanish steed, with saddle and golden harnesses of foreign make: He holds the reins in one hand, and in the other a staff, with which he commands and rules the field. The splendid animal, fleet and nimble, fiercely beats the ground with iron-shod hooves, champing at the bit, covered in dry, thick, white foam. [...] The king's handsome face radiates a strange delight in this good and happy event: And in his dancing eyes a thousand rays of bright blazing flames gleam. O'er his head was fixed the shining star of his father. His strong, spirited, capable captains were gathered round about him.[26]

The picture that Corte-Real paints of Philip, though clearly drawing on the description of his father a few lines earlier, is not that of a bellicose monarch about to enter the battle fray, but that of a dignified king whose right hand firmly holds and restrains the fury symbolised by the horse. Though present and surrounded by his men on the battlefield, Corte-Real's Philip, whose 'handsome face radiates a strange delight', does not have the same attitude towards war as his father, although his own success rests on that paternal legacy. Thus, when the city surrenders, and he is once again surrounded by his men and we read that 'the shining star of his father' beams over his head. The scene therefore clearly contrasts the horrors of combat with the stern, dignified presence of a king who need not draw a sword to wield his authority.

The last work to mention here is *La Araucana* by Alonso de Ercilla y Zúñiga, which narrates the conquest of Chile and the war waged by the Spaniards against the Mapuche people. Published in three parts (in 1569, 1578 and 1589), the poem informs readers of a bloody conflict—

---

26 Jerónimo Corte-Real, *Felicísima victoria concedida del cielo al señor don Iuan d'Austria, en el golfo de Lepanto de la poderosa armada Othomana* (Lisbon: Antonio Ribero, 1578), VI, vv. 622–633, vv. 663–669. 'Estaba en otra parte el Rey potente / de fortísimas armas todo armado. / Y a la limpia celada guarnescida / De oro y perlas, ornaban ricas plumas. / En caballo Español blanco, y con silla, / y guarniciones d'oro, de obra estraña: / Las riendas una mano lleva, y otra / un bastón, con que manda y rige el campo. / El hermoso animal, ligero y suelto, / con los herrados pies la tierra bate / feroz, tascando el freno, lo envolvía / en una seca, espesa, blanca espuma. / [...] / El qual deste felice y buen suceso, / su rostro hermoso muestra un gozo estraño: / Y en sus alegres ojos centellaban / mil rayos de lumbrosas vivas llamas. / Tenía fixa sobre su cabeça, / la estrella rutilante de su padre. / Cercado estaba en torno de sus fuertes, / animosos, y diestros capitanes'.

witnessed and narrated in first person by the author—characterised by the cruelty and injustice of the Spaniards, especially under the command of Pedro de Valdivia. As we will see, Ercilla attempted to contrast this vision of war with a very specific idea of royal pacifism in keeping with the king's desired image. At certain points in the second part of La Araucana (1578), the poet strayed from his Chilean subject matter to reference events taking place in Europe. This happens in Cantos XVII and XVIII, where the Ercilla of poetic fiction says that he has been visited in dreams by Bellona, who promises to show him several recent events that have transpired across the ocean, including the Battle of Saint-Quentin. When he narrates this episode, the poet hints that the memory of his retired father's deeds spurred Philip to emulate him and muster his armies, on that 'first occasion', to defeat France. These verses convey the idea that the king needed to go to war at the beginning of his reign for the sake of his reputation, which was literally built on Charles's legacy.

> The son, seeing the prosperous career of his victorious retired father, and wanting to fulfil the true hope his deeds had always given, in the beginning [of his reign] and on the first occasion, he has mustered that great army to bring low the conceit, pride and arrogance of France the foe.[27]

However, Ercilla does not show us a triumphant Philip, armed and on horseback, before entering the fray. Instead, Bellona gives the narrator a vision of his troops taking the town. The poet's verses give detailed descriptions of the fighting, the havoc, the sacking—in short, the horrific consequences of the use of force. Alonso de Ercilla the soldier makes no attempt to conceal from readers the destruction caused by artillery, the rage, death and ruin visible everywhere, and speaks of 'untamed fury' (XVIII, xi, v. 1) violently breaking through the city's defences. The poet devotes eighteen long stanzas to describing the cruelty of war, which only ceases when the king finally intervenes to protect the maidens fleeing in terror, as recounted in this following excerpt:

> The women blindly stumbling hither and yon, driven by fear, were at Philip's order gathered and removed to a safe place, where defended from the rage of war by loyal guards they found succour; for though their houses be sacked, their virtue would remain intact.[28]

---

27 Alonso de Ercilla y Zúñiga, *Segunda parte de La Araucana* (1578), eds. Morínigo-Lerner (Madrid: Castalia, 1987), XVII, lv. 'Viendo el hijo la próspera Carrera / del vitorioso padre retirado, / por hacer la esperanza verdadera / que siempre de sus obras había dado, / en el principio y ocasión primera / aquel copioso ejército ha juntado, / para bajar de la enemiga Francia / la presunción, orgullo y arrogancia.'

28 Alonso de Ercilla y Zúñiga, Segunda parte de La Araucana, XVIII, xxiv. 'Las mujeres que acá y allá perdidas, / llevadas del temor, sin tiento andaban, / por orden de Felipe recogidas /

When the maids and nuns fled from the soldiers, 'pious Philip' ordered his men to shield them from the 'rage of war' and let no man defile the holy places; they immediately obeyed. Finally, we see the town's desperate inhabitants throwing themselves upon the weapons of their adversaries. At that point Philip intervenes a second time, now as a 'merciful' monarch.

> But the pious King's great mercy had blunted the fierce blades, and with great promptness and diligence all fury and fire was extinguished; in the end, facing no further opposition or resistance, he entered into Saint-Quentin, with the key to France already in his hand, and the way to Paris clear before him.[29]

The king's clemency 'blunted' the weapons' sharp edges and brought the siege to a swift conclusion. Here Philip is not the victorious warrior but a pious monarch who puts an end to armed violence, whose mere presence imposes discipline on the rage of war, and whose intervention halts the destructive rampage of the victors and curbs their excesses.[30] The king's mercy exhibits a different way of waging war that contrasts with the methods employed by the Spanish conquistadors in Chile. The image of the triumphant warrior, though symbolically present, is tempered by that of the peaceful monarch.

After reading these excerpts, it seems clear that Spanish epic poets fully embraced the image of Philip II as a peaceful king, an image constructed during his years in England and the Low Countries and for a very similar purpose. It was there, over the course of the 1550s, that the vision of Philip as a second Solomon took shape, intimated by the magnificence celebrated in his *Felicissimo viaje* and visibly emphasised in various artworks commissioned in later years. Instigated by the king and his counsellors and magnified in courtly circles, the influence of this image, destined to symbolically define Philip's politics, made itself felt in the work of court poets like Luis Zapata, nobles like Jerónimo Corte-Real, high-born military men like Jerónimo Jiménez de Urrea, and even lowly soldiers like Alonso de Ercilla. All, despite their very different approaches to epic poetry, chose to portray their king as the embodiment of Solomonic virtues and helped to spread the idea that royal justice and pacifism win victories greater than those achieved by force.

---

en seguro lugar las retiraban, / donde de fieles guardas defendidas / del bélico furor las amparaban; / que aunque fueron sus casas saqueadas, / las honras les quedaron reservadas'.
29 Alonso de Ercilla y Zúñiga, *Segunda parte de La Araucana*, XVIII, xxviii. 'Mas del piadoso Rey la gran Clemencia / había las fieras armas embotado, / que con remedio presto y diligencia / todo el furor y fuego fue apagado; / al fin, sin más defensa y resistencia, / dentro de San Quintín quedó alojado, / con la llave de Francia ya en la mano, / hasta París abierto el paso llano'.
30 See A. Plagnard, *Une épopée ibérique : Alonso de Ercilla et Jerónimo Corte-Real (1569–1598)* (Madrid: Casa de Velázquez, 2019), 235–239 and 299.

Notes on the Contributors

Patricia Andrés González is professor of Art History at Valladolid University, and member of its research group *Art, power and society in the Modern Age*. Doctor in Art History, with the doctoral thesis *Guadalupe, a religious center for artistic and cultural development*, her research focuses on iconography, emblematic literature and its impact on the arts, and historical-artistic heritage. She has more than fifty publications (among his latest monographs, those dedicated to the custody of Arfe in Valladolid or to the facade of the Valladolid University).

Christian Beaufort-Spontin is the former director of *Hofjagd und Rüstkammer*, Kunsthistorisches Museum in Vienna. His research has focused on the world of weapons and luxury armor in the Habsburg sphere.

Fernando Bouza Álvarez is professor at the University Complutense de Madrid, and editor of the journal *Cuadernos de Historia Moderna*. His research focuses on early modern Iberian culture and politics. He is the author of, among others, *Communication, Knowledge, and Memory in Early Modern Spain* (2004) and co-editor of *The Iberian World (1450–1820)* (2019).

Fernando Checa is full professor of Art History at the University Complutense in Madrid, Spain, and a former director of the Prado Museum in Madrid. Checa is recipient of the prestigious Prize in History awarded by Spanish Ministry of Culture for his ground-breaking study on Philip II of Spain as patron of the arts (*Felipe II, mecenas de las artes*). He has published extensively on the artistic patronage of the Spanish House of Habsburg, especially during the rule of Emperor Charles V and Philip II of Spain. She is also an active guest curator having curated major exhibitions on the Royal Collections of the Habsburgs and their extended family in Madrid, Vienna, Paris, Gent, Roma, Innsbruck, Puebla (Mexico) and Dallas (TX). Checa's most recents monographs explores Titian's production for the European courts (*Tiziano y las cortes del Renacimiento*), and the role of Philip II around the artistic image (*Renacimiento habsbúrgico. Felipe II y las imágenes*). Paul Mellon Senior Fellow at CASVA (Washington) and Visiting professor at the Université de Geneve (Switzerland) and Oklahoma State.

José Luis Gonzalo Sánchez-Molero is professor of Complutense University of Madrid, in Faculty of Library and Information Studies. His research deals are the courtly bibliophilia in the Spanish sixteenth-century, the Erasmismus in Spain, Miguel de Cervantes and the ancient book in East Asia. He received the "Bibliography Prize of the National Library" in Spain (1997) and the "Bartolomé José Gallardo Award" for his investigations on the royal libraries in the Spanish sixteenth-century (2002).

Antonio Gozalbo Nadal: PhD Thesis in Art History from the Jaume I University of Castellón (UJI), with international and Cum Laude mention. He has a degree in Humanities (UJI) and a Graduate in Art History (UNED). Master's in Art History and Visual Culture (UJI-UV). He has several publications and participations in congresses, having collaborated in scholarships and R+D+i projects. He currently teaches Art History at the UJI and the Associated Center of the UNED in Vila-real (Castellón).

Matteo Mancini is professor of Art History at UCM, dedicating his studies and research to Venetian painting of the sixteenth and seventeenth centuries and its links and consequences in Spanish and European painting of the same era. At the professional level he emphasizes his work in the Museo Nacional del Prado as coordinator of cultural activities, and in National Heritage of Spain as coordinator of communication and dissemination of exhibitions.

Víctor Mínguez is full professor of Art History at the Universitat Jaume I. Specialist in the analysis of images of power. Among his most recent books are: *La invención de Carlos II. Apoteosis simbólica de la Casa de Austria* (2013) e *Infierno y gloria en el mar. Los Habsburgo y el imaginario artístico de Lepanto* (2017).

Jesús F. Pascual Molina is professor and academic secretary of the Department of Art History at the University of Valladolid in Spain. His research is focused in the connections between art and power, especially in the sixteenth century. In relation with this topic, has published many articles and being part of different research projects, and he is member of the *Art, Power and Society in the Modern Age Research Group*. Among his works, he has been co-editor of *Magnificencia y arte. Devenir de los tapices en la historia* (2018) and *El legado de las obras de arte. Tapices, pinturas, esculturas… Sus viajes a través de la Historia* (2017), and has co-authored with M. Á. Zalama, *Testamento y codicilos de Juan II de Aragón, y última voluntad de Fernando I: política y artes* (2017).

Vanessa Quintanar Cabello is a researcher specialized in the food representation in the European art from 16th to 18th century. She was actively involved in the development of the Virtual Library of the Royal Academy of Gastronomy of Spain. Additionally, she has published several scientific articles as well as participated in national and international conferences which focused on the role of art as a documentary source in the study of the food history.

Antonio Urquízar Herrera is full professor at the History of Art Department of the UNED, Madrid. He has published several works on Early Modern Art in Spain, among them *Admiration and Awe. Morisco Buildings and Identity Negotiations in Early Modern Spanish Historiography* (Oxford University Press, 2017), and *Coleccionismo y nobleza. Signos de distinción social en la Andalucía del Renacimiento* (Marcial Pons, 2007). He is currently PI of a research group on Early Modern Art in Spain, and Chair to the COST Action CA18129 *Islamic Legacy: Narratives East, West, South, North of the Mediterranean (1350–1750)*, that brings together more than 150 researchers coming for 38 European and Mediterranean countries.

María José Vega Ramos is full professor of Literary Theory and Comparative Literature at the Universidad Autónoma de Barcelona. She is founder and director of the Seminario de Poética del Renacimiento, a research group on Early Modern literary theory and criticism. She has worked mainly on literary theory and comparative literature in Early Modern Europe (XVIth century). M. J. Vega is author of several monographs on literary theory, censorship and expurgation in the 16th century. She has been editor of several monographic issues of academic journals and has translated into Spanish Latin and Italian texts of the XVth and XVIth Century. She has published papers and review articles on Early Modern European literature in academic journals since 1992. In the last five years she has developed research projects in UK, Germany, and Spain. She has received the Humboldt Research Award (2012, RFA), the Mercator Gastprofessur (2011, Deutsche Forschungsgemeinshaft) and the ICREA Acadèmia Research Award (calls 2008, 2014, 2019).

Lara Vilà lectures Literature in Universitat de Girona (UdG). She earned her PhD in 2001 with a thesis devoted to the study of the imitation of Vergil in 16th Century Spanish Epics, a subject approached and deepened in her subsequent publications. She has also studied Ethnographic texts about Spanish colonialism in Asia and her more recent essays focus on the importance of war and the military in Early Modern Spanish Literature.

Miguel Ángel Zalama is full professor and Director of the Department of Art History at the University of Valladolid and and director of the

Tordesillas Center for Relations with Latin America. He has been a researcher at the Institute of Fine Arts at the University of New York and later moved to the University of La Sapienza, Rome, as well as a visiting professor at the Université Catholique de l'Ouest, Angers (France), and the University of Monterrey (Mexico). Specializing in the history and theory of late medieval and Renaissance art, he has published numerous works in this regard and directed successive research projects.

Index of names

Achilles 232, 234
Adrianssen, Alexander van 92
Aeneas 112, 223, 247
Aglaia 183
Agricola, Johannes 160, 175
Agrippa 112
Álava, Diego de 230
Albert III, Duke of Austria 203
Albert, Margrave of Brandenburg 248
Albert of Austria, Archduke, Viceroy of Portugal 22, 141
Alberti, Leon Battista 28, 39, 47
Alciato, Andrea 120, 179-180, 186
Aldobrandini, Pietro 124
Alencastre, Juliana de 24
Alexander (Alessandro) Farnese, Duke of Parma 140-141, 168-169, 214
Alexander the Great 232
Alfian, Antonio de 120
Alfonso I d'Este, Duke of Ferrara 123
Alfonso V the Magnanimous, King of Aragon 192, 200
Alonso, Agustín 224-225, 228, 234
Alonso de Santa Cruz 34, 92-93, 95, 98, 100-101, 103-104
Altdorfer, Albrecht 37, 127, 189
Altdorfer, Erhard 130
Álvarez-Ossorio, Antonio 93
Álvarez, Vicente 92, 96, 98-101
Álvarez de Toledo, Diego 230
Álvarez de Toledo y Pimentel, Fernando, 3rd Duke of Alba, *aka* Grand Duke of Alba 134, 136, 139-140
Amberger, Cristoph 201
Andreas of Austria, *see* Burgau, Andreas of Austria, Margrave of Burgau
Andrés, Patricia 14
Anguissola, Sofonisba 24
Anna of Habsburg (or Austria), Archduchess and Queen of Spain 16, 123
Anne de Croÿ, Princess of Chimay 210
Anne de Montmorency, Constable of France 136
António of Aviz, Prior of Crato 139
Apollodorus, 120
Aquiles, Julio 117, 133
Archias 232
Arcimboldo, Giuseppe 24, 39, 202, 220
Arias Montano, Benito 215
Aristotle 33, 50, 74, 224
Arroyo, Diego 30
Augustus, Roman Emperor 221
Austria, House of *see* Habsburgs
Ávila y Zúñiga, Luis de 32, 132, 134, 226-227, 247
Áviz, House of 182

Bacon, Francis 149
Balthasar Charles, Prince of Spain 195
Barbarossa 115-116, 131
Batteux, Charles 48

Battisti, Eugenio 71
Bazán, Álvaro 119, 139
Beaufort-Spontin, Christian 13
Beham, Barthel 130
Beham, Hans Sebald 130
Bellona 121, 251
Benedictine monks 210
Bennewitz, Peter 113
Białostocki, Jan 11
Biondo, Flavio 42, 149
Blondeel, Lancelot 129
Blotius, Hugo 217, 219
Boccaccio 60
Bodar, Diane 91
Bona, Giovanni 172
Bonacina, Elisabetta 25
Bonet Correa, Antonio 35
Borghini, Vincenzo 178
Borja, Juan de 183
Bosch 36, 39
Boschini, Marco 65, 67-69
Bouza, Fernando 12-13, 114
Bramante 42
Breu the Younger, Jörg 37
Breu the Elder, Jörg 128
Bronzino 170
Brueghel the Elder, Pieter 39, 105, 143
Brunelleschi, Filippo 51
Burckhardt, Jacob 12, 45, 46
Burgau, Andreas of Austria, Margrave of Burgau, Cardinal Bishop of Constance and Brixen 172
Burgau, Karl von Burgau, Margrave of Burgau 172
Burgkmair, Hans 37, 182, 188, 190-191, 205
Bustamante García, Agustín 138
Busto, Bernabé de 226

Cabezón, Antonio 30
Cabrera de Córdoba, Luis 18, 35
Caesar 112, 113, 134, 223

Calvete de Estrella, Juan Cristóbal 29-31, 35, 92-99, 101, 105-106, 158, 161, 192-193, 239
Calvi, Lazzaro 121
Cambiaso, Luca 121-122, 138
Cambiaso, Orazio 138
Copernicus, Nicolaus 113
Caravaggio, Michelangelo Merisi da 71
Caravaggio, Polidoro da 116
Cardinal of Augsburg 99
Cardinal of Mantua 97
Carducci, Vicenzo 71, 123
Carlos, Prince of Spain 215
Carpio, Bernardo del 222
Cartari, Vincenzo 121
Casas, Cristóbal de 120
Cassirer, Ernst 45
Castel Bolognese, Giovanni Bernardi da 128, 132, 134
Castello, Fabrizio 138
Castello, Giovanni Battista, Il Bergamasco, 119
Catherine of Aragon, Queen consort of England 182
Catherine of Lancaster, Queen of Castile 181
Catholic Monarchs 78, 82, 85, 88, 181, 234
Cavagna, Giovanni Battista 170
Ceballos Escalera, Alfonso 188
Celtis, Conrad (Konrad) 37, 199, 203
Cennini, Cennino 59
Cervantes, Miguel de 73
Cervera Vera, Luis 35
Charlemagne 207
Charles I, King of England 114
Charles II, Archduke of Austria and Duke of Styria 38, 217
Charles IV, King of Spain 54
Charles V, Emperor and King of Spain 16-17, 19, 29, 31-32, 37,

45, 51, 54, 67, 77-78, 80, 82-86,
88, 97, 100, 104-106, 109-118,
123, 127-135, 139, 141, 146-148,
150-151, 155-158, 161, 165, 168,
177, 182-183, 187, 192, 194-195,
199, 201, 205, 208-214, 216,
221-223, 226, 229, 231-232,
234-235, 237-240, 246-251
Charles VIII, King of France 50, 205, 207, 212
Charles de Cröy, Prince of Chimay 206
Charles Emmanuel I, Duke of Savoy 119
Charles the Bold, Duke of Burgundy 76, 78, 206
Chasseneuz, Barthélemy de 149
Chassincourt, Jeanne de 24
Checa, Fernando 12, 88, 123, 146, 149
Christmas, John 114
Christmas, Mathias 114
Christus, Petrus 75
Cicero 76, 120, 232
Cimabue 42
Cisneros, Francisco Jiménez de Cisneros, Archbishop of Toledo 151
Cobos y Molina, Francisco de los 132
Cock, Hieronymus 136, 148
Coecke van Aelst, Pieter 52, 118, 212, 241
Colbert, Jean-Baptiste 49
Collin, Alexander 128
Colón, Hernando 211
Colón de Toledo, Luis 212
Colonna, Fabrizio 95, 99
Columbus, Christopher 110
Constable of Castile 84
Coornhert, Dirck 117
Corte Real, Jerónimo 223, 225, 249, 250, 252

Cortés, Hernán 155, 156, 225, 230, 234
Cosimo I de' Medici, Great Duke of Tuscany 37, 59, 167, 169, 178
Count of Benavente 84
Count of Fuentes 141
Count of Tendilla 159
Covarrubias, Sebastián de 180
Crabeth, Dirck 243, 245
Craesbeecks 24
Cranach the Younger, Lukas 170
Croce, Benedetto 47, 64
Curzio, Caio Cesare 170
Custos, Dominicus 38, 174

D'Alembert, Jean le Rond 47-48
D'Este, House of 165
DaCosta Kaufmann, Thomas 13
Dante 42, 60
David, King of Israel 242-243
Davis, Elizabeth 227-228
De'Barbari, Jacopo 208
Dermoyen, William 129
Diana 103
Díaz de Vivar, Rodrigo, *aka* El Cid 222
Díaz Tanco de Frexenal, Vasco 150
Dietrichstein, Anna 24
Dietrichstein, Barbara 24
Dietrichstein, Hippolyta 24
Dioscorides 120
Dirikse, Rodrigo, *see* Holanda, Rodrigo de
Dolce, Ludovico 134
Dominicans 120
Donado, Lunardo 166
Dondini, Guglielmo 141
Doria, Andrea 94, 111, 116
Doria, Giovanni Andrea 121
Duccio 44
Duchess of Lorraine 97
Duke Maurice of Saxony 99
Duke of Alba 97, 118, 156, 161, 168

Duke of Bavaria 100, 165
Duke of Berry 88
Dukes of Burgundy 195, 203, 206, 209, 214
Duke of Ferrara 94, 97
Duke of Mantua 94, 96,-97, 117, 145, 158
Dukes of Burgundy 49, 51, 91
Dulle Griet 143, 144
Durantino, Francesco 134
Dürer, Albrecht 37, 44, 127, 188, 208

Egmont, Count of 137, 140
El Greco 24, 69
Eleanor of Austria, Queen of Portugal and France 100, 103-105, 118, 211
Elias, Norbert 13, 200
Elizabeth I Tudor, Queen of England 17
Emmanuel Philibert, duke of Savoy 136, 244
Erasmus of Rotterdam 120, 195, 208-209, 239
Ercilla, Alonso de 223, 226, 228, 235, 250-252
Escalante, Bernardino de 229
Escobar, Baltasar 225
Espinosa, Nicolás 228, 235
Euphrosyne 183

Fame 121
Federico da Montefeltro, Duke of Urbino 50, 200
Federico II Gonzaga, Marquis of Montferrato 109
Ferdinand I of Habsburg, Emperor 16, 45, 165, 171, 185, 199-200, 211, 216-217, 238, 247
Ferdinand I, King of Naples 50
Ferdinand II of Tyrol, Archduke 38, 88, 158-159, 165-172, 175, 217
Ferdinand II the Catholic, King of Aragon 115, 149, 168

Ferdinand of Austria, Cardinal-Infante 112
Ferdinando of Austria, Prince of Spain 121, 123-124
Fernández Albaladejo, Pablo 18
Fernández de Córdoba, Gonzalo 162
Fioravanti, Leonardo 24
Flacus, Valerius 120
Flandes, Juan de 50
Fontana, Giovanni Battista 38, 174
Fontana, Giulio 123
Fortune 121
Fox Morillo, Sebastián 234
Francesco de Medici 167, 178
Francis I, King of France 77, 128 129, 183, 212, 231
Francken, Frans 156
Frederick II, Count Palatine of the Rhine 131
Frederick III, Emperor 191, 203

García de Paredes, Diego 230
Garnode, Laureus de 84
Garrido de Villena, Francisco 228
Gartner, Simon 174
Geizkofler, Zacharias 170
Geneli, René 25
Gesio, Giovanni Battista 24
Gesner, Conrad 213
Gheeraerts the Elder, Marcus 19
Ghersem, Géry de 25
Ghislain de Busbecq, Augier 217
Gilbert, Creighton 28
Giordano, Luca 127
Giotto 42, 44
Giovanni de' Medici 49
Giovio, Paolo 37, 147, 162, 170-171, 182
Giunti 43
God 26
Goethe, Johann Wolfgang von 44
Gombrich, Ernst 45-46
Gómez de Silva, Ruy 24

Gonin, Francesco 62-63
Gonzaga, Caterina 172
Gonzaga, Ferrante 95, 97-99, 136
Gonzaga, House of 165, 170
González de León, Fernando 229
Gonzalo Sánchez-Molero, José Luis 14
Goya, Francisco de 54-55
Gozalbo Nadal, Antonio 13
Gracián Dantisco, Antonio 215
Gracián de Alderete, Diego 149
Granello, Niccolò 138
Grapheus, Cornelius 241
Guarino, Giovanni Battista 203
Guazzo, Stefano 64
Guevara, Felipe de 132
Guicciardini, Francesco 222
Guldenmundt, Hans 130
Guzmán de Silva, Diego 123

Hablot, Laurent 180
Habsburg (Habsburgs) 12-13, 17, 24, 28-32, 35-39, 45, 60-61, 64, 66-68, 77-78, 86, 88- 89, 97, 101, 107, 112, 115, 119, 123, 125, 127, 134, 136-137, 139, 141, 150-151, 158, 167, 170, 178, 183-184, 186, 195, 197, 199-201, 203-204, 207-208, 213, 219-223, 228, 231, 236, 243
Habsburg dynasty *see* Habsburg
Habsburg Renaissance *see* Habsburg
Hasan, King of Tunis 116, 131
Hassan, Mulay, *bey* of Tunis *see* Hasan, King of Tunis
Helmschmied, Desiderius Kolman (Colman) 247
Heemskerck, Maarten van 117, 134-135, 148, 155
Heere, Lucas de 243-244
Hegel, Georg Wilhelm Friedrich 46
Heller, Ruprecht 129

Henry II, King of France 136-138, 177
Henry III, Emperor 208
Henry III, King of Castile 181
Henry IV, King of Castile 78, 181
Henry IV, King of France 49
Henry VIII, King of England 50, 77
Hercules 17-18, 26, 30, 109, 114
Herrera, Fernando de 233
Herrera, Juan de 35, 39, 215
Hesse, Philip of 248
Heywood, Thomas 114
Hieronymites 36
HM Master 134
Hoefnagel, Joris 24
Hogenberg, Frans 117, 133, 137, 139-140
Holanda, Rodrigo de, *aka* Rodrigo Diriksen 137, 139
Holy League 121
Homer 112, 129, 232-233
Hooghe, Romeyn 141
Horn, *see* Philip de Montmorency, Count of Horn
Hörnqvist, Mikael 148
Horopollo 193
Horozco y Covarrubias, Juan de, Bishop of Guadix 180
House of Austria *see* Habsburg
House of Habsburg, *see* Habsburg
Hubert, Wolfgang 130
Huizinga, Johan 46, 51
Hurtado de Mendoza, Diego 215
Hurtado de Mendoza, Francisco, Count of Monteagudo 119

Iñiguez, Francisco 35
Isabel Clara Eugenia, Governess of the Netherlands 53-54
Isabella I the Catholic, Queen of Castile, 50, 81
Isabella of Portugal, Empress 183

Jacincourt *see* Chassincourt, Jeanne de
James VI Stuart, King of Scotland 17
Jason 112
Jiménez de Ayllón, Diego 228
Jiménez de Urrea, Jerónimo 248, 252
Joanna I the Mad, Archduchess and Queen of Spain 16, 80, 214, 238
Joanna of Habsburg-Jagiellon 178
John II, King of Aragon 78
John II, King of Castile 78, 138
John Chrysostom, Saint 209
John Frederick I, Elector of Saxony 133
John of Austria, stepbrother of Philip II 119-120, 123, 140, 168, 186, 249
John of Trastámara, Prince of Spain 80, 205
Jonghelinck, Jacques 139
Juan, Honorato 239
Juana Enríquez, Queen of Aragon 78
Julius Caesar 223
Junius, Hadrianus 181
Jupiter 114, 159

Kelley, Donald R. 15
Khewenhüller, Hans 168
Knights Hospitaller 115
Koenigsberger, Helmut G. 17
Kölderer, Jörg 30, 37
Kranz, Rolf 245
Krautheimer, Richard 28
Kruse, Georg 171
Kurz, Otto 34-35
Kurz, Sebastian 113

L'Alouëte, François de 161
L'innominato 61, 63
Ladislaus the Posthumus, Duke of Austria and King of Hungary and Bohemia 203
Laetus, Julius Pomponius 203

Lalaing, Antoine de 82
Lamberg, Caspar von, *aka* Gašper Lamberger 190
Lamberger, Gašper *see* Lamberg, Caspar von
Lamoral, Count of Egmont *see* Egmont, Count of
Lasso de la Vega, Gabriel Vega, 225
Lautensack, Hans Sebald 130
Lazius, Wolfgang 217
Le Brun, Charles 49
Ledda, Giuseppina 179
Ledesma, Juan de 141
Leo X, Pope 49
Leonardo da Vinci 42, 59, 70
Leoni, Leone 39, 134, 136, 183
Leoni, Pompeo 24, 134, 136
Leopold of Austria, Archduke 68, 219
Leyva, Antonio de, Prince of Ascoli 168
Livy 151
Locle, Camille du 64
Lomazzo, Giovanni Paolo 67, 87, 145-146
López de Gómara, Francisco 130
López de Mendoza, Íñigo, Duke of El Infantado 159
López de Mendoza, Marquis of Santillana 233
López de Palacios Rubios, Juan 229
Lorenzo de' Medici, the Magnificent 49
Louis II Jagiellon, King of Hungary 130, 209
Louis IX, King of France 156
Louis XII, King of France 162
Louis XIV, King of France 48-49
Lucan 223
Ludovico il Moro, Duke of Milan 50
Luna, Álvaro de, Constable of Castile 78
Luther, Martin 45, 209

Machiavelli, Niccolò 144, 148-149
Magellan 112
Mal Lara, Juan de 119-120, 186
Mancini, Matteo 12
Mann, Thomas 44
Mantegna, Andrea 145, 150
Manzoni, Alessandro 60-64, 69
Marche, Olivier de la 147
Margaret of Austria, Archduchess and Princess of Spain 39, 80, 85, 199, 204-209, 211, 214
Margaret of Austria, Queen of Spain 119
Margaret of York, Duchess of Burgundy 206
Margaret, Duchess of Florence 87
Maria Manuela of Portugal, Princess of Spain 86
Maria of Habsburg, Empress 16
Mariana, Juan de 234
Marmolejo, Pedro Villegas 120
Marquis of Mondéjar, Governor of Granada 117
Marquis of Vasto 116
Marquis of Villena 84
Martínez, Miguel 227
Mary of Austria, Empress 38
Mary of Burgundy, Archduchess 16, 78, 188, 203
Mary of Hungary, Queen 31-32, 39, 45, 85, 97, 100-101, 103-106, 118, 133-134, 199, 209-211, 214
Mary Tudor, Queen of England 17, 119, 184, 242-243
Mary Tudor, Queen of England 86
Master of the Virgin of the Catholic Monarchs 79
Matthias Corvinus, King of Hungary 50, 200, 203
Matthias, Archduke 38
Maurice, Elector of Saxony 238
Maximilian I of Habsburg, Emperor 16, 29-30, 36-39, 78, 85, 109, 112, 115, 127, 145-146, 158, 169, 172, 182, 186-191, 199-201, 203-204, 206, 209, 213, 216-217
Maximilian II of Habsburg, Emperor 15-16, 18-19, 38, 123, 166, 185-186, 199-200, 203, 217, 219
Mayer, Pol 244
Mayner, Alejandro 133
Medicis 49-50, 146, 148, 152, 165
Meiner, Alejandro 117
Meldemann, Niklas (Nikolaus) 130-131
Mennel, Jakob 37
Merian, Matthäus 117
Méry, François Joseph 61
Mexía (Mejía), Pedro 149, 226
Michelangelo 42, 48-49, 59, 71
Michelet, Jules 12
Michiel, Zuan 166
Mielich, Hans 133
Milanesi, Gaetano 57-59, 64, 70
Milick, Nickel 134
Milieu, Christophe 15
Minerva 123-124
Mínguez, Víctor 13
Modius, Franciscus 151
Mondella, Lucia 61-62
Monogramist AW 130
Monogramist MS 130
Mor, Antonis 24, 39, 51, 136
Moses 36
Mosquera de Barnuevo, Francisco 228
Moura, Cristóvão de 24
Mulcahy, Rosemarie 121-122, 125
Münster, Sebastian 137
Musi, Agostino de' (*aka* Agostino Veneziano) 133
Musurus, Marcus 203
Mylaeus, Christophe *see* Milieu, Christophe

Napoleon 171, 174

Negroli, Filippo 132
Negroli, Francesco 132
Neptune 121, 125
Noah 36
Norwich, John Julius 111
Núñez de Oria, Francisco 235

O'Reilly, William 14
Oña, Pedro de 228
Orange, William of 19
Ossola, Carlo 13
Ostendorfer, Michel 131
Ovid 120

Páez de Castro, Juan 213, 214
Pannemaker, Willem de 52-53, 118, 133-134
Panofsky, Erwin 45-46, 69
Pantin, Pierre 24
Pantoja de la Cruz, Juan 218
Panvinio, Onofrio 150, 153-154
Pareja, Juan de 61
Parker, Geoffrey 107
Partridge, Loren 146
Pascual Molina, Jesús F. 13-14, 30
Passini, Cristoforo 134
Paul III, Pope 116-117, 133
Paul IV, Pope 20, 136
Pérez, Antonio 121-122
Pérez de Guzmán, Fernán 233
Pérez de Villagrá, Gaspar 228
Perrenin, Antoine 132
Perrenot de Granvelle, Antoine, Cardinal 24, 134
Perret, Pieter 24
Peruzzi, Baldassare 116
Petrarch 60, 145
Pett, Phineas 114
Philbert, Duke of Savoy 205
Philip de Montmorency, Count of Horn 140

Philip I of Habsburg, King of Portugal *see* Philip II, King of Spain
Philip I the Fair, Archduke and King of Castile 16, 78, 80, 205-206
Philip II, King of Spain 15-21, 23, 29, 31, 34-39, 45, 51-53, 64, 77, 85-88, 92-101, 103, 105-107, 110, 112, 114-115, 118-119, 121-124, 135-139, 141, 156, 161, 165, 168, 172, 177, 184-185, 187, 192, 199-200, 213-215, 217-219, 221, 225, 229, 231-232, 235-237, 239-252
Philip III, King of Spain 119
Philip IV, King of Spain 53-54, 68, 112, 141, 219
Philippe II de Croÿ, Duke of Aarschot 210
Philip of Habsburg, Prince of Spain *see* Philip II, King of Spain
Philip the Good, Duke of Burgundy 51, 76, 112, 200
Piccolomini, Alessandro 120
Piero de' Medici, the Gouty 49
Pino, Paolo 28
Pius V, Pope 120
Plantin, Christophe 185
Pliny 120, 151-152, 159, 161
Plutarch 112, 149, 151
Pole, Reginald, Cardinal and Archbishop of Canterbury 242-243
Pontano, Giovanni 74-75
Popper, Karl 46
Porras de la Cámara, Francisco 25-26
Profiti, Agostino 25
Ptolemy 114
Pufendorf, Samuel 22
Pujol, Joan 225
Pulgar, Fernando del 81
Puys, Remy du 147, 149

Queen of Sheba 243-244
Quintanar Cabello, Vanessa 13
Quondam, Amadeo 13

Raimondi, Marcantonio 44
Ranke, Leopold von 46
Rantzau, Heinrich von 167, 171
Raphael 42, 49
Renzo 61
Requesens y Zúñiga, Luís de 141
Rhodes, Apollonius 119
Rico, Francisco 188
Ridolfi, Carlo 65
Riegl, Alois 46
Rochlitz, Elisabeth von 248
Rodríguez, Jerónimo 225
Rogier, Philippe 24
Romano, Giulio 109, 115
Romulus 150
Rosa, Pietro 170
Rubens, Peter Paul 54, 65, 68-69, 102, 105
Rudolf II of Habsburg, Emperor 18, 37-39, 88, 144, 165, 172-174, 183, 199, 219
Rufo, Juan 225, 228
Russell, Daniel 193
Rüxner, Georg 107

Saavedra Fajardo, Diego 112-113, 195-196
Saavedra y Guzmán, Antonio de 225, 228
Saint Augustine 120
Saint Bernard 120
Saint Laurence 35
Sain Louis, *see* Louis IX, King of France
Salazar, Eugenio 25
Sallust 233
Sambucus, Johannes, *aka* János Zsámboky 185
Samosata, Lucian of 33-34

Sanabria, Alonso de 156
Sánchez Cantón, Francisco Javier 35
Sánchez Coello, Alonso 39
Sandbichler, Veronika 101
Sansovino, Francesco 157, 171
Santa Cruz, Alonso de 132-133, 226
Santo Tomé (the Apostle Thomas) 26
Santos, Francisco de los 122
Savonarola 149
Saxon dinasty 170
Schäufelein, Hans Leonhard 128
Schiller, Friedrich 64
Schön, Erhard 130
Schönsperger, Johannes 204
Schlosser, Julius von 12, 27, 28, 34-35, 67, 88
Schnaase, Karl 46
Schopenhauer, Arthur 46
Schoöpfer, Hans 170
Schottus, Andreas 24
Schrenck von Notzing, Jacob 38, 160, 167, 171, 175
Scipio Africanus 109, 116
Sebastián, Santiago 186
Sebastian I of Aviz, King of Portugal 17
Sempere, Jerónimo de 147-148, 155, 224
Sennacherib, Assyrian King 130
Sepúlveda, Juan Ginés de 226, 234, 239
Serojas, Juan de 30
Sgrooten, Christiaan 114
Siegmund of Tyrol, Archduke 172
Sigismund II, King of Poland 50
Sigüenza, Fray José de 34-36, 67, 122
Silver, Larry 29, 201
Sittow, Michel 50
Sluter, Claus 51
Snyders, Frans 102
Society of Jesus 120
Sohm, Philip 66

Solis, Virgil 134
Solomon, King of Israel 242-244, 252
Spanish Empire 111
Spanish Monarchy 111
Spranger, Bartholomeus 24, 39
Stabius, Johannes 37
Starn, Randolph 146
Strada, Famiano 141
Strada, Jacopo 219
Suárez de Figueroa, Lorenzo 96
Suleiman the Magnificent, Sultan of the Ottoman Empire 130-131
Surian, Michiel 244

Tassis, Johann Baptista de 160
Tasso, Torquato 222
Tavarone, Lazzaro 138
Taylor, René 35
Tempesta, Antonio 117, 135
Teniers, David 68
Terzio, Francesco 38, 170, 174
Tessitore, Fulvio 64
Teufl, Heinrich 170
Thalia 183
Theotokópoulos, Doménikos see El Greco
Tibaldi, Pellegrino 216
Tirol, Hans 37
Titian 20, 32, 36, 39, 51, 54, 67, 69, 122-123, 134-136, 237
Titus Livius 148
Toledo, Juan Bautista de 215
Tortello, Benvenuto 120
Trastámara, House of see Trastámaras
Trastámaras 78, 80, 181
Treitzsauerwein, Marx 37
Trezzo, Jacopo da 24-25, 184-185
Truchsess, Otto 37
Typotius, Jacobius 38

Ulysses 112
Urquízar-Herrera, Antonio 13
Urrea, Jerónimo de 228, 248-249

Valdivia, Pedro de 251
Valdivieso, Luis de 120
Valera, Diego de 204
Valeriano, Pierio 120-121
Valois dinasty 128, 130, 136
Valturius, Robertus 147, 157, 162
Van Aytta van Zuychem, Wigle see Zuichemus ab Aytta', Viglius
Van der Weyden, Rogier 31, 51, 77
Van Dyck, Anthony 69
Van Mâle, Guillaume 132
Van Mander, Karel 143-144
Van Orley, Bernard 129, 208
Van Veen, Otto 140
Van Vlierden, Daniël 211
Vargas Machuca, Bernardo de 228
Varro 151
Vasari, Giorgio 12,-13, 28, 36-37, 39, 41-45, 47-49, 51, 55, 57-60, 67, 71, 79
Vázquez, Juan Bautista 120
Vecilla Castellanos, Pedro de la 224, 228, 234-235
Vega, Garcilaso de la 233
Vega, María José 13, 246
Velázquez, Diego 54, 61, 64-65, 68-69, 125
Veneziano, Agostino see Musi, Agostino de'
Venus 249
Verdi, Giuseppe 61, 64
Vermeyen, Jan Cornelisz 31-33, 39, 52, 116-118, 132-133
Vico, Enea 134
Victory 121
Vilà, Lara 14
Virgil 120, 122, 223
Virués, Cristóbal de 225, 228
Vital, Laurent 82-83
Vitruvius 28
Vulcan 247, 249

Wavrin, Jean de 206

Waiss, Anton 170
Warburg, Aby 71
Welser, Philippine 172
Wenceslaus I, King of Bohemia 203
Whaley, Joachim 14
Wilhelm of Jülich, Kleve and Berg 168
Winckelmann, Johann 41
Wölfflin, Heinrich 46
Worringer, Wilhelm 45
Wyngaerde, Anton van den 136-138

Yates, Francis
Young, Alan R. 188

Zalama, Miguel Ángel 12
Zapata, Luis 159, 224-226, 228, 235-236, 247-249, 252
Zenoi, Domenico 134
Zuccaro, Federico 117
Zuccaro, Taddeo 117
Zsámboky, Jámos *see* Sambucus, Johannes
Zuichemus ab Aytta', Viglius *aka* Wigle van Aytta van Zuychem 214
Zurita, Jerónimo 226